P9-CQV-449

America's Best Day Hiking Series

Hiking MICHIGAN

ROGER E. STORM

SUSAN M. WEDZEL

Human Kinetics

Library of Congress Cataloging-in-Publication Data

Storm, Roger.
    Hiking Michigan / Roger E. Storm, Susan M. Wedzel.
        p.   cm. -- (America's best day hiking series)
    ISBN 0-88011-583-1
    1. Hiking--Michigan--Guidebooks.   2. Parks--Michigan--Guidebooks.
3. Wilderness areas--Michigan--Guidebooks.   4. Michigan--Guidebooks.
I. Wedzel, Susan M., 1953-   . II. Title. III. Series.
GV199.42.M5S86   1997   96-51873
796.51'09774--DC21   CIP

ISBN: 0-88011-583-1

Copyright © 1997 by Roger E. Storm and Susan M. Wedzel

All rights reserved. Except for use in a review, the reproduction or utilization of this work in any form or by any electronic, mechanical, or other means, now known or hereafter invented, including xerography, photocopying, and recording, and in any information storage and retrieval system, is forbidden without the written permission of the publisher.

Acquisitions Editor: Patricia Sammann
Developmental Editor: Julie A. Marx
Assistant Editors: Coree Schutter, Andrew Smith, and Jacqueline Eaton Blakley
Editorial Assistant: Jennifer Jeanne Hemphill
Copyeditors: Anne Mischakoff Heiles and Joyce Sexton
Graphic Designer: Robert Reuther
Graphic Artists: Sandra Meier and Yvonne Winsor
Cover Designer: Jack Davis
Cover Photograph: Lake Michigan at Harbor Springs; courtesy of Michigan Travel Bureau/Thomas A. Schneider
Interior Photographs: Roger E. Storm and Susan M. Wedzel
Illustrator: Tim Shedelbower
Printer: Versa Press

The maps on the following pages were adapted from maps from the Michigan Department of Natural Resources: 8, 24, 40, 46, 58, 68, 76, 78, 82, 86, 90, 94, 104, 108, 114, 126, 134, 156, 160, 168, 172, 188, 200, 204, and 210 (Warren Dunes State Park).

Human Kinetics books are available at special discounts for bulk purchase. Special editions or book excerpts can also be created to specification. For details, contact the Special Sales Manager at Human Kinetics.

Printed in the United States of America

10 9 8 7 6 5 4 3 2 1

Human Kinetics
Web site: http://www.humankinetics.com/

United States: Human Kinetics
P.O. Box 5076
Champaign, IL 61825-5076
1-800-747-4457
e-mail: humank@hkusa.com

Canada: Human Kinetics, Box 24040
Windsor, ON N8Y 4Y9
1-800-465-7301 (in Canada only)
e-mail: humank@hkcanada.com

Europe: Human Kinetics, P.O. Box IW14
Leeds LS16 6TR, United Kingdom
(44) 1132 781708
e-mail: humank@hkeurope.com

Australia: Human Kinetics
57A Price Avenue
Lower Mitcham, South Australia 5062
(08) 277 1555
e-mail: humank@hkaustralia.com

New Zealand: Human Kinetics
P.O. Box 105-231, Auckland 1
(09) 523 3462
e-mail: humank@hknewz.com

Valeria, you'll always be at home in our hearts.

Acknowledgments

This collection of Michigan day hikes came about by combining two of our passions—Michigan and hiking. Our thanks go to the many staff and volunteers we had the pleasure to meet at the various parks and nature centers across the state. By giving so freely of their time in providing information, answering our questions, and pointing us in the right direction, they made our task easier, as well as more enjoyable.

Special thanks go to Dean Sandell for his early advice, to Dick Anderson for his enthusiasm, and to Kathleen Przylylski, Les Walstrom, Scott Bauchsmiller, Mary Zelinski, Kathy Gottsacker, Wil Shapton, Ann Stephens, Sarah Hopkins, Brandi Robinson, Jennifer Portwine, Rex Hubbard, Sherri Pingil, Diantha Martin, Duane Hoffmann, Matt Heumann, Kenneth Teysen, Lawrence Goldmann, Linda Koski, Romona Venegas, and Peg Rowley for their special attention. Thanks also to Carol Wilson for taking us in on a crowded holiday weekend and letting us hang out until the rain stopped.

Our deepest appreciation goes out to Kirsten Williams and Donald Stahlbaum for stepping in as hiking partners, to Marty Powers for taking care of Stasha and the kids, and to Norm Cox for giving so unselfishly of his time and talents at critical times during our absence.

Michigan Park Locator

Map numbers correspond to the park numbers
in the Contents and the Trail Finder.

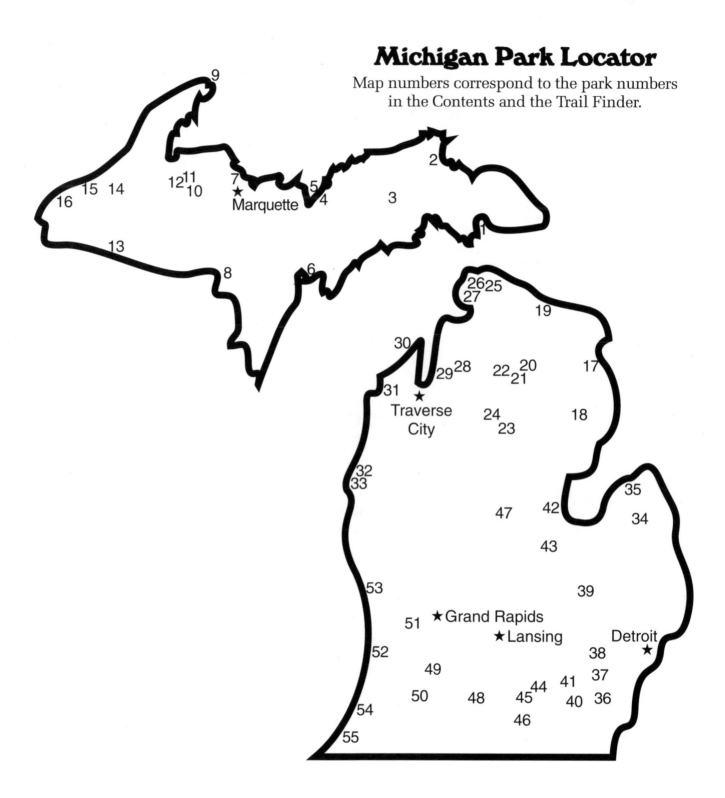

Contents

How to Use This Book	vi
Trail Finder	vii

Upper Peninsula   **1**

1. Mackinac Island State Park — 3
2. Tahquamenon Falls State Park — 7
3. Seney National Wildlife Refuge — 11
4. Pictured Rocks National Lakeshore — 15
5. Grand Island National Recreation Area — 19
6. Fayette Historic State Park — 23
7. Little Presque Isle Tract — 27
8. Fumee Lake Natural Area — 31
9. Estivant Pines Nature Sanctuary — 35
10. Van Riper State Park — 39
11. McCormick Wilderness — 43
12. Craig Lake State Park — 45
13. Sylvania Wilderness — 49
14. Ottawa National Forest — 53
15. Porcupine Mountains Wilderness State Park — 57
16. Black River Harbor National Forest Recreation Area — 61

Northern Lower Peninsula   **65**

17. Negwegon State Park — 67
18. Hoist Lakes Foot Travel Area — 71
19. Ocqueoc Falls Bicentennial Pathway — 75
20. Sinkhole Area — 77
21. Clear Lake State Park — 81
22. Pigeon River Country State Forest — 85
23. George Mason River Retreat Area — 89
24. Hartwick Pines State Park — 93
25. Mill Creek State Historic Park — 97
26. The Village of Mackinaw City — 101
27. Wilderness State Park — 103

28. Jordan River Pathway — 107
29. Grass River Natural Area — 109
30. Leelanau State Park — 113
31. Sleeping Bear Dunes National Lakeshore — 117
32. Nordhouse Dunes Wilderness — 121
33. Ludington State Park — 125

Southern Lower Peninsula   **129**

34. Sanilac Petroglyphs State Historic Park — 131
35. Port Crescent State Park — 133
36. William P. Holliday Forest and Wildlife Preserve — 137
37. West Bloomfield Woods Nature Preserve — 141
38. Indian Springs Metropark — 145
39. For-Mar Nature Preserve and Arboretum — 149
40. Parker Mill Park — 153
41. Island Lake Recreation Area — 155
42. Bay City State Recreation Area — 159
43. Shiawassee National Wildlife Refuge/ Green Point Environmental Learning Center — 163
44. Pinckney Recreation Area — 167
45. Waterloo Recreation Area — 171
46. Hidden Lake Gardens — 175
47. Chippewa Nature Center — 179
48. Whitehouse Nature Center — 183
49. Yankee Springs Recreation Area — 187
50. Kalamazoo Nature Center — 191
51. Aman Park — 195
52. Saugatuck Dunes State Park — 199
53. P.J. Hoffmaster State Park — 203
54. Sarett Nature Center — 205
55. Warren Dunes State Park/Warren Woods Natural Area — 209

How to Use This Book

Hiking is an antidote to modern life. It gives the body some much-needed (and enjoyable) exercise, and it gives the mind both rest and stimulation. It even lifts the spirit to connect again with this earth that we're a part of but seldom have time to think about. With the America's Best Day Hiking Series, we hope to provide you with an incentive to start or continue hiking, for the pleasure and the challenge of it.

Each book in the series offers information on more than 100 of the most interesting and scenic trails in a particular state, as well as notes about recreational, historical, and sightseeing destinations located near the trails. The assortment of trails ranges from short, easy hikes for occasional hikers and families with young children to longer, more rugged ones for the experienced trailblazer. None of the trails takes more than a day to hike, although some trails may be linked together to create a hike of several days.

The trails in *Hiking Michigan* are divided into three main areas—Upper Peninsula, Northern Lower Peninsula, and Southern Lower Peninsula. Within each area, trails are listed from east to west. Divider pages signal the beginning of each new area, and those pages include information on the local topography, major rivers and lakes, flora and fauna, weather, and best features of the area.

The innovative format is designed to make exploring new parks and trails easy. Information on each park or other nature area always appears on a right-hand page. It begins with the park's name and a small state map that shows the park's general location. Bulleted highlights then point out the trails' most interesting features. A description of the park's history and terrain comes next, with practical information on how to get to the park and the park's hours, available facilities, permits and rules, and the address and phone number of a contact who can give you more information. The section entitled "Other Points of Interest" briefly mentions nearby parks and recreational opportunities, with phone numbers to call for more information.

After the general information follows a selected list of trails in the park. The length and difficulty of hiking each is given, along with a brief description of its terrain. The difficulty rating, shown by boot icons, ranges from one (the easiest) to five (the most difficult).

On the other side of the page is a full-sized map of the park. Our book's larger format allows us to provide clear, readable maps that are easy to follow.

easiest					most difficult
1	2	3	4	5	

The next right- and left-hand pages are usually descriptions of the two best hikes in that park, along with a trail map at the bottom of each page (a few parks have only one hike, with just one map that primarily shows the trail). Each hike begins with information on the length and difficulty of the trail, and the estimated time to walk it, plus cautions to help you avoid possible annoyances or problems. The description of the trail provides more than directions; it's a guided tour of what you will see as you hike along. The scenery, wildlife, and history of the trail are all brought to life. Points of interest along the trail are numbered in brackets within the text, and those numbers are shown on the trail map to guide you. The approximate distance from the trailhead to each point of interest is given.

The park descriptions, maps, and trails are all kept as a unit within an even number of pages. Parks for which only one trail is highlighted take up only two pages; those with the regular two trails cover four pages. We've perforated the book's pages so you can remove them if you like, or you can copy them for your personal use. If you carry the pages with you as you hike, you might want to use a plastic sleeve to protect them from the elements. You also can make notes on these pages to remind you of your favorite parts of the park or trail.

If you want to quickly find a park or trail to explore, use the trail finder that appears on the next pages. It gives essential information about each highlighted trail in the book, including the trail's length, difficulty, special features, and park facilities.

We hope the books in the America's Best Day Hiking Series inspire you to get out and enjoy a wide range of outdoor experiences. We've tried to find interesting trails from all parts of each state. Some are unexpected treasures—places you'd never dream exist in the state. Some may be favorites that you've already hiked and recommended to friends. But whether you live in a city or in the country, are away vacationing or are at home, some of these trails will be near you. Find one you like, strap on your hiking boots, and go!

Trail Finder

Continued ☞

KEY

🚐	RV camping
⛺	tent camping
🏊	swimming
🛶	canoeing
🎣	fishing
🚣	boating
⛱	picnicking
🚲	biking

	Trail Sites and Trails	Park Facilities	Miles	Trail Difficulty Rating	Hills	Escarpment	Forest	Lake	Wetlands	Overlook	River/Stream	Page #
1	**Mackinac Island State Park**	picnicking, biking										
	Natural and Historical Features Tour		3.2	🥾🥾🥾	✓	✓	✓	✓		✓		5
	Tranquil Bluff Trail		3.2	🥾🥾🥾	✓	✓	✓	✓		✓		6
2	**Tahquamenon Falls State Park**	RV camping, tent camping, swimming, canoeing, fishing, boating, picnicking										
	Giant Pines Loop With Upper Falls Tour		4	🥾🥾🥾	✓	✓	✓		✓	✓	✓	9
	Clark Lake Loop		5.2	🥾🥾🥾	✓		✓	✓	✓	✓		10
3	**Seney National Wildlife Refuge**	canoeing, fishing, biking										
	Pine Ridge Nature Trail		1.4	🥾			✓	✓	✓			13
	C-3 Pool Trail		5.8	🥾			✓	✓			✓	14
4	**Pictured Rocks National Lakeshore**	tent camping, canoeing, fishing, picnicking										
	Chapel Basin Trail		9.8	🥾🥾	✓	✓	✓	✓	✓	✓	✓	17
	Beaver Basin Loop		5.5	🥾🥾	✓	✓	✓	✓	✓	✓	✓	18
5	**Grand Island National Recreation Area**	tent camping, fishing, picnicking, biking										
	East Ridge Trail		10.6	🥾🥾	✓	✓	✓	✓	✓	✓	✓	21
	West Ridge Trail		10	🥾🥾	✓	✓	✓	✓	✓	✓	✓	22
6	**Fayette Historic State Park**	RV camping, tent camping, swimming, fishing, boating, picnicking										
	Townsite Trail		1.3	🥾	✓	✓	✓	✓		✓		25
	Overlook Trail and Loop 1		2.6	🥾🥾	✓	✓	✓	✓		✓		26
7	**Little Presque Isle Tract**	fishing, boating										
	Lake Superior—Little Presque Isle Point to Wetmore Landing	picnicking, biking	3.8	🥾🥾	✓	✓	✓	✓		✓		29
	Hogsback Mountain Loop	swimming	5.2	🥾🥾🥾🥾🥾	✓	✓	✓	✓	✓	✓	✓	30

#	Trail Sites and Trails	Park Facilities	Miles	Trail Difficulty Rating	Hills	Escarpment	Forest	Lake	Wetlands	Overlook	River/Stream	Page #
8	**Fumee Lake Natural Area**	[canoe, bicycle]										
	Little Fumee Lake Trail		1.8	🥾			✓	✓	✓		✓	33
	Big Fumee Lake Trail		6	🥾🥾	✓	✓	✓	✓	✓	✓	✓	34
9	**Estivant Pines Nature Sanctuary**											
	Cathedral Loop Trail		1.5	🥾🥾🥾	✓		✓		✓		✓	37
	Memorial Loop Trail		1.5	🥾🥾🥾	✓		✓		✓		✓	38
10	**Van Riper State Park**	[RV, tent, swim, canoe, fish, camp, picnic]										
	Upper Loop		2.2	🥾🥾🥾	✓	✓	✓		✓	✓	✓	41
	Lower Loop		3.1	🥾🥾	✓		✓		✓	✓	✓	42
11	**McCormick Wilderness**	[fish, canoe, tent]	6	🥾🥾	✓	✓	✓	✓			✓	44
12	**Craig Lake State Park**	[canoe, tent, fish]										
	Crooked Lake Trail		4	🥾🥾	✓	✓	✓	✓	✓			47
	Craig Lake Trail		6.1	🥾🥾🥾	✓	✓	✓	✓	✓	✓	✓	48
13	**Sylvania Wilderness**	[tent, swim, fish, camp, picnic]										
	Clark Lake Trail		7.1	🥾🥾	✓		✓	✓	✓	✓	✓	51
	Unnamed Trail—Loon Lake Access		4.6	🥾🥾	✓		✓	✓	✓	✓		52
14	**Ottawa National Forest**	[tent, swim, canoe, fish, camp, picnic, bicycle]										
	Beaver Lodge Nature Trail		1.4	🥾🥾	✓		✓	✓	✓	✓		55
	Cascade Falls Hiking Trail		1.7	🥾🥾🥾🥾🥾	✓	✓	✓			✓	✓	56
15	**Porcupine Mountains Wilderness State Park**	[RV, tent, fish, camp, picnic]										
	Overlook Trail		3.6	🥾🥾🥾🥾	✓		✓		✓	✓	✓	59
	Escarpment Trail		4.2	🥾🥾🥾🥾	✓	✓	✓	✓	✓	✓	✓	60
16	**Black River Harbor National Forest Recreation Area**	[RV, tent, camp, picnic]										
	North Country Trail to Sandstone, Gorge, Potawatomi, and Conglomerate Falls		3.9	🥾🥾🥾	✓	✓	✓		✓	✓	✓	63
	North Country Trail to Rainbow Falls—West and East		3.2	🥾🥾🥾🥾	✓	✓	✓	✓	✓	✓	✓	64
17	**Negwegon State Park**	[swim, fish, tent, picnic]										
	Potawatomi Trail		3.3	🥾				✓	✓	✓		69
	Algonquin Trail		6.7	🥾🥾				✓	✓	✓	✓	70

	Trail Sites and Trails	Park Facilities	Miles	Trail Difficulty Rating	Hills	Escarpment	Forest	Lake	Wetlands	Overlook	River/Stream	Page #
18	**Hoist Lakes Foot Travel Area**											
	Hoist Lakes Little East Loop		4.9	boot boot boot	✓		✓	✓	✓			73
	Hoist Lakes Little West Loop		6.5	boot boot boot	✓		✓	✓	✓	✓		74
19	**Ocquecoc Falls Bicentennial Pathway**		4.2	boot boot	✓		✓		✓	✓	✓	76
20	**Sinkhole Area**											
	Sinkholes Pathway— Short Loop		.8	boot boot boot	✓		✓	✓		✓		79
	Sinkholes Pathway— Long Loop		2	boot boot boot	✓		✓	✓		✓		80
21	**Clear Lake State Park**											
	Clear Lake Nature Trail		4.5	boot boot	✓		✓	✓		✓		83
	Clear Lake–Jackson Lake Trail—Southern Loop		4.4	boot boot	✓		✓	✓	✓			84
22	**Pigeon River Country State Forest**											
	Shingle Mill Pathway— Upper Loop		5.9	boot boot	✓		✓	✓	✓	✓	✓	87
	Shingle Mill Pathway— Middle Loop		6.3	boot boot	✓		✓	✓	✓	✓	✓	88
23	**George Mason River Retreat Area**											
	Mason Tract Pathway—North		2.7	boot boot	✓		✓			✓	✓	91
	Mason Tract Pathway—South		6.4	boot boot	✓		✓		✓	✓	✓	92
24	**Hartwick Pines State Park**											
	Virgin Pines Foot Trail		1.2	boot	✓		✓					95
	Au Sable River Foot Trail		3.8	boot boot	✓		✓			✓	✓	96
25	**Mill Creek State Historic Park**											
	Evergreen Trail With Sugar Shack Forest Trail		1.9	boot boot	✓		✓		✓	✓	✓	99
	Beaver Pond Trail		1.7	boot boot	✓		✓		✓	✓	✓	100
26	**The Village of Mackinaw City**		2.2	boot				✓		✓		102

Continued ☞

#	Trail Sites and Trails	Park Facilities	Miles	Trail Difficulty Rating	Hills	Escarpment	Forest	Lake	Wetlands	Overlook	River/Stream	Page #
27	**Wilderness State Park**											
	East Ridge/Nebo/South Boundary/East Boundary Trails Loop		4.6	▲▲▲	✓		✓		✓			105
	Big Stone/Pondside/Red Pine/Hemlock Trails Loop		4.2	▲▲	✓		✓	✓	✓		✓	106
28	**Jordan River Pathway**		3.3	▲▲▲	✓		✓		✓	✓	✓	108
29	**Grass River Natural Area**											
	Woodland/Wildfire Trail		1.3	▲			✓		✓	✓	✓	111
	Cabin/Sedge Meadow/Tamarack/Fern Trails Loop		1.3	▲			✓	✓	✓	✓	✓	112
30	**Leelanau State Park**											
	Lake Michigan Trail		2.4	▲▲	✓		✓	✓		✓		115
	Mud Lake Trail		3.2	▲▲	✓		✓	✓	✓			116
31	**Sleeping Bear Dunes National Lakeshore**											
	Dunes—Sleeping Bear Point Hiking Trail		2.2	▲▲▲	✓		✓	✓		✓		119
	Pyramid Point Hiking Trail		2.7	▲▲▲	✓		✓	✓		✓		120
32	**Nordhouse Dunes Wilderness**											
	Four-Mile Loop		4.1	▲▲▲	✓		✓	✓	✓	✓		123
	Six-Mile Loop		5.9	▲▲▲	✓		✓	✓	✓	✓		124
33	**Ludington State Park**											
	Skyline/Sable River/Island/Lost Lake Trails		3.7	▲▲	✓		✓	✓		✓	✓	127
	Big Sable Point Lighthouse Loop		4.9	▲▲	✓		✓	✓	✓			128
34	**Sanilac Petroglyphs State Historic Park**		1.4	▲▲	✓		✓		✓		✓	132
35	**Port Crescent State Park**											
	Camping Area Trail		2.1	▲▲	✓		✓	✓		✓	✓	135
	Day-Use Area Trail		2.8	▲▲	✓		✓	✓	✓	✓	✓	136
36	**William P. Holliday Forest and Wildlife Preserve**											
	Tulip Leaf/Beech Trails		1.9	▲	✓		✓		✓		✓	139
	Tonquish Trail		5.8	▲▲▲	✓		✓		✓	✓	✓	140

	Trail Sites and Trails	Park Facilities	Miles	Trail Difficulty Rating	Terrain/Landscape							Page #
					Hills	Escarpment	Forest	Lake	Wetlands	Overlook	River/Stream	
37	**West Bloomfield Woods Nature Preserve**											
	West Bloomfield Woods Nature Preserve Trail	⛺🏕	2.2	🥾	✓		✓		✓	✓	✓	143
	West Bloomfield Trail Network	🚲	4.3	🥾			✓	✓	✓	✓		144
38	**Indian Springs Metropark**	⛺🏕										
	Woodland Trail		3.7	🥾	✓		✓	✓	✓	✓	✓	147
	Farmland Trail	🚲	1.6	🥾🥾	✓		✓		✓			148
39	**For-Mar Nature Preserve and Aboretum**											
	Ground Water Pond and Hawthorn Trail		1.2	🥾			✓		✓	✓	✓	151
	Ground Water Pond and Sugar Bush Trail		.7	🥾🥾	✓		✓		✓	✓	✓	152
40	**Parker Mill Park**	🚲⛺🏕	1.6	🥾			✓		✓	✓	✓	154
41	**Island Lake Recreation Area**	🏕🏊										
	West Loop	🛶	9.5	🥾🥾	✓		✓	✓	✓	✓	✓	157
	East Loop	⛺🏕🚲	5.6	🥾🥾	✓		✓	✓	✓	✓	✓	158
42	**Bay City State Recreation Area**	🚐🏕										
	Frank N. Andersen Nature Trail	🏊	3.2	🥾				✓	✓	✓	✓	161
	Tobico Marsh Loop	⛺🏕🚲	4.9	🥾				✓	✓	✓	✓	162
43	**Shiawassee National Wildlife Refuge/Green Point Environmental Learning Center**	🚲										
	Ferguson Bayou Trail		4.8	🥾			✓	✓	✓	✓	✓	165
	Songbird/Duck Trails		1.5	🥾			✓		✓	✓	✓	166
44	**Pinckney Recreation Area**	🚐🏕										
	Crooked Lake Trail	🏊🛶	5.1	🥾🥾🥾	✓		✓	✓	✓	✓	✓	169
	Losee Lake Hiking Trail—Red Loop	⛺🏕🚲	3.3	🥾🥾🥾	✓		✓	✓	✓	✓		170
45	**Waterloo Recreation Area**	🚐🏕										
	Waterloo-Pinckney Hiking Trail—Portage Lake to Sackrider Hill	🏊	5.9	🥾🥾🥾	✓		✓	✓	✓	✓	✓	173
	Waterloo-Pinckney Hiking Trail—Horseman's Camp to Green Lake	⛺🏕🚲	8.3	🥾🥾🥾	✓		✓	✓	✓	✓	✓	174

Continued ☞

	Trail Sites and Trails	Park Facilities	Miles	Trail Difficulty Rating	Hills	Escarpment	Forest	Lake	Wetlands	Overlook	River/Stream	Page #
46	**Hidden Lake Gardens**	🌲⛱										
	Pine-Tree Trail		1.3	🥾🥾	✓		✓	✓				177
	Hikers' Trail		3	🥾🥾🥾	✓		✓	✓	✓			178
47	**Chippewa Nature Center**											
	Woodland Trail		2	🥾			✓		✓		✓	181
	Blue Loop		2.9	🥾🥾			✓	✓	✓	✓	✓	182
48	**Whitehouse Nature Center**											
	River's Edge Trail		.9	🥾			✓		✓		✓	185
	Prairie Trail		1	🥾			✓		✓		✓	186
49	**Yankee Springs Recreation Area**	🏊🚐⛺🐟🪵🌲⛱🚲										
	Hall Lake Trail		3.7	🥾🥾	✓		✓	✓	✓	✓	✓	189
	Long Lake Trail		6.8	🥾🥾	✓		✓		✓	✓	✓	190
50	**Kalamazoo Nature Center**											
	Beechwood Trail		.8	🥾🥾🥾	✓		✓		✓	✓	✓	193
	Fern Valley Trail		.6	🥾🥾🥾	✓		✓		✓	✓		194
51	**Aman Park**	🐟🌲⛱										
	Yellow Trail		1.1	🥾🥾	✓		✓			✓	✓	197
	Red Trail		1.5	🥾🥾	✓		✓			✓	✓	198
52	**Saugatuck Dunes State Park**	🏊🌲⛱										
	North Trail With Spur to Lake—Outer Loop		2.9	🥾🥾🥾🥾	✓		✓	✓		✓		201
	Beach Trail		2.5	🥾🥾🥾	✓		✓	✓		✓		202
53	**P.J. Hoffmaster State Park**	🚐⛺🏊🌲⛱	2.6	🥾🥾🥾	✓		✓	✓		✓		204
54	**Sarett Nature Center**											
	River/Gentian/Two-Board Trails Loop		.6	🥾🥾	✓		✓		✓	✓	✓	207
	Lowland/Upland Trails Loop		2	🥾🥾🥾	✓		✓		✓	✓	✓	208
55	**Warren Dunes State Park/ Warren Woods Natural Area**	🚐⛺🏊🐟🌲⛱										
	Nature/Blue Jay/Beach/ Mt. Randal Trails Loop		3.8	🥾🥾🥾	✓		✓	✓	✓	✓	✓	211
	Warren Woods Natural Area Trail		1.2	🥾🥾	✓		✓		✓	✓	✓	212

Upper Peninsula

Promoted as "Nature's Theme Park," Michigan's Upper Peninsula became part of the state as a consolation prize in a boundary dispute between Michigan and Ohio in the mid-1830s. Ohio got to keep Toledo. Michigan was granted statehood as well as the vast land and riches of the Upper Peninsula.

Topography

Known as the U.P., not northern Michigan, the peninsula contains one-third of Michigan's total land area. Long and narrow, the U.P. stretches over 380 miles from Ironwood on the west to the tip of Drummond Island on the east, and is surrounded by three of the Great Lakes—Superior, Michigan, and Huron.

The eastern end of the U.P. is low lying, often swampy, cut by small streams, and carpeted by marshland and woodland. Rolling limestone hills, part of the Niagara Escarpment, stretch across its south side. To its north, multicolored sandstone formations tower 50 to 200 feet above Lake Superior at the Pictured Rocks National Lakeshore.

Unlike any other part of the state, the western U.P., with its rugged hills and escarpments (rock cliffs), contains outcroppings of some of the oldest known rocks on earth. West of Marquette, in the Huron Mountains you find the state's highest elevations. The western U.P. also has vast iron ore deposits. The discovery of a copper strip in the Keweenaw Peninsula enabled Michigan to be the number-one copper-producing state for 40 years.

Major Rivers and Lakes

Lakes Superior, Michigan, and Huron define much of the U.P.'s shape and provide the Peninsula with 1,700 miles of coastline. The shores are rocky and picturesque, varying from beach to dune to precipice.

Over 4,300 inland lakes speck the peninsula. Lake Gogebic is the largest. The Manistique Lakes, Indian Lake, and Lake Michigamme are some other large lakes.

The U.P. has 12,000 miles of rivers and streams that, while generally short, in their haste to reach the lakes are wildly boisterous. Some 250 waterfalls exist across the U.P., with most located in the western and central portions. The eastern U.P. has the mighty Tahquamenon Falls.

Common Plant Life

Forests of virgin white pine dominated much of the U.P. before the lumber era. Today, over 85 percent is forested by what is broadly termed the north woods, a zone between the needleleaf, boreal forest of Canada and the broadleaf trees that stretch south.

Here in the north woods, the species of both forest communities flourish. Sugar maple, basswood, beech, and the red maple reach northward into the region typified by white spruce, balsam fir, tamarack, and quaking aspen. Also found in the zone are red pine, eastern hemlock, yellow birch, and eastern white pine.

Having been logged out, pockets of old-growth forest persist, but only three large tracts of old-growth forest remain. They are found in the Porcupine Mountains Wilderness, the Sylvania Wilderness, and on the private lands of the Huron Mountain Club.

In the spring, a profusion of wildflowers blossoms across the U.P. While arbutus and violets scent the air, look for trillium, marsh marigold, blue carpets of forget-me-nots, the purple coneflower, over 30 species of wild orchids, and one of the rarest plants in the world—the Michigan monkey-flower, found only in a couple of counties near the Straits of Mackinac. These are followed in early summer by daisies, hawkweeds, fireweeds, sunflowers, and then the goldenrods of September. The thimbleberry is a U.P. specialty. Blueberries are also plentiful in sandy soils and bog environments.

A bog is a unique wetland habitat often occupying a glacial depression. Sphagnum moss grows in thick, floating mats on the water's surface and is often mistaken for solid ground. The floating mats hold in the cold of winter and allow tundra shrubs like Labrador tea and leatherleaf to survive far south of their normal range. Carnivorous pitcher plants are also common in the bog environment.

Common Birds and Mammals

In Michigan, to view moose or catch a glimpse of a wolf in the wild, you once had to travel to the remote setting of Isle Royale. Set in Lake Superior about

50 miles northwest of the Keweenaw Peninsula, Isle Royale is a rugged island wilderness. It is 45 miles long and 9 miles wide, with over 160 miles of some of the authors' favorite hiking trails. But in 1985, and again in 1987, moose were reintroduced to the U.P. from Canada and are thriving in their new home. Wolves also came back to the U.P. as they expanded their range from Minnesota during the 1980s.

As romantic as the notion of seeing moose or wolf is, you have a much better chance of seeing white-tailed deer or even black bear. Other mammals to look for include coyote, red fox, bobcat, beaver, porcupine, fisher, and snowshoe hare. At an old iron ore mine in Iron Mountain, up to one million big and little brown bats—one of the largest concentrations of bats in the world—gather to hibernate for the winter.

Birds are the most visible of wild animals, but unlike what occurs with a soaring eagle, a perched hawk, or circling vultures, you are more likely to hear the call of the loon, the honking of Canada geese, or the caw of a raven long before you see them. In the spring, thousands of birds congregate at Whitefish Point during the migration north. Over 230 bird species have been recorded there. The tip of the Keweenaw Peninsula is an important spring migration route for raptors. For a migration of a different type, monarch butterflies congregate at Peninsula Point in the fall before crossing Green Bay into Wisconsin.

A note about insects: Be prepared. Late May to mid-July is considered the peak season for an assortment of critters such as the black fly, mosquito, no-see-um, deerfly, and stable fly. As a consolation, there are no poisonous snakes in the U.P.

Climate

It is said that the U.P. has two seasons, shoveling and swatting. In truth, the U.P.'s weather is highly impacted by the Great Lakes that surround it. Temperature extremes are moderated by the presence of the lakes, and in the winter they help generate the highest snowfalls in the Midwest. The average maximum January temperatures range between 20 and 25 degrees Fahrenheit, while the lows average between −1 and 11 degrees. In July the average maximum temperatures range from 75 degrees to 79 degrees Fahrenheit, with the lows averaging between 50 and 58 degrees. Annual snowfall totals vary from 51 inches at Escanaba, to 150 inches at Ironwood, to nearly 200 inches in the snowbelt of the Keweenaw Peninsula.

Best Natural Features

- Lakes Superior, Michigan, and Huron
- Pictured Rocks multicolored sandstone cliffs
- Grand Sable Dunes
- Tahquamenon Falls
- Isle Royale, an International Biosphere Reserve
- Porcupine Mountains Wilderness
- 4,300 inland lakes
- 12,000 miles of rivers and streams
- 250 waterfalls
- Keweenaw Peninsula, the U.P.'s Upper Peninsula
- Brockway Mountain

1. Mackinac Island State Park

- Step back in time to experience an era before the automobile.
- Enjoy historic reenactments at Fort Mackinac.
- Visit unique geologic formations.

Park Information

This state park makes up over 80 percent of the small island located in the Straits of Mackinac. The world-renowned retreat has more history than just the 18th-century fort within its bounds.

Before it became Michigan's first state park in 1895, it had been Mackinac National Park, the country's second national park, after Yellowstone. For history buffs, there's history on the bluffs. Fort Mackinac, perched on the bluff overlooking the Straits, was built by the British in 1780. Cannon and musket firings and period reenactments offer visitors a taste of yesteryear.

Fort Mackinac, Fort Holmes, and a plethora of barracks, missions, and old cemeteries also take you back. Add to that palatial Victorian cottages, the stately Grand Hotel, the clip-clop of hooves, and creaking harness leather from horse-drawn carriages, and you live a bygone era.

Directions: Ferry transportation is available from St. Ignace and Mackinaw City. Three ferry lines service the island. For information on schedules and rates, contact Arnold Transit at 800-542-8528, Shepler's at 800-828-6157, or Star Line at 800-638-9892.

Hours Open: The state park is open daily, but Fort Mackinac is open from 9:00 A.M. to 6:00 P.M. from June 15 to Labor Day, with hours reduced in spring and fall.

Facilities: Hiking, biking, cross-country skiing, snowmobiling, bridle paths, picnicking, interpretive trails, interpretive center.

Permits and Rules: There is no charge for Mackinac Island State Park, but there is a charge for admission to Fort Mackinac. This is $6.75 for adults, $4.00 for children 6 to 12, or $20 per family. Combination packages, which allow seasonal access to Fort Mackinac, Colonial Michilimackinac, and Historic Mill Creek are available at $13.00 for adults, $7.50 for children, or $38.00 for a family.

Further Information: Contact Mackinac State Historic Parks, P.O. Box 873, Mackinaw City, MI 49701-0873; 616-436-5563.

Other Points of Interest

The Mackinac Island Chamber of Commerce can provide you with information on horse and buggy sight-seeing tours, bicycle rentals, island hotels and guest houses, and horse-drawn taxi services. Contact Mackinac Island Chamber of Commerce, Mackinac Island, MI 48757; 800-4-LILACS or 906-847-6418.

Other state parks are nearby: **Wilderness State Park** (see park #27), **Mill Creek State Historic Park** (see park #25), and **Colonial Michilimackinac State Historic Park** are located in the Lower Peninsula. Only Wilderness State Park provides camping facilities. Colonial Michilimackinac provides a view of the British, French, and Indians in the 18th century. For more information, contact Colonial Michilimackinac, c/o Mackinac State Historic Parks, P.O. Box 873, Mackinaw City, MI 49701-0873; 616-436-5563.

Camping is also available in the Upper Peninsula's **Straits State Park,** which has an awesome view of the Mackinac Bridge. For more information, contact Straits State Park, St. Ignace, MI 49781; 906-643-8620.

Mackinaw City has parks, museums, walks, and points of interest. For more information, contact the Mackinaw City Chamber of Commerce, Mackinaw City, MI 49701; 616-436-5574.

Park Trails

Although most people arriving at the Island scurry about Huron Street, weaving in and out of the clapboard buildings that house fudge and souvenir shops, relief from the crowds and mayhem of peak tourist visitation is available. With over 100 miles of non-motorized roads or trails, there are plenty of opportunities for bicycling, hiking, or horseback riding—set out and explore. Be sure to stop at the Visitor Center across from Marquette Park, near the docks, for more trail information.

Round the Shore —8.2 miles—A favorite hiking and bicycle route. It hugs the shoreline as it encircles the island on M-185, the only highway in Michigan where automobiles are banned.

British Landing Nature Trail —.5 mile—Learn about the natural history of the island on this interpretive trail located at the British Landing Nature Center.

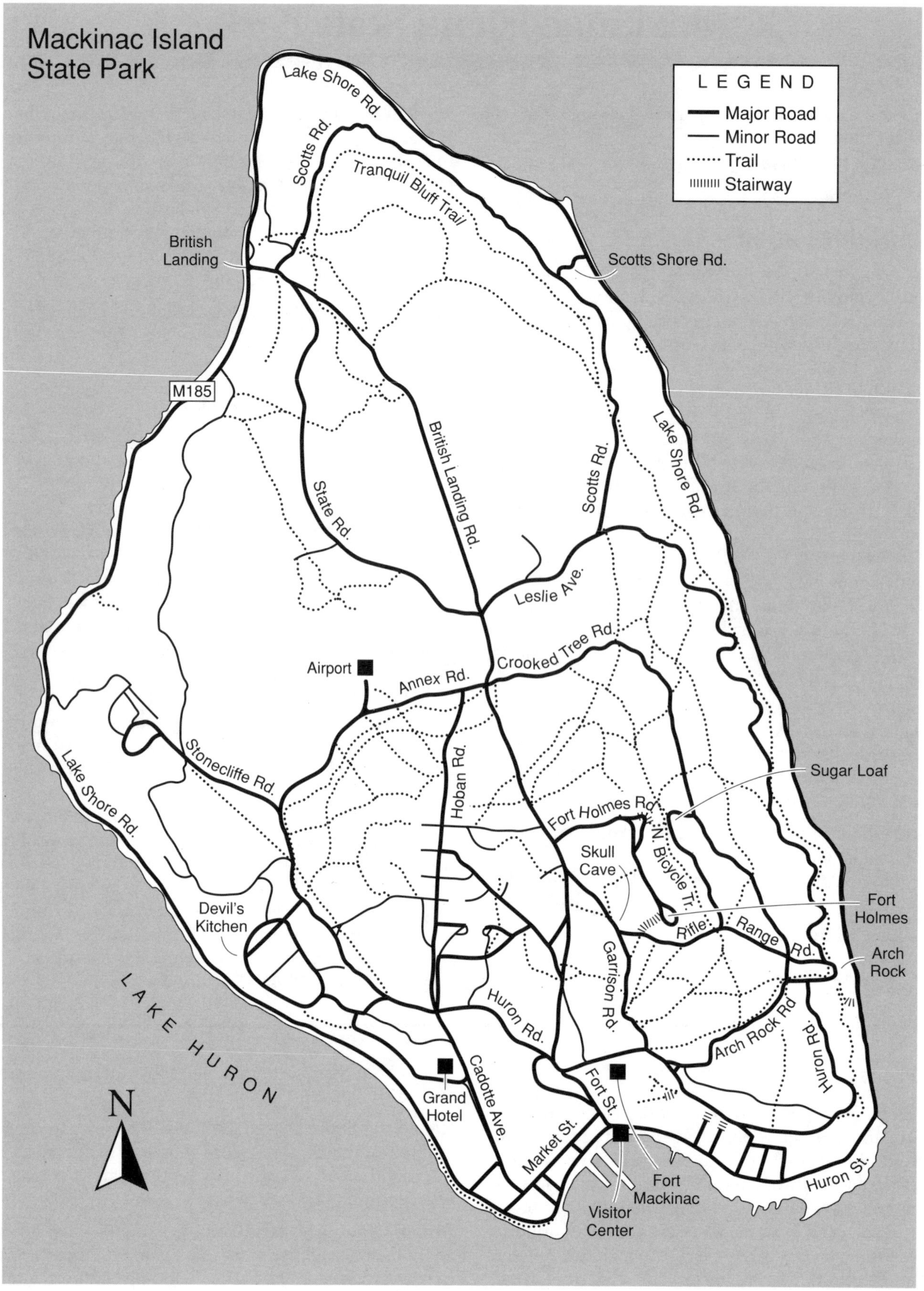

Mackinac Island State Park

LEGEND
— Major Road
— Minor Road
······ Trail
|||||| Stairway

Lake Shore Rd.

Scotts Rd.

Tranquil Bluff Trail

British Landing

Scotts Shore Rd.

M185

British Landing Rd.

Scotts Rd.

Lake Shore Rd.

State Rd.

Leslie Ave.

Crooked Tree Rd.

Airport

Annex Rd.

Stonecliffe Rd.

Hoban Rd.

Lake Shore Rd.

Sugar Loaf

Fort Holmes Rd.

N. Bicycle Tr.

Skull Cave

Fort Holmes

Devil's Kitchen

Rifle   Range Rd.

Arch Rock

Garrison Rd.

Arch Rock Rd.

Huron Rd.

Huron Rd.

L A K E   H U R O N

Grand Hotel

Cadotte Ave.

Market St.

Fort St.

Fort Mackinac

Huron St.

N

Visitor Center

Natural and Historical Features Tour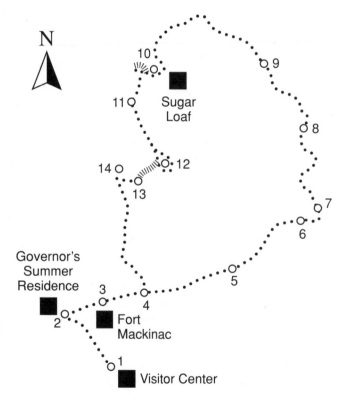

Distance Round-Trip: 3.2 miles

Estimated Hiking Time: 1.5 to 2 hours

Cautions: Both hiking and bicycling are permitted on the trails. Be careful. You cross roads that are shared with horses. Watch your step. Steps are slippery when wet. Take care and take insect repellent.

Trail Directions: Start at the Visitor Center at the southeast corner of Fort and Huron Streets **[1]**. Cross Huron Street and head up the sidewalk along Fort Street. This climb up the hill takes you past Marquette Park, past a replica of a bark missionary chapel and then past the entrance to Fort Mackinac. The governor's summer residence is at the top of the hill (.2 mi.) **[2]**. This is open to the public from 9:30 A.M. to 11:30 A.M. on Wednesdays during the summer.

Turn right and stroll over to Fort Mackinac (.3 mi.) **[3]**. Keep walking to the junction with a directional board. It directs you straight to the pedestrian and bicycle path (.4 mi.) **[4]**. Stroll through the wooded setting where white cedars are predominant. White pine and spruce help perfume the air.

A narrow path cuts across the trail just before you curve left to parallel Arch Rock Road (.7 mi.) **[5]**. Listen for the touring carriages as the horses clop down the road. After passing a bench, you begin to descend. A sign warns, "Danger, Bicycles Slow" (.9 mi.) **[6]**. A sharp turn awaits you just before you reach the busy circle at Arch Rock Road.

Carriages line up as they wait for the tourists viewing Arch Rock (1 mi.) **[7]**. The arch-shaped rock rises 146 feet above the water. Nicolet Watch Tower adjoins the rock. Named after John Nicolet, the first white man to enter the Old Northwest, it offers a climb of almost 60 steps to a bluff overlooking Lake Huron.

Head back down, follow around the circle, and continue north along Leslie Avenue. The trail winds through woods. Occasionally, you get tree-silhouetted views of the lake. Follow along the ridge. A rail fence protects you from getting too near the steep bluff at about 1.3 mi. **[8]**.

Take the left fork at the Y-junction (1.5 mi.) **[9]** and roll along the North Bicycle Trail through the shade of the woods. At 2 mi., you reach Sugar Loaf **[10]**. The towering stack of 75-foot-high rock was once a tiny island when water levels were much higher.

Turn around and you'll notice steps. Take them up the steep slope, past the sheer rock wall with cavelike

holes, and onto the bluff for a different view of the Sugar Loaf formation.

Turn left on Fort Holmes Road (2.2 mi.) **[11]** and go on to Fort Holmes (2.3 mi.) **[12],** which is situated on the island's highest point. In the War of 1812, the British moved to this high ground overlooking Fort Mackinac. The Americans were taken by surprise, and they surrendered. Surrender to the heights and take in the spectacular view—Bois Blanc Island amid a Lake Huron that is punctuated with boulders and a lighthouse.

Backtrack to the steps along the southwest side of the fort and take them down to Rifle Range Road (2.4 mi.) **[13]**. Turn right. Just to the right, on Garrison, is Skull Cave (2.5 mi.) **[14]**. Read the plaque about why it is called Skull Cave.

Head south on Garrison Road as it descends back to the information board by the bicycle and pedestrian trail (2.8 mi.) **[4]**. From here, retrace your steps back to the Visitor Center.

1. Trailhead
2. Governor's summer residence
3. Fort Mackinac
4. Directional board
5. Intersection with path
6. Descent
7. Arch Rock
8. Rail fence
9. Y-junction
10. Sugar Loaf
11. Fort Holmes Road
12. Fort Holmes
13. Rifle Range Road
14. Skull Cave

Tranquil Bluff Trail 👢👢👢

Distance One-Way: 3.2 miles

Estimated Hiking Time: 1.5 to 2 hours

Cautions: This point-to-point trail starts at the southeast side of the island, near Arch Rock, and ends at the northwest side of the island, near the British Landing Nature Center. Getting to and from the trail will more than double your mileage. Plan your time accordingly.

There are a number of steep climbs and descents on the eastern portion of the trail that are very slippery when wet. The trail has exposed rocks and roots, and portions of the trail will flood when it rains. Wear appropriate footgear. This section of the trail is also along the edge of steep cliffs. Watch your step. Finally, take along insect repellent.

Trail Directions: Climb the steps to the Nicolet Watch Tower, which is next to the Arch Rock viewing area. The sign for the trail is to the left of the rock with the plaque commemorating John Nicolet, the first white man to enter Michigan and the Old Northwest **[1]**.

The Tranquil Bluff Trail, the longest hiking trail on the island, provides an opportunity to walk the island in relative tranquillity. Unlike its name, the first part of the trail contains some of the least tranquil hiking on Mackinac Island. The trail follows the edge of the cliffs along the east side of the island, rising and falling as it provides a number of scenic overlooks. This is not the Mackinac Island that most tourists will see or remember. If the trail is more than you bargained for, Leslie Avenue is close by on the left. The trail does pop out onto this paved road briefly (.2 mi.) **[2]**, then veers right to climb to a cedar-scented overlook (.3 mi.) **[3]**.

The next mile is the roughest part of the trail as it rises and falls along the edge of the cliff. You are rewarded for your efforts with numerous scenic views opening through the trees that cling to the rocky ledge. About 1 mi. into the hike, enjoy a series of spectacular views of Lake Huron from the bluff **[4]**.

When you reach the junction with the Murray Trail (1.3 mi.) **[5]**, the Tranquil Bluff Trail has left the bluffs behind. It now becomes a peaceful walk through the woods. At 1.7 mi., cross the dirt road known as Scotts Road **[6]**. This road is again accessible when it

appears below on the right as you reach an opening in the trees (2.1 mi.) **[7]**.

You are near the northernmost point of the trail at 2.5 mi., and Big St. Martin Island is visible on the northern horizon **[8]**. The trail soon swings wide to the left and you find yourself heading south toward the junction with Porter Hank's Trail (3 mi.) **[9]** and the British Landing Nature Trail (3.1 mi.) **[10]**. If you are interested, the .5 mi. long nature trail has numerous nature displays and identified trees that give users a better appreciation of the island's natural heritage. An inexpensive trail map can be obtained at the Nature Center.

Continuing past the nature trail, the Tranquil Bluff Trail ends when you reach British Landing Road (3.2 mi.) **[11]**. This road was used by the British to reach the high ground above Fort Mackinac, an action that resulted in the fort's surrender during the War of 1812. From here you can take the shore route along the west side of the island or follow British Landing Road through the center of the island, back to the village.

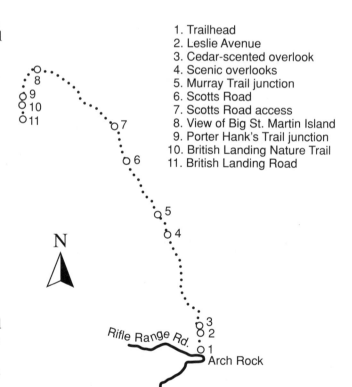

1. Trailhead
2. Leslie Avenue
3. Cedar-scented overlook
4. Scenic overlooks
5. Murray Trail junction
6. Scotts Road
7. Scotts Road access
8. View of Big St. Martin Island
9. Porter Hank's Trail junction
10. British Landing Nature Trail
11. British Landing Road

N

2. Tahquamenon Falls State Park

- Visit the land of Longfellow's Hiawatha.
- Watch root-beer–colored water plunge over one of the largest waterfalls east of the Mississippi.
- Tiptoe through bogs.

Park Information

With nearly 40,000 acres, Tahquamenon Falls State Park is the second-largest state park in Michigan. Much of the park is undeveloped. The lifeblood of the park is the Tahquamenon River, which flows through the park and twice plunges into dramatic waterfalls.

The Upper Falls, sometimes called the Little Niagara, is one of the largest waterfalls east of the Mississippi River. It is over 200 feet across and has a vertical drop of nearly 50 feet. Hiking and cross-country ski trails start from the Upper Falls parking area. Gift and food concessions are located here, along with a picnic area.

The Lower Falls are a series of smaller falls that cascade around an island. While these are less dramatic than the Upper Falls they are no less scenic. Rent a boat and row out to the island for a unique way to view the falls. Hiking trails, a restaurant, picnic area, and campgrounds are located at the Lower Falls.

Tannin leached from the spruce, cedar, and hemlock swamps that drain into the Tahquamenon River gives the water its amber, or root beer, color. Another trademark, the foam beneath the falls, is the result of the soft waters being whipped as they tumble over the falls.

The park offers more than waterfalls. Camping, hiking, backpacking, fishing, canoeing, and nature study are activities during the warmer months. Autumn brings beautiful color to the trees, and snowshoeing, cross-country skiing, and snowmobiling are available in the winter.

Two modern campgrounds are located at the Lower Falls. Modern and rustic campgrounds are located at the Rivermouth site.

Directions: From Paradise, the Lower Falls entrance is 10 miles west on M-123. The Upper Falls are about 4 miles farther west. The Rivermouth unit is 4 miles south of Paradise on M-123.

Hours Open: Open year-round from 8:00 A.M. to 10:00 P.M.

Facilities: Hiking, cross-country skiing, snowshoeing, snowmobiling, swimming, fishing, hunting, picnicking, boat launch, boat rental, canoeing, camping (tent and RV), sanitation station, and interpretive trails.

Permits and Rules: A park fee is required per motor vehicle ($4 daily, $20 annually). Camping is permitted in established areas only.

Further Information: Contact Tahquamenon Falls State Park, Star Route 48, PO Box 225, Paradise, MI 49768; 906-492-3415.

Other Points of Interest

At **Whitefish Point,** visit the **Great Lakes Shipwreck Museum.** From the 1816 wreck of the *Invincible* to the wreck of the *Edmund Fitzgerald,* experience the tales of ships and men who braved Lake Superior's cold, deep waters and violent storms. For more information, call 906-635-1742. In the spring, visit **Whitefish Point Bird Observatory** to watch the birds migrating at one of Michigan's premier bird-watching sites. For more information, call 906-492-3596.

The **Tahquamenon River Logging Museum and Nature Study Area,** north of Newberry, invites you to venture into the robust life of the lumberjack. For more information, call 906-293-3700.

Park Trails

Tahquamenon River Trail 👢👢—4 miles—This trail runs along the Tahquamenon River between the Upper and Lower Falls.

Overlook Campground Nature Trail Loop 👢👢— 2 miles—This trail begins near campsite #179 in the Overlook Campground and winds its way to the Lower Falls.

Wilderness Loop 👢👢👢👢—6 miles—The park's most primitive trail, it is well marked. But there are few footbridges and no boardwalks. It traverses pine ridges, peat lands, and old-growth hemlocks.

North Country National Scenic Trail 👢👢👢👢— 20 miles—Linking the Lewis and Clark National Historic Trail in North Dakota with New York's Crown Point Historic Site on Lake Champlain, this 3,200-mile-long trail includes 20 miles within Tahquamenon Falls State Park.

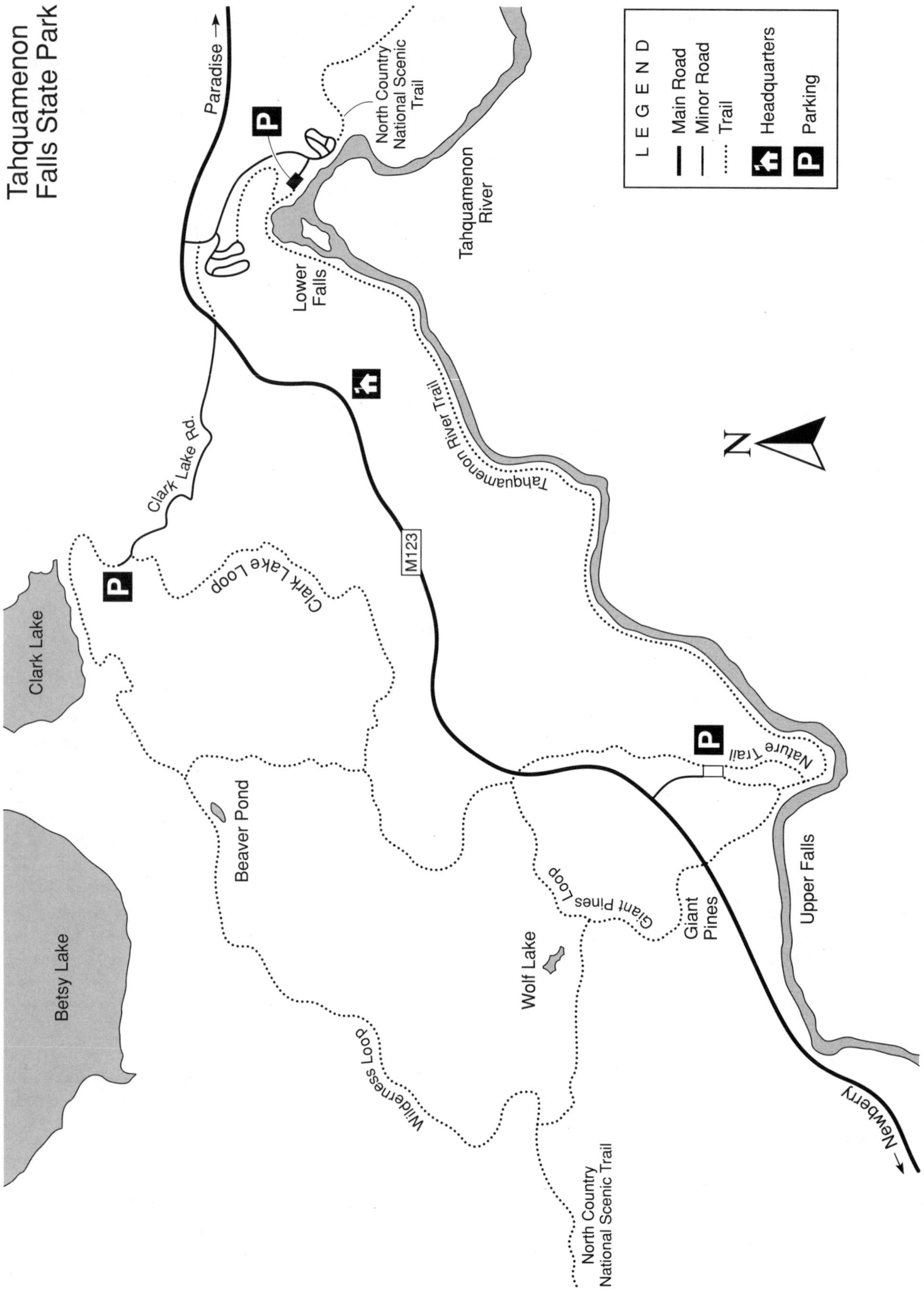

Tahquamenon Falls State Park

Paradise →

North Country National Scenic Trail

Tahquamenon River

Lower Falls

Clark Lake Rd.

Clark Lake Loop

M123

Tahquamenon River Trail

Clark Lake

Betsy Lake

Beaver Pond

Wilderness Loop

Wolf Lake

Giant Pines Loop

Giant Pines

Nature Trail

Upper Falls

North Country National Scenic Trail

Newberry →

N

LEGEND

——	Main Road
——	Minor Road
····	Trail
🏠	Headquarters
P	Parking

Giant Pines Loop
With Upper Falls Tour 👢👢👢

Distance Round-Trip: 4 miles

Estimated Hiking Time: 2 to 3 hours

Cautions: The trail may be intermittently wet. Wear hiking boots and be prepared to cross logs and rocks. Take insect repellent. You don't want mosquitoes and black flies to ruin your hike through one of Michigan's finest examples of primeval beech/sugar maple/hemlock forest.

Trail Directions: Take the Old Growth Forest Nature Trail at the southeast corner of the Upper Falls parking lot **[1]**. This trail rolls and winds through old-growth woods past interpretive boards and benches. The old growth here includes beech, sugar maple, eastern hemlock, and yellow birch.

At .4 mi., turn left on the paved path that leads to viewing points along the Tahquamenon River **[2]**. This leads you to a staircase that takes you 116 steps down to a boardwalk (.6 mi.) **[3]**; here you can view the root-beer–colored water as it cascades over the edge, frothing as it plunges into the river below. Rest on one of the benches before climbing back up to the trail.

Follow the falls-viewing trail on its ridge above the river, stopping at the many viewing spots. From up here, the falls sounds like wind whispering through the trees.

At 1 mi., another staircase takes you almost 100 steps down to a platform right at the falls **[4]**. Watch the river rush by you before it spills down below. Climb back up. There's a bench where you can rest if you wish before continuing to the northwest to plunge onto the Giant Pines Trail.

Step into the old-growth forest on a trail that may, at various times of the year, be wet, and revere the large beeches and sugar maples around you. Your boots will get muddy on this loop, but the experience is worth it. Hemlocks mix in with the other trees before you carefully climb out of the woods to cross M-123 (1.3 mi.) **[5]**.

Dip back into the forest and arrive at one of the trees that gave the trail its name, a giant white pine (1.5 mi.) **[6]**. Stare up in silence at the 120-foot-high tree with its 4-foot, 8-inch diameter. Combined with its mate down the trail, there is enough board feet to build a five-room house. One can only imagine what the forest looked like before giants like these were depleted.

As it winds through the forest, the trail crosses firm ground, then grassy, log-strewn mud. At 1.9 mi., the trail, cut away like a channel, is carpeted with red-brown needles **[7]**. Hemlocks line the way.

The trail descends and winds right. This next stretch is particularly intermittent with wet and dry patches. This continues even after the North Country Trail joins in at 2.3 mi. **[8]**. Well, maybe it intensifies. Wet patches have rocks, logs, and planks bridging the way. Depending upon the season or how long it has been since a rainfall, some pools form on the trail. If there has been a recent wet spell, check to see if there's a pool boiling with life near the planks (2.4 mi.) **[9]**.

After passing under overhead wires, you arrive at the junction for the Wilderness and Clark Lake Loops (3.1 mi.) **[10]**. A picnic area is here; to its right is M-123. Cross the highway and jog to the right to pick up the trail on the other side and enter the dark cover of hemlock and beech.

At times lined with ferns, the trail is drier here. Maple saplings work hard for a comeback at about 3.5 mi. **[11]**. The trail gently descends, and at about 3.7 mi. you may have to maneuver around one more wet area **[12]** before winding down to the north end of the parking lot.

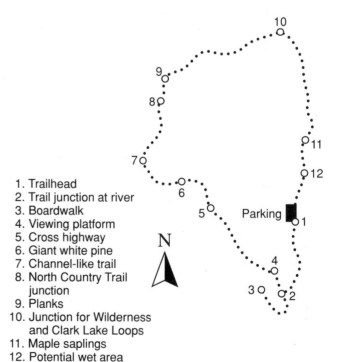

1. Trailhead
2. Trail junction at river
3. Boardwalk
4. Viewing platform
5. Cross highway
6. Giant white pine
7. Channel-like trail
8. North Country Trail junction
9. Planks
10. Junction for Wilderness and Clark Lake Loops
11. Maple saplings
12. Potential wet area

Clark Lake Loop 👢👢👢

Distance Round-Trip: 5.2 miles

Estimated Hiking Time: 3 to 4 hours

Cautions: Be prepared for wet trail conditions and bog walking. Wear appropriate footgear. Take insect repellent. Mosquitoes, black flies, and deer flies are numerous, particularly from mid-May to mid-July.

Trail Directions: From the Lower Falls, take M-123 west to Clark Lake Road. Follow Clark Lake Road, a single-lane, dirt road, to its terminus at a small parking area for the Tahquamenon Natural Area **[1]**.

Enjoy the wide, sandy trail as it rises from the southwest end of the parking area and skirts a bog. Look to your left for a narrow footpath, your gateway to a boardwalk excursion out onto a bog (.1 mi.) **[2]**. The Tahquamenon Falls State Park is home to the largest contiguous ecosystem of this type in the state. The Clark Lake Loop will let you experience a portion of this unique landscape firsthand.

Clark Lake first comes into view as the trail rises onto a ridge of red pine. The best view of the pristine lake comes after a slight descent to trail marker post #5 (.4 mi.) **[3]**. Take pleasure in the solitude of the lake as the trail rolls along the uneven shore, on a ridge cushioned with sand and pine needles.

After crossing a boardwalk over root-beer–colored water, look for a blue-tipped post that guides you away from the lake (.7 mi.) **[4]**. You are now entering landscapes dominated by ferns, patchworks of silver and green lichens, blueberries, ridges of red pine, jack pine uplands, and sphagnum-moss–carpeted lowlands.

By the time you reach trail marker #4, (1.6 mi.) **[5]**, you will have walked on logs to cross several low-lying wet areas. Enjoy the spartan log crossings while you can, because you will soon be walking on less log and more bog.

Turn left at trail marker #4 and walk the perimeter of a beaver pond with the skeletons of dead trees still standing like a forest of ghosts. The trail shortly makes a sudden right, so be looking for blue paint on the trees. Arrive at the first of many bog crossings (1.7 mi.) **[6]**. You will remember this unique and squishy experience.

By the time you reach trail marker #7 (2.6 mi.) **[7]**, the experience may not be so unique anymore; the bogs are becoming ubiquitous. Turn left at the post, proceed past a wet area, and descend into a forest of large hemlock trees (2.8 mi.) **[8]**.

At 3 mi., the trail swings left as you approach a utility corridor **[9]**. Continue to cross a number of bogs in this section. The third crossing is a particularly long one (3.3 mi.) **[10]**. Look for the blue markers after crossing as the trail turns sharply left. After passing a number of stumps, you may notice that some carry the scars of an old forest fire (3.6 mi.) **[11]**.

Continuing past ridges of fern, lichen, and blueberries, and over low-lying wet areas, the trail eventually enters a white cedar swamp on an old logging railroad corridor (4.6 mi.) **[12]**. Chugging in on the old corridor, you reach trail marker #6 at Clark Lake Road (5 mi.) **[13]**. Turn left to return to the parking area.

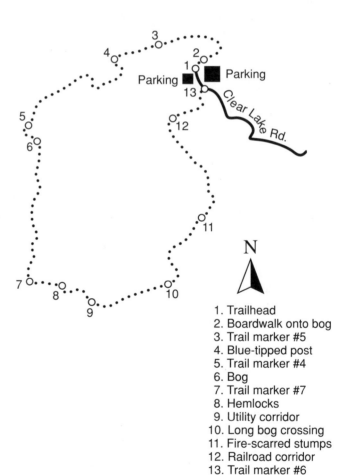

1. Trailhead
2. Boardwalk onto bog
3. Trail marker #5
4. Blue-tipped post
5. Trail marker #4
6. Bog
7. Trail marker #7
8. Hemlocks
9. Utility corridor
10. Long bog crossing
11. Fire-scarred stumps
12. Railroad corridor
13. Trail marker #6

3. Seney National Wildlife Refuge

- Learn about nature from displays, multimedia shows, and a touch table at the Visitor Center.
- Hike or bike on over 60 miles of trails through woods, past rivers, or along pools.
- Discover an abundance of wildlife.

Park Information

Wisconsin. Minnesota. Alaska. Ontario. These are some of the license plates you may see at the Visitor Center parking lot of the Seney National Wildlife Refuge. What makes this place such a desirable destination? Only 95,455 acres of land intricately mottled with marsh, bog, swamp, and forest. Drive, bike, or hike through the refuge and you'll get a feel for what makes up the bulk of the landscape: wetlands. Pools—some green with algae, some blanketed with floating pads, some interrupted with small nesting islands or turtle-encrusted logs—envelop you. Two-thirds of the refuge is wetlands.

Wetlands are what the refuge was. Many of the northern hardwoods and swamp conifers that covered the area about a century ago were depleted by lumbermen. Fires and drainage of the land followed, clearing the land for farming. But the soil was poor. As is the case with much of the public land in Michigan, because of failure to pay taxes the lands reverted to the state. The federal government was encouraged to take over the land, and in 1935 the refuge was created. The Civilian Conservation Corps stepped in and the restoration began. Roads, dikes, and ditches were established, making an intricate water-control system. All of this maintains the refuge and its diverse habitat. Wetlands are what the refuge will remain.

Visitors in vehicles are not the only migrants to pass through the refuge. The biological diversity within the refuge provides suitable habitat for over 200 species of birds. Viewing opportunities are plentiful for common loons, bald eagles, trumpeter swans, and sandhill cranes, as well as white-tailed deer. The refuge also embraces black bear, river otters, beavers, and bobcats—even wolves, although a sighting would be a rare privilege.

At the Visitor Center there are multimedia shows, displays and audio presentations, and a touch table with various animal furs and print molds for deciphering various animals' footprints.

More than 60 miles of trails provide plenty of viewing or recreational ground for hikers or bikers.

One of the trails is an interpretive nature trail. Canoeists can seek refuge along the Driggs and Manistique Rivers. There's also a 7-mile auto tour, the Marshland Wildlife Drive. A brochure assists visitors in understanding the refuge and its wildlife, and observation decks provide an opportunity for taking the two-dimensional brochure to another dimension—viewing wildlife in their habitat.

Winter gives rise to different opportunities—cross-country skiing and snowshoeing. Trails are groomed from mid-December to mid-March.

Directions: The Visitor Center is located about 5 miles south of Seney on M-77 (or about 2 miles north of Germfask). The entrance is on the west side of the highway.

Hours Open: The refuge is open year-round from dawn until dusk, while the Visitor Center is open only from 9:00 A.M. to 5:00 P.M. from May 15 through October 15. The auto tour also runs from May 15 through October 15.

Facilities: Hiking, biking, cross-country skiing, fishing, hunting, canoeing, interpretive trails, interpretive center.

Permits and Rules: No fee is required. Off-road biking is not permitted. Keep your pets on a leash. Pick up your trash. Allow others room to pass you on the road. Leave all plants and animals as you found them. Roads or trails are periodically closed; respect that they are closed.

Further Information: Contact Seney National Wildlife Refuge, HCR #2, P.O. Box 1, Seney, MI 49883; 906-586-9851.

Other Points of Interest

Canoes may be rented locally from Big Cedar on M-77 in Germfask (906-586-6684) or Northland Outfitters on M-77 in Germfask (906-586-9801). Northland Outfitters also rents mountain bikes. The **Fox River Pathway** stretches 27.5 miles from north of Seney to the Kingston Lake campground in the Pictured Rocks National Lakeshore. For more information, contact Shingleton Forest Area, Lake Superior State Forest, West M-28, P.O. Box 67, Shingleton, MI 49884, 906-452-6236; or Lake Superior State Forest, Rte. #4, Box 796, South M-123/M-28, Newberry, MI 49868, 906-293-5131.

Seney National Wildlife Refuge

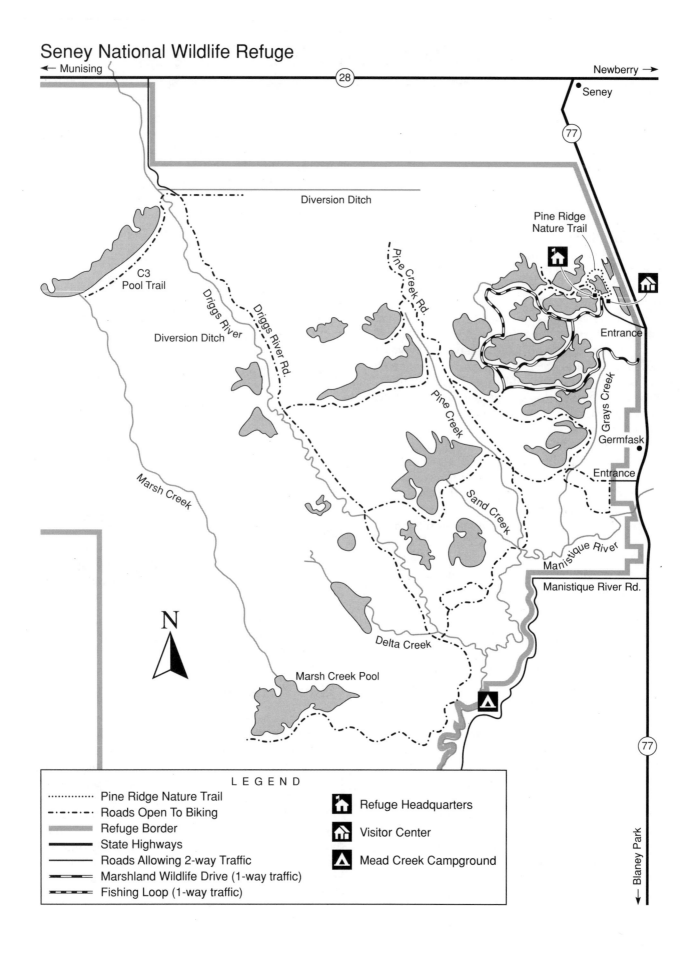

← Munising

(28)

Newberry →

Seney

(77)

Diversion Ditch

Pine Ridge
Nature Trail

C3
Pool Trail

Pine Creek Rd.

Driggs River

Driggs River Rd.

Diversion Ditch

Entrance

Grays Creek

Pine Creek

Germfask

Marsh Creek

Sand Creek

Entrance

Manistique River

Manistique River Rd.

N

Delta Creek

Marsh Creek Pool

(77)

Blaney Park

L E G E N D

.... Pine Ridge Nature Trail
–·–·–·– Roads Open To Biking
▬▬▬ Refuge Border
▬▬▬ State Highways
——— Roads Allowing 2-way Traffic
▬ ▬ ▬ Marshland Wildlife Drive (1-way traffic)
▬ ▬ ▬ Fishing Loop (1-way traffic)

🏠 Refuge Headquarters

🏠 Visitor Center

⛺ Mead Creek Campground

Pine Ridge Nature Trail 🥾

Distance Round-Trip: 1.4 miles

Estimated Hiking Time: 1 hour

Cautions: The trail is in wet terrain. Not only does this make the area a magnet for mosquitoes, but certain portions of the trail also are prone to flooding. Take plenty of insect spray. Black flies, deer flies, and wood ticks may also be a problem.

Trail Directions: The trail starts at the north end of the Visitor Center **[1]**. Head off through the grass between two pools; the one on your right has a green, textured cover of lily pads. Step onto a small bridge between the two pools and admire the handiwork of the Civilian Conservation Corps that helped to establish the elaborate water-control system within the refuge. Much of the trail is on dikes. Hence you are surrounded by water as you circle around one of the pools.

At about .1 mi., the trail wraps around the pool to your left **[2]**. Along your right side, grasses, reeds, and cattails wave at you from the marsh. An interpretive sign discusses beavers (.2 mi.) **[3]**. Maybe the pile of twigs and debris located on a small island in the pool had something to do with the placement of the sign. Look for other signs of beavers along the way, such as shaggy, conical stumps.

Pass the ghost forest of drowned trees and get a brief respite from the sun under a tunnel of brushy foliage before emerging to a small, sandy reprieve with a bench (.3 mi.) **[4]**. This is a great spot for watching turtles clumped on logs that protrude from the pool.

The trail takes you past some paper birches before curving left (.5 mi.) **[5]**. A bridge crosses over a pool of lily pads before depositing you on an extensive boardwalk where you can hear the hollow clump of your passage for almost .25 mi. A sea of cattails fences you in along the way.

Just before you step back onto terra firma on an island of pine needles the color of burnt sienna, the boardwalk bends left and you cross another footbridge (.7 mi.) **[6]**. The trail continues along this red carpet laid out for you through woods and over another bridge; then it passes an interpretive board letting you know that the small shrub you are walking by is Juneberry (.8 mi.) **[7]**.

Cross a boardwalk, pass a small pool as thick and colorful as pea soup, then cross another boardwalk to view the large pool to your right. After a few steps more of the red-carpet treatment, a knob of land forms a point into the large pool. Here a bench awaits you (0.9 mi.) **[8]**. Use it while you view the many nesting islands in this pool. Listen for sandhill cranes or watch the bobbing buoys of geese and duck tails as they submerge their heads in the water searching for food.

Over the next stretch, you walk along a dike between two pools until you arrive at a service road (1.1 mi.) **[9]**. Turn left. Within 200 feet or so, watch for the sign that directs you back onto a path to the left. Depending upon the season or weather conditions, it could be wet and muddy just before you cross the footbridge. The reason for this may be obvious at the next bridge, where you clearly see the engineering exploits of beavers (1.2 mi.) **[10]**. Dam. Soon after, a sign describes a marsh as an area where plants extend above water. Look out over the pool at the spikes of cattails doing just that.

A grassy path winds you back to the Visitor Center but first passes the refuge headquarters (1.3 mi.) **[11]**. An information board sheds some light on a 1976 fire in the refuge. Read about it and about the Canada geese reintroduction before heading back to the left along the road to the parking lot of the Visitor Center.

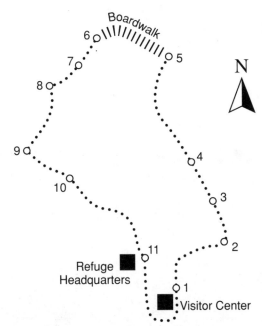

1. Trailhead
2. Trail bends left
3. Interpretive sign
4. Bench
5. Trail curves left
6. Footbridge
7. Interpretive sign
8. Bench
9. Service road
10. Beaver dam
11. Refuge headquarters

C-3 Pool Trail 🥾

Distance Round-Trip: 5.8 miles

Estimated Hiking Time: 3 hours

Cautions: This hike on a dike is often in open sun. Wear a hat, carry sunscreen, and take plenty of insect spray. Black flies, deer flies, and mosquitoes can be plentiful.

Trail Directions: From the Visitor Center, take M-77 north to M-28. Head west on M-28 for 7.5 mi. and turn south on Driggs River Road. Travel along this dirt road for 2 mi. Turn right after crossing over the Diversion Ditch. Cross the Driggs River and arrive at a small parking area near the gate for the dike road **[1]**.

This easy hike provides a good opportunity for viewing wildlife, so don't forget your binoculars. You may also want to pack a picnic lunch. Proceeding past the gate, all you have to do is follow the dike road and look for wildlife. There is little chance to make a wrong turn on this hike.

At .2 mi., note the beaver lodge in the small pool to your right **[2]**. Then get your binoculars ready as a larger pool comes into view. Look for deer feeding along the edge of the far side of the pool, for ducks floating in the cattails, for turtles sunning themselves on stumps, or for great blue herons fishing in the shallow water (.3 mi.) **[3]**.

After the trail makes a little jog, a large wetland opens up on the left side of the dike (.7 mi.) **[4]**. Listen for deer thrashing through the wetland as you approach. Then scan the pool for loons, geese, sandhill cranes, and, if you are lucky, river otters playing in the water. You might even see a bald eagle soaring overhead.

At 1.2 mi. you cross part of the water-level control system **[5]**. Here, water is rushing over a dam to flow south. You can hear the water crashing over the dam. On your right, several nesting islands rest quietly in contrast.

When you reach a muddy stream of brown water as it flows through a sea of green grass to your left, watch for a position marker on the right (2.6 mi.) **[6]**. This marker is your key to spotting a bald eagle nest in a pine tree on the far side of the pool. While this nest had seen activity in the past, for some reason it was not put to use in 1996.

The trail soon snakes left, then right, to a red pine growing next to the water (2.8 mi.) **[7]**. This spot, tempting for a picnic, is located just before the trail ends at the closed bridge over Marsh Creek (2.9 mi.) **[8]**. Kick back and enjoy the spot before retracing your steps back.

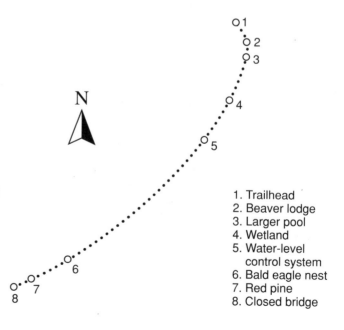

1. Trailhead
2. Beaver lodge
3. Larger pool
4. Wetland
5. Water-level control system
6. Bald eagle nest
7. Red pine
8. Closed bridge

4. Pictured Rocks National Lakeshore

- Explore colored cliffs, pebbled beaches, white sand dunes, and waterfalls.
- Discover the shipwrecks of the Alger Underwater Preserve.
- Cruise the waters along this unforgettable Lake Superior coastline.

Park Information

This 43-mile strip along Lake Superior's shoreline offers such splendor that in 1966 it was designated as the country's first national lakeshore. At the forefront are its cliffs, rising from Lake Superior to heights of 200 feet. Sculpted by water and weather, the arches and caves resemble castles and battleships. Water mixed with minerals seeps from the rocks, staining the cliffs with various hues. The earthy palette of colors changes as shadow and light continually alter the picture. But there's more than just the pictured rocks.

The mosaic of aqua-, blue-, and emerald-colored Lake Superior waters needs no introduction. Spray, exploding from cliffs, paints another scene. Waterfalls add a tint and the massive Grand Sable Banks offer a softer contrast to the rigid cliffs of the pictured rocks. Weave in forests and inland lakes for a multilayered work of art—Pictured Rocks National Lakeshore.

Some park highlights include the Au Sable Light Station; a shoreline accentuated with shipwrecks; natural features like Sable Falls, Miners Castle, and Chapel Falls; the Munising Falls Interpretive Center; the Log Slide; the white sand and pebbled Twelve-Mile Beach; and the Grand Marais Maritime Museum.

Three campgrounds can be reached by vehicle; there are also 7 group and 13 backcountry camps.

Directions: The Visitor Information Center is located on H-58, just east of M-28 in Munising. The Grand Sable Visitor Center is located on H-58 about 5 miles west of Grand Marais. The Munising Falls Interpretive Center is located on Sand Point Road, north of H-58, about 2 miles east of downtown Munising.

Hours Open: The park is open year-round. The Visitor Information Center is open daily, except on January 1, Thanksgiving Day, and December 25, and is closed on Sundays during the winter. Grand Sable Visitor Center is open during the summer and only periodically throughout the rest of the year. The Munising Falls Interpretive Center is open during the summer, as is the Grand Marais Maritime Museum.

Facilities: Hiking, cross-country skiing, snowshoeing, snowmobiling, fishing, hunting, canoeing, camping (tent and backcountry), picnicking, interpretive trails, and interpretive centers.

Permits and Rules: There is a fee for camping. Do not climb on cliffs. Bicycles are permitted only on roads where automobiles are permitted. Wheeled or motorized vehicles and pets are not allowed in the backcountry. Do not disturb shipwreck remains or remove plants.

Further Information: Contact Pictured Rocks National Lakeshore, P.O. Box 40, Munising, MI 49862-0040; 906-387-3700.

Other Points of Interest

Pictured Rocks Boat Cruises offers narrated tours, leaving Munising Bay every day from June to mid-October. For more information, contact Pictured Rocks Cruises, Inc., P.O. Box 355, Munising, MI 49862; 906-387-2379.

Grand Island Shipwreck Tours offers tours for viewing the shipwrecks of the **Alger Underwater Preserve.** Tours run from June through September. For details, contact Grand Island Shipwreck Tours, 1204 Commercial Street, Munising, MI 49862; 906-387-4477.

A publicly operated **shuttle bus** offers transportation for point-to-point hikers who need transportation back to their vehicles. For more information, contact ALTRAN, P.O. Box 69, Munising, MI 49862; 906-387-4845 or 800-562-7814 (in Michigan).

Park Trails

Over 50 miles of trails traverse the park. Pick up a map at one of the visitor centers to plan other hikes.

Lakeshore/North Country Trail 👢👢👢—42.8 miles—This trail follows the cliffs and shore of Lake Superior from Munising to Grand Marais and is the backbone of the trail system. Many day hikes incorporate portions of this trail.

Mosquito Falls Trail 👢👢—3.8-mile round-trip— This trail, which starts at the Chapel Falls parking area, provides views of the Mosquito River, its series of waterfalls, and the Mosquito River canyon.

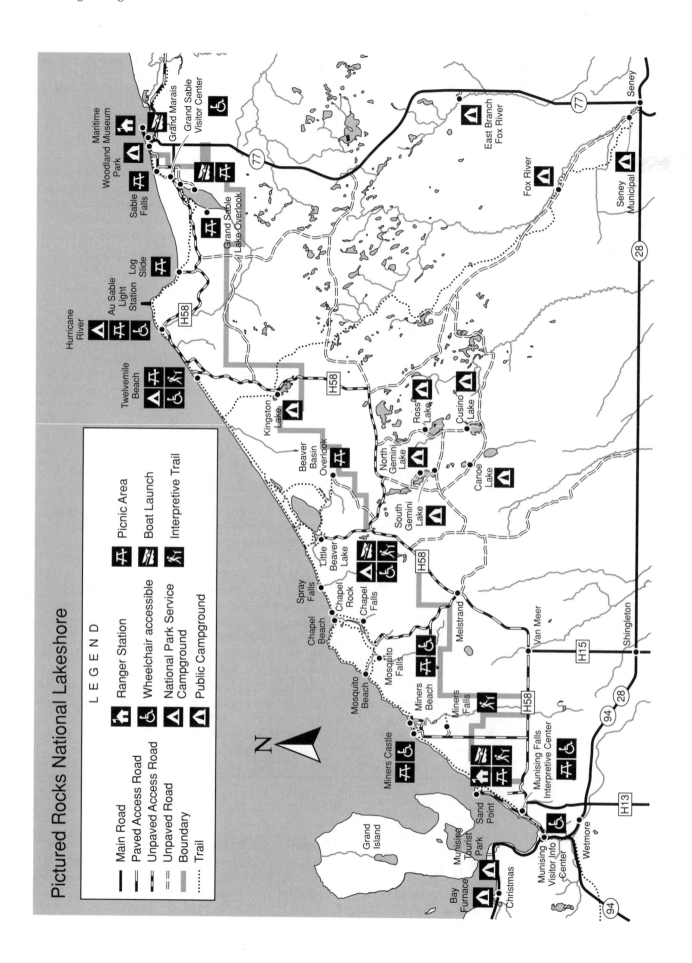

Pictured Rocks National Lakeshore

L E G E N D

Main Road
Paved Access Road
Unpaved Access Road
Unpaved Road
Boundary
Trail

Ranger Station
Wheelchair accessible
National Park Service Campground
Public Campground

Picnic Area
Boat Launch
Interpretive Trail

N

Chapel Basin Trail 🥾🥾

Distance Round-Trip: 9.8 miles

Estimated Hiking Time: 5.5 to 6.5 hours

Cautions: The trail winds along cliffs. Stay away from edges. Rocks and roots are sometimes exposed, and some parts of the trail may be wet. Wear proper footgear. Mosquitoes and black flies can be a problem. Use insect repellent. Take along some water.

Trail Directions: Start this trail from the Chapel Falls parking area, just right of the information map **[1]**, and follow it through the dense hardwoods. At .4 mi., the trail veers left and narrows **[2]**. It rolls along before arriving at the Chapel Lake overlook spur (.8 mi.) **[3]**. Follow this short path to a rocky perch for a view of Chapel Lake far below.

You hear the falls before you reach their overlook spur at 1.2 mi. **[4]**. A viewing platform gives you a close-up of water free-falling over a 90-foot sandstone cliff.

Back on the main trail, cross the footbridge and take the root-laden path to a clearing on a bluff (1.4 mi.) **[5]**. This opens up another view of the falls. Follow the trail to the left. Planks usually support your steps through wet areas. After a fairly steep descent, you arrive at Chapel Rock (3.2 mi.) **[6]**.

Walking the ridge above Lake Superior, you soon cross a bridge over Chapel River as it rushes into the turquoise waters of the lake (3.3 mi.) **[7]**. Step onto a carpet of pine needles and reach a clearing. Welcome the pine perfume and the rainbow colored cliffs below.

Pass through the Chapel Beach camping area where there are steps down to Lake Superior (3.5 mi.) **[8]**; For the next 4.3 miles, walk the ridge overlooking Lake Superior. Near the end of Chapel Beach, the trail takes a short left where the cliffs jut out into the water. You need to watch for a close right, which takes you down what may or may not be a dried-up streamed (3.6 mi.) **[9]**. Climb steeply out of this ravinelike trench and veer to the right, along the cliff.

The trail rolls through forest, occasionally weaving to clearings along the cliffs. One clearing reveals coves where the cliffs resemble battleships (3.7 mi.) **[10]**. Taking a few steps more reveals pottery-colored cliffs, etched with bowls and arches standing erect in mottled green and aqua water. Take a few steps more for another clearing and another formation. Each time you move on, the colors and shapes are different.

If you packed a lunch, enjoy it at Grand Portal Point (4.8 mi.) **[11]**. Here, you get a sweeping view of Lake Superior and its ragged shoreline of cliffs. Stay clear of the edge as you work your way back into the woods at the end of this sandy ledge (5 mi.) **[12]**.

The trail rolls through a carpet of bunchberries spilling down the steep slopes (5.2 mi.) **[13]**. At your next overview, gull sounds echo from the caves of the rocky ledge below (5.3 mi.) **[14]**.

Cut across another sandy opening (6 mi.) **[15]**. Look back at the previous cliff that is carved like an Indian's head with a Mohawk haircut of foliage. At 6.5 mi., the trail cuts very close to the edge **[16]**. From here you can see Grand Island. Ensuing overviews reveal cliffs etched with caves. Travel through more trees, pass another sandy stretch, and then arrive at Mosquito Camp. Pass straight through the camp to the junction for the trail that leads back (8 mi.) **[17]**.

Turn left and follow along the north side of Mosquito River, through the camp, and over a series of planks that cross over wet areas in the woods, until you arrive at the spur to Mosquito Falls (9.3 mi.) **[18]**. Stay straight. You soon reach the trail that leads back to the parking area (9.5 mi.) **[19]**. Turn right and follow it down, over a bridge, then up rocky steps to the parking area.

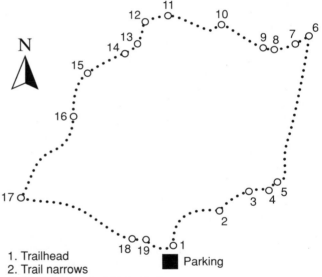

1. Trailhead
2. Trail narrows
3. Chapel Lake overlook spur
4. Chapel Falls overlook
5. View of Chapel Falls
6. Chapel Rock
7. Chapel River
8. Steps to Lake Superior
9. Ravine
10. Overlook with view of coves
11. Grand Portal Point
12. Reenter woods
13. Bunchberries
14. Overlook with view of rocky ledge
15. Sandy opening
16. Cliff edge
17. Mosquito Beach trail junction
18. Mosquito Falls spur
19. Parking lot trail junction

Beaver Basin Loop 👢👢

Distance Round-Trip: 5.5 miles

Estimated Hiking Time: 3 to 3.5 hours

Cautions: Rocks and roots are sometimes exposed on the trail. Some parts of the trail can be wet or muddy; wear proper footgear. Take insect repellent, as mosquitoes and black flies may be abundant, especially in the warmer months. Take along a hat and some water.

Trail Directions: Start from the west end of the parking area for the Lakeshore Trail, located just south of the Little Beaver Lake Campground. A mile-marker post indicates that it is 1.5 mi. to the Lakeshore Trail and Lake Superior and 1.4 mi. to Beaver Lake **[1]**.

Step into the dark, beech/maple forest and step down a series of ledges to a trail marker for the White Pine Trail (.1 mi.) **[2]**. Follow this numbered trail in reverse order. The trailhead for this interpretive loop actually begins at the Little Beaver Lake Campground, where a self-guiding brochure is available. Of the 13 numbered posts along the White Pine Trail, you pass posts #10 through #5 on this hike. Continue past the marker and descend to cross a boardwalk.

At .2 mi., the trail descends sharply, switching back and forth below a rocky ledge. On the hill are a number of white pines estimated to be around 300 years old **[3]**. At the bottom of the descent, a boardwalk awaits to carry you alongside a rushing stream. You soon cross this stream by a footbridge just past the trail junction to the Little Beaver Lake Campground (.4 mi.) **[4]**.

The trail levels out. Step across a lengthy boardwalk that deposits you by a sandstone outcrop. Swing around the outcrop, passing several sea caves cut into the rock that was deposited in shallow seas some 500 to 600 million years ago (.6 mi.) **[5]**.

The trail descends to cross over another boardwalk, leading you to a small footbridge over open water (.7 mi.) **[6]**. When climbing away from the boardwalk, the trail swings right, passes a number of fire-scarred stumps, and reaches a trail junction overlooking Little Beaver Lake (.9 mi.) **[7]**. Stay to the right and look for waterfowl as you follow along the north side of the lake on this trail cushioned with pine needles. Also note the trees, or what is left of them, showing evidence of the mammal from which the lake got its name—the beaver (1.2 mi.) **[8]**.

After you walk the length of Little Beaver Lake, the trail soon reaches a sandy beach (1.4 mi.) **[9]** along the shore of the much larger Beaver Lake. Rise above the clear lake; from a distance, you can see the bottom. At 2.2 mi., you reach a trail marker near the creek that drains Beaver Lake **[10]**. Turn left. You are now headed toward Lake Superior. Before reaching it, you come to a trail junction (2.7 mi.) **[11]**. If you were to go left on the Lakeshore Trail, you would get to the Little Beaver Trail in 1.4 mi. Go right. When the trail turns right again, toward Beaver Creek, continue straight on a well-worn, but unmarked, path that provides a shortcut to Lake Superior. Soon, perched on a sand dune, you get an overview of the beach. Climb down the dune and turn left at the lake (2.8 mi.) **[12]**. From here, that protruding point of land you see off in the distance is Grand Portal Point.

Walking the Lake Superior beach amid driftwood, listening to the pounding surf, and hunting through the myriad rocks scattered about your feet make a pleasant diversion. Looking for the correct turnoff from the beach to the trail, on the other hand, is a lesson in futility. When you come upon three wooden posts just before reaching a rocky point, you know you have gone too far (3.8 mi.) **[13]**. That's okay. Climb the steep, sandy trail behind the posts to reach the Lakeshore Trail. Then turn left to arrive at the junction for Little Beaver Camp (4 mi.) **[14]**.

Hike inland .6 mi. to return to the trail junction that overlooks Little Beaver Lake (4.6 mi.) **[7]**. Turn right and retrace your steps to the parking area.

1. Trailhead
2. White Pine Trail junction
3. White pines
4. Little Beaver Lake Campground trail junction
5. Sea caves
6. Footbridge
7. Trail junction
8. Beaver activity
9. Beach
10. Trail marker near Beaver Creek
11. Lakeshore Trail junction
12. Lake Superior
13. Three wooden posts
14. Trail junction

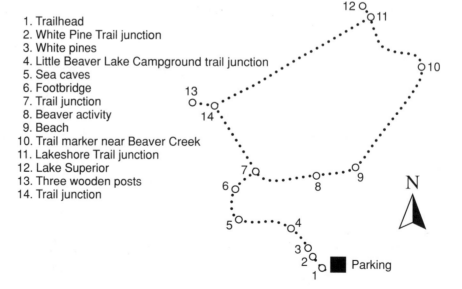

5. Grand Island National Recreation Area

- Escape to this 13,500-acre island of 300-foot cliffs, sandy beaches, inland lakes, and lush forests.
- Walk along bluffs high above Lake Superior.
- Dip your toes into the cold waters of Lake Superior as you stroll a sandy beach.

Park Information

Situated in Lake Superior .5 miles offshore from Munising, this 13,500-acre island mirrors the Pictured Rocks National Shoreline that faces it from the mainland. Sandstone cliffs rising up to 300 feet rival those of Pictured Rocks. Sandy beaches and forests of pine, beech, and hemlock cutting through rugged hills, and interior lakes all combine to make this retreat a real treat.

The Cleveland-Cliffs Iron Company acquired the island in 1900 and used it as a corporate retreat. In 1990 the federal government purchased the island and it was designated a national recreation area, a component of the Hiawatha National Forest.

Over 40 miles of trails embrace the ridges of the island or cut through its interior. Most run north-south and can be linked to form large loops. The north end of the island displays the cliffs. The trail along the tombolo, or the bar of sand that ties the large island to its thumb, is through dune swales, or shallow depressions.

Grand Island National Recreation Area is in its infancy. No water is provided, and camping at one of the two designated areas is primitive. Backcountry camping is also allowed. There are only two designated camping areas, which have a limited number of sites. Trails, trail use, and camping facilities will be changing as the recreation area matures.

Directions: Grand Island is located about .5 miles from the mainland community of Munising. Grand Island Landing is located on M-28, about 4 miles west of the blinking light at H-58 and M-28 in Munising.

Hours Open: Although open year-round, weather conditions limit use of the area. Winter freeze-ups and spring ice break-ups limit the period of use. Unpredictable Lake Superior weather can also render the island inaccessible at times. Ferry service is available only from the Friday before Memorial Day through October 9.

Facilities: Hiking, mountain biking, cross-country skiing, snowshoeing, snowmobiling, ATVs, fishing, hunting, camping (tent and backcountry), and picnicking.

Permits and Rules: No entrance fee is charged, but this may change in the future. Presently no fee or permits are required for the designated or random camping sites. Random sites must not be on the tombolo and must be more than 100 feet from Lake Superior or its cliff edges, other campsites, private property, trails, inland lakes and named creeks, and the Research Natural Area.

Be careful; this is a primitive island. Rescues could take half a day. Use caution on the cliff edges. Bears inhabit the island; don't feed or harass them. No water is currently available, so bring your own. Advise someone on the mainland of your travel plans and be prepared to spend at least an extra day in case Lake Superior weather fouls up boating schedules. Stay on the identified trails and respect the private property of the island residents. Pets must be on leashes.

Further Information: Contact Hiawatha National Forest Visitor Center, Munising Ranger District, Route 2, P.O. Box 400, Munising, MI 49862; 906-387-3700.

Other Points of Interest

Grand Island Ferry Service schedules trips to the island from the Friday before Memorial Day through October 9. The ferry leaves Grand Island Landing in Munising at 9:00 A.M., 12:00 P.M., 3:30 P.M., and 6:30 P.M. through September 2. After September 2, no 6:30 P.M. service is offered. The return trip leaves Williams Landing on the island 15 minutes later than the Mainland departure schedule. But don't count on the ferry being there at these times unless you've made prior arrangements.

A shuttle service offers **Grand Island Sight-Seeing Tours**. They are scheduled to depart Williams Landing on the island at 9:30 A.M. and 12:30 P.M, but arrangements must be made ahead of time. An express run also offers service up to the north end of the island. It leaves Williams Landing at 9:30 A.M. if advance reservations have been made. Make arrangements at least a day ahead of time. For more information, contact ALTRAN, P.O. Box 69, Munising, MI 49862; 906-387-4845 or 800-562-7814 (in Michigan).

Pictured Rocks Boat Cruises offers narrated tours, leaving Munising Bay every day from June to mid-October. For more information, contact Pictured Rocks Cruises, Inc., P.O. Box 355, Munising, MI 49862; 906-387-2379.

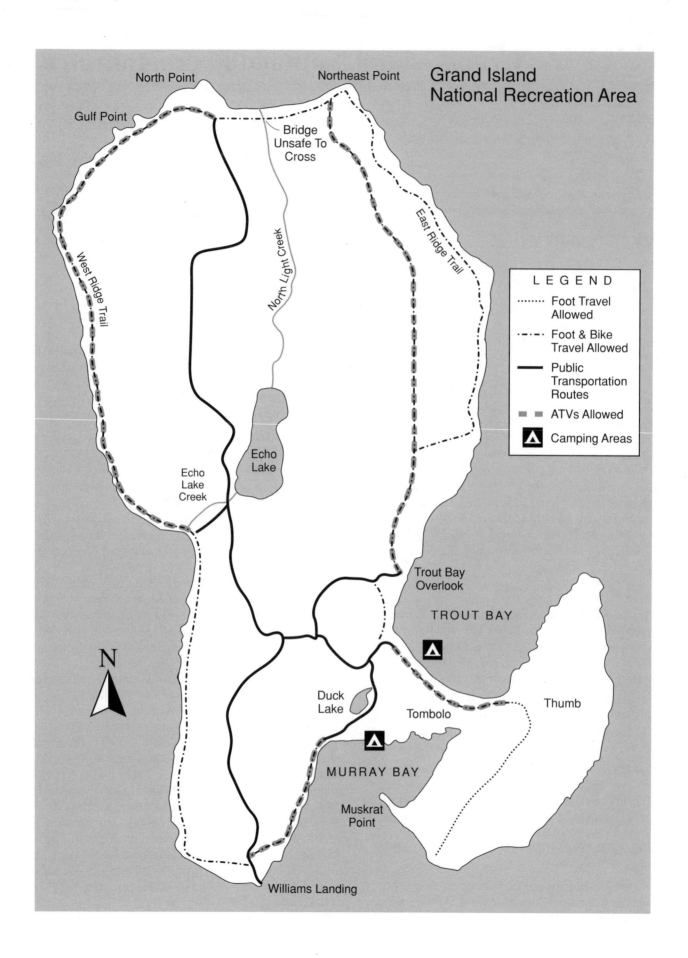

Grand Island National Recreation Area

North Point

Northeast Point

Gulf Point

Bridge Unsafe To Cross

West Ridge Trail

North Light Creek

East Ridge Trail

Echo Lake

Echo Lake Creek

LEGEND

⋯⋯ Foot Travel Allowed

–·–·– Foot & Bike Travel Allowed

—— Public Transportation Routes

■ ■ ■ ATVs Allowed

▲ Camping Areas

Trout Bay Overlook

TROUT BAY

Thumb

N

Duck Lake

Tombolo

MURRAY BAY

Muskrat Point

Williams Landing

East Ridge Trail 🥾🥾

Distance Round-Trip: 10.6 miles

Estimated Hiking Time: 5.5 to 6.5 hours

Cautions: Be careful on the cliffs. The bridge over North Light Creek is unsafe. Be prepared to ford through the creek or to cross on rocks and logs. Bears inhabit the island. Don't feed or harass them. No water is available, so bring your own. Pack a lunch and all the gear you need for a day. Parts of the trail may be wet, so wear proper footgear. Insects will be a problem. Take insect repellent or netting. Advise the ferry service of your plans to return to the mainland.

Trail Directions: Arrange an express run to pick you up at the dock at Williams Landing and take you to the north end of the island **[1]**. Once there, head east along the old carriage road through second-growth hardwoods. The trail winds north and takes you near the cliffs at about .2 mi.; this will give you a sense of the rim you will be walking **[2]**.

At .5 mi., a short spur leads down to the sandy beach along Lake Superior's shoreline **[3]**. Relax in the sand and listen to the waves rushing in as a breeze off the water brushes your cheeks. But don't get too comfortable. You've only just begun. Head back up to the trail.

Roll up your pant legs. North Light Creek dares you to cross it—by fording it, by stepping from stone to stone, or by balancing across a log (.6 mi.) **[4]**. Just don't use the unsafe bridge. While you're down at the creek bed, look to the northwest at the tree-topped cliffs of North Point.

The trail ascends, at times getting near the edges where fences keep you from getting too close. At 1.3 mi., the trail veers right, exposing a wall of sandstone that drops off to the lake below **[5]**. At 2 mi., overlook a cove where a cave has been battered into the cliff **[6]**. The trail diverts from the lake, cuts through maples, then swings back. Across Lake Superior you can view Pictured Rocks off in the distance (3.1 mi.) **[7]**.

The cliff-hanger continues as the trail ebbs and flows near the lakeside ridge. At 3.9 mi., listen to the stream spilling over rocks in the rolling terrain to your right; you can also hear water gently rushing down the steep ravine on your left **[8]**.

More lake views present themselves before the trail veers inland (4.9 mi.) **[9]** and cuts through woods as it subtly descends, passing streams, hills, and ravines. Under a canopy of darkness, the hill on your left looks like a fortress surrounded by a moat (5.8 mi.) **[10]**. The trail ascends to a small meadow at the junction (5.9 mi.) **[11]**.

Turn left on the grassy two-track through mature hardwoods, and descend in and out of tunnels of trees. Pass a dark pool littered with moss-covered logs. You continue rolling through woods before reaching the Trout Bay overlook (7.1 mi.) **[12]** where trees frame the blue waters of the bay.

At 7.4 mi., a trail board announces a footpath on the left **[13]**. Turn down this narrow, rolling, muddy path as it passes ephemeral pools. The trail gently descends, cuts across planked boards over a spring stream, and arrives at a dirt road (8.1 mi.) **[14]**. Follow the tree-lined road to the right to the next trail board (8.2 mi.) **[15]**, where you turn left.

The dirt road passes through some large hemlocks. Duck Lake soon comes into view (8.4 mi.) **[16]**. Listen. Let the quiet envelop you like a warm blanket.

Soon the blue from Murray Bay comes into view. Relax at one of the picnic tables (9 mi.) **[17]** before continuing on to the right, where you'll pass an old cemetery. The trail continues its gentle descent. Winding down, you pass some of the few remaining residences on the island before arriving at a road (10.6 mi.) **[18]**. Turn left and follow it back to Williams Landing.

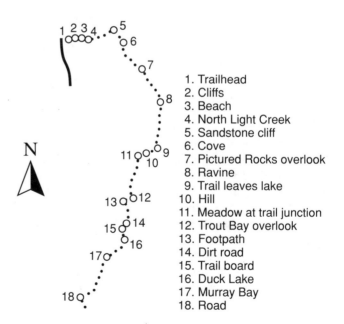

1. Trailhead
2. Cliffs
3. Beach
4. North Light Creek
5. Sandstone cliff
6. Cove
7. Pictured Rocks overlook
8. Ravine
9. Trail leaves lake
10. Hill
11. Meadow at trail junction
12. Trout Bay overlook
13. Footpath
14. Dirt road
15. Trail board
16. Duck Lake
17. Murray Bay
18. Road

West Ridge Trail 👢👢

Distance Round-Trip: 10 miles

Estimated Hiking Time: 5.5 to 6.5 hours

Cautions: Be careful on the cliffs. Bears live on the island; don't feed or harass them. Bring your own water, as none is currently available. Pack a lunch and all the gear you need for a day. Some parts of the trail tend to be wet or muddy, so proper footgear is important. Since there will be mosquitoes and black flies in the warmer months, take insect repellent or netting. Advise the ferry service of your plans to return to the mainland.

Trail Directions: You need to arrange an express run to pick you up at the dock at Williams Landing and take you to the north end of the island **[1]**. Once there, head west along the old carriage road through second-growth hardwoods. You break out of the trees for a view of Lake Superior from behind the security of the safety fencing placed along the edge of the highest cliff of the hike (.3 mi.) **[2]**.

The trail takes you back into the woods, swings inland, and crosses a small stream. This section is prone to flooding. You soon see the lake and can hear it pounding the cliffs. There are several small side paths from the trail to the edge of the cliff for adrenaline-pumping views from the edge (.7 mi.) **[3]**. Watch your step.

At 1 mi., you descend and cross an old bridge **[4]**. Here, through the ravine that the bridge spans, you get a peephole view of Lake Superior and a section of cliff. This is just a tease. Climb from the bridge to gain an unobstructed view from the top of a cove that has been carved out by the constant pounding of Lake Superior waters (1.1 mi.) **[5]**. This is the first of several coves that you will pass. Take your time and enjoy the sights and sounds.

Not straying too far from the edge, where there are little step-out areas from which to view the cliff and Lake Superior, hang in there, for you soon reach the next cove (1.5 mi.) **[6]**. At 2.2 mi., you reach a third cove **[7]**, and then a fourth one only .1 mi. beyond that **[8]**. Notice that Wood Island and the mainland are now visible to the southwest.

Having moved inland and having hiked several straight sections of trail, you find yourself climbing as you pass an escarpment (rock cliff) on your left (3.2 mi.) **[9]**. The trail then levels off as you hike through the woods to a sign that cautions of an upcoming cliff area (4 mi.) **[10]**. The next 1.4 mi. contains a number of opportunities for stepping out to view the ragged edge of the island. How tenuous-looking is the grasp of some trees as they cling to the cliff's edge. At 5.4 mi., just before you swing left away from the edge, is a lookout point. Here, amid red pine, hemlock, and paper birch, you can see a good portion of the western shore of the island to the south **[11]**.

Descending to cross Echo Lake Creek (5.7 mi.) **[12]**, the trail bypasses a private residence by cutting left at the post with a blue arrow. After looping around the private residence, through the hemlock trees on your right, you soon spot a wooden deck with steps down to a sandy Lake Superior beach (6.1 mi.) **[13]**. This beach is worth a little side trip. Did you bring your swimsuit? Can you spell C-O-L-D?

As you continue southward, the cliffs may be less dramatic, but watching your step is still necessary. At 8.3 mi., waves crash on rocks almost at the trail's edge **[14]**, while other portions of the trail are eroding away. As you approach the southwest end of the island, step out on the beach that is a magnet for driftwood and pebbles (8.9 mi.) **[15]**. The trail then swings left. You veer away from the lake and eventually pass through a gate near several large white pines before arriving at a road (9.8 mi.) **[16]**. Turn right and follow it back to Williams Landing.

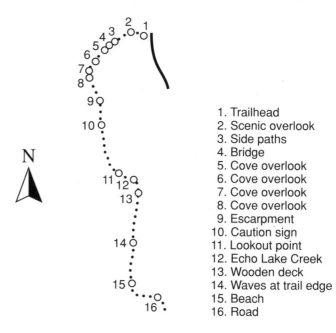

1. Trailhead
2. Scenic overlook
3. Side paths
4. Bridge
5. Cove overlook
6. Cove overlook
7. Cove overlook
8. Cove overlook
9. Escarpment
10. Caution sign
11. Lookout point
12. Echo Lake Creek
13. Wooden deck
14. Waves at trail edge
15. Beach
16. Road

6. Fayette Historic State Park

- Hike along limestone bluffs overlooking an historic townsite.
- Walk amid the standing structures and ruins of a once bustling industrial community.
- Visit the Interpretive Center for a glimpse into the life of a 19th-century company town.

Park Information

Once a bustling village of 500 people, the historic Fayette townsite is preserved as a museum village within Fayette Historic State Park. This ghost town, with more than 20 of the original town buildings—some restored to their 1870s utility—rests along the Garden Peninsula along Big Bay de Noc. Old blast furnaces, the ruins of the company store, charcoal kilns, the town hall, and homes and lodging places stand in contrast to the 90-foot-high limestone cliffs that were once essential to the town's success.

Limestone, plentiful hardwood forests for making charcoal, and a deep harbor once made this a profitable iron-smelting town, run by the Jackson Iron Company. But not for long. Coke iron became more efficient and cheaper to produce than charcoal iron, and in 1891 the company closed its smelting operations and left Fayette. The town took on a new life in the 1960s when it became part of a state park.

Self-guided tour maps allow visitors to stroll through the townsite on their own; guided tours are also available. The Interpretive Center displays artifacts and photographs that paint a picture of the rise and fall of the town.

There's more than an historic townsite at this park of 700-plus acres. Hike along the limestone cliffs that line Snail Shell Harbor, where scuba diving is allowed. Camping, a sandy beach with picnic area, a boat launch, over 5 miles of hiking trails, and boat camping at Snail Shell Harbor are also available.

Directions: Follow US-2 about 15 miles west of Manistique to M-183. Take this south for about 15 miles.

Hours Open: The park is open year-round from 8:00 A.M. to 10:00 P.M.; the buildings are open from mid-May through mid-October from 9:00 A.M. to 7:00 P.M.

Facilities: Hiking, cross-country skiing, swimming, fishing, hunting, boat launch, camping (RV and tent), picnicking, interpretive trail, and interpretive center.

Permits and Rules: A park fee is required per motor vehicle ($4 daily, $20 annually). A fee and use permit are required for scuba diving. All submerged artifacts are to remain in place; nothing is to be removed from the harbor bottom.

Further Information: Contact Fayette Historic State Park, 13700 13.25 Lane, Garden, MI 49835; 906-644-2603.

Other Points of Interest

Bay de Noc Grand Island Trail is a 40-mile trail that runs from Rapid River to Munising. It overlooks the Whitefish River basin. Although open for hiking and mountain biking, it is primarily used for horseback riding, so portions of the trail are sandy. For more information, contact the Hiawatha National Forest, 8181 US-2, Rapid River, MI 49878; 906-474-6442.

A 1.5-mile trail, **Peninsula Point Lighthouse Interpretive Trail,** points out historical and geographical features along Big Bay de Noc. The trail is about 19 miles south of Rapid River on County Road 513. For more information, contact the Hiawatha National Forest, 8181 US-2, Rapid River, MI 49878; 906-474-6442.

Twelve miles west of Manistique at **Palms Book State Park** is Kitch-iti-kipi, Indian for "big spring." Here, ride the self-propelled observation raft that you pull along a cable from shore to shore over this crystal-clear spring where you can view the depths. The park has a picnic area and concession. For more information, contact Palms Book State Park, c/o Indian Lake State Park, Route 2, P.O. Box 2500, Manistique, MI 49854; 906-341-2355. Or you can contact the Schoolcraft County Chamber of Commerce, P.O. Box 72, Manistique, MI 49854; 906-341-5010.

Park Trails

Camp to Beach 🥾—.3 miles—The trail provides access from the campground to the sandy beach at the day-use area.

Camp to Townsite 🥾—.4 miles—This trail provides a hiking link from the campground to the townsite and Visitor's Center.

East Trail 🥾🥾—1.8 miles—A connector from the campsite accesses this loop through hardwood forest. Another connector accesses the northern loop that goes along the limestone cliffs.

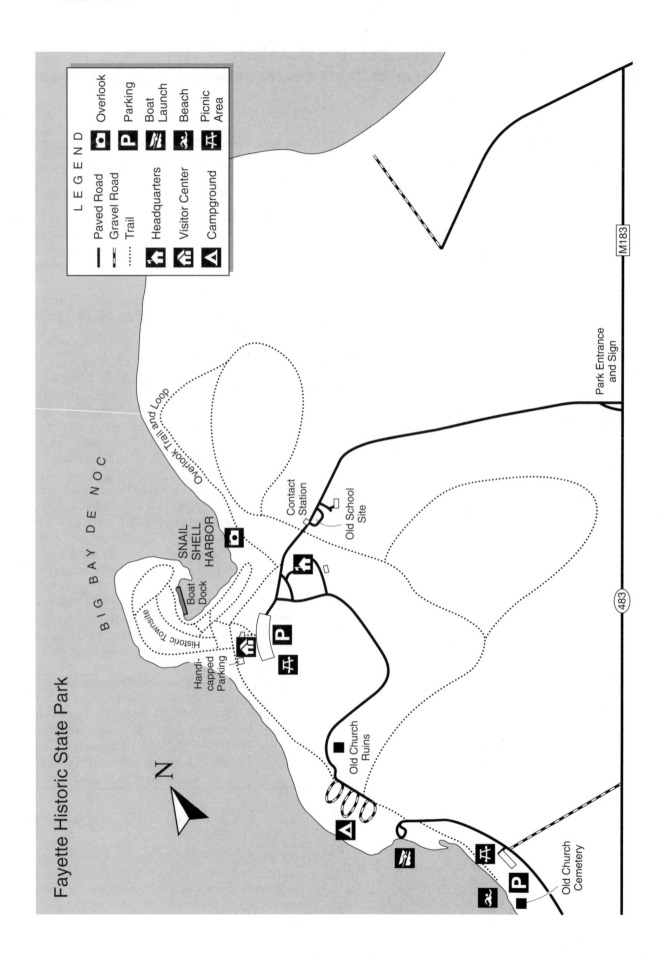

Fayette Historic State Park

BIG BAY DE NOC

SNAIL SHELL HARBOR

Overlook Trail and Loop

Boat Dock

Historic Townsite

Handi-capped Parking

Contact Station

Old School Site

Old Church Ruins

Old Church Cemetery

Park Entrance and Sign

M183

483

N

LEGEND

Paved Road
Gravel Road
Trail
Headquarters
Visitor Center
Campground
Overlook
Parking
Boat Launch
Beach
Picnic Area

Townsite Trail 🥾

Distance Round-Trip: 1.3 miles

Estimated Hiking Time: 1 to 1.5 hours

Cautions: Mosquitoes and black flies will be bothersome. Bring insect repellent. Horse-drawn carriages share the roads with you. Watch your step.

Trail Directions: Start in front of the Visitor Center **[1]**. Head down the hard-surfaced trail alongside the bluff. Take the gravel path at the bottom to the left, into the historic townsite nestled on a hook of land that juts out into Big Bay de Noc.

This ghost of a town has a haunting mix of walled remains and restored structures from its short-lived past as an industrial town. The deep, blue waters of Snail Shell Harbor form a backdrop to the townsite, and windows from crumbling structures frame the limestone cliffs that rise along the east shore of the harbor. Kilns and furnace complexes stand strong along the south end of the harbor.

Interpretive plaques present information about the surroundings. For example, you can read about the 6 mi. railroad grade that serviced the townsite, or about the town's water system.

At .1 mi., follow the road to the left **[2]**. Pass the reconstructed machine shop, pass the two roads by the hotel, and continue to the plaque that overlooks beautiful Big Bay de Noc (.2 mi.) **[3]**. Listen to the waves as they roll onto the pebbled beach. Then read that this was a 19th-century industrial dump site for glasslike slag, or cinder.

Turn around and head back to the middle road in front of the hotel, and take the north fork to the harbor. View the cliffs through the windows of the walled ruins of the company store (.3 mi.) **[4]**.

Backtrack to the middle road by the hotel, and follow it to the northwest as it takes you by the town hall and by foundations and homes of the company supervisors. Farther removed from these is the foundation of a boardinghouse for workers (.4 mi.) **[5]**. Soon the road forks. Turn right and follow it between the houses to the harbor, where you get a first-class view of the cliffs (.5 mi.) **[6]**, as did the superintendent who once lived in the large house

you just passed. To the south, at the bend in the harbor, the stone furnace complex stands like a fortress.

Follow to the left along the bay where trees shade the trail. Openings in the canopy remind you that you are on a ridge along the bay. Waves, and the resonating dong from a bouy's bell, also remind you.

Cross the road that leads down to what was the doctor's house (.6 mi.) **[7]**. Stay on the bay-side road as it takes you past the structural ghosts that house secrets from the past. At the end of this row of structures, a well-worn path cuts across the grass just before the hotel (.8 mi.) **[8]**. Take this back to the company store and down to the road by the harbor (.9 mi.) **[9]**.

Turn left and walk alongside the floating dock. Picnic tables provide opportunity for a break. Take in the harbor's cliffs, cool waters, and striking remnants. Views are particularly striking from the tip of the land hook, where the warehouses once stood (1 mi.) **[10]**.

Turn back and stroll along the harbor and back up the road to the company store (1.2 mi.) **[4]**. Retrace your steps back to the asphalt-paved trail, and climb back up to the Visitor Center.

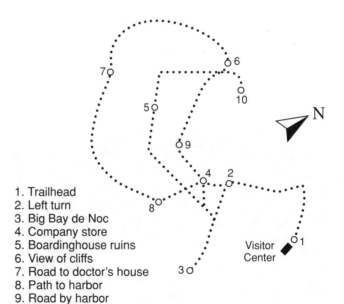

1. Trailhead
2. Left turn
3. Big Bay de Noc
4. Company store
5. Boardinghouse ruins
6. View of cliffs
7. Road to doctor's house
8. Path to harbor
9. Road by harbor
10. Warehouses site

Overlook Trail and Loop 1

👢👢

Distance Round-Trip: 2.6 miles

Estimated Hiking Time: 1.5 to 2 hours

Cautions: Mosquitoes and black flies could be a nuisance in the warmer months. Bring along insect repellent and a hat. Some sections of the trail have exposed roots and rocks. Wear appropriate footgear.

Trail Directions: Start from in front of the Visitor Center **[1]** and head down the asphalt walkway alongside the bluff. At the gravel path, turn right and climb past sumac and quaking aspen toward the drive into the Visitor Center. Turn left at the gate and follow the sign for the Overlook Trail.

You have just climbed Furnace Hill. In the old days this gravel path served as Fayette's primary link to the outside world during spring and late fall when the ice on the lake was either breaking up or forming. Escanaba, a three-hour trip by boat, took two days to reach by stage along this wagon road.

As you approach the first overlook of the townsite, you enter an open area where a 100-foot-long barn once stood. The Jackson Iron Company housed as

many as 60 teams of horses and five yoke of oxen here (.2 mi.) **[2]**.

You soon find yourself leaning to look over the barrier at the first of two scenic overlooks that provide views of the ghost town, Snail Shell Harbor, and also of Lake Michigan (.4 mi.) **[3]**. At the second overlook, the Overlook Trail ends. You have the option of heading back to the Visitor Center or continuing your hike by following the blue boot prints on the wooden posts.

Walking near the edge of the cliff, you can hear the waves crashing and the bell on the buoy clanging in the harbor. Stop and carefully take a look over the edge to see how steep the cliff is. Also, note the limestone cliffs on your right that show the effects of wave action from an earlier period when Lake Michigan water levels were higher (.5 mi.) **[4]**.

The trail swings slightly right, and after a very short distance you leave the mostly white cedar environment of the cliff and enter a beech/maple forest (.6 mi.) **[5]**. The change in the vegetation is quite dramatic. Watch your step on the roots and moss-covered rocks as songbirds welcome you into their home.

The trail climbs gradually and you reach a junction with a map board posted to a trail marker. Following Loop 1 in a counterclockwise manner, you turn right (.9 mi.) **[6]**.

At 1.2 mi., make a sharp hairpin turn to the left **[7]**. (An alternative would be for you to continue straight and return via the paved road to the Visitor Center.) This section of trail appears to get little use as moss carpeting and limestone slabs compete to guide your feet along the way. You complete the loop at 1.7 mi. **[6]**, where you turn right to retrace your steps back to the Visitor Center. Listen as the bell of the buoy guides you back.

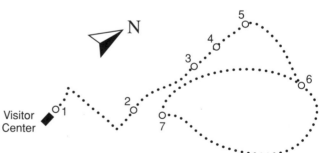

1. Trailhead
2. Barn site
3. Scenic overlooks
4. Limestone cliffs
5. Beech/maple forest
6. Trail junction
7. Trail junction

7. Little Presque Isle Tract

- Enjoy sandy beaches along the rugged Lake Superior shoreline.
- Climb to spectacular overlooks.
- Hike across a beaver dam.

Park Information

Only 3.5 miles north of Marquette, sheer cliffs, sandy beaches, and old growth forests of hemlocks and red pines are accessible via the network of hiking, bicycling, and cross-country skiing trails that weave through 3,040 acres of Little Presque Isle Tract.

Four miles of Lake Superior shoreline, with rugged cliffs, rocky escarpments, and pockets of soft sand, are the focus of the tract—and a forecast of the diversity that lies in store inland. The 64-acre Harlow Lake provides for quiet contemplation and non-motorized boating. Hogsback Mountain, 600 feet above Lake Superior, offers challenging hiking and a dramatic view of the lake and surrounding area.

Most of the public use is at Little Presque Isle Point, which overlooks the 8.6-acre island the tract is named for, and Wetmore Landing. Both have sandy beaches, vault toilets, and parking.

More than 18 miles of trails cross Hogsback Mountain, loop Harlow Lake, traverse ridges along Lake Superior, and link with other trails. Six rustic cabins are available along the Harlow Lake ski trail.

The tract, acquired by the state in three separate exchanges from 1976 through 1979, is managed by the Escanaba River State Forest for low-intensity recreational development and use. There is no camping, and motorized vehicles are not allowed except in designated areas.

Directions: The tract is 3.5 miles north of Marquette. Three parking areas are located off County Road 550: at Wetmore Landing, at Little Presque Isle Point, and at Clark's Gravel Pit.

Hours Open: The park is open year-round.

Facilities: Hiking, mountain bicycling, cross-country skiing, swimming, fishing, boat launch, cabins, picnicking, and interpretive trail.

Permits and Rules: No park fee is required. No camping is allowed. Fires must be contained in designated fire pits or grills. Motorized vehicles are permitted only on designated roads and parking areas.

Further Information: Contact Ishpeming Forest Area, Escanaba River State Forest, Ishpeming Field Office, 1985 US 41, Ishpeming, MI 49849; 906-485-1031.

Other Points of Interest

The City of Marquette's 328-acre **Presque Isle Park** offers cliffed and sandy Lake Superior shoreline, dense northern forests, numerous vehicular turnouts for taking in panoramic views, short trails with overlooks, and a 160-foot water slide. In the evening, Sunset Point is an elegant spot in which to pull the shade down for the day. Follow Lakeshore Boulevard to the park's entrance. For more information, contact Marquette Parks and Recreation, 300 West Baraga, Marquette, MI 49855, or call Marquette County Convention and Visitors Bureau, 800-544-4321.

Sugarloaf Recreational Trail winds up over .5 miles to the peak of Sugarloaf Mountain, where panoramic views of Lake Superior, its rugged shore, the City of Marquette, and its surrounding hills and forests abound. The trail is located north of the city off County Road 550.

Just south of Presque Isle Tract is the **Mead-Wetmore Pond Nature Trail.** Access is on the west side of County Road 550. Wetmore Pond is a floating bog. Some trails are interpretive, and they link with the trails of Presque Isle Tract as well as with the North Country Trail. For more information, contact Mead Paper, Woodlands Department, P.O. Box 238, Champion, MI 49814; 906-786-1660, extension 2194.

Get a taste of the history of the city's past at the **Marquette Maritime Museum.** It is open daily from 10:00 A.M. to 5:00 P.M. from June through September. The museum is located on East Ridge at Lakeshore Boulevard. For more information, call 906-226-2006.

Park Trails

Song Bird Trail 🥾🥾—1.1 miles—This interpretive trail passes thickets, wetlands, and a river delta. It starts from the Little Presque Isle Point area parking lot. A brochure helps you to identify the habitats and the various birds that are likely to inhabit them.

Harlow Lake Trail 🥾🥾—6 miles—This trail is notable for its Nordic use. Parking is near a gravel pit on the west side of County Road 550, near Wetmore Landing.

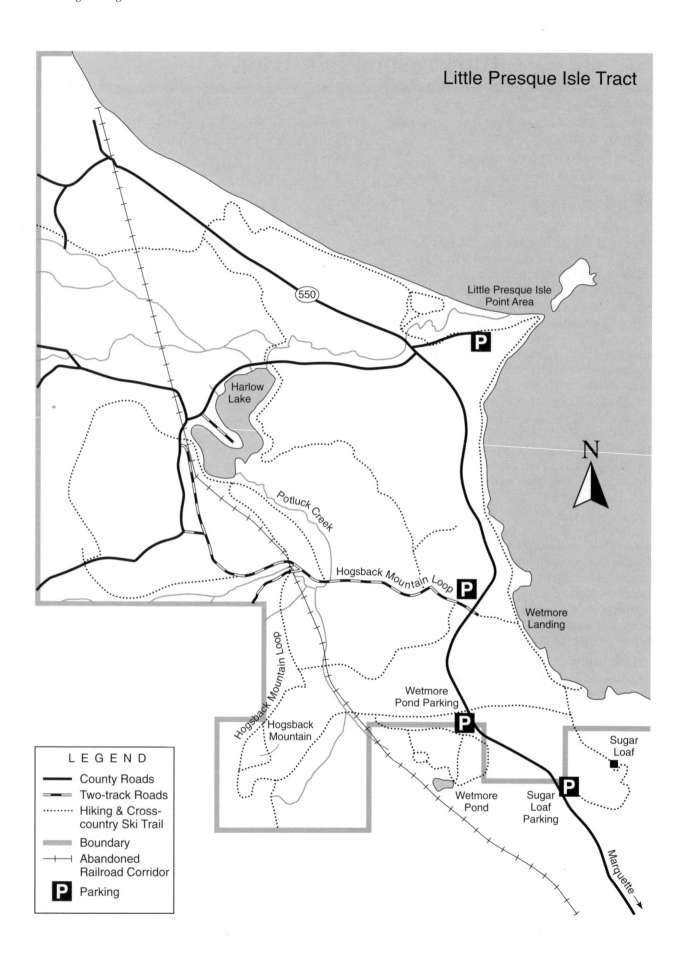

Little Presque Isle Tract

Little Presque Isle Point Area

550

Harlow Lake

Potluck Creek

Hogsback Mountain Loop

Hogsback Mountain Loop

Hogsback Mountain

Wetmore Landing

Wetmore Pond Parking

Wetmore Pond

Sugar Loaf

Sugar Loaf Parking

Marquette

N

LEGEND
— County Roads
— Two-track Roads
····· Hiking & Cross-country Ski Trail
— Boundary
—|—| Abandoned Railroad Corridor
P Parking

Lake Superior—Little Presque Isle Point to Wetmore Landing

Distance Round-Trip: 3.8 miles

Estimated Hiking Time: 2 to 3 hours

Cautions: At times you are near the cliff's edge. Be careful. Roots and rocks crop up along the trail, so watch your step. Mosquitoes and black flies could be a problem in the warmer months. Bring along insect repellent and use it.

Trail Directions: Start from the north side of the parking area at the Little Presque Isle Point area **[1]**. Although the trail heads east along the Lake Superior shoreline, succumb to the temptation of the lake and head north for a short shoreline visit. The beach is an intriguing mix of sand and shore that is under the cover of red pines. You don't need to draw out the visit too long; this hike keeps you along the lake. Head back to the pine-carpeted trail toward the point, where you can see the island, Little Presque Isle.

A blue mark on a tree alerts you to follow the trail to the right, but go on out to the point for a closer view of the 8.6-acre island (.2 mi.) **[2]**. The view through pine and birch is tough to resist.

Follow to the right, and the trail eventually cuts near the lake. A few trails pass through here. Your path takes you under the cover of trees, but near the shore. After passing cobblestones near the lake's edge, you reach a fork (.3 mi.) **[3]**. Follow the blue markings and stay near the line of the shore. From here you see the burnt-umber rock outcroppings along the shore ahead of you.

The trail ascends, and at about .4 mi. you walk along the sinuous line of coves that have been eroded into the ridge **[4]**. Gently rolling along the trail, you pass many more coves as you wind in and out of the trees. When you walk into darkness, notice the prevalence of hemlocks. Some of them look as though they are about to dive off the cliff into the cold waters of Lake Superior (.7 mi.) **[5]**.

The shoreline continues, ragged, with a sawtooth edge of coves. Red cliffs drop to the depths of the lake below, only a few feet from your boots. Boulders pounded by waves below signal that you are near the steps that take you to a higher ridge (.8 mi.) **[6]**. Climb

up and continue left through the mixed hardwoods. Notice that the forest floor is bright with foliage where an uprooted tree exposed a hole of sunlight (.9 mi.) **[7]**.

Roll along through the woods, passing an area with many fallen birches (1 mi.) **[8]**. This is your cue that a clear view of the lake is close. Very close. Watch that edge; it's a sheer drop over. Continue along, dipping down a small ravine, then crossing the footbridge over another (1.1 mi.) **[9]**. This takes you to a viewing area with a seat and security railing. From here, past the steep escarpment (rock cliff), you view the sandy beach below.

Thereafter the trail gradually descends until you reach the almost 100 steps that take you down to the boulder-strewn edge of the lake (1.5 mi.) **[10]**. Climb over these massive reminders of the cliffs of yesteryear. Wind around these giants, and then pass along the pebblestone shore, which gives way to the sandy beach at Wetmore Landing (1.9 mi.) **[11]**. A path leads less than .2 mi. to the parking area—or you can rest in the sand before turning around and heading back to Little Presque Isle Point for a different perspective of the Lake Superior shoreline.

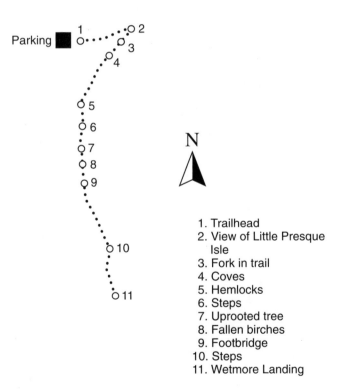

1. Trailhead
2. View of Little Presque Isle
3. Fork in trail
4. Coves
5. Hemlocks
6. Steps
7. Uprooted tree
8. Fallen birches
9. Footbridge
10. Steps
11. Wetmore Landing

Hogsback Mountain Loop

Distance Round-Trip: 5.2 miles

Estimated Hiking Time: 4.5 to 5.5 hours

Cautions: There are steep climbs and descents on rock. You cross a pond on a beaver dam. Wear appropriate footgear. Bring insect repellent, a hat, and water.

Trail Directions: The parking area is 5 mi. north of Marquette on County Road 550. The trail begins on the west side of the parking area **[1]**. Cross County Road 550 and head westerly down a "seasonal" county road, past map board #1 (.1 mi.) **[2]**. When you reach the next trail junction, swing left and descend through red pine (.3 mi.) **[3]**.

At .8 mi., you cross a one-lane bridge over a stream **[4]** to reach the junction to Harlow Lake. Stay to the left, then go left again at the next junction to cross a culvert over running water (1 mi.) **[5]**.

After crossing an abandoned railroad corridor, look left for post #5. Head for the sign nailed to a tree beyond post #5. It points in the direction of the ski-trail short loop (1.1 mi.) **[6]**. Then climb over a dirt mound to enter the woods, and soon cross over a stream on a footbridge (1.2 mi.) **[7]**. You then climb into a hemlock grove, descend past a pond, and swing around a rock outcrop to find yourself in a stand of red pine at the junction for Hogsback Mountain (1.5 mi.) **[8]**. Go right.

Cross a couple of muddy sections before starting to climb the Hogsback. The trail is eroded, and many roots and rocks are exposed, making the climb treacherous (1.7 mi.) **[9]**. At 2 mi., you reach a map board **[10]**. Go left. This is the most difficult section of the trail. You may find that you need to use your hands as you climb up the steep grade over bare rock.

You are well rewarded for your effort when you reach the summit (2.2 mi.) **[11]**. A panoramic view of Lake Superior and the Marquette environs awaits you.

Getting down from the peak is no less difficult than the climb. Watch your step. There are many blue marks along the summit, but they are hard to follow over the bare rock. Take your time.

As you descend, you come upon a trail map board (2.7 mi.) **[12]**. Stay to the left and continue downward. It isn't until you see the top of the handrail from the submerged footbridge sticking out from the middle of a pond that you realize that the climb down has ended. Don't panic. You don't have to turn around and climb back up, but you do have to use the beaver dam to cross the pond (3.2 mi.) **[13]**. It's on your left. Dam. It's almost 150 feet wide. Step carefully. When you reach solid ground, you step onto an abandoned railroad corridor. Turn right along the corridor to pick up the trail again (3.2 mi.) **[14]**. Turn left.

Climb over the low end of a rock outcrop to the junction with the Mead Nature Trail (3.4 mi.) **[15]**. Stay left to climb along another rock outcrop. At the next outcrop take a look behind you for a scenic view of Hogsback Mountain (3.7 mi.) **[16]**.

Cross County Road 550 (3.9 mi.) **[17]** and start up another rock ridge. Snaking around the backside, you'll descend through a narrow ravine between rock outcrops. When the trail levels out, you swing right along the backside of an outcrop in a hemlock grove (4.2 mi.) **[18]**.

At 4.5 mi., after hiking through a wet area, watch for a map board **[19]**. Turn left and descend toward Lake Superior. A remnant walkway leads you from the ridge toward the beach (4.7 mi.) **[20]**. The trail now parallels the lake. Watch for blue markers on the trees (5.1 mi.) **[21]** that lead you away from the beach and back to the parking area.

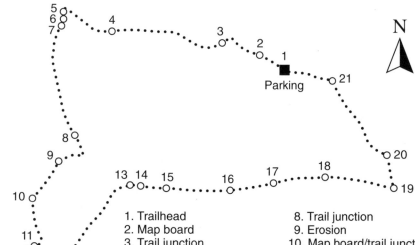

N

1. Trailhead
2. Map board
3. Trail junction
4. Bridge
5. Culvert
6. Sign for ski-trail short loop
7. Footbridge
8. Trail junction
9. Erosion
10. Map board/trail junction
11. Hogsback Mountain summit
12. Map board/trail junction
13. Beaver dam crossing
14. Return to trail
15. Mead Nature Trail junction
16. Scenic look over your shoulder
17. County Road 550
18. Hemlocks
19. Map board/trail junction
20. Walkway to beach
21. Trail to parking area

8. Fumee Lake Natural Area

- Hike around lakes uncluttered with cabins or motorboats.
- Canoe the quiet waters of the pristine Fumee Lakes.
- Enjoy the call of a loon or the sight of an eagle soaring above the lakes.

Park Information

Tucked away, within 5 to 10 minutes of three of Dickinson County's cities, are over 1,000 acres of serenity—the Fumee Lake Natural Area. This Dickinson County park with two pristine lakes, significant wetlands to recharge the water, and over 270 plant and wildflower species provides a peaceful refuge for animals and other visitors to the area.

Seven species of fish may swim easy in the no-fishing lakes, and at least 26 species of mammals may pass through without the threat of being hunted. With more than 5 miles of shoreline between the two lakes, over 137 species of birds visit or find a home here. The bald eagle and common loon discover prime nesting habitat within the natural area.

From midsummer through September, canoeists may enjoy the setting from their quiet watercraft in the lakes. Throughout the year, 10 miles of trails open the natural area to hikers, bicyclists, and cross-country skiers. Most of the trail system encircles one of the two lakes.

The two lakes, Little Fumee Lake and Fumee Lake, make up the bulk of this natural area. The area came about as a natural extension of what was once city-owned property. Around the turn of the century, the City of Norway needed a safe water source. In 1910 an underground pipeline was completed from Little Fumee Lake. It and its watershed became important to the locale. A 500-foot canal was dug between this lake and Fumee Lake so lake levels could be regulated. This life source, the water and its surrounding area, was protected.

Newer well and groundwater systems paved the way for a change. Because the lakes and their surrounding watershed had been preserved in a natural state for so many years, residents of Dickinson County voted in 1992 to purchase the land for this, the Fumee Lake Natural Area.

Directions: To get to this site located between Norway and Quinnesec, take Upper Pine Creek Road about 1 mile north from US-2 to the road in. It's about .25 miles west to the parking area.

Hours Open: Open year-round.

Facilities: Hiking, mountain bicycling, cross-country skiing, and canoeing.

Permits and Rules: No park fee is required. This is a nonmotorized area. No fishing or hunting is allowed. Canoeing is permitted from midsummer through September.

Further Information: Contact Tourism Association of the Dickinson County Area, 600 South Stephenson Avenue, Iron Mountain, MI 49801; 906-774-2945 or 800-236-2447.

Other Points of Interest

The **Merriman East Pathway** has almost 7 miles of trail for hiking and cross-country skiing. The pathway is located northeast of Iron Mountain. From Iron Mountain, take M-95 6 miles north to Merriman East Truck Trail; then go east about 7 miles. For more information, contact Norway Forest Area, Copper Country State Forest, P.O. Box 126, Norway, MI 49870; 906-563-9247.

Explore 400 feet below the ground in the tunnels and drifts of the **Iron Mountain Iron Mine.** Located on US-2 in Vulcan, it is open from Memorial Day weekend through October 15, from 9:00 A.M. to 5:00 P.M. For more information, call 906-563-8077.

Park Trails

South Ridge 🥾—2 miles—All three of the trails start from the northwest end of the parking area. This trail traverses the south portion of Little Fumee Lake, swings through forest, and skirts along a portion of Fumee Lake.

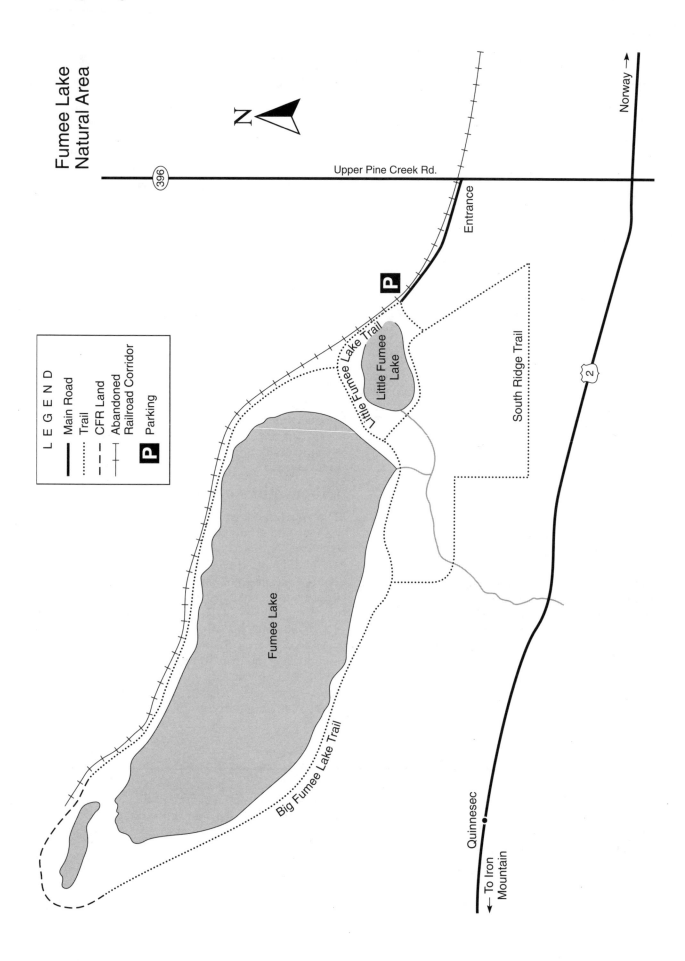

Fumee Lake
Natural Area

N

LEGEND
Main Road
Trail
CFR Land
Abandoned
Railroad Corridor
P Parking

396

Upper Pine Creek Rd.

Entrance

P

Little Fumee Lake Trail

Little Fumee
Lake

South Ridge Trail

2

Fumee Lake

Big Fumee Lake Trail

Norway →

Quinnesec

← To Iron
Mountain

Little Fumee Lake Trail 👢

Distance Round-Trip: 1.8 miles

Estimated Hiking Time: 1 hour

Cautions: Mosquitoes and black flies will be a problem in the warmer months. Bring insect repellent.

Trail Directions: Start through the gate from the northwest corner of the parking area **[1]**. The dirt road you follow parallels the abandoned rail corridor that once serviced the Chicago and North Western Railroad. No motorized vehicles are allowed within the natural area, but this corridor, located just outside, is a snowmobile trail in the winter.

Along the south side of the trail is a wetland; cattails wave in the breeze. Look closely and you can see nesting boxes perched among them. On the other side, lily pads float in the channel between the old grade and the trail. Pass under the buzzing high wires, and you'll then arrive at the trail junction where all three loops begin and end (.2 mi.) **[2]**.

Stay straight, proceeding alongside the old rail corridor. Little Fumee Lake comes into view through a window of trees (.3 mi.) **[3]**. The small lake remains in view, passing in and out of the windows formed by the trees. Listen for the haunting cry of loons and watch for them as they float and dive in the water.

The trail passes through a dense mix of hardwoods, then veers left before arriving at the junction for the Big Fumee Lake Trail (.5 mi.) **[4]**. Follow the two-track to the left as it cuts through the hardwoods. As you get nearer to Little Fumee Lake, grasses form the forefront to cattails, which precede the lake. Between the two lakes now, at times they afford you a view.

A stream crosses between the two lakes at .9 mi. **[5]**. This is also the canoe portage point. Near here, you can take in the big picture—both lakes—until you reach the next junction (1 mi.) **[6]**.

Follow to the left, where you walk between the cattails of Little Fumee Lake and the low, lush wetlands to your right. Soon you'll hear the trickle of a stream before you finally reach it (1.2 mi.) **[7]**. It connects Little Fumee Lake, which you see framed in cattails, with the wetland that is profuse with foliage. The trail flanks the lake as it wraps around to the northeast. Along this stretch, you get vivid views of this secluded little lake. Woods encircle the trail, which encircles the lake. A small concrete building, a relic from the natural area's water-provision days, stands strong along the shore (1.4 mi.) **[8]**. From this vantage point, this is the only improvement visible.

The trail curves to the south, away from the lake, and heads under a canopy of trees. At 1.5 mi., the South Ridge Trail cuts to the southeast through the fence **[9]**. Follow along to the northeast through the hardwoods, which soon give way to red pines. A canoe route appears to your left near the lake. Here, another building stands—a log cabin. This was built after the depression by the Works Progress Administration as a warming shack for men engaged in other WPA projects. In this area, the project was the installation of 8 miles of gravel roads around the lakes. Red pine needles continue to cushion your steps until you arrive at the junction that closes the loop around Little Fumee Lake (1.6 mi.) **[2]**. Turn right and cut again through the wetlands, passing under the high wires and alongside the abandoned rail corridor until you return to the parking area.

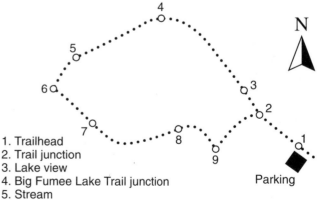

1. Trailhead
2. Trail junction
3. Lake view
4. Big Fumee Lake Trail junction
5. Stream
6. Trail junction
7. Stream
8. Concrete building
9. South Ridge Trail junction

Parking

N

Big Fumee Lake Trail 🥾🥾

Distance Round-Trip: 6 miles

Estimated Hiking Time: 2.5 to 3.5 hours

Cautions: Mosquitoes and black flies will be a nuisance in the warmer months. Bring insect repellent. The western end is on private property and may be muddy. Wear appropriate footgear.

Trail Directions: Start from the gate at the northwest corner of the parking area **[1]**. The dirt road you follow parallels an abandoned railroad corridor. No motorized vehicles are allowed within the natural area, but this corridor, located outside, serves as a snowmobile trail.

To the south of the trail, moved by the breeze, cattails wave at you from a wetland. Nesting boxes, unmoved by the moment, sit perched, quietly waiting. Look to the north. Lily pads float in the channel between the old rail grade and the trail. Pass under the buzzing high wires to arrive at a trail junction (.2 mi.) **[2]**. Stay to the right.

Little Fumee Lake comes into view through a window of trees (.3 mi.) **[3]**. Listen for the machine-gun "rat-a-tat-tat" of the kingfisher as it flies away, startled by your approach. The trail then passes a dense mix of hardwoods before arriving at the junction with the Little Fumee Lake Trail (.5 mi.) **[4]**. Follow the two-track to the right. Fumee Lake soon reveals itself, and the trail comes right up to the edge for an intimate viewing (.9 mi.) **[5]**. Hiking along Fumee Lake, you will find that it is something of a tease, often hidden behind a veil of trees.

At 1.3 mi., a side path leads to the lake **[6]**. Boulders that lie partially buried in the soil along the water's edge make great seats. Further down, the trail is again right up to the edge of the lake (1.6 mi.) **[7]**. It then climbs to reach another side path (1.7 mi.) **[8]**. Paper birch logs border this walkway.

The trail again descends and you find yourself at the lake's shore for your last view from the north side (1.8 mi.) **[9]**. The trail soon leaves the natural area. Stay to the right when the trail first splits and go through an opening among some boulders (2.2 mi.) **[10]**. At the second split, go left and soon cross a creek (2.3 mi.) **[11]**. You are no longer on the old road, and the trail may be muddy.

A barbed-wire fence separates you from the water-filled pit of the old Indiana Mine (2.4 mi.) **[12]**. The mine is now home to beavers, Canada geese, and other wild critters. When the fence ends, go straight through the tall grass. After passing two large pine trees, turn left where the trail widens as a result of ATV use. Descend to a wet area past a running spring (2.8 mi.) **[13]**.

White cedars now dominate the landscape, and small creeks flow along both sides of the old corridor that the trail follows along (3 mi.) **[14]**. At 3.4 mi., the trail swings left from the old corridor to reenter the Fumee Lake Natural Area **[15]**.

The south side of the lake is not as accessible as the north side. At 3.7 mi., a side path takes you for your first view of the lake **[16]**. As you wind your way through the forest on the old road system, stay to the left at the junction with the South Ridge Trail (4.7 mi.) **[17]**. At 5 mi., you cross over a culvert with water rushing away from Fumee Lake **[18]**. Stop at the bench and enjoy the view (5.1 mi.) **[19]**.

Just past the bench, stay left at the junction to reach the drain where canoeists portage between the two lakes (5.2 mi.) **[20]**. At the next junction you find that you have completed your loop of Fumee Lake (5.7 mi.) **[4]**. Turn right and retrace your steps back to the parking area.

1. Trailhead
2. Trail junction
3. Lake view
4. Trail junction
5. Lake view
6. Side path
7. Lake view
8. Side path
9. Lake view
10. Boulder
11. Creek
12. Barbed-wire fence
13. Running spring
14. White cedar
15. Reenter Fumee Lake Natural Area
16. Side path
17. South Ridge Trail junction
18. Culvert
19. Bench
20. Canoe portage

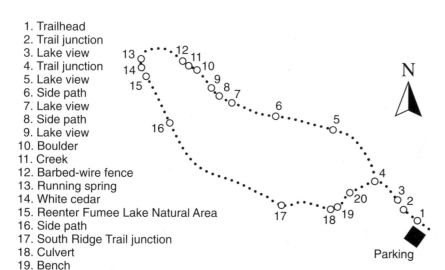

9. Estivant Pines Nature Sanctuary

- Experience a virgin forest.
- Catch a glimpse of what much of Michigan once looked like.
- Gaze skyward in awe at 100-foot-tall white pines.

Park Information

A visit to the Estivant Pines Nature Sanctuary is like stepping back in time. With 377 acres, it is the largest preserve of old-growth eastern white pine in Michigan. Scattered in a virgin forest of northern hardwoods, this sanctuary provides you with a sense of how Michigan looked when 100-foot-high white pine dominated much of the landscape.

The sanctuary is named after Edward A.J. Estivant, a French man who purchased 2,400 acres south of Copper Harbor in 1861. The land was held in the Estivant family until 1947, when it was sold to the Calumet and Hecla Mining Company. In 1970, when logging operations threatened the remaining old-growth forest, local citizens and the Michigan Nature Association organized a campaign to save the large trees. Three years later, 200 of the acres were purchased for the establishment of the sanctuary. An additional 177 acres were purchased in 1988 when logging operations encroached on the sanctuary property.

Located on the spine of the Keweenaw Peninsula, the sanctuary is an area of rugged rock outcroppings and ragged hillsides. There is a softer side; 23 fern species and 13 species of native orchids are found in the sanctuary. And 85 bird species nest here, including 14 species of warblers.

Maintained by the Michigan Nature Association, the sanctuary is intended to provide visitors with a true wilderness experience. The trails are rugged and are designed for foot traffic only. People who intend to explore off the marked trails are advised to carry a compass and U.S. Geological Survey maps for the Fort Wilkins and Lake Medora quadrangles.

Directions: From the junction of US-41 and M-26 in Copper Harbor, travel east .2 miles and turn south (right) toward Lake Manganese. Then follow the signs to Estivant Pines. The last leg of the drive into the sanctuary is over an improved backwoods road. The road is narrow and bumpy. Drive carefully.

Hours Open: Open year-round from dawn to dusk.

Facilities: Hiking.

Permits and Rules: There is no admission fee. Foot traffic only; bicycles and motorized vehicles are strictly prohibited. Camping and fires are not allowed. Pack out all litter. To prevent damage to rare plants and maintain respect for the wildlife, pets are prohibited in the sanctuary.

Further Information: Contact Michigan Nature Association, P.O. Box 102, Avoca, MI 48006; 810-324-2626.

Other Points of Interest

Fort Wilkins State Park offers camping, hiking, and fishing, but the park's centerpiece is the restored Fort Wilkins. Built in 1844 to keep the peace in Copper Country, it was abandoned two years later. The fort was briefly regarrisoned in the 1860s. Today 18 buildings survive, 12 of them original structures dating from the 1840s. Museum exhibits, audiovisual programs, and costumed interpretations show the rough life that soldiers had to endure here. This state park is located 1 mile east of Copper Harbor on US-41. For more information, contact Fort Wilkins State Park, US-41 East, Copper Harbor, MI 49918; 906-289-4215.

Brockway Mountain Drive ranks as one of the most scenic drives in America. This 9.5-mile roadway is higher above sea level than any other between the Rockies and Alleghenies. To reach the drive, take M-26 .5 miles south from Copper Harbor or 5 miles north from Eagle Harbor. For more information, contact the Keweenaw Tourism Council, P.O. Box 336, Houghton, MI 49931; 800-338-7982.

Isle Royale National Park, the only island national park, is located 50 miles off the Keweenaw Peninsula in Lake Superior. It is reachable by boat from Copper Harbor and Houghton, or by seaplane from Houghton. While seeing moose is pretty common, the resident wolves are more elusive and you'd be lucky to spot one. The park has over 160 miles of trail, offering a variety of options for trip length and difficulty. For more information, contact Isle Royale National Park, Houghton, MI 49931; 906-482-0984.

In addition to the Estivant Pines Nature Sanctuary, the **Michigan Nature Association** has more than a dozen other preserves in the Keweenaw Peninsula. To obtain a copy of "Walking Paths in Keweenaw," contact the Michigan Nature Association, P.O. Box 102, Avoca, MI 48006; 810-324-2626.

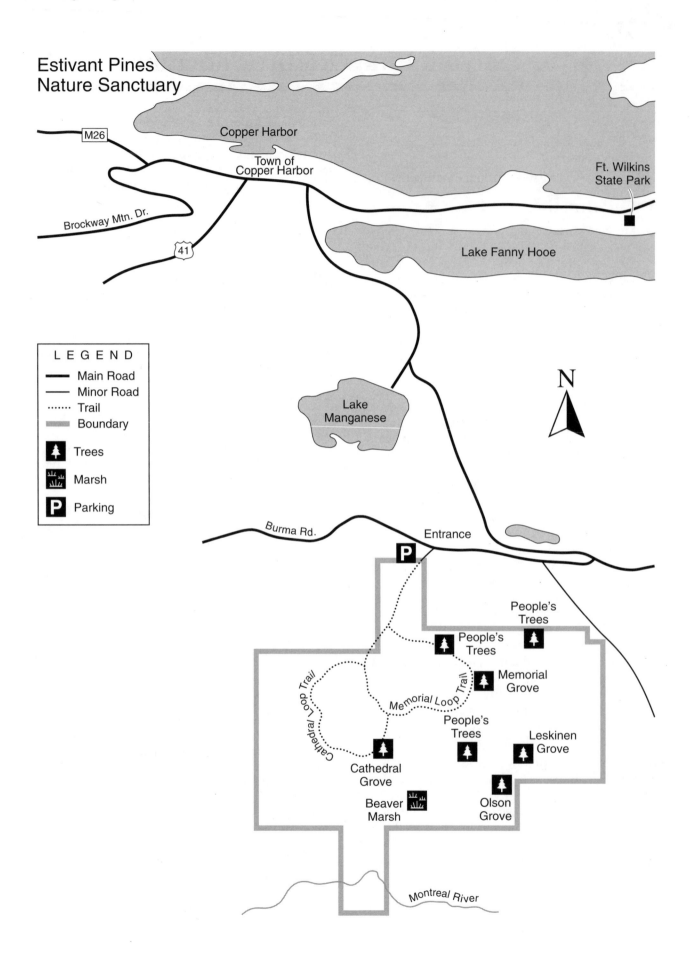

Estivant Pines
Nature Sanctuary

Cathedral Loop Trail 👢👢👢

Distance Round-Trip: 1.5 miles

Estimated Hiking Time: 1 hour

Cautions: Roots and rocks are often exposed on the trail. Most wet areas are covered with boardwalks, but other areas are also prone to be wet or muddy. At times there are steep climbs and descents. Proper footgear is a must. Another must is insect repellent and a hat or netting. Be prepared for mosquitoes and black flies in season.

Trail Directions: The trail starts from the south end of the small parking area on Burma Road. There is a signboard here that lists the Sanctuary Manners, or rules **[1].**

The trail from the parking area is on an old mining road dating back to the mid-1800s. If you are observant, you may see scars on the base of the big trees; the scars were left by wagons that were used for the

small copper mine explorations that were conducted in the area.

After crossing a small stream, the trail swings right to skirt a hill on the left and climbs into the forest. You cross three boardwalks to arrive at a posted sign showing the sanctuary's trails and your present location (.2 mi.) **[2].** The Memorial Loop goes to the left here. Go past this junction, cross another boardwalk, and walk through some large white pines before arriving at the junction for the Cathedral Loop Trail (.4 mi.) **[3].** Turn right, cross over wood planks, and climb a rocky, root-laden hill.

While only a small percentage of the big pines are visible from the trail, take time to gaze skyward at the old giants you encounter. Be careful though; the trail also commands your attention.

Shortly after descending to cross a boardwalk over a small stream (.7 mi.) **[4],** you turn left where an unmarked trail goes to the right (.8 mi.) **[5].** Climb into the area known as the Cathedral Grove (.9 mi.) **[6].** Cloistered in this grove are some of the largest and oldest white pines in the sanctuary. Some measure over 4 feet in diameter and 125 feet in height, and are 500 years in age.

Leaving the Cathedral Grove, you quickly reach the junction with the Memorial Loop (1 mi.) **[7].** Turn left and follow the old mining road for .5 mi. back to the parking area.

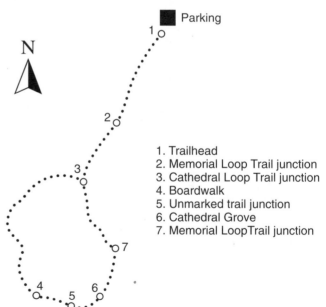

N

1. Trailhead
2. Memorial Loop Trail junction
3. Cathedral Loop Trail junction
4. Boardwalk
5. Unmarked trail junction
6. Cathedral Grove
7. Memorial LoopTrail junction

Memorial Loop Trail 👢👢👢

Distance Round-Trip: 1.5 miles

Estimated Hiking Time: 1 hour

Cautions: Roots and rocks are often exposed on the trail. Most wet areas are covered with boardwalks, but other areas may be wet or muddy. At times there are steep climbs and descents. Proper footgear is a must, as are insect repellent and a hat or netting. There will be mosquitoes and black flies in season.

Trail Directions: The trail starts from the south end of the small parking area on Burma Road. There is a signboard here with the Sanctuary Manners, or rules **[1]**. From the parking area, the trail follows the route of an old mining road that dates back to the mid-1800s. The road was used for small copper mine explorations conducted in the area. You may notice that some of the big trees have scars that were left by the wagons.

The hike starts as you cross a small stream and follow the trail as it veers right around a hill and climbs into the forest. After crossing a number of boardwalks, you arrive at a posted sign showing the sanctuary trails and your present location (.2 mi.) **[2]**. To your left is where you will finish this hike.

Continue past the junction, cross another boardwalk, pass some large white pines, and arrive at the junction for the Cathedral Loop Trail (.4 mi.) **[3]**. Keep going straight as the trail follows on the old mining road to the second junction with the Cathedral Loop Trail (.5 mi.) **[4]**. The Cathedral Grove is just a short distance on your right and well worth the side trip. Some of the largest and oldest white pines in Michigan are clustered here, measuring over 4 feet in diameter and 125 feet in height. Some are 500 years old.

Beyond the junction, the trail rises and swings left. After it levels off, you find yourself walking along the edge of a ridge before swinging left and descending toward the area known as Memorial Grove (.9 mi.) **[5]**. This is an area of 200-year-old white pines. They filled in after a fire burned out all of the competing hardwoods, exposing the thin soil. Through this section the trail is rugged, with some steep descents and climbs. Take your time and revere this remnant of the area as much of it looked before majestic trees were leveled by axes.

At 1.3 mi., you complete the Memorial Loop, arriving at the first junction **[2]**. Turn right and follow the old mining road back to the parking area.

1. Trailhead
2. Map board/return point from Memorial Grove
3. Cathedral Loop Trail junction
4. Side trip to Cathedral Grove
5. Memorial Grove

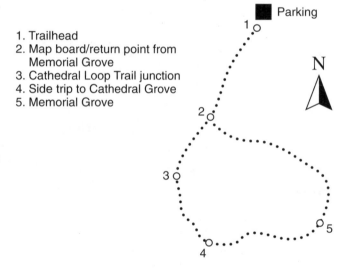

10. Van Riper State Park

- See evidence of century-old mining ventures.
- Canoe, fish, or boat the Peshekee River and Lake Michigamme.
- Learn about moose.

Park Information

This park claims to be in the heart of moose country. It is. In 1985 and 1987, moose, once popular in the region, were reintroduced 6 miles north of the park. (The demands for iron ore, copper, and timber near the turn of the century had devastated their habitat.) In 1995, their numbers were estimated at about 378. The park has an information kiosk with pictures and information on the transplant, a video story of the moose lifts, and maps and boards showing potential viewing areas.

The 1,200-acre park also boasts a .5-mile stretch of frontage on Lake Michigamme. Visitors can swim at a sandy beach where lake temperatures are moderate. There are also 1.5 miles of park frontage on the Peshekee River.

The park is bisected by US-41/M-28. South of the highway the park has been developed and has modern and rustic campsites, a boat launch, a beach, a park store, and picnic shelters. North of the highway, the park is barely developed. About 4.5 miles of trails cut through rolling, forested woods, along and above the river's banks, up to ridges with panoramic overviews, and to mine shafts abandoned long ago.

Directions: The park is located about 1.5 miles west of Champion. The entrance to the day-use and camping area is on the south side of US-41/M-28.

Hours Open: Open year-round, but the campground is open only from May 15 through October 15.

Facilities: Hiking, swimming, fishing, hunting, boat launch, canoeing, camping (tent and RV), sanitation station, picnicking, and cabins.

Permits and Rules: A park fee is required per motor vehicle ($4 daily, $20 annually).

Further Information: Contact Van Riper State Park, P.O. Box 66, Champion, MI 49814; 906-339-4461.

Other Points of Interest

Craig Lake State Park, administered by Van Riper State Park, offers rustic camping, canoeing, and hiking opportunities (see park #12). Access to the park is off an old logging road that is about 8 miles west on US-41/M-28.

The **McCormick Wilderness** (see park #11), a 27-square-mile preserve, serves as partial headwaters for four rivers and offers rocky cliffs, forests, waterfalls, and lakes, all in a rugged wilderness. Those who prefer a remote setting for hiking, backpacking, hunting, fishing, cross-country skiing, or snowshoeing are sure to enjoy this tract. It is located northwest of Van Riper State Park on County Road 607. For more information, contact Ottawa National Forest, Kenton Ranger District, Kenton, MI 49934; 906-852-3501.

Two rail-trails are located near Champion. Both allow hiking, bicycling, horses, snowmobiles, and off-road vehicles. The **Peshekee to Clowry ORV Trail** is 6.1 miles long; the **Republic-Champion Grade Trail** runs 8.1 miles. For more information, contact Ishpeming Forest Area, Escanaba River State Forest, Ishpeming Field Office, 1985 US-41, Ishpeming, MI 49849; 906-485-1031.

Park Trails

Four trails, covering about 4.5 miles, may be combined to form various hikes. They may be accessed from the south unit by crossing the highway near the entrance road or from the loop that leads to the rustic cabin in the north section of the park.

Old Wagon Road Trail 👢—1.5 miles—As the name of this point-to-point trail indicates, it is an old wagon road. It starts on the north side of the highway near the south unit and moves through woods. It is a connector for other trails.

Main Trail 👢👢—.5 miles—This point-to-point trail is also a connector. It can be picked up from the Old Wagon Road Trail or at the campground trailhead. It climbs to a scenic overlook with a view of a beaver pond.

Miners Loop 👢👢—.3 miles—This loop, accessed from the Old Wagon Road or the Main Trail, passes through an old mining area.

River Trail 👢👢👢—1.5 miles—This loop, accessed from the rustic cabin cul-de-sac, passes through woods, along the Peshekee River, and onto high ridges.

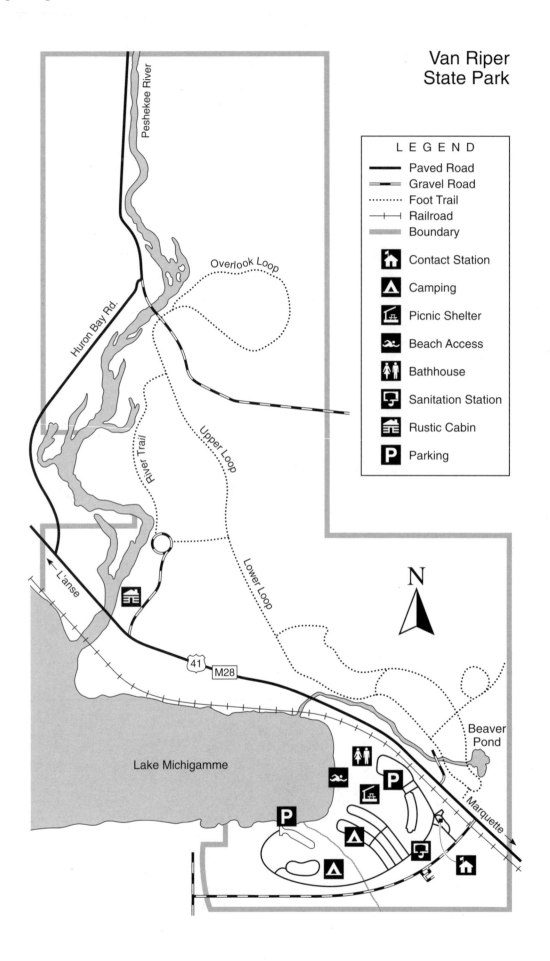

Van Riper
State Park

LEGEND

——	Paved Road
———	Gravel Road
··········	Foot Trail
—+—+—	Railroad
▬▬▬	Boundary
🏠	Contact Station
▲	Camping
🏚	Picnic Shelter
🏊	Beach Access
🚻	Bathhouse
🚮	Sanitation Station
🏠	Rustic Cabin
P	Parking

Peshekee River

Overlook Loop

Huron Bay Rd.

River Trail

Upper Loop

Lower Loop

N

L'anse

41 M28

Beaver Pond

Lake Michigamme

Marquette

Upper Loop—River Trail With Old Wagon Road Trail Loop

Distance Round-Trip: 2.2 miles

Estimated Hiking Time: 1.5 to 2 hours

Cautions: Roots and rocks are exposed on the trail. Other areas are wet. There are steep climbs and descents. Proper footgear is a must. Bring insect repellent during the warmer months.

Trail Directions: Start at the northwest end of the cul-de-sac that leads to the cabin north of the highway **[1]**. The trail forks, but don't worry. It merges back together. The left fork, however, takes you to the river's edge where a bench invites you to sit and enjoy the sights and sounds of the river.

Descend the trail cushioned with pine needles as grasses wave at you from the river's edge. The trail rises gently as it veers left, giving you an overview of the river and grasses below (.1 mi.) **[2]**. Soon the red-brown, mottled bark of tall red pines surrounds you as you walk the ridge, gazing in duplicate at your surroundings—on a sunny day the reflection off the calm river is striking (.2 mi.) **[3]**.

As the trail nears the river bank, you leave the red pine monoculture and enter a mixed forest where bunchberries line the trail (.3 mi.) **[4]**. The trail ascends through ferns and enters the dark cover of conifers before descending to Old Wagon Road Trail (.5 mi.) **[5]**.

Turn left down this grassy way, pass high wires, and soon cross the small footbridge over a dammed pool. The trail veers left and becomes muddy, a precursor of what is to come. A footbridge keeps your feet dry over the foreshadowed wet stretch (.6 mi.) **[6]**.

At .7 mi., you reach a gravel road and a trail information board **[7]**. Cross the road and roll with the trail before arriving at the overlook loop (.8 mi.) **[8]**. Take the right fork and climb up the steep ridge that will serve as your lookout platform along this loop. A bench at the top lets you catch your breath. You'll need it—what a view of the river and escarpments below!

This platform you're on is not of flat form. The terrain undulates as you wind through woods and valleys of ferns. At 1 mi., you reach a spur (marked by a boulder) that takes you to an overlook **[9]**. From here you see a rolling green carpet of treetops for miles. Back on the trail, you come to another over-look. Rocks and outcroppings here make great seats. Use them.

The trail winds down steeply. Don't slip on the moss-covered rocks or roots that prevail along this stretch. At 1.3 mi., a large, mossy boulder with a flat-top haircut of ferns **[10]** marks your entrance to a wet, rocky adventure that is lush with vegetation. Maneuver through the mud, the rocks, and the logs set in place over particularly wet spots, and enjoy this short but wild section.

Soon you reach a junction (1.4 mi.) **[11]**. Turn left and climb to a ridge overlooking the Peshekee River. You can see river grasses clumped on small islands. Downstream a steel bridge crosses the river. The views change as you continue to climb up the steep steps alongside a wall of rock. Wind steeply down to close the overlook loop (1.5 mi.) **[8]**.

Retrace your footsteps back to the junction with Old Wagon Road Trail (1.7 mi.) **[5]**. Go straight. Your legs get a break on the ensuing flat stretch. You can really pamper them if you choose. A bench is located in a clearing at 1.8 mi. **[12]**.

After the clearing, enter the cool, dark shade of pines. Luxuriate in this until you reach the closing spur to this trail at 2.1 mi. **[13]**. Turn right and enjoy the shade of the mixed forest as you wind your way back to the cul-de-sac where you left your vehicle.

1. Trailhead
2. Overview
3. Red pines
4. River's edge
5. Old Wagon Road Trail junction
6. Footbridge
7. Gravel road
8. Overlook loop trail junction
9. Overlook
10. Fern-topped boulder
11. Trail junction
12. Bench
13. Trail junction

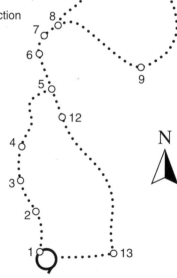

Lower Loop—Old Wagon Road Trail/Main Trail/Miners Loop/River Trail Spur 🥾🥾

Distance Round-Trip: 3.1 miles

Estimated Hiking Time: 2 to 2.5 hours

Cautions: Roots and rocks are exposed on some sections of the trail. Wear proper footgear. You also need insect repellent during the warmer months.

Trail Directions: Start at the northeast end of the cul-de-sac that provides access to the rustic cabin north of US-41/M-28 **[1]**. A sign points in the direction of Old Wagon Road Trail. Proceed past the two red pine trees that flank the trail on either side.

This section of trail, a spur of the River Trail, leads you through a mix of hardwoods and pines to the Old Wagon Road Trail (.1 mi.) **[2]**. Turn right on the old wagon road and enjoy examples of large white pine, maple, and paper birch as you stroll down this old thoroughfare. At .4 mi., a bench waits for you at the junction with the Main Trail **[3]**. Stay right and pass a second junction with a bench and the first of many interpretive signs along the hike (.7 mi.) **[4]**. Swing left and enjoy the sounds of a babbling brook as it competes with the nearby highway for your attention.

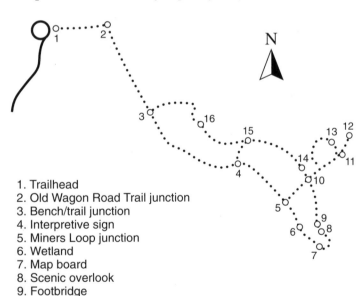

1. Trailhead
2. Old Wagon Road Trail junction
3. Bench/trail junction
4. Interpretive sign
5. Miners Loop junction
6. Wetland
7. Map board
8. Scenic overlook
9. Footbridge
10. Miners Loop junction
11. Mine pit
12. Spring
13. Old foundation
14. Footbridge
15. Lower Trail junction
16. Footbridge

Next, enjoy the aromatic pine as you approach the junction with the new Miners Loop (.9 mi.) **[5]**. Continue right and skirt a wetland (1 mi.) **[6]**, just before arriving at the park's trail map board in an opening near the highway (1.1 mi.) **[7]**. This is the trailhead for people camping at the park. This is also the end of your hike on the Old Wagon Road Trail.

Proceed past the signboard to reenter the woods on a footpath, which is the Main Trail. Swing left, climb over a couple of small ridges, turn right, and climb steeply onto a ridge above the beaver pond. Turn left to follow the ridge and emerge from the trees for a scenic overlook of the pond below (1.2 mi.) **[8]**.

Leaving the ridge, you walk through lush ferns that take advantage of the additional light coming through a hole in the forest canopy. Then cross a footbridge over a stream that drains the beaver pond (1.3 mi.) **[9]**. You pass several pits before turning right at the junction with the Miners Loop (1.4 mi.) **[10]**. Stay right when the trail splits and loop to the left to eventually walk upon an old corridor now lined by pine trees. You soon arrive at another junction that provides the option of continuing along the old corridor. This takes you past an old mine pit (1.5 mi.) **[11]** and ends at a spring (1.7 mi.) **[12]**. You are cautioned from going any further by a sign that reads, "Danger, Caving Ground, No Trespassing."

Double back and turn right to continue on the Miners Loop. You pass a small stone foundation, a relic from the mining that occurred in the area almost 100 years ago (1.9 mi.) **[13]**. Iron ore was first discovered in the Lake Superior region only a few miles east of here in 1845.

Proceeding past a pit in the center of a small open area, the trail swings left past a bench and descends back to the junction with the Main Trail. Turn right and descend to cross a footbridge (2 mi.) **[14]**. At 2.4 mi., after you have climbed and emerged into an open area, the view of Lake Michigamme is obscured by trees. At the junction, you have the option of taking the Lower Trail to the old wagon road or of continuing right to complete the Main Trail (2.4 mi.) **[15]**.

Staying right, you pass more pits before descending sharply to cross a footbridge (2.5 mi.) **[16]**. The trail then swings left and climbs up from the small stream. Turn left when the trail reaches an old forest road. This takes you back to the Old Wagon Road Trail (2.7 mi.) **[3]**. From here, retrace your steps to the River Trail spur that returns you to the parking area.

11. McCormick Wilderness

- Find solitude in the rugged, yet peaceful wilderness.
- Discover varied landscapes—rocky cliffs, swamps, pristine lakes, islands, waterfalls, northern woods.
- Track moose whose release site was in the immediate area.

Park Information

The 16,850-acre McCormick Wilderness area is a part of the Ottawa National Forest. It offers rugged outdoor enthusiasts almost 27 square miles of glacially shaped landscape containing northern hardwoods, lowland conifers, rocky cliffs, swamps, streams, rivers, waterfalls, lakes, and plenty of wildlife.

Although the area was logged in the early 1900s, regenerated trees have been left undisturbed for at least 70 years. Patches of white pines somehow survived. Enthusiasts with acute survival skills may seek them out to view what few people have seen since before the logging era.

The wilderness serves as the divide between the Lake Michigan and Lake Superior watersheds. It also serves as partial headwaters for four rivers—Huron, Yellow Dog, Dead, and Peshekee—and cradles 18 lakes. Waterfalls are secretly tucked away on Yellow Dog River. A compass, boots, a good map, and experience in orienteering can help you unearth these secrets.

This rugged, serene treat was once the vacation retreat of the McCormicks, descendants of Cyrus H. McCormick, who invented the reaping machine. Buildings of the estate once stood near White Deer Lake. It was the wish of the tract's last owner, Gordon McCormick, to donate the estate to the U.S. Forest Service upon his death, which occurred in 1967. In 1987, the unique property became part of the National Wilderness Preservation System.

As this is a wilderness, there are few improvements. A parking area (with a very primitive toilet) is located off County Road 607. An information board stands before a gated bridge, which forms part of the old road that once led to the estate on White Deer Lake. This 3-mile road and a portion of the North Country Trail are the only foot trails. Although over 100 miles of trails once weaved through the site in its vacation-retreat heyday, these are overgrown. The joy held out by this tract is for experienced hikers who like blazing their own trails.

In 1985 and 1987, moose were reintroduced near the wilderness. The moose were lifted by helicopter from the Algonquin Provincial Park in Ontario, Canada, carted by truck, and then dropped off nearby; 29 were released in 1985 and 30 were released in 1987. By 1995, their numbers were estimated to be about 378.

Directions: The park is located about 12 miles north of Champion. Take US-41/M-28 about 2 miles west of Champion to County Road 607. Take this road 9.3 miles north to the parking area, which is accessed via a drive on the east side of the road.

Hours Open: Open year-round.

Facilities: Hiking, cross-country skiing, snowshoeing, fishing, hunting, canoeing, and camping (back-country).

Permits and Rules: Although no fee is required for backcountry camping, registration cards containing information about your intentions should be filled out and deposited in a container by the information board. Motorized and mechanized vehicles or equipment are not allowed. Leave no trace. Carry out what you carry in and don't cut down live trees or other plants.

Further Information: Contact McCormick Wilderness, Ottawa National Forest, Kenton Ranger District, Kenton, MI 49943; 906-852-3501.

Other Points of Interest

Van Riper State Park (see park #10) provides modern camping facilities, a boat launch and swimming beach on Lake Michigamme, picnic facilities, and hiking trails. Here one can also look at a kiosk of information about the moose lifts.

Craig Lake State Park (see park #12), administered by Van Riper State Park, offers rustic camping, canoeing, and hiking opportunities. Access to the park is off an old logging road that is about 8 miles west on US-41/M-28.

Near Champion are two rail-trails. Both allow hiking, bicycling, horses, snowmobiles, and off-road vehicles. **The Peshekee to Clowry ORV Trail** is 6.1 miles long; the **Republic-Champion Grade Trail** runs 8.1 miles. For more information, contact, Ishpeming Forest Area, Escanaba River State Forest, Ishpeming Field Office, 1985 US-41, Ishpeming, MI 49849; 906-485-1031.

White Deer Lake 👢👢

Distance Round-Trip: 6 miles

Estimated Hiking Time: 2.5 to 3 hours

Cautions: The trail is not marked, so carefully follow along the worn path. Some sections are prone to flooding; wear appropriate footgear. At times you may need to maneuver over fallen trees. Take along insect repellent during the warmer months.

Trail Directions: Start by crossing the bridge over the Peshekee River next to the information board on the east side of the small parking area **[1]**. The trail, which follows the old access road to White Deer Lake where the McCormick estate once stood, parallels the pristine Baraga Creek. You may hear the creek before you see it, but look for the beaver dam when the creek first comes into view on your left (.3 mi.) **[2]**.

Follow the trail to the right as it guides you around a small rock outcrop (.4 mi.) **[3]**, which hints at things to come. Having descended to cross a small stream, you soon arrive alongside the rocky cliffs of an escarpment (.6 mi.) **[4]**.

As if the cliffs aren't awesome enough by themselves, the creek reappears to complete the scene. You now walk on a trail nestled on a strip of land that is sandwiched between the flowing waters of Baraga Creek and the steadfast rock of the escarpment (.7 mi.) **[5]**. Hop on the rocks by the creek and take in the view.

You leave the creek and cliffs behind as you continue along the trail to the lake. At 1 mi., you pass through a couple of downed trees where openings have been cut for ease of passage **[6]**. It's not until you've hiked 1.2 mi. that you enter the woods **[7]**. Enjoy the shade as you pass several large white pines before the trail crosses a small stream and then makes the steepest climb on the walk to the lake (1.3 mi.) **[8]**.

At 1.6 mi., the trail passes between a stream and an escarpment. As the stream opens to a large, grassy wetland, the trail hugs the escarpment and swings around the edge of the wetland **[9]**. This section of the trail is prone to flooding, so watch your step.

Snaking over a series of ridges, the trail finally emerges into the meadow that is slowly reclaiming the foundations of the McCormick estate (2.9 mi.) **[10]**. Walk across this meadow and descend to the lake (3 mi.) **[11]**. Just offshore stands the island that once supported the estate's lodge. Stay and enjoy the serenity of the wilderness. Have a picnic. After all, it is a 3 mi. hike back to your vehicle.

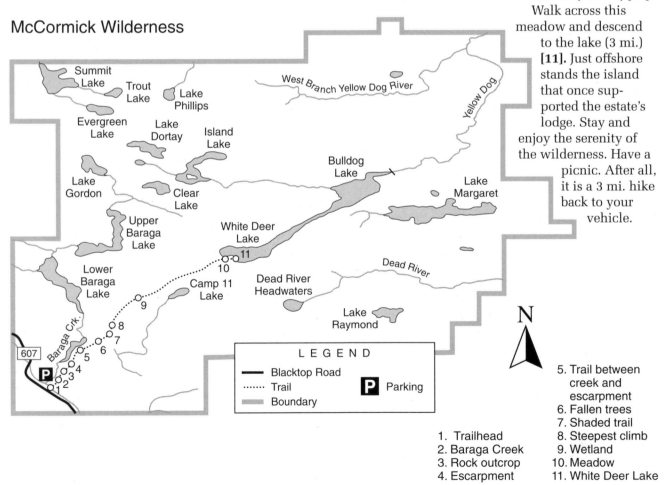

McCormick Wilderness

Summit Lake
Trout Lake
Lake Phillips
West Branch Yellow Dog River
Yellow Dog
Evergreen Lake
Lake Dortay
Island Lake
Lake Gordon
Clear Lake
Bulldog Lake
Lake Margaret
Upper Baraga Lake
White Deer Lake
Lower Baraga Lake
Camp 11 Lake
Dead River Headwaters
Dead River
Lake Raymond
Baraga Crk.
607
P

N

LEGEND

— Blacktop Road
⋯⋯ Trail
▓ Boundary
P Parking

1. Trailhead
2. Baraga Creek
3. Rock outcrop
4. Escarpment
5. Trail between creek and escarpment
6. Fallen trees
7. Shaded trail
8. Steepest climb
9. Wetland
10. Meadow
11. White Deer Lake

12. Craig Lake State Park

- Accept the challenges posed by this remote, rugged, primitive state park.
- Canoe, fish, or hike within this serene wilderness.
- Meet moose. Maybe.

Park Information

This park may not get much of a workout, but you and your vehicle will. Access to this wilderness area is over old logging roads that put your shocks to the test. Even the park brochure warns that some of the roads may be impassable, or passable by four-wheel drive only. Although we found them rugged (to say the least), our rear-wheel drive minivan successfully got us to the Craig Lake parking area.

The only improvements in the park consist of two rugged cabins, a water pump, and outhouses at the campsites along Craig Lake. Another campsite is located at Crooked Lake. But you'll have to backpack in to reach any of them, or you may backcountry camp anywhere within the park.

Craig Lake State Park is primitive. It's also rugged and serene. If you are willing to travel the 7 miles over beat-up roads to a park with minimal facilities, and are willing to haul your canoe, gear, or self over this nonmotorized wilderness, then pristine lakes, quiet, pine-perfumed forests, sparkling Peshekee River waters, and perhaps a chance meeting with a moose await you. Although two marked trails weave around Craig Lake for 7 miles of secure hiking, backcountry hiking potentials throughout the park are limitless. Parts of the marked trail system are incorporated into the North Country Trail.

This is moose country. In 1985 and 1987, moose, once popular in the region until the demands for iron ore, copper, and timber devastated their habitat, were reintroduced near the park. The moose were lifted by helicopter from the Algonquin Provincial Park in Ontario, Canada, and dropped off about 5 miles from here. By 1995, their numbers were estimated at about 378.

Marked trails assist you over about 7 miles of terrain, but almost 7,000 acres are available for backcountry exploration. Eight lakes provide fishing and boating opportunities; three of these are connected by portages for broadened canoeing experiences.

Directions: The park is located about 10 miles west of Champion. The access road is about 8 miles west of the entrance to Van Riper State Park. Van Riper State Park administers Craig Lake State Park. Stop at Van Riper and pick up a map (and ask about the current road conditions to Craig Lake). Take US-41/M-28 about 8 miles west of Van Riper to Chitin Lake Road (which, as a part of a network of logging roads, is not likely to be marked). This road is about 1 mile west of a Mobil station. Take this road about 2.7 miles north to Craig Lake Road (again not marked; turn left as shown on the map you picked up at Van Riper) and take this corrugated road to the parking lot.

Hours Open: Open year-round. Cabins are available from May 15 through October 15 each year.

Facilities: Hiking, fishing, hunting, canoeing, camping (backcountry), and cabins.

Permits and Rules: A park fee is required per motor vehicle ($4 daily, $20 annually). Camping is on a self-registration basis. Cabin users must check in at Van Riper State Park. You may backcountry camp as long as you set up camp at least 150 feet away from water and stay away from the immediate area of the cabins. No motors are allowed except on Lake Chitin and Thomas Lake. No live bait may be used for fishing. Carry out what you carry in. Finally, the island on Clair Lake is private property; respect this as such.

Further Information: Contact Van Riper State Park, P.O. Box 66, Champion, MI 49814; 906-339-4461.

Other Points of Interest

Van Riper State Park (see park #10) provides modern camping facilities, a boat launch and swimming beach on Lake Michigamme, picnic facilities, and hiking trails. A kiosk of information about the moose lifts is set up there.

The **McCormick Wilderness** (see park #11) is a 27-square-mile preserve that serves as the divide between the Lake Michigan and Lake Superior watersheds. In addition, it offers rocky cliffs, forests, waterfalls, and lakes, all in a rugged wilderness. It is located east of Craig Lake State Park on County Road 607. For more information, contact Ottawa National Forest, Kenton Ranger District, Kenton, MI 49934; 906-852-3501.

Near Champion are two rail-trails where hiking, bicycling, horses, snowmobiles, and off-road vehicles are allowed. The **Peshekee to Clowry ORV Trail** is 6.1 miles in length, and the **Republic-Champion Grade Trail** is 8.1 miles long. For more information, contact Ishpeming Forest Area, Escanaba River State Forest, Ishpeming Field Office, 1985 US-41, Ishpeming, MI 49849; 906-485-1031.

Craig Lake State Park

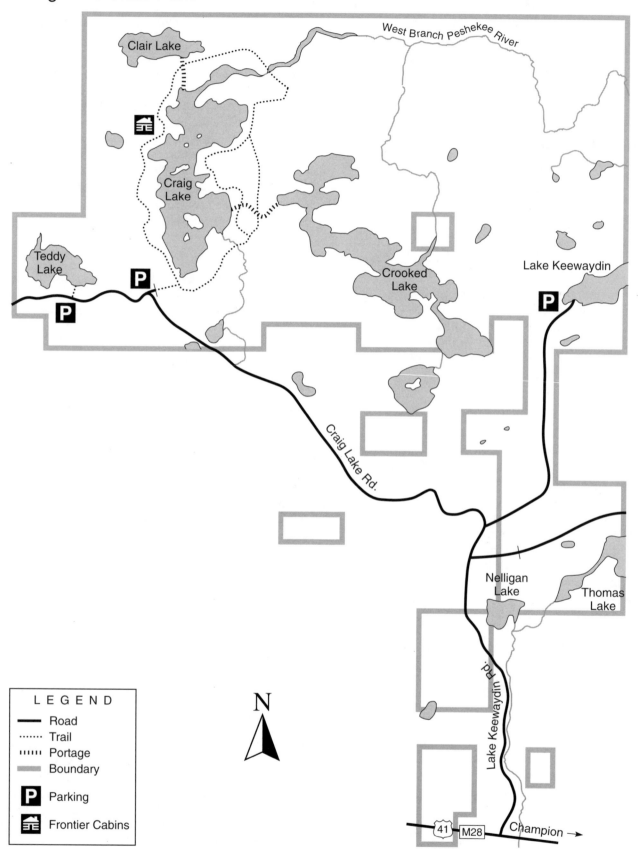

Crooked Lake Trail 🥾🥾

Distance Round-Trip: 4 miles

Estimated Hiking Time: 2.5 to 3 hours

Cautions: Roots and rocks are exposed along the trail, and some areas are wet. Wear proper footgear. Take along insect repellent in the warmer months. The maps here and onsite are not to scale; lengths alluded to may not be indicative of distances traveled.

Trail Directions: The trail starts at the map board located at the east end of the Craig Lake parking lot **[1]**. Step through the gate and descend a remnant service road that flanks rolling hills, passes through mixed hardwoods, and proceed past a bowl-shaped pool strewn with logs to arrive at the posted junction (.2 mi.) **[2]**.

Turn to the right and soon pass the spur that leads to campsites on Craig Lake as the trail rolls and snakes through hilly terrain, passing a moss-covered boulder before you notice a steep hill to your right. More noticeable is what's in front of the hill. A tree once grew on the huge boulder; now the root remnants cling to the boulder like huge talons of a bird of prey (.4 mi.) **[3]**.

Pass the other end of the campsite spur before crossing the footbridge that parallels a beaver dam along a pond (.8 mi.) **[4]**. The trail swings left to another junction (.9 mi.) **[5]**. Go right along the grassy trail as it passes the rigid, gray ghosts of trees; then duck under cover of pine woods.

At 1.1 mi., the portage between Crooked and Craig Lakes crosses the trail **[6]**. Turn right and transport yourself over to Crooked Lake (1.3 mi.) **[7]**. The quiet lake enveloped with pines, boulders, and rock escarpments will have you whispering, "This is why I come to the wilderness." Enjoy the tranquillity before returning to the trail (1.5 mi.).

Roll up and down the trail that is tightly embraced with pines. Climb up the trail, round the bend to the left past scattered boulders, and wind down to the junction (1.9 mi.) **[8]**. Turn left, pass through a manageable muddy area, and stop at the large boulder (2 mi.) **[9]**. Now look up the trail at the steep hill you'll climb. Climb. The top of the hill is punctuated by a dead tree that has been pounded by woodpeckers. The trail rolls over a few small ridges, then begins a gradual descent that culminates where fallen trees line the trail (2.2 mi.) **[10]**.

Continue along, dipping in and out of the cool cover of trees. Descend sharply as the trail bends right. It rolls along through pine before reaching the scene of a forest massacre where many trees and logs are strewn about (2.3 mi.) **[11]**. Look closely for beaver activity. Soon you reach the portage. Turn right and stroll the couple of hundred feet to Craig Lake (2.4 mi.) **[12]**.

Back on the trail, cross a wet area on precarious logs before arriving at the junction that closes the Crooked Lake loop (2.8 mi.) **[5]**. Retrace your steps from earlier, over the bridge with the beaver dam **[4]**, and stop at the campsite spur (3 mi.) **[13]**. You can either continue straight (shaving .8 mi. off the hike), or turn right for a hike along the lake. Turn right, winding through hardwoods until you get to the campsite trail junction (3.2 mi.) **[14]**. The spur continues left, and you hike along a ridge overlooking the lake. A steep hill is your backdrop to the left.

At 3.5 mi., follow the sharp bend to the right over a boardwalk **[15]**. A sheer wall of moss awaits you at 3.6 mi. **[16]**. This rock escarpment marks the beginning of a fairly steep climb. Soon the trail levels; then it descends to the main trail (3.8 mi.) **[17]**. Turn right and retrace your steps to the parking lot.

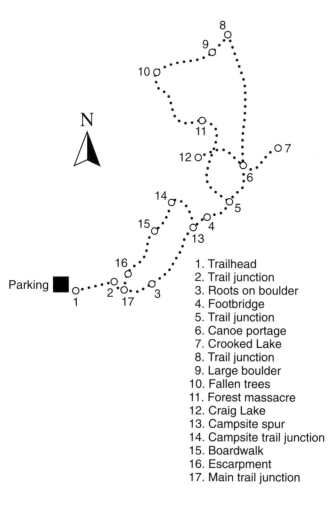

1. Trailhead
2. Trail junction
3. Roots on boulder
4. Footbridge
5. Trail junction
6. Canoe portage
7. Crooked Lake
8. Trail junction
9. Large boulder
10. Fallen trees
11. Forest massacre
12. Craig Lake
13. Campsite spur
14. Campsite trail junction
15. Boardwalk
16. Escarpment
17. Main trail junction

Craig Lake Trail 👢👢👢

Distance Round-Trip: 6.1 miles

Estimated Hiking Time: 4 to 5 hours

Cautions: Roots and rocks are exposed along the trail, and some areas are wet. Wear proper footgear. Insect repellent is necessary during the warmer months. The maps here and onsite are not drawn to scale; lengths alluded to may not be indicative of distances traveled.

Trail Directions: Start at the gate on the east end of the small parking area for Craig Lake **[1]**. Follow the orange diamond-shaped markers as you step out on an access road that doubles as the trail. Stay to the right at the first trail junction (.2 mi.) **[2]**, and again as you pass the two footpaths (.3 mi.) and (.7 mi.) that loop to the sandy-beach campsites **[3]**. When you cross a footbridge near a beaver dam (.8 mi.) **[4]**, the trail leaves the access road behind and becomes more of a footpath. Watch out for roots and rocks. Shortly the trail swings left and you reach a posted trail junction (.9 mi.) **[5]**. Go left.

At 1 mi., you pass a large white pine on the left **[6]** before descending into maples. Cross over a wet area on logs and pass by a number of fallen trees before reaching the canoe portage between Craig and Crooked Lakes (1.2 mi.) **[7]**. Craig Lake is only a couple of hundred feet down the portage, and is well worth a peek. Otherwise, cross the well-worn portage and veer right to pass through another area of fallen trees. Note the evidence of beaver activity.

Cross a series of small ridges before descending sharply. Tread through a muddy stretch before you come to the second junction with the Crooked Lake Trail (1.6 mi.) **[8]**. Turn left. At 1.9 mi., the trail climbs sharply alongside trees that are perched on boulders, their roots gripping the rocks like talons of a predatory bird grasping its prey **[9]**. This is your cue that you are about to enter Mother Nature's rock garden. Rocks and boulders are strewn about erratically.

After the trail levels off, veer left near the large hemlock trees and begin a steep descent. Soon you reach a wet area; you cross it on moss-covered rocks, then swing right in a valley to cross it again (2 mi.) **[10]**. The trail climbs, then swings left to where the forest floor undulates with rocks, boulders, and fallen trees. Veering left again, the trail begins a steep descent near a large, rotting stump; it then bottoms out in a valley of giant, moss-covered boulders (2.3 mi.) **[11]**.

Climbing again, you are teased by views of the lake that are silhouetted through the trees. As you approach a steep rock outcropping, the trail cuts

sharply to the right. Thus you avoid another climb by crossing through a wet area on more moss-covered rocks. The trail veers left and descends before climbing through pine trees and swinging around the low side of a ridge, which directs you to a trail marker. Turn left and cross the West Branch Peshekee River on a single-log bridge (2.8 mi.) **[12]**.

Climbing away from the river, the trail crosses a series of rock outcroppings. At 3.5 mi., the effort expended to hike this section is rewarded when a steep climb takes you to a scenic overlook with a view of the lake **[13]**. Take a break here and enjoy the solitude.

At 3.7 mi., cross the portage between Craig and Clair Lakes **[14]**. It's a short walk over to Craig Lake. Go and enjoy it before continuing on, then climb to another scenic overview of the lake.

When you reach the rustic cabins, stay to the right and follow the road that doubles as the trail (4.5 mi.) **[15]**. After passing the North Country Trail junction (5.8 mi.) **[16]**, you soon reach the Craig Lake State Park camping area (5.9 mi.) **[17]**. From here, it is just a short hike back to where you parked.

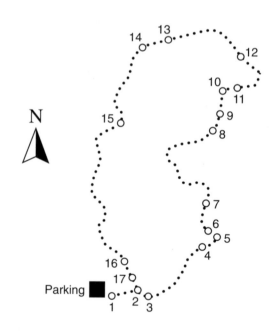

1. Trailhead
2. Trail junction
3. Campsite trail junction
4. Footbridge
5. Trail junction
6. White pine
7. Canoe portage
8. Trail junction
9. Roots on boulders
10. Wet area
11. Moss-covered boulders
12. Single-log bridge
13. Scenic overlook
14. Canoe portage
15. Frontier cabins
16. North Country Trail junction
17. Camping area

13. Sylvania Wilderness

- Find solitude in the wilderness for a day, or plan to stay at a designated wilderness campsite.
- Hike through old-growth forests and along lakeshores.
- Canoe the pristine lakes.

Park Information

Part of the Ottawa National Forest, this 18,327-acre wilderness provides outstanding opportunities for outdoors enthusiasts. With this acreage and that of the Sylvania Recreation Area, which provides campgrounds and a lake that may be reached by vehicles, over 21,000 acres of pristine beauty await you.

More than 25 miles of trails and portages provide access to old-growth forests and to 34 named lakes. In keeping with its designation, this is a place not to be controlled or modified by humans. Such a place offers outstanding opportunities for solitude and primitive recreation experiences. These include wilderness camping, canoeing, fishing, and cross-country skiing. If you do not stay at one of the 48 auto-accessible camping sites, be prepared to be self-sufficient in this land of deer, bears, coyotes, and loons.

The scars of past human interventions are eventually fading out. Buildings, roads, and trail markings have been removed, or they will be allowed to revert back to a wild state.

In 1895, A.D. Johnston purchased 80 acres near Clark Lake with the intent of cutting mature pines. Finding them too beautiful to cut, he made the tract his retreat. Friends and acquaintances found the land impressive, and they too bought land. Collectively they formed the Sylvania Club. This jewel was well preserved by the time the U.S. Forest Service purchased it in 1967. It was designated a federal wilderness 20 years later.

Directions: From Watersmeet, go west on US-2 for about 4 miles to County Road 535. Turn south (left) and go about 4 miles to the entrance.

Hours Open: Open year-round.

Facilities: Hiking, cross-country skiing, swimming, fishing, hunting, boat launch, camping (tent and backcountry), and picnicking.

Permits and Rules: Visitors are required to register. Campers must register in person at the main entrance station between May 15 and September 30. There is no fee except for auto-access camping in the Recreation Area. Otherwise, motorized and mechanized vehicles or equipment are not allowed. Leave no trace. Carry out what you carry in, and don't disturb live vegetation. Pets must be on a six-foot leash. Fires are allowed in fire rings only; drown fires with water before leaving. Because of nesting loons, islands are off limits from ice-off to July 15.

Further Information: Contact Watersmeet Visitor Center, Watersmeet, MI 49969; 906-358-4724. For campsite availability, call 906-358-4404. Or contact the Watersmeet Ranger Station, Ottawa National Forest, Watersmeet, MI 49969; 906-358-4551.

Other Points of Interest

Also a part of the Ottawa National Forest, the **Watersmeet Visitor Center,** located on the corner of US-2 and US-45, has exhibits, interpretive materials, slide shows, and nature programs. For more information, contact Watersmeet Visitor Center, Ottawa National Forest, Watersmeet, MI 49969; 906-358-4724.

Three rail-trails, or sections thereof, are near Watersmeet. The **Watersmeet/Land O' Lakes Trail** starts on the west side of US-45 at the north end of Watersmeet. This 8.8-mile trail runs down to Land O' Lakes, Wisconsin. It is a multiuse trail, as is the **Little Falls Trail.** Pick up this trail 3 miles east of Watersmeet off the State Line Trail (on Buck Lake Road). For more information, contact the Watersmeet Ranger Station, Ottawa National Forest, Watersmeet, MI 49969; 906-358-4551. The **State Line Trail** is over 100 miles long; more than 92 miles are on abandoned rail corridor. Access to this trail is just north of US-2, near the Watersmeet/Land O' Lakes Trail. This trail is managed by the Copper Country State Forest, located on 1420 US-2 West, Crystal Falls, MI 49920. For more information, call 906-875-6622.

Park Trails

More than 25 miles of trails weave through the wilderness as a part of a network. Trails build upon each other, so innumerable combinations are possible. Access points with parking include County Road 535 at Forest Road 6380; at the Clark Lake day-use area and at the campgrounds nearby; east of the entrance station between Katherine and Crooked Lakes; at the north end of Crooked Lake; on the east side of Forest Road 6324; and south of Drone Lake, east of Forest Road 6320.

Sylvania Wilderness

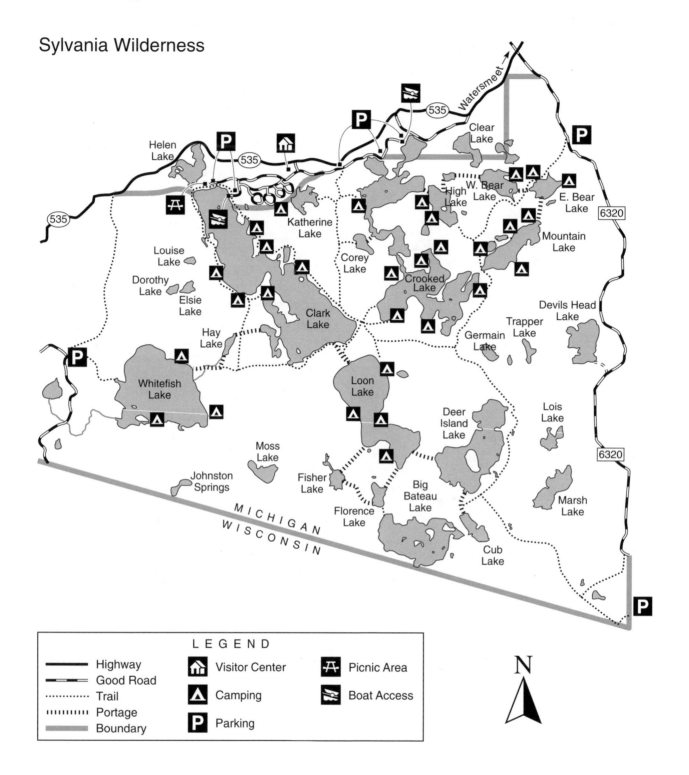

LEGEND

——— Highway		Visitor Center			Picnic Area
=== Good Road		Camping			Boat Access
········· Trail					
ııııııııı Portage		Parking			
——— Boundary					

Clark Lake Trail 👢👢

Distance Round-Trip: 7.1 miles

Estimated Hiking Time: 4 to 5 hours

Cautions: Remnant blue blazes are still on trees, but as these fade, new marks will not be made along the trails. Take along a map and compass. Streams overflow, so you may find yourself sloshing through water or crossing over logs or rocks. You must have appropriate footgear. Insects will be a problem in the warmer months, so take insect repellent.

Trail Directions: Park at the Clark Lake day-use area and head south to the lake from the picnic shelter [1]. Follow the shoreline to the right, go past the swimming beach, cut through a small meadow, and then swing left into the woods onto a cushion of pine needles (.2 mi.) [2].

Get a taste of the wilderness as you step on stones to cross a small stream; then take the root stairs down, then up, a small depression. Although surrounded by trees, you are near the lake and will often get sneak previews through the trees. Several large trees, including many hemlocks, remind you that even lumbermen could find value in keeping a tree standing.

The trail skirts the lake along a ridge, then passes through moss-covered lumps of fallen trees that look like rolling velvet (.4 mi.) [3]. Test your balance at .8 mi. when you very carefully cross the logs and rocks that bridge a spillover from the pond that flanks the trail [4]. Pass over more rolling velvet and through more wet areas until you wind into Cedar Campground (1.4 mi.) [5].

Just past the camp post, you cross a small stream. Here a narrow trail, suitable for goats, goes straight while another trail heads right. Follow to the right, and climb to a bluff for a view overlooking the lake (1.5 mi.) [6].

You need to cross another small stream bed. Use your ingenuity. This alerts you that you are near the Maple Campground. A post confirms this at 1.9 mi. [7]. Soon the trail passes through another rolling stretch of green velvet that has burnt-umber pockets of pine needles. The trail will veer away from the lake. Watch for a ridge on your right. The trail cuts up between it and the lake, heading into the woods. Notice the quiet.

At 2.5 mi., the portage from Glimmerglass Lake crosses your path [8], signaling a stretch of trail with wetland foliage that brightens up the forest floor. Turn left at the junction (2.9 mi.) [9]. The grassy two-track passes through woods and wetlands and approaches the lake at 3.6 mi. [10]. The trail weaves on a ridge along the lake's edge. Just after you enter a pine forest, the portage to Loon Lake crosses your way (4.1 mi.) [11].

A narrow strip of sandy beach is the convergence point for the paths to Loon and Crooked Lakes (4.4 mi.) [12]. Walk along the ridge through the woods. Just after the trail swings to the right away from the lake, take the narrow path on the left (4.6 mi.) [13].

Pass a small bay. A view of the lake opens up through the trees (4.8 mi.) [14]. Reenter the forest before winding down to the Pine Campground (5 mi.) [15]. Follow the trail around a small lake named Golden Silence, then climb to a vantage point where silence rules (5.3 mi.) [16].

The trail rolls, winds through woods, then climbs again to overlook the lake before starting its descent to pass by a tree whose trunk has formed a natural seat (5.6 mi.) [17]. Pass through rolls of velvet and more wet areas to arrive at Balsam Campground (5.9 mi.) [18], and then Ash Campground (6.2 mi.) [19]. Roll along, dipping down streambeds and along ridges. At 6.7 mi., you arrive at the boat launch [20]. You are not far from the beach where you started. Wind along the grassy, almost meadowlike beach and then back up to your starting point, the picnic shelter.

1. Trailhead
2. Entrance to forest
3. Moss-covered logs
4. Wet area
5. Cedar Campground
6. View of lake
7. Maple Campground
8. Canoe portage
9. Trail junction
10. Approach to lake
11. Canoe portage
12. Beach
13. Trail junction
14. View of lake
15. Pine Campground
16. View of small lake
17. Tree seat
18. Balsam Campground
19. Ash Campground
20. Boat launch

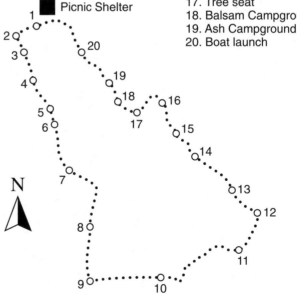

Unnamed Trail—Loon Lake Access 🥾🥾

Distance Round-Trip: 4.6 miles

Estimated Hiking Time: 2 to 3 hours

Cautions: The remnant blue blazes on trees along this trail are fading, and new marks will not be made, so you may need to blaze your own trail. Take along a good map and compass. Portions of the trail may be muddy. Wear appropriate footgear. Insects will be a problem during the warmer months, so take insect repellent.

Trail Directions: From the Sylvania Wilderness entrance station, head east about .25 mi. to a small unmarked parking area on the north side of the road. Begin your hike by crossing the road, passing a gate, and descending into the woods on what once was a single-lane road **[1]**.

Not a difficult hike, this trail gives you a good opportunity to access the center of the wilderness, away from the Sylvania Recreation Area and the boat launch. You may want to pack a picnic lunch to enjoy at one of a number of lakes that can be reached from this trail. Loon Lake is your destination.

If you are really hungry, or just curious, there are a couple of side-trip opportunities you quickly reach. The first one heads east to the Porcupine Campground on Crooked Lake (.4 mi.) **[2]**. The second, less than .1 mi. further, heads west to Katherine Lake **[3]**.

A large white pine stands guard at the trail junction to Corey Lake (.8 mi.) **[4]**. Note the number of large trees along this trail. At 1 mi., take pleasure as you pass more tall white pines **[5]**. Cross a small moss-covered footbridge (1.3 mi.) **[6]**. The trail then climbs into mostly hardwoods. Note the large maple on your right before you begin your descent to merge with the Clark Lake Trail (1.6 mi.) **[7]**.

Head left to follow along the edge of Clark Lake. Look for canoeists and loons and other waterfowl as they glide across the pristine water. At 1.8 mi., you reach a meadow and a sandy beach at the southeast end of the lake **[8]**. This area is a major unsigned junction. Two trails head left. Another goes to the beach on your right. A fourth trail parallels the beach on the right. This is the one to follow, and it may be hard to spot. It is the path least traveled.

Leaving the meadow behind, hike along an old lakeshore road past smaller meadows interspersed among the pines. The next junction is the canoe portage to Loon Lake (2.1 mi.) **[9]**. Turn left, climb the ridge through pines, cross a meadow, and descend through the woods to the small sandy beach at Loon Lake (2.3 mi.) **[10]**. Just in time for lunch. Take a break and enjoy the wilderness before packing up and heading back the way you came in. This different perspective sheds a whole new light on the scenery.

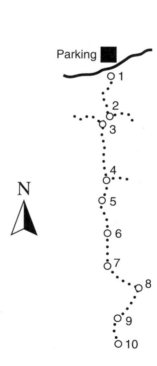

Parking

N

1. Trailhead
2. Crooked Lake trail junction
3. Katherine Lake trail junction
4. Corey Lake trail junction
5. White pines
6. Footbridge
7. Clark Lake trail junction
8. Unsigned trail junction
9. Canoe portage
10. Loon Lake beach

14. Ottawa National Forest

- Seek solitude in the three designated wilderness areas.
- Visit some of the nearly 80 waterfalls located in or near the forest.
- Canoe up to seven major river systems.
- Learn more about the region's resources at the Watersmeet Visitor Center.

Park Information

There is something for everyone in the 953,000-plus acres of the Ottawa National Forest. This mesh of forest that blankets Michigan's western Upper Peninsula has waterfalls; gorges; wilderness areas; more than 2,700 miles of streams and rivers; over 500 lakes; forests of pine, maple, spruce, birch, and fir; and rugged terrain that was shaped by retreating glaciers thousands of years ago. An abundance of recreational opportunities await fishermen, hunters, hikers, backpackers, mountain bicyclists, canoeists, kayakers, snowmobilers, and cross-country skiers.

A few of the highlights within the forest are three wilderness areas (Sturgeon River Gorge, Sylvania Wilderness [see park #13], and McCormick Wilderness [see park #11]); a scenic drive (Black River Scenic Byway); more than 50 waterfalls (Cascade, Agate, and the five falls along the Black River Scenic Byway, to name a few); around 200 miles of hiking trails (Gogebic Ridge Trail, North Country National Scenic Trail, Sturgeon Falls, and Imp Lake Interpretive Trail, for example); over 1,000 miles of snowmobile trails; and mountain bicycling trails (the Pines and Mines Mountain Bike Trail System, which includes the Ehlco Mountain Bike Complex and the Henry and Pomeroy Lake Mountain Bike Complex). In addition, 27 campgrounds provide serene and scenic camping that ranges from rustic to semideveloped. Backcountry camping adds another dimension.

Directions: Facilities and points of interest are spread out over a large area. Contact the forest supervisor's office or the individual district offices of the Ottawa National Forest for more information.

Hours Open: Most facilities are open year-round.

Facilities: Hiking, mountain bicycling, cross-country skiing, snowshoeing, snowmobiling, swimming, equestrian, fishing, hunting, boat launch, canoeing, camping (tent and backcountry), picnicking, interpretive trails, and interpretive center. These vary depending upon facility or location.

Permits and Rules: Generally, there are no fees or permits for hikers, canoeists, or other users. Camping fees vary by site. No fee is required for backcountry camping. Motorized and mechanized vehicles or equipment are not allowed in the wilderness areas. Leave no trace. Carry out what you carry in, and don't cut down live trees and other plants. Don't feed the bears; keep food out of their reach.

Further Information: Contact Ottawa National Forest, Forest Supervisor's Office, Ironwood, MI 49938; 906-932-1313. Or you may contact the various district offices of the Ottawa National Forest: Bergland Ranger District, M-28, Bergland, MI 49910 (906-575-3361); Bessemer Ranger District, 500 North Moore Street, Bessemer, MI 49911 (906-667-0261); Iron River Ranger District, 990 Lalley Road, Iron River, MI 49935 (906-265-5135); Kenton Ranger District, Kenton, MI 49943 (906-852-3500); Ontonagon Ranger District, 1209 Rockland Road, Ontonagon, MI 49953 (906-884-2411); Watersmeet Ranger District, Old US-2, P.O. Box 276, Watersmeet, MI 49969 (906-358-4551).

Other Points of Interest

The Ottawa National Forest covers a huge territory. For more information about what's available in the area, contact Upper Peninsula Travel and Recreation Association, 618 Stephenson Avenue, P.O. Box 400, Iron Mountain, MI 49801 (800-562-7134); Iron County Tourism Council, 100 East Aurora Street, Ironwood, MI 49938 (906-932-1000); Western Upper Peninsula CVB, 137 East Cloverland Drive, P.O. Box 706, Ironwood, MI 49938 (906-932-4850); and Ontonagon Tourism Council, 600 River Road, P.O. Box 266, Ontonagon, MI 49953 (906-884-4735).

Park Trails

Hiking opportunities within the forest seem endless. There are about 200 miles of trails that range from easy to difficult. Some of these are interpretive trails, such as Deer Marsh Interpretive Trail at Lake Ste. Kathryn and the Connection Interpretive Trail at the Watersmeet Visitor Center. Some are scenic, such as Sturgeon Falls or Wolf Mountain. Some are historic, like Gogebic Ridge Trail; others are for backpacking, like the 118 miles of the North Country Trail that passes through the forest. Finally, the potential in the wilderness is limitless. Contact the supervisor's office or one of the district offices of the forest service for potential routes.

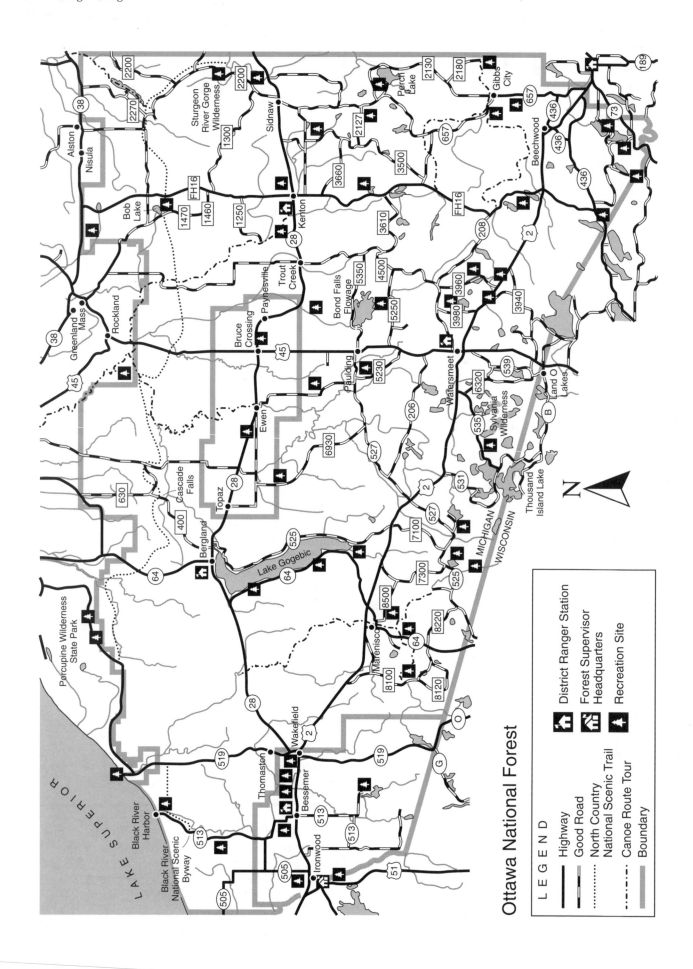

Ottawa National Forest

LEGEND

Highway	District Ranger Station
Good Road	Forest Supervisor Headquarters
North Country National Scenic Trail	Recreation Site
Canoe Route Tour	
Boundary	

Beaver Lodge Nature Trail 🥾🥾

Distance Round-Trip: 1.4 miles

Estimated Hiking Time: 45 minutes to 1.5 hours

Cautions: Take along insect repellent during the warmer months. And be careful; you are in bear country.

Trail Directions: The trail is accessed from Bob Lake Campground, which is located north of Kenton and east of Greenland. From Kenton, take Forest Highway 16 north from M-28 to Pori Road. From Greenland, head west on M-38 to Forest Highway 16 and then south to Pori Road. Follow the signs to Bob Lake west 4 mi.; then turn left on Forest Road 1478 and proceed for 2 miles to the campground.

The trail begins at the trail information board located at the parking lot for the beach/picnic area on the east end of the campground **[1]**. Look closely at the information board to see the outline of the trail's route. Located along the trail are 24 high-quality interpretive stops that enhance your hiking experience. The trail also has its own trail marker. White on brown, the square marker depicts a beaver chewing a tree.

The trail starts out level, skirts a floating bog, and swings southward. The first .1 mi. contains a number of interpretive stops, so take your time. That odd-looking device you come upon is a tree finder. Take aim at a nearby tree, and the tree finder will identify it **[2]**.

When you reach the trail junction next to the yellow birch interpretive stop, turn left (.1 mi.) **[3]**. This section of the trail is part of the North Country National Scenic Trail. It also once served as a railroad grade for the logging activities carried out in this area earlier in the century.

As you cross the road to the beach/picnic area, veer right to climb 32 steps along the side of a rather steep hill. At the top is a bench if you need to catch your breath (.2 mi.) **[4]**. The forest floor here is literally littered with maple saplings. Just past a large white pine stump, the trail swings left to skirt a small pond that is labeled a pothole (.3 mi.) **[5]**. These potholes result from pits that formed in glacial deposits and filled with water. These areas also brighten up a dark forest by allowing sunlight to break through the otherwise dense forest canopy.

At .5 mi., while descending, the North Country Trail cuts off to the left before you reach a pond **[6]**. Step across the single-plank boardwalk to a series of three interpretive boards that describe how this locale has changed over time **[7]**. You then cross another boardwalk, skirt a wetland, and swing right to cross a footbridge at the beaver dam and large, almost lake-like pond (.6 mi.) **[8]**. The trail then takes you left; from a ridge, follow along the pond to the next interpretive stop (.8 mi.) **[9]**, which educates you on the beaver, "the furry woodsman."

From here, the trail turns right and climbs away from the beaver pond. At .9 mi., you cross a small footbridge, swing right around another wetland, and then climb into a hemlock grove **[10]**. Note the lack of growth on the forest floor.

After descending from the ridge on your way down to the campground road, look back at the ravine that was on your left to notice that it is shaped like a natural amphitheater (1.1 mi.) **[11]**. Then cross the road and turn right at the trail junction to once again find yourself walking along the old logging railroad corridor. Turn left at the next trail junction by the yellow birch interpretive stop (1.3 mi.) **[3]**, and retrace your steps back to the parking area. Before leaving the campground, walk down to the beach area and enjoy the small, pristine lake in one of the most serene settings that you can drive to. You may even want to set up camp.

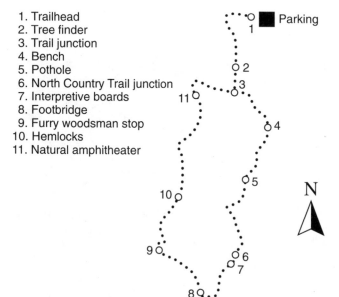

1. Trailhead
2. Tree finder
3. Trail junction
4. Bench
5. Pothole
6. North Country Trail junction
7. Interpretive boards
8. Footbridge
9. Furry woodsman stop
10. Hemlocks
11. Natural amphitheater

Cascade Falls Hiking Trail

👢👢👢👢👢

Distance Round-Trip: 1.7 miles

Estimated Hiking Time: 1 to 1.5 hours

Cautions: The trail provides you with some steep climbs and descents, it has you stepping over roots and rocks, and it has you walking through areas that are prone to be wet. Wear appropriate footgear. Take along insect repellent during the warmer months. Be careful: This is bear country.

Trail Directions: The Cascade Falls Hiking Trail is located northeast of Bergland. From M-28, take Forest Road 400 north for about 7 mi. to the sign for the falls and turn right to access the drive into the parking area. The trail starts at the information board on the south end of the small parking area **[1]**.

This trail consists of two trails that, when looped together, create an unforgettable hiking experience. Near the trailhead, stay to the right to bypass the Bluff Trail as it climbs that rocky escarpment on your left **[2]**. You will come back that way. For now, take the Valley Trail to seek the falls.

The trail swings left to head east, roughly paralleling the ridge to your left and Cascade Creek flowing unseen on your right. Aspens are prevalent as you snake along on the gravel trail. You cross a series of four boardwalks before reaching the junction with the other end of the Bluff Trail (.4 mi.) **[3]**. Turn right and descend to cross a small footbridge.

At .5 mi., you cross another footbridge over a small stream **[4]**. The forest canopy soon opens and the trail becomes grassier and wetter as you hike through the shrubs and small trees toward the increasing roar of the falls.

At the falls, the scene changes to water cascading over rocks, which drowns out the silence of the stoic pines that crowd the edge of the creek for a peek to see what all the commotion is about (.7 mi.) **[5]**. Take your time and scramble over the exposed rock to gain different vantage points from which to witness the water of Cascade Creek tumbling over rock.

Leaving the falls behind, retrace your steps to the second junction with the Bluff Trail (1 mi.) **[3]**. Continue straight as you climb past the junction and then swing to the left. Don't be fooled into thinking that you have reached the top once you start descending. You are soon climbing steeply to reach an overlook with a view of the surrounding forest (1.2 mi.) **[6]**. When you finish huffing and puffing, you may hear the roar of the falls off in the distance.

Turn right at the blue diamond trail marker and descend, only to climb another escarpment. Once again, a scenic overlook is waiting for you. This time, it's a view of forested hills to the north (1.4 mi.) **[7]**. The trail then descends slightly and swings left to provide a panoramic view of the surrounding area **[8]**. This is the place to stop to enjoy the incredible view. It's all downhill from here.

The descent is very steep and is often on bare rock that can be slippery. Take your time and watch your step. At 1.6 mi., you emerge at another lower overlook **[9]** before making the last steep descent to the first trail junction **[2]**. Turn right and return to the parking area.

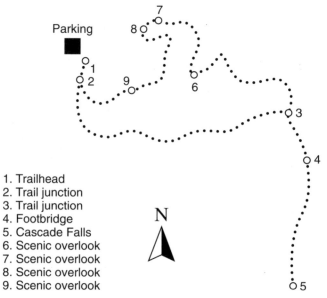

1. Trailhead
2. Trail junction
3. Trail junction
4. Footbridge
5. Cascade Falls
6. Scenic overlook
7. Scenic overlook
8. Scenic overlook
9. Scenic overlook

N

15. Porcupine Mountains Wilderness State Park

- Enjoy panoramic views from the Lake of the Clouds overlook and from Summit Peak Tower.
- Explore the park's wilderness on more than 90 miles of hiking trails.
- Visit the impressive Presque Isle waterfalls.

Park Information

More than 25 miles of Lake Superior shoreline stretch across this 60,000-acre wilderness, Michigan's largest state park. Across its vast, rugged terrain are over 90 miles of trails that open up the park's remote interior of secluded lakes, streams, rivers, waterfalls, and virgin timber. The ruggedness and remoteness helped to spare the timber from the saw.

Although the network of point-to-point trails encourages backcountry exploration, day users have much to see and do. The Visitor Center, located near the junction of South Boundary Road and M-107, has wildlife exhibits and a relief map of the park. A multi-image slide program gives information on the park's history and provides data on the myriad recreational opportunities the park offers. For example, Summit Peak Tower, a 40-foot observation structure, provides a view of the park and the surrounding area. There is also the ski area, which has a 640-foot drop over a 5,800-foot run for Alpine skiing. In addition, there are over 26 miles of cross-country ski trails weaving through the area.

Two campgrounds provide ample accommodations for visitors. There are also 16 rustic trailside cabins, backcountry campsites, and trailside camping sites. Trailside camping is allowed throughout the park as long as it is done .25 miles from cabins, scenic areas, shelters, or roads.

Directions: The east entrance to the park is about 17 miles west of Ontonagon on M-107. The Visitor Center is located just south of M-107 on South Boundary Road. About 15 miles north of Wakefield, at the end of County Road 519, is the Presque Isle River Unit.

Hours Open: The park is open year-round, but the campgrounds are open only from early May through mid-October. Some of the roads are limited seasonally. South Boundary Road is plowed only through the end of November. M-107 is plowed only to the ski area.

Facilities: Hiking, cross-country skiing, snowshoeing, snowmobiling, fishing, hunting, boat launch, camping (tent, RV, and backcountry), sanitation station, picnicking, cabins, interpretive trails, and interpretive center.

Permits and Rules: A park fee is required per motor vehicle ($4 daily, $20 annually). Overnight hikers must register. Motorized vehicles are not allowed on the trails. Pack out what you pack in. Fires are allowed in designated areas only. No fires are allowed if there is a high fire danger alert. Burn only downed trees; don't cut down live trees.

Further Information: Contact Porcupine Mountains State Park, 412 South Boundary Road, Ontonagon, MI 49953; 906-885-5275.

Other Points of Interest

The **Ehlco Mountain Bike Complex** of the Pines and Mines Mountain Bike Trail System is located south of the park. Access is from Forest Road 360, which is west of M-64. For more information, contact the Ottawa National Forest, Bergland Ranger District, Bergland, MI 49910; 906-575-3361.

Park Trails

Most of the trails within the park are point-to-point trails that can be connected to form innumerable loops. Although most of these will form longer loops that appeal to the backpacker, there are some shorter options.

Summit Peak Tower Trail 👢—.5 miles—Midway along South Boundary Road is Summit Peak Road. From this, a .5-mile trail, with benches for resting, leads the way to the 40-foot-high Summit Peak Tower.

Lake of the Clouds 👢👢—.3 miles—A paved trail from the parking lot at the end of M-107 leads up to the rocky escarpment that serves as the overlook for Lake of the Clouds. From here, you get a view of the Big Carp River Valley hundreds of feet below.

East and West River Trails 👢👢—1 mile each— Both start from the Presque Isle day-use area. Each flows along the Presque Isle River, and the two can be combined to form a 2-mile loop. They take you past the Manabezho, Manido, and Nawadaha Falls, which together make up the Presque Isle Falls.

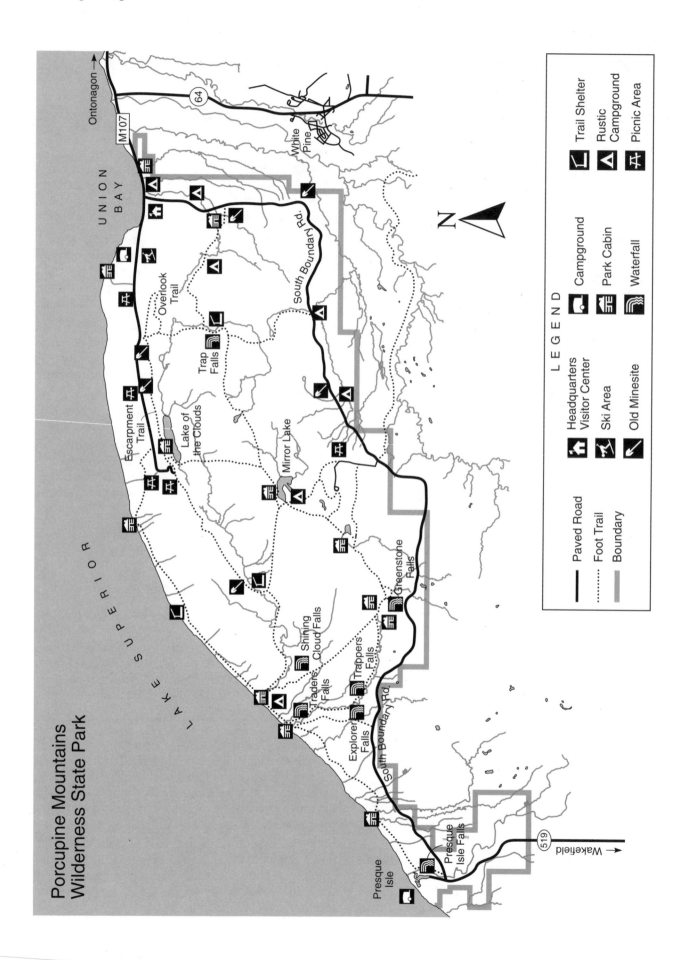

Porcupine Mountains
Wilderness State Park

LAKE SUPERIOR

UNION BAY

Ontonagon →

M107

64

White Pine

South Boundary Rd.

Overlook Trail

Trap Falls

Escarpment Trail

Lake of the Clouds

Mirror Lake

Shining Cloud Falls

Traders Falls

Trappers Falls

Greenstone Falls

Explorer Falls

South Boundary Rd.

Presque Isle

Presque Isle Falls

519

Wakefield →

L E G E N D

Paved Road		Headquarters Visitor Center	Campground	Trail Shelter
Foot Trail		Ski Area	Park Cabin	Rustic Campground
Boundary		Old Minesite	Waterfall	Picnic Area

N

Overlook Trail 👢👢👢👢

Distance Round-Trip: 3.6 miles

Estimated Hiking Time: 2.5 to 3.5 hours

Cautions: This trail has some steep climbs and descents; it goes through long, muddy stretches; has roots, rocks, and loose planks; and has fallen trees to climb over. Wear proper footgear. Mosquitoes and black flies can be a problem in the warm months. Bring insect repellent. Take water. Be careful; this is bear country.

Trail Directions: The trail starts at the Government Peak parking area off M-107 **[1]**. Head south, through the hardwoods, and up the stony path of the Government Peak Trail. The cobblestones mark an ancient beachline from a time when lake waters were much higher. Climb past the junction for the Escarpment Trail and past what will be your return loop on the Overlook Trail, until the hill crests and you notice more hemlocks (.3 mi.) **[2]**. Start heading down and to the left; then cross muddied planks by a small stream. Notice the huge hemlocks here.

Follow along through more mud, cross over wobbly planks, and continue through another stand of hemlocks before arriving at the south junction for the Overlook Trail (.5 mi.) **[3]**. Turn left onto the needle-carpeted trail and wind along under the cover of hemlocks.

At .8 mi., the trail climbs **[4]** and then veers to the left up and around through more hemlocks. The climb gets steeper until you reach the crest at 1.2 mi. **[5]**. From here you can see light through the trees. Follow the light to an overlook devoid of trees that offers a somewhat obscured view of the interior of the park. Foliage from trees may block an otherwise bird's-eye view.

The trail makes a sharp left here and descends as a narrower path, leaving the hemlocks behind. At times, with maple saplings hugging your knees, it seems as though you've strayed off the trail. You haven't. Just make sure that you watch for the blue marks on the trees. A blue mark on a huge hemlock announces that you are on the right path (1.4 mi.) **[6]**.

Although the trail dips down, and then up, its general tendency is a climb—sometimes gentle, sometimes steep—until it reaches another crest (1.8 mi.) **[7]**. Here, a bench faces to the west. On a clear day, this west vista overlooks the park's rugged interior and the Big Carp River Valley.

The trail swings left, cutting through hardwoods, and merges with a wide cross-country ski path (1.9 mi.) **[8]**. Keep to the left, heading down through maple saplings. Your steep descent culminates at a small stream (2 mi.) **[9]**. Climb again and dip to another stream (2.2 mi.) **[10]**. Start up again. After you notice you are on a ridge, the trail rolls down, steeply, and you step from rock to rock to cross a stream that is lined with moss-covered rocks (2.4 mi.) **[11]**.

Large conglomerates along the trail make hard but secure seats if you need a break. The scattering of large boulders continues, even when you reenter the darkness of hemlocks (2.5 mi.) **[12]**. The trail rolls through the dark forest, past huge boulders that look as though they had been strewn about by an angry giant. It continues past moss-covered logs, along a web of exposed roots through huge thimbleberry leaves, and then down a moderately steep slope (2.8 mi.) **[13]**. Now roll up your pant legs. For the next .5 mi. you will be trudging through mud and water, balancing over logs, and climbing over trees that have fallen over in the wet soil.

At 3.3 mi., the trail descends steeply to a stream you can probably jump over **[14]**. Climb up the bank and you soon see the sign for the Government Peak Trail up ahead. At its junction (3.4 mi.) **[15]**, turn right and head down on the cobblestones back to where you left your vehicle.

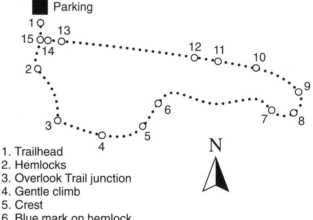

■ Parking

1. Trailhead
2. Hemlocks
3. Overlook Trail junction
4. Gentle climb
5. Crest
6. Blue mark on hemlock
7. Crest/bench
8. Junction with ski path
9. Stream
10. Stream
11. Stream
12. Hemlocks
13. Steep slope
14. Stream
15. Government Peak Trail junction

Escarpment Trail 👢👢👢👢

Distance One-Way: 4.2 miles

Estimated Hiking Time: 2.5 to 3.5 hours

Cautions: This trail provides you with some steep climbs and descents. You will step over roots and rocks and hike through rough areas prone to wetness. Wear proper footgear. There may be mosquitoes and black flies, especially in the warmer months, so take along insect repellent. Take some water. This is bear country, so be careful.

Trail Directions: Begin at the North Mirror Lake trailhead, which is at the east end of the parking lot for the Lake of the Clouds overlook [1]. You start out with a brief climb on rock. Follow the blue blaze to the left to avoid climbing to the top. Then, make a rather steep descent. At .3 mi., you reach a posted junction. The North Mirror Lake Trail splits off to the right; the Escarpment Trail continues straight [2]. Just up the trail is the sign for the Escarpment Trail indicating that it is 4 mi. to M-107.

M-107 is the other end of this point-to-point trail, so plan your hike accordingly. Options include making arrangements to be dropped off or picked up at either end, using two vehicles, or simply turning around at any point to return to where you started. However you make your plans, you don't want to miss this hike. Most people think the Escarpment Trail is the most scenic trail in the park.

At .5 mi. you have climbed to your first scenic peek at the park's interior [3]. Follow the blue blazes as you step over rocks and roots, then swing left to descend into the woods. You soon make a steep climb before breaking out to a spectacular view of the Lake of the Clouds and its surrounding area (.9 mi.) [4]. Stop, sit down on a rock, catch your breath, and enjoy the view.

After following along the open escarpment, you slip back into the woods and descend before reemerging at another overlook (1.2 mi.) [5]. At 1.6 mi., after a particularly long descent, you start the climb up Cloud Peak [6]. When you complete the climb, you are rewarded with a view from the site of the original overlook for the Lake of the Clouds (2 mi.) [7]. Visitors used to have to hike .5 mi. from M-107 to enjoy this view before the road was extended and the current overlook was opened.

You soon reach a post that points to the left (2.1 mi.) [8], away from the rocks and toward the woods for a long descent. At 2.3 mi., you reach a trail junction [9]. Going left, the halfway turnoff to M-107 allows you to hike out to the road and return to the parking area along that route. Going right is a side trip to the site of the Carp Lake Mine established in 1858. An old stamp mill still sits where it was abandoned when the mine closed years ago.

Continue straight—a short cutoff to the right takes you to a fenced-off cistern—and start your steep climb up Cuyahoga Peak. With an elevation of just over 1,600 feet, it is the tallest hill along the trail. At 2.7 mi., having completed the climb, enjoy views of the Carp River Valley below as you walk along the edge of the escarpment [10].

The last mile of the trail is a long descent, so you may want to turn around here if you plan to hike back to the starting point. If not, you descend sharply before leveling out to walk over the scattered tailings, remnants of the Cuyahoga Mine of 1856 (4 mi.) [11].

Cross a boardwalk and turn left at the junction with Government Peak Trail (4.1 mi.) [12]. You finish by hiking down the steep slope to M-107. This is the end of the trail, but not the end of your hike if you must head back to the Lake of the Clouds parking area for your vehicle.

1. Trailhead
2. North Mirror Lake Trail junction
3. Scenic overlook
4. Scenic overlook
5. Overlook
6. Beginning of climb
7. Cloud Peak overlook
8. Post with arrow left
9. Trail junction
10. Scenic overlook
11. Cuyahoga Mine
12. Government Peak Trail junction

16. Black River Harbor National Forest Recreation Area

- Explore five scenic waterfalls as the Black River plunges toward Lake Superior.
- Drive the Black River National Scenic Byway.
- Hunt for agates along the Lake Superior shore.

Park Information

Take one harbor at the mouth of the Black River where it spills into Lake Superior, add a succession of waterfalls with ample access points, provide a sprinkling of campsites, link this all together with a scenic byway, and you have a recreation recipe for success. Spice this up with a hiking trail that links the scenic waterfalls for invigorating viewing, and this recreation area is a splash.

Five picturesque waterfalls may be viewed from County Road 513, otherwise known as Black River Road. Because of the area's beauty, in 1992 the area was dedicated as a national scenic byway. Short trails from a series of parking areas lead to viewing platforms for all of the falls: Rainbow, Sandstone, Gorge, Potawatomi, and Great Conglomerate.

The harbor, which opens up access to Lake Superior, has a boat ramp that can accommodate most crafts that are trailered in. There is no launching fee, and a concessionaire offers limited supplies for boaters and picnickers, provides fuel for boaters, and regulates boaters who need transient docking. A picnic shelter, picnic area, Rainbow Falls, and Lake Superior beach are accessible from the harbor.

A .25-mile hike away is the Black River Harbor Campground, which in addition to half-acre sites offers a scenic overlook of the Lake Superior Apostle Islands and has a hike down to Lake Superior.

Several short hikes from various parking stops lead to the observation decks of the falls. All of these are linked via the North Country Trail, which passes through the recreation area.

Directions: The harbor and campgrounds are located about 15 miles north of Bessemer. They are accessed from Black River Road, or County Road 513. Parking areas for the falls are off this road as well.

Hours Open: The trails have no posted hours, but the campground is open from mid-May through mid-October. At the harbor, the concessionaire offers services from Memorial Day through September.

Facilities: Hiking, boat launch, camping (tent and RV), and picnicking.

Permits and Rules: There is no trail fee, but there is a charge for camping. Keep pets on a leash. Do no cut or carve any live trees. When hiking to the falls, keep children nearby.

Further Information: Contact Ottawa National Forest, Bessemer Ranger District, 500 North Moore Street, Bessemer, MI 49911; 906-667-0261.

Other Points of Interest

With rugged hills and rocky bluffs, the area is a mecca for winter skiing. **Big Powderhorn Mountain** is nearby, as are several lodges and resorts. Also nearby is the **Copper Peak International Ski Flying Facility,** the largest ski jump in the Northern Hemisphere. For more information on these attractions, or for information on canoeing, horseback riding, fishing, and other recreational activities, contact Bessemer Chamber of Commerce, Bessemer, MI 49911; 906-663-4542. Or contact Ironwood Chamber of Commerce, 100 East Aurora, Ironwood, MI 49938; 906-932-1122.

Park Trails

Black River Harbor Recreation Area Self-Guided Neotropical Breeding Bird Tour 👢👢—1 mile— This interpretive trail starts just beyond the gate into the campground. The trail consists of two loops and is part of a watchable-wildlife site. A cassette tape of bird sounds awaits you at the trailhead. Bring your own cassette player, and please rewind the tape when you are done.

North Country Trail 👢👢👢—12.5 miles—The trail is a segment of what will be the 3,200-mile trail that is to extend from the Lewis and Clark Trail in North Dakota to the Appalachian Trail in New York State. About 5 miles of the North Country Trail traverses the Black River and its waterfalls, then crosses a footbridge over the river and moves upstream along the other side of the river just past the Rainbow Falls.

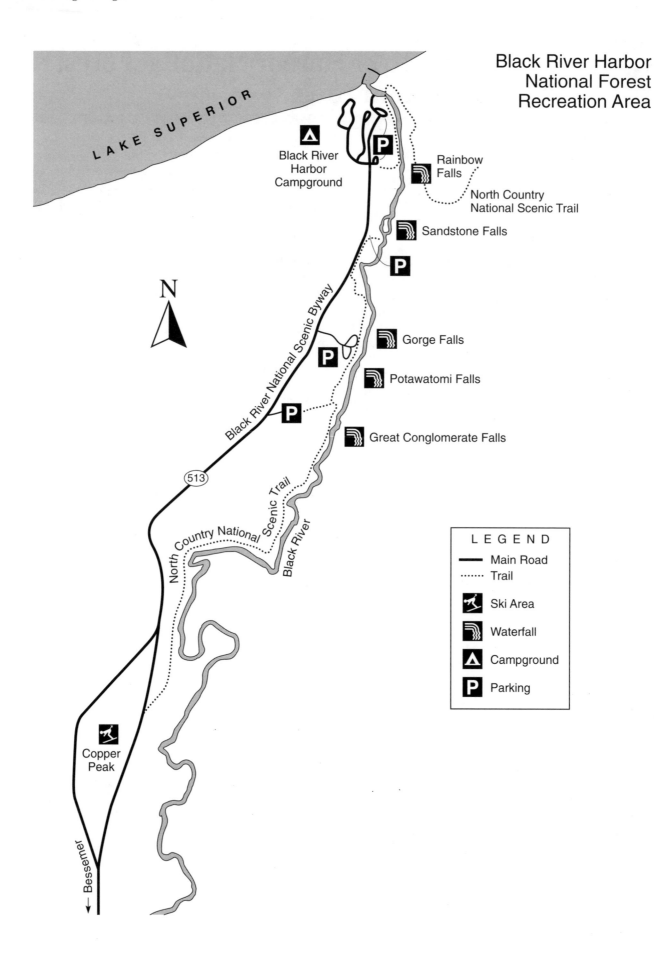

Black River Harbor
National Forest
Recreation Area

LAKE SUPERIOR

Black River
Harbor
Campground

Rainbow
Falls

North Country
National Scenic Trail

Sandstone Falls

N

Black River National Scenic Byway

Gorge Falls

Potawatomi Falls

Great Conglomerate Falls

513

North Country National

Scenic Trail

Black River

LEGEND
—— Main Road
······ Trail
Ski Area
Waterfall
Campground
P   Parking

Copper
Peak

Bessemer

North Country Trail to Sandstone, Gorge, Potawatomi, and Conglomerate Falls

Distance Round-Trip: 3.9 miles

Estimated Hiking Time: 2 to 3 hours

Cautions: This trail has steep climbs and descents. Hikers encounter muddy stretches, step over roots and rocks, and move along ridges that at times are near the river's edge. Wear proper footgear. In warm months, mosquitoes and black flies can be a nuisance. Take insect repellent. And take care; this is bear country.

Trail Directions: Although there are parking areas from which to access all of the falls, this trail begins at the Sandstone Falls parking lot. Start at the east end of the lot [1]. Enter the woods and descend what is for the most part a staircase down to the falls. The steep slopes can be very slippery. Switch back and forth down to the river's edge, then head north. A platform offers a view of the water as it drops over sandstone, then rushes between conglomerate cliffs to plunge about 20 feet (.2 mi.) [2].

Head back to the parking lot to pick up the North Country Trail, which will weave you around to the other falls. It's located near the road (.4 mi.) [3]. Go south through the hardwoods. The trail parallels the road for about .1 mi., then swings away from it through the old-growth hemlocks.

The trail cuts down ravines, passes through spindly maples, then crosses a footbridge over a stream flowing into the Black River (.9 mi.) [4]. As you follow the river ridge, cross more steep ravines while catching glimpses of the caves cut into the river canyon. Hear the thunder of the falls before you arrive at the Gorge Falls parking junction (1.2 mi.) [5].

Go down the steps to the viewing platform. Through a narrow canyon, the water drops 24 feet, stirring up foam in the amber waters below. Go downstream to another viewing platform to see the deep gorge cut by the river. Gorgeous.

Continue south on the main trail. It winds around for more views, then cuts down stairs and a steep slope to arrive at another platform (1.5 mi.) [6]. Look downstream as the waters disappear over the edge.

Go down the next stairway off the main trail to view the Potawatomi Falls. Water, spread over a width of 130 feet, rushes over rock rubble as it drops 30 feet. Head back up to the main trail and continue south to an information board. Read about the geology of the river before pressing on. More viewing platforms await you.

At 1.6 mi., an overview shows you the full breadth of the falls [7]. Go up more stairs, merge with the trail, then reach another overview. At 1.7 mi., pass the spur from the Potawatomi Falls parking lot and continue along the rugged trail [8].

Climb down, then up, steep root steps (1.9 mi.) [9]. At 2 mi. cross a stream by stepping from stone to stone [10]. The trail is muddy through here and you soon cross another stream, this time over logs. Then climb to a challenging overlook.

You are in for more challenges. Cross a stream on slippery logs; then climb up a mountain of roots to a point where you get a glimpse of the next falls (2.1 mi.) [11]. Round a bend, maneuver down a steep web of roots, and then cross the footbridge over a stream to arrive at Great Conglomerate Falls (2.2 mi.) [12]. From a natural platform of rock, view the water as it splits around a mass of rock into two waterfalls and plunges about 40 feet. Then follow the North Country Trail back to Sandstone Falls.

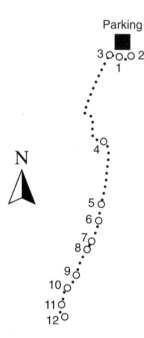

1. Trailhead
2. Sandstone Falls
3. North Country Trail junction
4. Footbridge
5. Gorge Falls
6. Lookout platform
7. Potawatomi Falls
8. Potawatomi Falls spur
9. Root steps
10. Stream
11. Roots to climb
12. Great Conglomerate Falls

North Country Trail to Rainbow Falls— West and East 👢👢👢👢

Distance Round-Trip: 3.2 miles

Estimated Hiking Time: 2 hours to 2.5 hours

Cautions: This trail has some steep climbs and descents, on stairs and on slopes. Some stretches are muddy, some have roots and rocks to step over, and some are along ridges near the river's edge. Take care and wear proper footgear, and keep children close by. Take insect repellent because of mosquitoes and black flies, particularly in the warmer months. You are in bear country, so be careful.

Trail Directions: Start from the information board at the parking area for Rainbow Falls [1]. Head into the woods for a short, level walk. About halfway to the falls, cross a footbridge over calm water as you move rapidly toward the thunderous roar of the falls ahead of you.

The stairs down to the falls are reached in less than .2 mi. [2]. To see a display of the falls' awesome power up close, climb down the nearly 200 steps to the observation deck below. The noise is deafening as you get almost close enough to touch the frothing water tumbling over the rock.

Look to the top of the cliff on the opposite bank of the river. That observation area is a better place from which to see the falls. It's also where you are headed. Climb up the steps, catch your breath, and then turn right to follow along the North Country National Scenic Trail. Watch your feet as you walk along the edge of the gorge and step over roots and around fallen trees. Gradually the roar of the falls dies down and you find yourself descending steeply toward the parking area for the Black River Harbor. Head for the information board in front of you (.7 mi.) [3].

Follow the path through the picnic area to cross the Black River on a pedestrian suspension bridge (.8 mi.) [4]. From the bridge, enjoy your view of the harbor as the frothy Black River empties into Lake Superior.

Stepping off the bridge, you head left to where the trail splits. Going left takes you to the Lake Superior beach. Veer to the right, and climb steeply through paper birch. Where the trail makes a hairpin turn to the right, there is a bench where you can rest and take in the view the harbor (.9 mi.) [5].

Completing the climb, a side trail cuts off to the left and you get a view of Lake Superior from your perch on the ridge. Turn right and pass a bench overlooking the river valley (1.1 mi.) [6]. You should hear a dull roar off in the distance. This section of the trail is very scenic. The trail snakes its way along the edge of the river valley, crossing a number of footbridges and boardwalks, heading down steps, and proceeding past large white pines and hemlocks. The roar of the falls gets louder as you approach them.

At 1.6 mi., you arrive at the falls [7]. If the sun is shining, look for a rainbow in the mist emanating from the water as it tumbles more than 40 feet over the rock. Hence the name—Rainbow Falls. Enjoy the sights and sounds for a while before retracing your steps back to your vehicle. You may even want to take a side trip over to the Lake Superior beach.

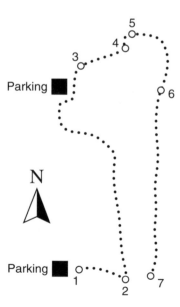

1. Trailhead
2. Steps
3. Information board
4. Suspension bridge
5. Bench/view of harbor
6. Bench/view of river valley
7. Rainbow Falls overlook

Northern Lower Peninsula

Michigan's northern section extends from the knuckles of the Lower Peninsula's mitten (roughly north of a line from Pentwater to Saginaw Bay) to the Straits of Mackinac at the tip of the mitt.

Topography

Glaciers created much of the state's general topography. Large sections of broad plains are covered with rocky glacial deposits. In many areas, the glacial plains are level to gently rolling, with occasional higher hills. Specific features include belts of morainic hills, ridges, kames, terraces, sinkholes, hollows, and kettle-shaped depressions. A ridge of glacial deposit extends from Mackinac to central Michigan, approximately bisecting the northern Lower Peninsula. The highest point is near Cadillac, where the morainic mass reaches over 1,700 feet above sea level.

The two Great Lakes, Michigan and Huron, border the northern Lower Peninsula and join at the Straits of Mackinac. It is here, too, that Michigan's two peninsulas were joined by the completion of the Mackinac Bridge in 1957. Dubbed the "Big Mac," it is the longest suspension bridge in the world.

Michigan's unique sand dunes reach their peak along Lake Michigan at the Sleeping Bear National Lakeshore. Here, sand is perched on top of glacial features that had been near the water's edge at a time when the lake was higher. The top of Sleeping Bear Dune towers 450 feet above Lake Michigan. Less than 4,500 years old, Michigan's coastal dunes are relatively topographical youngsters.

Major Rivers and Lakes

Lakes Michigan and Huron define the tip of Michigan's mitten. Among inland water bodies, Houghton Lake is the state's largest lake. Other large lakes include the Crystal, Torch, Charlevoix, Burt, and Mullet. The Burt and Mullet lakes are part of the 40-mile Inland Waterway.

Most of Michigan's rivers are "extended." As the levels of the Great Lakes lowered, the rivers lengthened their channels to reach the lakes. Along Lake Michigan, sand dunes tended to block the rivers' openings to the lake. This resulted in most of the rivers emptying first into a natural impoundment before flowing into the lake. Pentwater, Hamlin, and Manistee are examples of these natural reservoirs.

Ocqueoc Falls in Presque Isle County is the only significant waterfall in the Lower Peninsula. The Au Sable River, a favorite with canoeists, is the swiftest river, dropping over 600 feet along its length, which stretches from near Grayling to Lake Huron. Close to the town of Frederick, the upper Au Sable is only a few miles away from the upper Manistee River (another favorite of canoeists). For centuries, Native Americans would portage through the area, using the two rivers to canoe across the peninsula.

Common Plant Life

The northern Lower Peninsula lies between the needleleaf, boreal forest of Canada and the broadleaf trees that stretch south. Known as the north woods, here the species of both forest communities flourish. Sugar maple, basswood, beech, and the red maple reach northward into the territory of the white spruce, balsam fir, tamarack, and quaking aspen. Also found in this zone are red pine, eastern hemlock, yellow birch, and eastern white pine.

During the logging era, the best of Michigan's pines—in both quality and quantity—came from the center of the Lower Peninsula. Today, a small stand of virgin white pine, preserved at Hartwick Pines State Park, serves as a reminder of Michigan's natural beauty before it was logged over.

Among the state's wildflowers a popular spring bloom to look for is the dwarf lake-iris, which grows around the shores of Lakes Michigan and Huron near the Straits. Others to sight include the trillium, bird's-eye primrose, pitcher's thistle, Houghton's goldenrod, ram's-head orchid, yellow lady's slipper, marsh

marigold, and the scented trailing arbutus. In May, seek out morel mushroom near Mesick, the capital of Michigan's morel mushroom; then head for the National Morel Mushroom Hunting Championship, held in Boyne City.

Common Birds and Mammals

Elk is the northern Lower Peninsula's exotic mammal. It was reintroduced into the Pigeon River Area in 1918. Today the elk herd numbers about 1,200 animals. Other mammals to look for include the white-tailed deer, black bear, red fox, coyote, bobcat, raccoon, opossum, porcupine, beaver, mink, and weasel.

Northern Michigan is the only nesting area in the world for the endangered Kirtland's warbler. This bird enjoys nesting under 8- to 20-year-old jack pines that grow in the coarse Grayling sand. Wild turkey have become plentiful since they were reintroduced to the region in the 1950s. These large birds are often seen along roadsides in numbers varying from small

groups to large flocks. Other birds in the region include ruffed grouse, bald eagle, spruce grouse, upland sandpiper, eastern bluebird, herring gull, and various shorebirds and waterfowl.

Climate

Michigan is divided into the humid continental mild and humid continental hot summer climatic regions. The transition zone between them occurs along a line roughly parallel to the line used here to divide the Lower Peninsula into two regions. The mild-summer zone corresponds to the northern Lower Peninsula and is similar to Moscow, Russia, in having short, cool summers and long, cold winters. Temperatures are tempered by the presence of Lake Michigan. A climatic subregion exists one to two counties inland. In this so-called "fruit belt," the temperatures are altered by lake water's warming and cooling more slowly than its adjacent land. Because spring temperatures are delayed, so is the blossoming of the fruit trees until after the danger of frost. Later, warmer temperatures linger into fall, allowing the fruit time to ripen.

The average maximum temperature in January ranges between 25 °F and 29 °F, while the low averages between 9 °F and 16 °F. In July, the average maximum temperature ranges from 77 °F to 81 °F, with the low average ranging between 53 °F and 59 °F. Annual snowfall totals range from 51 inches at Gladwin to nearly 100 inches at Pellston. The moraine highlands of Crawford, Otsego, and Kalkaska counties receive an average annual snowfall of over 130 inches.

Best Natural Features

- Lakes Michigan and Huron
- Straits of Mackinac
- Sleeping Bear Dunes National Lakeshore
- North and South Manitou islands
- Pigeon River Country elk range
- Virgin white pine at Hartwick Pines State Park
- Au Sable, Manistee, and Pere Marquette rivers
- Ocqueoc Falls
- Sinkholes Natural Area
- Grand Traverse Bay

17. Negwegon State Park

- Enjoy a state park without crowds.
- Walk along a secluded Lake Huron beach.
- Hike to South Point for scenic views of the Lake Huron shoreline.

Park Information

This isolated park offers natural beauty to hikers who are willing to trade convenience for quiet, contemplative walks along 8 miles of sinuous Lake Huron shoreline, forests of birch and cedar, and more than 2,400 acres of nearly undeveloped splendor.

A challenging access has helped keep this park a serene retreat. Park brochures warn that Sand Hill Road, leading to the park's gravel road entrance, is so sandy that most two-wheeled vehicles are likely to get stuck. Our rear-wheel-drive minivan made it through, but we were probably lucky. And we were lucky enough to be one of only two vehicles parked in the gravel lot.

The park's limited development includes an information board with park data and trail maps, vault toilets, and a continually flowing water spigot. Around the spigot are telling footprints; if you take along a good guide on tracking, you can probably identify the tracks here from most of the types of animals found in the park! All that you're likely to miss in the mud are human tracks. Precisely this lack of noticeable human interaction enhances the beauty of this nature retreat.

Chippewa Indians once inhabited the area, and the park is named after Chief Negwegon, one of their leaders. Three hiking trails (covering more than 10 miles) are named after Indian tribes: the Algonquin, Chippewa, and Potawatomi.

There are no camping facilities here. There are no picnic tables. If you want a picnic, spread out a blanket and enjoy the remote serenity of the beach. There's no telling how long this unspoiled quiet will last: Plans have been suggested for rustic accommodations.

Directions: The park is located north of Harrisville. From Harrisville, take US-23 north for 12 miles to Black River Road, where you head east for about 1.5 miles to Sand Hill Road. This unmarked dirt road is by a cemetery, a good landmark. Go north (left) on Sand Hill Road about 2.5 miles to a gravel road and sign identifying Negwegon State Park. Turn right here and follow the road about 1.3 miles to the parking lot.

Hours Open: Open year-round.

Facilities: Hiking, swimming, fishing, hunting, and picnicking.

Permits and Rules: As with all state parks, visitors must pay a fee ($4 daily, $20 annually for each motor vehicle). There is no station here. The park is administered by Harrisville State Park.

Further Information: Negwegon State Park, c/o Harrisville State Park, P.O. Box 326, Harrisville, MI 48740; 517-724-5126.

Other Points of Interest

Harrisville State Park provides modern camping facilities with shaded sites, a sandy Lake Huron beach with picnic area, and a nature trail. It is about 1 mile south of Harrisville on US-23. For more information contact the Harrisville State Park (address above).

One mile east of the village of Ossineke, which is about 10 miles north of Black River Road, is the **Ossineke State Forest Campground**, part of the **Mackinaw State Forest**. In addition to 43 rustic campsites, this campground offers boating, fishing, and swimming on Lake Huron. Hiking and cross-country skiing enthusiasts can enjoy the Ossineke Pathway. For more information call the Mackinaw State Forest, 1732 West M-32, P.O. Box 667, Gaylord, MI 49735; 517-732-3541.

Sturgeon Point Lighthouse is located north of Harrisville, and tours are available at this 70-foot-high museum. For more information call the Harrisville Chamber of Commerce at 517-724-5107. For more information on the area, contact the Ossineke Chamber of Commerce, P.O. Box 164, Ossineke, MI 49766-0164.

Park Trails

Chippewa Trail 👢👢—3.5 miles—This trail is an inner loop, or shortened version, of the Algonquin Trail. You can begin hiking at either the north or the northeast end of the parking area. The trail loops through a hardwood forest of aspen, maple, and paper birch.

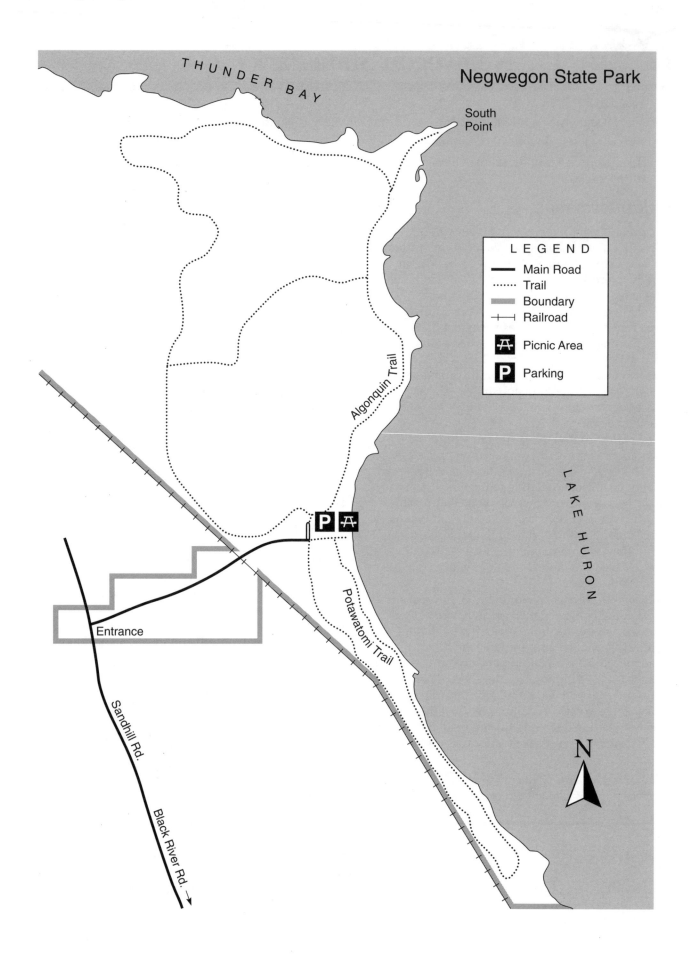

THUNDER BAY

Negwegon State Park

South
Point

LEGEND
Main Road
Trail
Boundary
Railroad
Picnic Area
P Parking

Algonquin Trail

LAKE HURON

P

Potawatomi Trail

Entrance

Sandhill Rd.

Black River Rd.

N

Potawatomi Trail 👢

Distance Round-Trip: 3.3 miles

Estimated Hiking Time: 1.5 to 2 hours

Cautions: Although this is mostly a sandy trail, an occasional root shows itself, so watch your footing. Some areas are apt to be muddy, depending on the weather or season; prepare accordingly. Take along insect repellent in warm months.

Trail Directions: Start this trail from the southeast end of the parking area and head through the gate toward the beach **[1]**. About half of this trail follows near Lake Huron, giving access to the beach, so you may want to bring along a blanket, towel, bathing suit, and lunch.

After you pass the water spigot, you will see the post for the trail, which directs you to the right. However, straight ahead, framed in the dark green of a tree, are the aqua waters of Lake Huron rolling onto the sandy beach and beach grasses beckoning to you. Give in!

Head south at the post along the grassy trail. The shore is often unmasked by openings in the trees that form a line between you and the lake. The first such unveiling is at .1 mi. **[2]**. Walking through cedars on a carpet of pine needles will entertain your nose and feet, and soon you will pass by a post with a blue triangle. Notice the trail is sandier than it had been.

White pine and cedar trees seem noticeably larger when you listen to the song of the beach here—waves gently breaking on shore (.3 mi.) **[3]**. Red pine mix in to frame the beach scene; white birch trees dominate along your right side. Pine perfumes the air as you peek again at the lake at .5 mi. **[4]**. The beach music intensifies and, at .7 mi., the trees open wide, allowing the cool breeze off the lake to brush past you **[5]**.

A trail post in the sand near the shore marks .9 mi. **[6]**. Weave into more pines, then break out to a prime beach access point (1.1 mi.) **[7]**. Although there are many more occasions to break for the beach, these taper off by the time you reach another post. Soon you enter the shade of the woods as the trail veers away from the lake. Walk through the tunnel of leaning cedars and a swampy area strewn with debris from fallen trees (1.4 mi.) **[8]**.

Take one last look at the lake before the trail veers right, takes you over roots, and through several cedars (1.5 mi.) **[9]**. The forest becomes a mix of pines, and their needles carpet the floor. Bunchberries on the forest floor inform you that the trail will become grassy. Pass a small, crescent-shaped pool enveloped by lush vegetation and enter an opening along the corridor of an active rail line (1.7 mi.) **[10]**. Turn right, following alongside the iron tracks. Look, too, for deer tracks here. The narrow opening lets in sunlight, encouraging meadow-like vegetation for browse, yet the forest also provides quick cover at its edges for the deer who picnic here.

The trail swings away from the tracks. You'll pass through large white pines and under a mixed canopy. As you roll along, the strong perfume of pines intermingle with the oily scent of the creosote from the railroad ties, never quite blending as one aroma.

Soon you pass through a dazzling display of white birches (2.3 mi.) **[11]**. A mixed forest appears, with plentiful aspens, and you pass through a wet area highlighted by irises (2.4 mi.) **[12]**. At 3 mi., on your right, a white pine looks like it's hugging a white birch tree **[13]**. The trail becomes sandy for a while and then presents some pine-needle carpeting. The end point along the trail is a mound of logs and dirt, built up to discourage motor vehicle entry (3.3 mi.) **[14]**. It brings you to the southwest end of the parking lot.

1. Trailhead
2. View of lake
3. White pines, cedars
4. View of lake
5. View of lake
6. Trail post
7. Beach access
8. Leaning cedars and swampy area
9. Trail veers right
10. Rail corridor
11. White birches
12. Wet area
13. Pine hugging a birch
14. End of trail

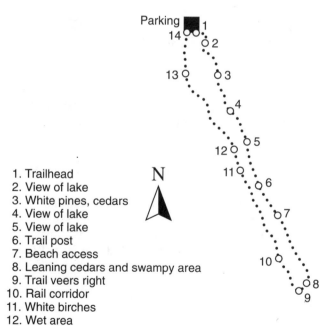

Algonquin Trail 🥾🥾

Distance Round-Trip: 6.7 miles

Estimated Hiking Time: 3 to 4 hours

Cautions: The trail has exposed roots and rocks, and some sections are apt to be wet and muddy. Wear appropriate footgear. Bring insect repellent in warm months.

Trail Directions: Start from the information board at the northwest end of the parking area **[1]**. You can orient yourself to the park's trails using the large map on the back of the board. Then head west into the mixed hardwood forest, crossing several small dune ridges and water-filled, swalelike features. This part of the trail doesn't get the traffic that the Lake Huron end does, and once you enter the park's interior, you may have the trail to yourself. Enjoy the solitude.

At 1.1 mi., hike through a striking forest of white paper birch **[2]**. Watch your step on the rocks. As the forest canopy opens to the delight of the local ferns and lichen, hike past the Chippewa Trail where it splits off to the right (1.4 mi.) **[3]**. Continue your hike north through red pine and then aspen. Continue past some oak trees and across an old forest road (1.6 mi.) **[4]**. Watch your step as you pass through a wet area and cross over loose rocks at the culvert (2.1 mi.) **[5]**.

At 2.8 mi. turn right with the trail to avoid trespassing onto private property **[6]**. Pass a large aspen, turn right again, and cross a footbridge (3 mi.) **[7]**, which brings you to a series of old dune ridges. Lake Huron soon becomes visible through the trees.

Cross a footbridge over a small stream (3.5 mi.) **[8]** and skirt a large, open area on the right as you walk through tall grass. Cross on yet another footbridge over a small stream (3.7 mi.) **[9]** and pass an old field on the left before walking the edge of another old field to arrive at the trail junction to South Point (4 mi.) **[10]**.

Turn left and hike the .5 mi. out to the tip of the rocky South Point for scenic views of the Lake Huron shoreline **[11]**. To the north are two islands. Bird Island is the closer; Scarecrow Island, the farther (part of the Michigan Island National Wildlife Refuge).

Enjoy the isolated splendor before retracing your steps back to the trail junction (5 mi.) **[10]**.

Turning left, you will travel along an old road leading through maple, oak, and paper birch trees to arrive at the junction with the Chippewa Trail (5.4 mi.) **[12]**. Even though you now hike parallel to the lake, you won't see much of it. Look for opportunities to take jaunts over to the shore. At 5.8 mi. a narrow, worn path beckons you to follow it over to a sandy beach **[13]**.

The remainder of the hike along the trail is fairly level despite some sand and wet areas. Watch your step as you walk on rocks or logs to get across standing water. When you reach the parking area (6.1 mi.) **[14]**, head over to the southeast end for a thirst-quenching drink from the constantly running spigot or continue out to the beach for a refreshing swim.

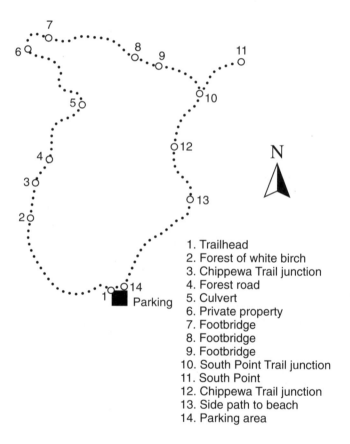

1. Trailhead
2. Forest of white birch
3. Chippewa Trail junction
4. Forest road
5. Culvert
6. Private property
7. Footbridge
8. Footbridge
9. Footbridge
10. South Point Trail junction
11. South Point
12. Chippewa Trail junction
13. Side path to beach
14. Parking area

18. Hoist Lakes Foot Travel Area

- Enjoy 10,600 acres set aside as a refuge for foot travel.
- Hike a day or longer on 20 miles of trail that wander the backcountry.
- Camp on ridges overlooking pristine lakes.

Park Information

As its name implies, the Hoist Lakes Foot Travel Area, comprising some 10,600 acres of the Huron National Forest, is maintained for pedestrian recreational travel only. If you enjoy hiking, snowshoeing, or cross-country skiing, this area has been set aside for your enjoyment. Motorized vehicles, mountain bicycles, and horses are banned.

Scattered among the area's forested hills are seven lakes and numerous wetlands, including some created by beavers. More than 20 miles of trails wander through this mix, providing ample opportunity for hikers and cross-country skiers to enjoy the backcountry. The trails, marked with blue diamonds, are easy to follow and have location maps at many junctions.

Primitive campsites and beaches are located at Byron and North and South Hoist Lakes. You'll need to pack in your own water because no portable water is available at the campsites and the area's water pumps don't work.

Directions: The east parking area is located on M-65 about .5 mile south of M-72. It is some 7 miles north of Glennie. You can reach the west parking area by taking M-65 south from the east parking lot about 2 miles to Sunny Lake Road. Head west about 5 miles to Au Sable River Road, and turn north for about 3 miles to the parking area.

Hours Open: Open year-round.

Facilities: Hiking, cross-country skiing, snowshoeing, swimming, fishing, hunting, and camping (backcountry).

Permits and Rules: There is no fee to use the park. No motorized vehicles, pack animals, or bicycles are permitted on the trails. Camping and fires are not permitted closer than 200 feet of trails or waterways. If you do make a fire, use fallen wood only: You may not cut standing timber, even if it is dead. Hunting and fishing are permitted in season; all Michigan Department of Natural Resources regulations apply. Parking for hunters is located along the area's boundary.

Further Information: Huron Shores Ranger Station, 5761 N. Skeel Road, Oscoda, MI 48750; 517-739-0728

Other Points of Interest

Reid Lake Foot Travel Area offers 6 miles of trail for nonmotorized recreation. It is located on M-72, east of the Hoist Lakes Foot Travel Area. For more information call the Huron Shores Ranger Station at 517-739-0728.

The **Jack Pine Wildlife Viewing Tour** is a self-guided, 48-mile auto tour that loops through the jack-pine ecosystem, home to the endangered Kirtland's warbler. The route is marked by special signs. Tour brochures are available from the U.S. Forest Service District Office (517-826-3232) or the Michigan Department of Natural Resources Office (517-826-3211). Both offices are located on M-33/72, north of Mio.

The **River Road Scenic Byway** is a 22-mile drive that parallels the scenic and historic Au Sable River and offers hiking trails, campsites, and numerous scenic overlooks. Other points of interest include Iargo Springs Interpretive Site, Canoer's Memorial, Lumberman's Monument and Visitor Center, and the Kiwanis Monument. For more information call the Huron Shores Ranger Station at 517-739-0728.

Park Trails

Twenty miles of trails weave through the Hoist Lakes Foot Travel Area. Although the park has five basic loops, they build on one another from the two access points. Innumerable combinations can be created from them, ranging from day hikes and cross-country ski excursions to backpacking excursions and overnight wilderness experiences. Because of the extensive cross-country usage, especially hilly portions of trails have lanes for two-way traffic.

Hoist Lakes Foot Travel Area

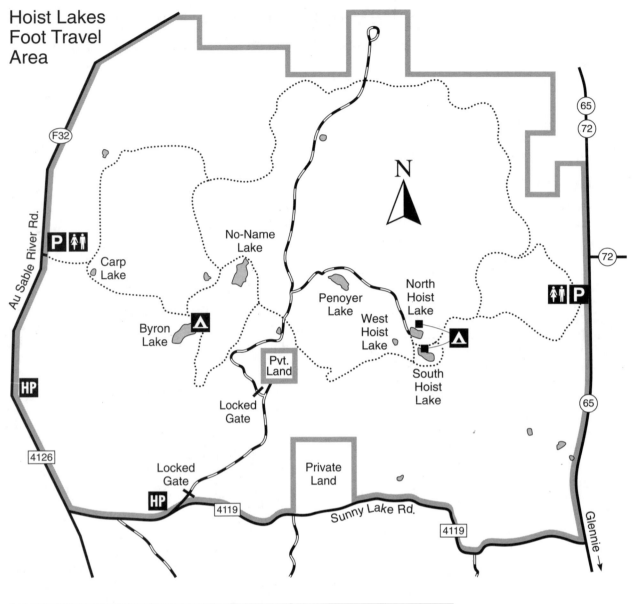

LEGEND

— Main Road

⊨ Two-Track or Sand Road

···· Hiking/Skiing Trail

━ Boundary

▲ Camping

🚹 Toilet

P Parking

HP Hunter Parking

Hoist Lakes Little East Loop

Distance Round-Trip: 4.9 miles

Estimated Hiking Time: 2.5 to 3 hours

Cautions: Many roots are exposed on the trail, and you hike through wet areas. Near the lake, water eroded the trail. Be careful and wear proper footgear. Take water and insect repellent.

Trail Directions: Parking for the trailhead is on the west side of M-65, just south of M-72. Start the trail from the west end of the parking area, immediately south of the information board **[1]**. Head through the metal gate to the three-way junction. Turn right.

Although the trail starts out rolling through a mix of aspen and pine, its general direction is down. Pass some blueberries before the trail bottoms out (.3 mi.) **[2]** and then heads back up. Red and jack pines prevail here, and a red-brown carpeting of pine needles rolls down the trail until it enters a red pine plantation (.4 mi.) **[3]**. At .5 mi., where the trail veers left, notice the corrugated landscaping, with red pines lined up in the furrows like soldiers standing in a row **[4]**.

After the plantation you pass through a thicket before arriving at post #2, where there's a bench. (.7 mi.) **[5]**. Go straight, or west, following the now moss-covered trail as it veers left and passes a marsh and a stand of paper birch (.9 mi.) **[6]**.

The trail continues its undulations, narrowing until ferns hug your knees (1.1 mi.) **[7]** as you pass through mixed hardwoods. Ferns give way to saplings and you veer left, beginning an ascent (1.2 mi.) **[8]** that continues for .1 mi. Your descent is gentle, ending at a wetland with a lawn of cattails and grasses (1.5 mi.) **[9]**. Start back up; pass a green pool strewn with fallen birch trees. Next head back down, past where the white bark of birch trees lights up the woods. Continue down the mossy trail until you reach the junction at post # 14 (1.7 mi.) **[10]**.

Turn right here. As you walk along, enjoy the views of the low-lying areas off to the west. The trail gently ascends through the hardwoods and reaches a fork (1.9 mi.) **[11]**. You can go either way. To the left is the high road, and the right is the low road. A boulevard of trees separates them. Go to the right; the paths meet again at the campsite spur (2.1 mi.) **[12]**.

Turn left to go south of South Hoist Lake. The trail rolls, passing through hardwoods softened by a feathering of pines (2.2 mi.) **[13]**. On one of the ascents, you get a peek at the lake through the trees (2.3 mi.) **[14]**. The trail passes a tree that uprooted in a wet area; violets grow in the moist soil (2.4 mi.) **[15]**. Follow it down, passing a green pool, with gray stumps and green islands of shrubs seeming to wade in it, and wind down to post #13 (2.7 mi.) **[16]**.

Turn right and hike the narrow, eroded trail until South Hoist Lake is at your side (2.8 mi.) **[17]**. The setting is serene. The lake mirrors protruding logs and lily pads on its crystal surface. Birches envelop the lake. Listen. The only sounds are of birds, frogs, and wind whispering in the trees.

Turn right at the junction at the north end of the lake (2.9 mi.) **[18]**. View North Hoist Lake to the left before reentering the woods and rejoining the trail **[12]** that will take you back to post #14 (3.5 mi.) **[10]**. Go straight, passing more wet areas. Continue past an uprooted tree and cross a small ridge that skirts a muddy area (3.8) **[19]**, before starting a gradual descent.

Roll through hardwoods, then red pine, and back into hardwoods. You pass through clear-cut rubble and into youthful stubble where young aspens have taken hold (4.7 mi.) **[20]**. Wildflowers lattice the trail before the edging becomes shrubby—a clue that you are near the end of the trail. Take the right fork up to the parking lot or continue straight for a few more feet to the three-way junction where you started.

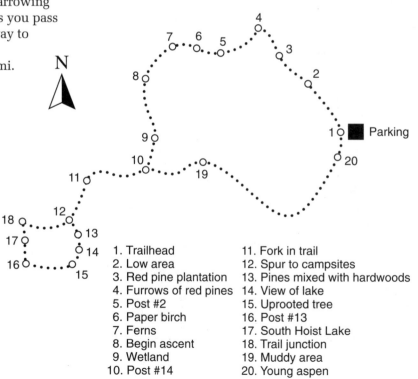

1. Trailhead
2. Low area
3. Red pine plantation
4. Furrows of red pines
5. Post #2
6. Paper birch
7. Ferns
8. Begin ascent
9. Wetland
10. Post #14
11. Fork in trail
12. Spur to campsites
13. Pines mixed with hardwoods
14. View of lake
15. Uprooted tree
16. Post #13
17. South Hoist Lake
18. Trail junction
19. Muddy area
20. Young aspen

Hoist Lakes Little West Loop

Distance Round-Trip: 6.5 miles

Estimated Hiking Time: 3 to 4 hours

Cautions: Wear appropriate footgear: You encounter loose stones on the steeper climbs and descents. Other sections of the trail may be wet. Take along insect repellent and water.

Trail Directions: Begin your hike at the information board in the parking area for the west side of the Foot Travel Area (where you can also find a vault toilet) **[1]**. Follow the well-worn path, which leads you east over gentle hills and past aspen, oak, and mixed pines. You quickly reach the junction with post #6 (.4 mi.) **[2]**. Turn right and descend on a carpet of pine needles.

Skirt Carp Lake, which lies hiding at the bottom of a small, bowl-shaped landform to your left. You barely see the lake through the trees until it finally pops into view (.6 mi.) **[3]**. Climb through aspen and maple to arrive at post # 8 and a nonworking water pump (.7 mi.) **[4]**.

Veer right and climb through young aspen growth to reach a mixed forest of oak and maple. Then descend into an area of dead trees, surrounded by growth on the forest floor fueled by the light that can penetrate these tree remains (1.2 mi.) **[5]**. Descend again to a stand of paper birch (1.3 mi.) **[6]**. Notice the wetland off to your left. Roll through the hills until you reach post # 9 at the north end of Byron Lake (1.6 mi.) **[7]**.

A side trail to the right provides the opportunity to explore the west shore of the lake. Continue along the north end of the lake less than .1 mi. to reach post #10, where you turn right **[8]**. It's easy to miss this marker if you've mistakenly followed the trail that splits to the right to access the campsites on the ridge between the lake and the trail. If you have missed post #10, you know you are still headed in the right direction if the trail you are on swings behind the campsites and past the small, sandy beach at the northeast end of the lake (1.7 mi.) **[9]**.

Continue along the ridge on the east side of the lake, then descend to cross an old access drive. Climb up from the drive, make a steep descent, then start a long climb to a scenic overlook. At the top of the hill, the trail splits off to the left before you reach the viewing area—an opening in the trees up ahead gives you a view of the Au Sable River Valley (2.3 mi.) **[10]**.

For the next .8 mi. you are heading downhill. During the descent the dominant tree changes from oak to maple. The forest canopy is now denser, and the trees, which include some red pines, are larger. At the bottom of the descent is a grassy opening from which you then climb to pass a small pond on your left (3.1 mi.) **[11]**. Look carefully and you might see a beaver dam in the distance.

The trail is fairly level as you pass fire-scarred stumps, trees toppled by the wind, and several bowl-shaped wetlands to arrive at post #12 (3.7 mi.) **[12]**. Turn left and descend into the woods.

At 3.9 mi. you reach No-Name Lake **[13]** and cross an opening of ferns, milkweed, and aspen saplings. You then walk between the lake and a swamp before swinging left to climb away from the lake and reach post #11 (4.4 mi.) **[14]**. Turn left to return to Byron Lake.

You soon find yourself walking between two small ponds where beavers have scarred the trees. Climb into the woods, then descend to find more beaver-gnawed aspen near a red pine plantation (4.7 mi.) **[15]**. Continue past a couple of wetlands to arrive back at post #10 (4.9 mi.) **[8]**. Linger and enjoy your second stop at sandy-bottomed Byron Lake. Then retrace your steps back to the parking area.

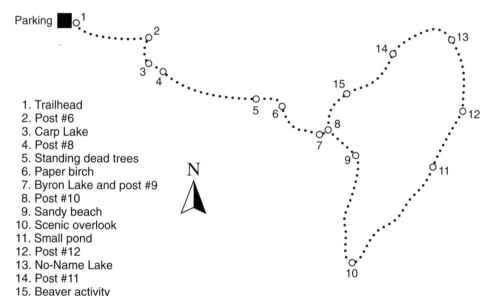

1. Trailhead
2. Post #6
3. Carp Lake
4. Post #8
5. Standing dead trees
6. Paper birch
7. Byron Lake and post #9
8. Post #10
9. Sandy beach
10. Scenic overlook
11. Small pond
12. Post #12
13. No-Name Lake
14. Post #11
15. Beaver activity

N

19. Ocqueoc Falls Bicentennial Pathway

- Swim in small pools as water cascades over the rocks around you.
- Picnic on a grassy riverbank along the falls.
- Hike or ski through forest or along the riverbank.

Park Information

Although waterfalls flow freely in Michigan's Upper Peninsula, the Lower Peninsula has only two waterfalls. One of them is Ocqueoc Falls, located in the Mackinaw State Forest. Not exactly the Niagara of northern Michigan, these falls make up with their personal touch what they lack in height and thunder. Jump in the river and let the waters caress you as they gently cascade about 10 feet down a series of three steps. You find no drama, no foam, no thunder—only the laughter and splashes of children intermingled with the comforting music of the falls' sounds (something like running bathwater).

Ocqueoc Falls Bicentennial Pathway was built, as the name implies, in 1976. About 6 miles of trails in the form of concentric loops provide recreational pathways for hiking, mountain bicycling, cross-country skiing, and snowshoeing.

Although the falls are the focal point here, the woods, banks along the Ocqueoc River, and abundant blueberry patches along the pathway are also great reasons to recreate here. If you wish to stay overnight, you can also avail yourself of the Ocqueoc Falls State Forest Campgrounds.

Directions: The pathway is located about 11.5 miles west of Rogers City. Take M-68 west. Where it curves sharply south, stay straight onto Ocqueoc Falls Road. The entrance is a few hundred feet farther on the north side of the road. The campgrounds are south of the entrance.

Hours Open: Open year-round.

Facilities: Hiking, mountain bicycling, cross-country skiing, snowshoeing, swimming, fishing, hunting, camping (tent), and picnicking.

Permits and Rules: Camping fee; no fee for the park. Keep trees and shrubs alive and growing. Motorized use is prohibited on the pathway.

Further Information: Department of Natural Resources, Onaway Field Office, P.O. Box 32, Highway M-211, Onaway, MI 49765; 517-733-8775 or call the Atlanta Forest Area at 517-785-4251.

Other Points of Interest

Black Mountain Forest Recreation Area, part of the Mackinaw State Forest, has a network of more than 30 miles of trails for hiking and cross-country skiing. Mountain bikers and equestrians may use trails and roads that are not posted as being specifically closed to them. All-terrain vehicles have their own system of trails—about 60 miles of them. In the winter some 80 miles of trails are groomed for snowmobiles. Black Lake and the Twin Lake Chain of Lakes provide choice fishing opportunities. Stay at one of two nearby state campgrounds. The Black Lake Campground has boat access and a swimming beach. Twin Lakes Campground provides canoe access to West Twin Lake. For more information contact the Atlanta Forest Area, Mackinaw State Forest, HCR 74, P.O. Box 30, Atlanta, MI 49735-9605; 517-785-4251.

About 6 miles north of Onaway is the **Onaway State Park**, located on the shores of Black Lake. The park has a small swimming beach, boat launch, picnic area, and campgrounds. For more information contact the Onaway State Park, Route 1, P.O. Box 188, M-211 North, Onaway, MI 49765; 517-733-8279.

P.H. Hoeft State Park, about 5 miles north of Rogers City, not only has campsites and a picnic area, over a mile of sandy Lake Huron shoreline, rolling sand dunes, and hiking trails. For more information contact P.H. Hoeft State Park, US-23 North, Rogers City, MI 49779; 517-734-2543.

Seagull Point Park is on Lake Huron, just north of Rogers City. A 2.3-mile, cedar-bark trail system weaves along the shore, through a forest, and past wildflowers and dunes. For more information contact City of Rogers City, 193 E. Michigan Avenue, Rogers City, MI 49779-1697; 517-734-2191.

Less than a quarter-mile west of Seagull Point Park is the **Herman Vogler Conservation Area,** which has more than 5 miles of nature study trails that range from .8 mile to 2.5 miles in length. For more information contact the Presque Isle Soil Conservation District, 240 W. Erie Street, Rogers City, MI 49779; 517-734-4000. Both parks are on Forest Avenue, off US-23.

Ocqueoc Falls Bicentennial Pathway—Medium Loop 👢👢

Distance Round-Trip: 4.2 miles

Estimated Hiking Time: 2.5 to 3 hours

Cautions: Roots are exposed, some areas are riddled with holes, slopes have loose stones, and some areas are wet, so wear appropriate footgear. Take insect repellent. The east bridge over Little Ocqueoc River looks rickety. Once it falls apart, it won't be replaced; you may have to alter your route.

Trail Directions: Start from the northeast corner of the parking lot, near the map board **[1]**. Turn right at the junction you immediately approach, heading up the grassy trail through mixed hardwoods and then red pines (.1 mi.) **[2]**. The undulating trail is lined with a soft carpeting of pine needles and pine cones.

Although the land rolls, it tends upward; soon you are on a ridge (.6 mi.) **[3]**. Other trails cut through, so watch for blue blazes on trees. At .9 mi. you pass an old road with a cul-de-sac and reenter red pines **[4]**.

Red pines stand straight in their planted rows as you round the curve to the left (1.1 mi.) **[5]**. Continue to watch for blue blazes as you wind through the forest; old roads cross the trail. At 1.5 mi. an opening in the trees allows you to look to your left at the grassy valley below **[6]**.

Continue past junction #2 (1.6 mi.) **[7]**, crossing a couple of wide paths and following the arrow at the fork, which directs you to the right. At 1.8 mi. another arrow directs you to swing left with the trail **[8]**.

The trail descends, passing several fallen trees, then levels out. You walk through a grassy, wet area before coming to the old footbridge at Little Ocqueoc River (2 mi.) **[9]**. Cross carefully over the tea-colored waters of what seems more like a stream than a river.

At 2.1 mi. the pathway makes a sharp left **[10]**, passing through an area of grass, ferns, and blueberries before reaching post #3 (2.3 mi.) **[11]**. The extension trail that forms a larger loop to the north, however, is another .1 mi. farther west. Continue straight past the extension path and wind left, then right, through mixed forest until you get to the junction that loops back to the south (2.5 mi.) **[12]**. Turn left, head down, and cross the footbridge back over the river.

Watch for blue blazes; other trails again cross your path. At 2.7 mi. follow the blazes directing you left **[13]**; soon ascend a steep incline with loose stones. Another trail crosses your path. By the time you notice you are walking a ridge, the trail descends through a mixed forest, and you wind down to junction #5 (2.9 mi.) **[14]**.

Go straight, down into the meadow; then wind along through the forest, cross a small culvert, and ascend with the trail. The river now winds to and from your side. At 3.3 mi. notice a large, sandy hill across the calm waters of the river **[15]**. Enjoy your riverside stroll before climbing up a steep hill, finding yourself then on a small ridge over the river's bend (3.5 mi.) **[16]**.

Pass through white pines and see other walls of sand across the river. As you wind along, notice the stumps and fallen logs—evidence of beavers (3.8 mi.) **[17]**. Pass a junction where you can listen as the falls grow louder. At 4.1 mi. a path cuts down to a small set of stairs; here you can head down to the bank and look upstream at the falls as they trip down their short, rocky steps **[18]**.

A grassy picnic area with tables and grills awaits you. First, however, take a few more steps over to the falls, kick off your boots, and sink your toes into the refreshing water. Enjoy. It's only a short walk back to your vehicle.

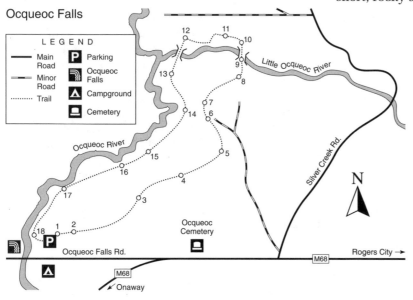

Ocqueoc Falls

LEGEND
— Main Road
— — Minor Road
.... Trail
🅿 Parking
Ocqueoc Falls
🅰 Campground
▣ Cemetery

Little Ocqueoc River
Ocqueoc River
Silver Creek Rd.
Ocqueoc Cemetery
Ocqueoc Falls Rd.
M68
M68
Onaway
Rogers City →
N

1. Trailhead
2. Red pines
3. Ridge walk
4. Red pines
5. Stand of pines and curve left
6. View of valley
7. Junction #2
8. Swing left
9. Footbridge
10. Sharp left
11. Post #3
12. Trail junction
13. Veer left
14. Junction #5
15. Sandy hill
16. Ridge
17. Beaver debris
18. Ocqueoc Falls

20. Sinkhole Area

- Hike the rim of five major sinkholes.
- Descend more than 100 feet to the bottom of a sinkhole.
- Enjoy 2,600 acres of nonmotorized serenity.

Park Information

Located within the Mackinaw State Forest, this 2,600-acre tract is an open textbook for hands-on geology. Its subject in general is glacial terrain and more specifically is karst topography. Don't close this book. The area is fascinating! Sinkholes are not mere holes; some are deep, conical depressions more than 100 feet deep and wide enough for you to jog around the periphery at the bottom (almost a tenth of a mile around one). Some sinkholes are awesome: You can look down at the tops of trees growing in them.

A *karst* is topography created by groundwater's having eroded the underlying bedrock (limestone, in this area). Water dissolves the rock into subterranean caves. Eventually these caves collapse, or sink. The glacial *till*, or *overburden*, which is comprised of sediments left over from the glaciers, collapses in as well, forming cones or depressions. Some of the holes get clogged so there is no drainage; they become lakes. Shoepac and Tomahawk are two such lakes.

Although you may explore the area with a compass and good map in hand, the Sinkholes Pathway leads you around five impressive sinkholes, one of which has a staircase down to the bottom. You'll also find old logging roads and forest trails to explore.

Directions: The area is about 10 miles south of Onaway. Take M-33 south to Tomahawk Lake Highway. Turn east, following the signs to Shoepac Lake State Forest Campground. Parking for the pathway is less than a mile past the campground, on the west side of the road by Shoepac Lake. The pathway begins on the east side of the road.

Hours Open: Open year-round.

Facilities: Hiking, mountain bicycling, cross-country skiing, snowshoeing, and hunting.

Permits and Rules: There is no fee. Motor vehicles are prohibited. Pack out whatever you pack in.

Further Information: Department of Natural Resources, Onaway Field Office, P.O. Box 32, Highway M-211, Onaway, MI 49765; 517-733-8775 or call the Atlanta Forest Area at 517-785-4251.

Other Points of Interest

Two nearby state forest campgrounds are also a part of the Mackinaw State Forest, located just outside of the Sinkhole Area, and a third is located about 3 miles southwest. **Shoepac Lake Campground** is located immediately south of the Sinkhole Area. In addition to campsites, it offers the lake for boating and fishing, the nearby sinkholes and High Country pathways, as well as off-road vehicle trails. **Tomahawk Lake Campground** on Tomahawk Lake Highway is less than a mile south of the Sinkholes Pathway. There you may camp, fish, boat, or swim. **Tomahawk Creek Flooding Campground** is south of Tomahawk Lake Road, about 1 mile east of M-33. The area's shallow waters, which afford fishing and boating, are also great for canoeing and wildlife viewing. The impounded Tomahawk Creek is a great habitat for wetland wildlife.

For more information on the three campgrounds, contact the Department of Natural Resources, Onaway Field Office, P.O. Box 32, Highway M-211, Onaway, MI 49765; 517-733-8775; or the Atlanta Forest Area, Mackinaw State Forest, HCR 74, P.O. Box 30, Atlanta, MI 49735-9605, 517-785-4251.

The **High Country Pathway** provides more than 70 miles for extended backpacking in the remote Pigeon River Area. Make one long adventure out of the single loop trail or break it into numerous shorter segments. The Shingle Mill, Sinkholes, and Clear Lake-Jackson Lake pathways all connect with or run close to the High Country pathway. For more information call the Pigeon River Country State Forest Headquarters at 517-983-4101.

Clear Lake State Park (park #21) is about 10 miles north of Atlanta on M-33. The park has campsites, swimming beach, boat launch, and hiking trails. For more information contact the Clear Lake State Park, 20500 M-33, Atlanta, MI 49709; 517-785-4388.

For other things to do in the area, contact: Onaway Chamber of Commerce, 310 West State Street, Onaway, MI 49675; 517-733-2874.

Sinkhole Area

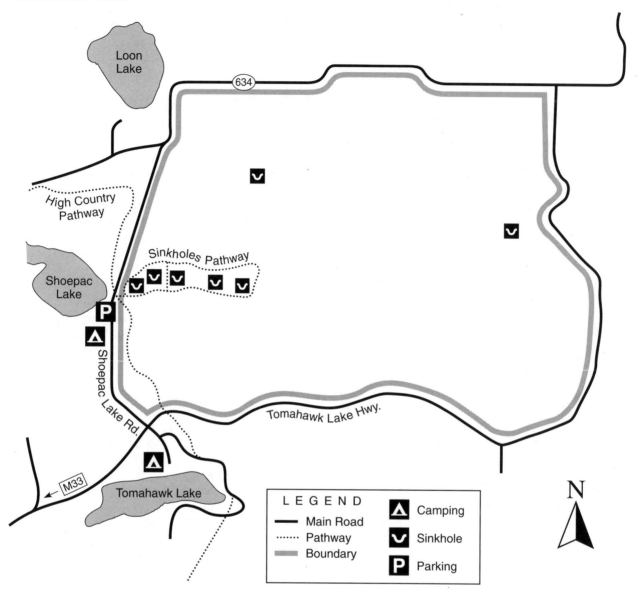

Sinkholes Pathway— Short Loop 👢👢👢

Distance Round-Trip: .8 mile

Estimated Hiking Time: 30 minutes to 1 hour

Cautions: Roots and loose stones are exposed along the trail, particularly on the steeper slopes. Take along insect repellent in warm months to ward off pesky insects. Don't overexert yourself climbing the steps out of the sinkhole.

Trail Directions: Cross the dirt road from the parking area at Shoepac Lake and head northwest to the information board, where the trail begins **[1]**. Walk down the path. You'll see a rustic, split-rail fence at your right side, protecting you from stepping too close to the depths and protecting the sensitive slopes of the sinkholes from you (a simple fence, split in what it protects but singular in its purpose—protection).

Round the bend of the trail; in less than .1 mi., descend the few steps on the slope that take you to the staircase of the observation deck that overlooks the first of five sinkholes **[2]**. Climb down 30 steps to the overlook—an awesome sight. You actually peer down at the tops of trees growing within this massive hole more than 100 feet deep. Awesome, too, is the erosion that occurred in the underlying limestone to produce a cave large enough that, once collapsed, it resulted in the interesting terrain you are about to descend. Take a deep breath, then start down the 181 steps to the bottom of the sinkhole. Take your time. A bench is positioned about halfway down the slope and another awaits you at the bottom, help for your shaky knees (0.1 mi.) **[3]**. Look up. Yes, you've come a long way!

A small trail loops through the brush and trees along the periphery of the hole. Stroll around this green cone. In less than a tenth of a mile you can loop it, getting your knees in shape to climb back up. That bench at the halfway mark may start to look golden. If you make it past that one, the observation deck has benches, too—to use as observation perches, of course (.2 mi.) **[2]**.

Head back up to the trail, turn right, and continue down the steps of the slope. Wind left with the trail, around the fencing that skirts the edge of the sinkhole. Soon you reach the overlook for the second sinkhole (.3 mi.) **[4]**, less deep than the first but no less interesting.

Wood chips line the trail as it continues through red pine, jack pine, and oak. At .4 mi. you wind down to post #2 **[5]**. This is your turnoff. Winding to the left with the trail would take you around the other three sinkholes. Turn right instead at this junction, descending along the trail before steeply ascending a land bridge that has you teetering between sinkholes #2 and #3.

Turn right onto the trail and stroll along the south side of the sinkholes (.6 mi.) **[6]**. Tall, slender aspens surround the trail as you hike westward toward Shoepac Lake. The trail descends, and at .7 mi. if you look across the gaping hole, you can see the steps and observation deck that you were on earlier **[7]**. Continue down the straight path. A tunnel of aspens silhouettes the lake that lies straight ahead of you. Step out onto the dirt road at about .8 mi. **[8]**. To the right in only a few steps is the parking area where you left your vehicle. After seeing the sinkholes, think about Shoepac Lake. The lake is a sinkhole, too, one filled with water. Swimming anyone?

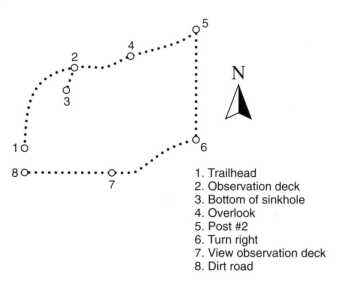

N

1. Trailhead
2. Observation deck
3. Bottom of sinkhole
4. Overlook
5. Post #2
6. Turn right
7. View observation deck
8. Dirt road

Sinkholes Pathway— Long Loop 👢👢👢

Distance Round-Trip: 2 miles

Estimated Hiking Time: 1 to 1.5 hours

Cautions: Roots and loose stones are exposed along the trail, particularly on the steeper slopes. Take along insect repellent in warm months. Don't over-exert yourself climbing the steps out of the sinkhole.

Trail Directions: Cross the dirt road from the parking area by Shoepac Lake and head northwest to the information board where the trail begins [1]. Head along the path with a rustic fence at your right side separating you and the sinkhole. Round the bend of the trail; in less than .1 mi., descend to the observation deck that overlooks the first of five sinkholes [2]. Climb down almost 30 steps to the platform and overlook the tops of trees that grow within the massive hole more than 100 feet deep. You can go to the bottom. A staircase of nearly 200 steps awaits you. Step down, passing a bench that is positioned about halfway. Another bench awaits you at the bottom (.1 mi.) [3]. Look up—way up. Take the short stroll that loops through the brush and trees around the bottom of this hole before climbing back up. Take a break at the halfway bench or at one of the benches on the observation deck (.2 mi.) [2].

Continue down the trail, winding left with it around the fencing that skirts the edge of the sink-

hole. Soon you reach the overlook for the second sinkhole, less deep than the first but no less interesting (.3 mi.) [4].

Wood chips line the trail as you continue your hike through red pine, jack pine, and oak. At .4 mi. you wind down to post #2 [5], which is the turnoff for the shorter hike. Wind around to the left first, through the occasional blueberry patches, then walk onto the observation deck for the third sinkhole [6].

You descend along the trail through a number of dead jack pines. Wood chips line the trail as it ascends to a point where you get an open view of the fourth sinkhole (.6 mi.) [7]. In less than .1 mi. you get a different perspective of this fourth hole, with eroded, sandy slopes. From here, the trail descends, passing through an area of pines impacted in 1939 by one of Lower Michigan's last major forest fires (it scorched nearly 40,000 acres) (.7 mi.) [8]. Soon after the pines, you are at the overlook for the fifth sinkhole, which is steeper than the last one.

Climb away from this overlook, through a mix of silvery-green lichen, moss, and blueberries, then past a meadow. The trail descends, levels out into a mix of grass and crunchy lichen, and is not well defined through here. Keep your eyes open for an old trail post, where you see the turnoff to the right (1 mi.) [9]. Turn right and climb through jack pine, past aspen growth, and then through paper birch as the trail gets steeper before it levels out (1.1 mi.) [10].

Another climb awaits you before you reach the south point of the junction, where you turn right (1.2 mi.) [11]. The trail descends through hardwoods, passes boulders (as you walk the rim), and descends through aspens and then jack pine, regenerated after the 1939 fire (1.6 mi.) [12]. At about 1.8 mi., you meet the junction from the shortcut trail [13]. The trail descends as you look through the tunnel of aspens silhouetting the lake straight ahead of you. Step out onto the dirt road by the lake at 2 mi. [14]; it's only a few steps to the right to your vehicle.

1. Trailhead
2. Observation deck
3. Bottom of sinkhole
4. Overlook
5. Post #2
6. Observation deck, third sinkhole
7. View of fourth sinkhole
8. Results of fire
9. Turn right
10. Paper birch
11. Turn right
12. Regenerated jack pine
13. Trail junction
14. Dirt road

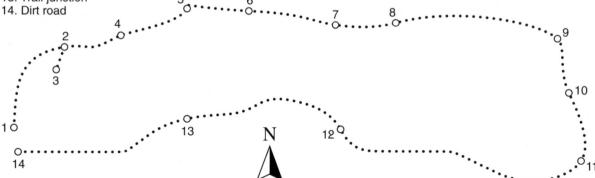

21. Clear Lake State Park

- Swim the crystal clear waters of Clear Lake.
- Listen for the majestic bugling of a bull elk.
- Gain access to more than 70 miles of hiking trails.

Park Information

Aptly named, the spring-fed Clear Lake is the centerpiece of Clear Lake State Park. Embracing more than half of the lake's shoreline, the park's 300 acres are accessed by two separate entrances. One serves the modern campground facilities on the north shore; the second serves the day-use area on the south shore.

The modern, year-round campsites are all within easy walking distance of the sandy beach and swimming area. Each campsite has an electrical hookup. Two restroom and shower buildings are located nearby. A minicabin that sleeps four is also available for rental.

The day-use beach and swimming area includes a pavilion, picnic areas, playgrounds, and horseshoe pits. You can reach the Clear Lake–Jackson Lake Trail from the day-use area. Stocked with a variety of fish species, Clear Lake itself is noted for its excellent smallmouth bass and trout fishing. Two paved boat launches provide boaters with access to the lake.

If you are lucky, you may spot an elk—or hear one bugling in the distance. Your best chance at the

encounter is in the early morning or evening hours during the spring or fall. Elk disappeared from Michigan more than 100 years ago, but 24 elk were reintroduced in 1918 and have grown to become a sizable herd.

Directions: The park is located about 10 miles north of Atlanta on M-33. The day-use entrance is on the south side of Clear Lake, and the campgrounds are on the north side of the lake.

Hours Open: Open year-round from 8:00 A.M. to 10:00 P.M.

Facilities: Hiking, mountain bicycling, cross-country skiing, swimming, fishing, boat launch, camping (tent and RV), sanitation station, picnicking, and cabin.

Permits and Rules: A park fee is required ($4 daily or $20 annually per motor vehicle).

Further Information: Clear Lake State Park, 20500 M-33, Atlanta, MI 49709; 517-785-4388.

Other Points of Interest

The **Jackson Lake State Forest Campground** is about 4 miles south of the Clear Lake State Park on M-33. Twenty-four campsites are available on the north shore of Jackson Lake. The Clear Lake–Jackson Lake Trail loops through the camp. For more information, call the Atlanta Forest Area, Mackinaw State Forest, HCR 74, P.O. Box 30, Atlanta, MI 49735-9605; 517-785-4252.

The **High Country Pathway** provides more than 70 miles of extended backpacking opportunities in the heart of Michigan's northern Lower Peninsula. Make one long adventure out of the single loop trail or break it into shorter segments. The Shingle Mill, Sinkholes, and Clear Lake–Jackson Lake pathways all connect with or run close to the High Country Pathway. For more information call the Pigeon River Country State Forest Headquarters at 517-983-4101.

The 48.5-mile **Clear Lake State Park and Mackinaw State Forest Scenic Drive** begins 3 miles north of Atlanta at the corner of M-33 and Voyer Lake Road. Marked by yellow-topped posts, the scenic route you are directed to follow is especially beautiful in the fall. For more information call Clear Lake State Park at 517-785-4388.

To get as close to the 45th Parallel as possible, hike the **Michigan Polar–Equator Trail.** For more information contact the Michigan Polar–Equator Club, Department of Zoology, Michigan State University, East Lansing, MI 48824.

Clear Lake State Park

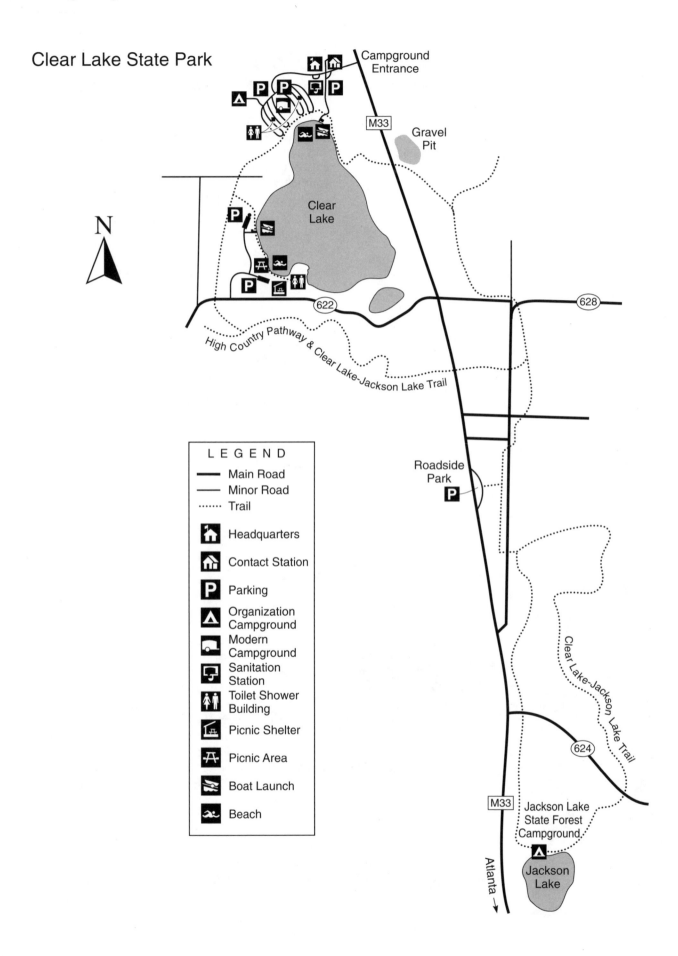

LEGEND

━━━ Main Road

─── Minor Road

······ Trail

Headquarters

Contact Station

Parking

Organization Campground

Modern Campground

Sanitation Station

Toilet Shower Building

Picnic Shelter

Picnic Area

Boat Launch

Beach

Campground Entrance

M33

Gravel Pit

Clear Lake

N

622

High Country Pathway & Clear Lake-Jackson Lake Trail

628

Roadside Park

Clear Lake-Jackson Lake Trail

624

M33

Jackson Lake State Forest Campground

Atlanta

Jackson Lake

Clear Lake Nature Trail 👢👢

Distance Round-Trip: 4.5 miles

Estimated Hiking Time: 2.5 to 3 hours

Cautions: Be prepared to walk over roots and rocks. Take along insect repellent in the warm months.

Trail Directions: The trail mostly follows around Clear Lake, but also combines with the High Country Pathway. The access point (one of several) starts near the boat launch from the north end of the lake. Park in the small lot south of the contact station in the northern unit and walk .4 mi. down to the boat launch on Clear Lake. And clear it is! The green waters are so crystalline that you can the see the rippled sandy bottom. Turn left **[1]**, and ascend the ridge along the lake.

The trail veers away from the lake into a mix of oaks, white pines, and gnarled jack pines (.3 mi.) **[2]**. It crosses under a high wire before winding to merge with another trail, old M-33 (.4 mi.) **[3]**.

Head right. Eventually you will swing around to the present M-33 (.5 mi.) **[4]**. Cross it to a dirt road that leads to the gravel pit, which is heavily used by all-terrain vehicles. Don't go that far! The hiking trail swings right, into the woods, and skirts the pit (.6 mi.) **[5]**. You come into the open, crunching over gravel. Keep heading straight and reenter the woods. Under the cool cover of trees, you'll wind up and around to a junction with the High Country Pathway (.8 mi.) **[6]**.

Turn right and descend to cross a dirt road, then climb to the crest of a hill (1 mi.) **[7]**. Swing down to where you catch a glimpse of a small valley before winding through white pines and several aspens to emerge onto another dirt road (1.3 mi.) **[8]**. An arrow will direct you left. Follow the road for about .1 mi. and turn right at the next dirt road.

Soon another road curves around from your left. At this point, look to your left across the road for blue marks that will lead you diagonally back into the woods (1.4 mi.) **[9]**. Look carefully because the trail is easy to miss. You go through the woods and to the junction for Jackson Lake (1.8 mi.) **[10]**. Turn right and within a couple hundred feet, cross the road **[11]**.

Follow through hardwoods and under high wires, then wind back down to M-33 (2.1 mi.) **[12]**. Cross back, meandering through the mixed hardwoods and then red pine and generally descending to a meadow, which is an old rail grade (2.3 mi.) **[13]**. The Valentine Branch of the Detroit Mackinaw Railroad passed through here during the logging era, 1880 through 1902.

Descend and cross the footbridge over an ephemeral stream (2.5 mi.) **[14]**. Take a sharp right at post #11 (2.7 mi.) **[15]**. This spot overlooks a pond holding the skeletal remains of trees. When you reach the dirt road (3.1 mi.) **[16]**, turn left onto it and pick up the trail again on the other side. Continue west through a grassy area, then past a baseball diamond built by the Civilian Conservation Corps (3.3 mi.) **[17]**. Soon you reach the junction for the High Country Pathway.

Follow to the right through scraggy jack pine and past new aspen growth before crossing County Road 622 (3.5 mi.) **[18]**. Red pine and blueberries are prominent along the next stretch, with silver-green lichen adding pockets of color and texture. You get a peek at the lake beyond the day-use area at 3.8 mi. **[19]**. Pass a gravel road and a handful of cottages. The trail then swings left and you continue your hike around the shores of Clear Lake (4.2 mi.) **[20]**.

When the light is right, you can witness a work of art. The lake displays a palette ranging from light green to aqua and blue-purple. Colors blend where they meet, like a rainbow. A couple of benches are placed on the western shore: Sit and enjoy the canvass. When you resume the hike, the trail winds around, passing through the camping area and beach to the boat launch (4.5 mi.) **[1]**. Turn left and hike the .4 mi. back up to where you left your vehicle.

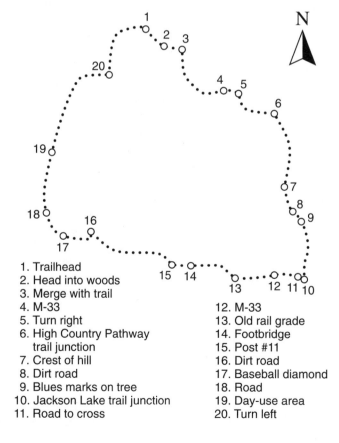

1. Trailhead
2. Head into woods
3. Merge with trail
4. M-33
5. Turn right
6. High Country Pathway trail junction
7. Crest of hill
8. Dirt road
9. Blues marks on tree
10. Jackson Lake trail junction
11. Road to cross
12. M-33
13. Old rail grade
14. Footbridge
15. Post #11
16. Dirt road
17. Baseball diamond
18. Road
19. Day-use area
20. Turn left

Clear Lake–Jackson Lake Trail—Southern Loop 👢👢

Distance Round-Trip: 4.4 miles

Estimated Hiking Time: 2.5 to 3 hours

Cautions: Some sections are overgrown. Look for blue blazes. Wear appropriate footgear, and take insect repellent.

Trail Directions: Begin at the roadside rest area on the east side of M-33, roughly halfway between Clear Lake State Park and the Jackson Lake State Forest Campground. Look for a lightly used path about 60 feet south of the toilets and for a tree with a blue paint mark **[1]**.

Enter the mixed woods, following the lightly used path for less than .1 mi. to the main trail. Turn right near a post with the number 20 on it **[2]**, a remnant of an interpretive trail marked by 25 numbered posts. You soon swing left between two large white pines to cross a dirt road.

On the other side you enter a utility corridor and arrive at a trail post with a map (.3 mi.) **[3]**. Head right down the utility corridor for a short distance before entering the woods on your left. Continue through lush ferns growing around the trunks of dead pine trees, cross a forest road, and exit the woods back onto the utility corridor (.7 mi.) **[4]**.

At .8 mi., as you cross a large meadow, you reach post #22 **[5]**. The Village of Valentine once stood here. During the lumber era, this settlement sported a post office, hotel, and general store. Leaving Valentine, swing right to cross a dirt two-track and walk among a strip of trees growing between the utility corridor and M-33. At .9 mi., as you cross County Road 624 **[6]**, on your left is a marker for the Polar-Equator Trail.

Don't stray to the left to follow a two-track; follow the blue blazes on the trees. At 1.3 mi. skirt a large wetland filled with ghost trees **[7]**. Head into the trees on the right, where the aspen are falling for beaver. Then turn left, cross over an old beaver dam, and follow along a drainage ditch past a series of small beaver dams.

Veer left through knee-grabbing ferns before you turn to enter the woods. Descend and cross a boardwalk through a wet area not far from Jackson Lake State Forest Campground (1.6 mi.) **[8]**.

Near the picnic area (1.7 mi.) **[9]**, look for the trail post with a map. Snake across a two-track and follow the narrow path left past several large oaks, before entering a clearing. At 2.1 mi. turn left onto an off-road vehicle (ORV) trail **[10]**, pass a red pine planta-

tion, and cross County Road 624 (2.2 mi.) **[11]** to reach a trail post with a map.

Pine needles cushion your steps as you parallel an ORV trail before crossing a series of boardwalks through a white cedar swamp (2.3 mi.) **[12]**. Cross the ORV trail and an old forest road before turning left on a second forest road (2.6 mi.) **[13]**. Be careful—the trail veers left, off the forest road, in less than .1 mi. Turn right past the old oak tree (2.8 mi.) **[14]**, then veer left again onto an old two-track where the trail climbs (2.9 mi.) **[15]**. At 3 mi. turn right on a moss-carpeted trail **[16]**.

At 3.3 mi. cross a utility corridor and cut across a cultivated field **[17]**. Look for the blue blaze as you finish crossing the field. Further on, you swing right at a blue-tipped post and climb slightly (3.5 mi.) **[18]**. At 3.6 mi., enter a red pine plantation with a mix of younger oaks and maples **[19]**. The trail undulates, then bursts into a logged area of ferns, shrubs, and small trees (3.7 mi.) **[20]**.

Cross the utility corridor and dirt track again before entering the woods (3.8 mi.) **[21]**. Swing left and descend through a mixed forest to the first trail post with the map that you had passed earlier (4.1 mi.) **[3]**. Stay right and retrace your steps to post 20 and then left, back to the roadside rest area.

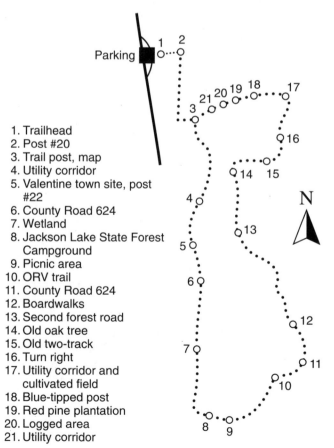

1. Trailhead
2. Post #20
3. Trail post, map
4. Utility corridor
5. Valentine town site, post #22
6. County Road 624
7. Wetland
8. Jackson Lake State Forest Campground
9. Picnic area
10. ORV trail
11. County Road 624
12. Boardwalks
13. Second forest road
14. Old oak tree
15. Old two-track
16. Turn right
17. Utility corridor and cultivated field
18. Blue-tipped post
19. Red pine plantation
20. Logged area
21. Utility corridor

22. Pigeon River Country State Forest

- View the largest elk herd east of the Mississippi River.
- Camp the backcountry along the High Country Pathway.
- Wander the nonmotorized tract of Green Timbers.

Park Information

The Pigeon River Country State Forest boasts two major distinctions. With more than 97,000 nearly contiguous acres, it is a large block of relatively undeveloped public forest land. It is also the center of Michigan's elk herd, the largest free-roaming elk herd east of the Mississippi River.

Logged out between 1860 and 1910, much of the forest area came to the state through tax reversion when later attempts at farming failed. The tax-reverted lands were designated a state forest in 1919, and tree planting soon began. The Civilian Conservation Corps built the Forest Headquarters in the 1930s, which has served also as a state fish research station and as the state's first conservation school.

Michigan's native elk disappeared about 1875, but in 1918, 24 western elk were released at three sites near the Pigeon River area. Today, the elk herd numbers about 1,200 animals. Your best opportunities to spot the elk are in September and early October and from late April through early May.

This beautiful area includes seven campgrounds; 27 miles of horse trails; 60 miles of trails for hiking, biking, and cross-country skiing; and excellent fishing and hunting locations.

Directions: Located primarily in Otsego and Cheboygan Counties, Pigeon River Country State Forest has many access points. The headquarters is located about 13 miles east of Vanderbilt. Take Sturgeon Valley Road east to Twin Lakes Road. Turn left and continue north about a mile to the headquarters.

Hours Open: Open year-round.

Facilities: Hiking, mountain bicycling, cross-country skiing, snowshoeing, swimming, fishing, hunting, camping (tent, RV, and backcountry), equestrian camping, and interpretive center.

Permits and Rules: In state forest campgrounds, you must camp at a designated site, register, and pay the camping fee. Wilderness camping on state forest land along the High Country Pathway is permitted. You are requested to camp no closer than 100 feet from any body of water or the pathway. A camp registration card is required to be posted at the campsite or register at a forestry field office. Fires are permitted: Keep them small and under control. Pack out what you pack in. In established campgrounds, pets must be on a leash. It is illegal to operate licensed vehicles on any roads not designated as open.

Further Information: Pigeon River Country State Forest Area, 9966 Twin Lakes Road, Vanderbilt, MI 49795; 517-983-4101 or Mackinaw State Forest, 1732 West M-32, P.O. Box 667, Gaylord, MI 49735; 517-732-3541.

Other Points of Interest

Connected to and managed by the Pigeon River Country State Forest is a 6,300-acre tract know as **Green Timbers,** closed to all motor vehicles. Hiking, mountain bicycling, cross-country skiing, horseback riding, camping, hunting, fishing, and wildlife viewing are emphasized. For more information contact the Pigeon River Country State Forest at 517-983-4101 or the Mackinaw State Forest at 517-732-3541.

Park Trails

Shingle Mill Pathway—This pathway provides hiking, mountain bicycling, cross-country skiing, and snowshoeing opportunities along five loop trails that build on each other from the Pigeon Bridge Campground. The loops range in length from .75 mile to 11 miles.

High Country Pathway—This pathway, which begins and ends at the Pigeon Bridge Campground, features more than 70 miles for extended backpacking in the heart of Michigan's northern Lower Peninsula. The single-loop trail can be hiked as one long adventure or broken into shorter segments.

Northern Spur of the Michigan Shore-to-Shore Riding and Hiking Trail—This spur extends through the forest and gives equestrians access to the Pigeon River Country. The trail stretches from Oscoda on the Lake Huron side of the state to Empire on the Lake Michigan side.

Pigeon River Country State Forest

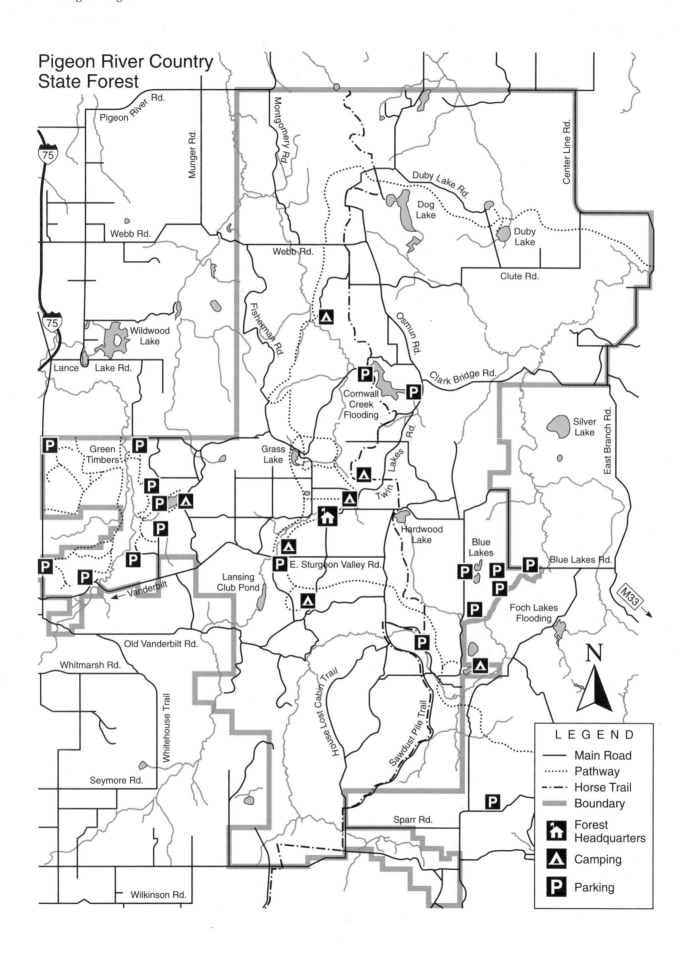

LEGEND

—— Main Road

········ Pathway

—·—·— Horse Trail

▬▬▬ Boundary

🏠 Forest Headquarters

⛺ Camping

🅿 Parking

Shingle Mill Pathway— Upper Loop 🥾🥾

Distance Round-Trip: 5.9 miles

Estimated Hiking Time: 3 to 3.5 hours

Cautions: Watch for roots and rocks exposed along the trail. You hike through wet areas, so wear proper footgear. Take along water and, in warm months, insect repellent.

Trail Directions: Start and park at the Pigeon River State Forest Campground, which is less than 1 mi. north of the headquarters (about 13 mi. east of Vanderbilt). Take Sturgeon Valley Road east to Twin Lakes Road. Turn left and go north about 1 mi. to the headquarters. Continue north. Turn west into the campground and follow Pigeon Bridge Road, crossing the Pigeon River (limited parking here). Follow the road a few hundred feet more until you arrive at the trailhead, where you see the path and blue-diamond trail marker. A couple of vehicles can park here. Head northeast through red pines **[1]**; you will see the post #6 location board up the way.

Veer left along the river, where blueberries and ferns intermingle along the trail. Ascend to walk the ridge overlooking the river plain, then pass through brush along the first crest (.2 mi.) **[2]**.

Follow along the ridge. At .3 mi. an equestrian trail crosses your path **[3]**. Continue on the ridge and pass the end of a dirt road (.6 mi.) **[4]**. Then descend into birches, aspens, and pines (.9 mi.) **[5]**. The trail gently undulates through red pines, then veers left to arrive at post #7 (1.1 mi.) **[6]**.

Head right through ferns, winding down to cross a boardwalk over a stream; then wind up to a junction (1.3 mi.) **[7]**. Turn right through a mixed forest. At the clearing is post #8 (1.5 mi.) **[8]**. This is the site of a former lumber mill, Cornwall Flats. Its old mill pond is now the alder swamp.

Cross another boardwalk, brush through lush ferns, then wind and climb through hardwoods before heading back down and over another boardwalk (1.8 mi.) **[9]**. Get ready for an arduous, two-tiered climb over roots and loose stones as the trail winds its way into a dark forest. Expect more undulations; after a two-track crosses your path, another steep climb awaits you (2.3 mi.) **[10]**. The trail levels out, then gently descends to the dirt road (2.7 mi.) **[11]**.

After you cross this road, you'll cross many logging roads; thinning pockets in the forest indicate that it is now being logged. The trail winds up to the junction at post #10 (3.1 mi.) **[12]**. You have three choices here: Go right to post #11, go left to post #9 (which you will do momentarily), or climb a few steps and go left to the overlook. For now, head over to the overlook for a stunning view of Grass Lake and the Pigeon River Valley. Even on a hazy day the smoky fog rolling from the backdrop of hills and wafting over the valley is breathtaking. Now go back and head down the trail as it descends steeply through the woods, bottoming out at about 3.3 mi. **[13]**.

Cross a dirt road (3.5 mi.) **[14]**, and soon cross it again. Youthful aspens and maples cluster near the road. The trail traverses boardwalks and a land bridge. Pass between beaver-dammed pools filled with the white ghosts of birches (3.7 mi.) **[15]**. Soon, you wind into the campground at post #9 (3.8 mi.) **[16]**.

Turn left, passing through red pines. Descend, cross the dirt road again (4.3 mi.) **[17]**, pass a clearing, and continue to descend to a junction near a lake (4.4 mi.) **[18]**. Swing left and walk along Section 4 Lake—such a nondescript name for a beautiful lake that defies description.

Murky aqua and seafoam-green waters mottle this bowl-shaped lake; fallen trees break up the surface like spokes in a wagon wheel. The colors (some as vibrant as spearmint mouthwash) vary with the depths within this watery sinkhole, yet still throw off crystal reflections of the surrounding forest. The trail continues rolling through the woods, follows along a ridge, and returns you to post #7 (4.7 mi.) **[6]**. From here, retrace your steps back to your vehicle.

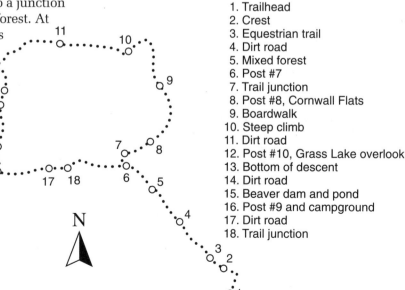

1. Trailhead
2. Crest
3. Equestrian trail
4. Dirt road
5. Mixed forest
6. Post #7
7. Trail junction
8. Post #8, Cornwall Flats
9. Boardwalk
10. Steep climb
11. Dirt road
12. Post #10, Grass Lake overlook
13. Bottom of descent
14. Dirt road
15. Beaver dam and pond
16. Post #9 and campground
17. Dirt road
18. Trail junction

Shingle Mill Pathway—
Middle Loop 👢👢

Distance Round-Trip: 6.3 miles

Estimated Hiking Time: 3 to 4 hours

Cautions: Wear proper footgear. Take water and insect repellent.

Trail Directions: Start and park at the Pigeon River State Forest Campground, which is less than 1 mi. north of the headquarters (about 13 mi. east of Vanderbilt). Take Sturgeon Valley Road east to Twin Lakes Road. Turn left for about 1 mi. to the headquarters. Keep going north, then turn west into the campground and follow Pigeon Bridge Road, crossing the Pigeon River (limited parking here). Follow the road a few hundred more feet until you arrive at the trailhead, where you see the path and the blue-diamond trail marker. A couple of vehicles can park here. Head northeast through red pines **[1]**; you will see the post 6 location board up the way.

Veer left along the river. The trail ascends to a ridge overlooking the grassy river plain, then passes through brush at the first crest (.2 mi.) **[2]**.

Follow along the ridge. At .3 mi. an equestrian trail crosses your path **[3]**. Continue on the ridge and pass the end of a dirt road (.6 mi.) **[4]**. Then descend into birches, aspens, and pines (.9 mi.) **[5]**. The trail gently undulates through red pines, then veers left to arrive at post #7 (1.1 mi.) **[6]**.

Head left and soon arrive at beautiful Section 4 Lake, a small, bowl-shaped body with jade-shaded water (1.4 mi.) **[7]**. The colors vary with the depths within this watery sinkhole, yet it still throws off crystal reflections of the surrounding forest. A number of trees, enamored of their reflections on the lake, met their demise by leaning over too far to look at their images.

At 1.6 mi. cross a dirt road **[8]**; then hike through a mixed forest to arrive at the campground at post #9 (2.1 mi.) **[9]**. Turn right to cross a land bridge, then descend through saplings to cross a boardwalk, then a footbridge. Alongside is a beaver dam to your left (2.2 mi.) **[10]**.

Cross a dirt road (2.3 mi.) **[11]**, and soon cross it again. You pass through a logged area and climb through a beech/maple forest to arrive at post #10 (2.8 mi.) **[12]**. Turn left at the junction for a magnificent view of Grass Lake and the Pigeon River Valley. Enjoy the view before you backtrack. Then head left to reach post #11 (3 mi.) **[13]**.

Turn left and descend steeply through the woods, then enter a recently logged area before you skirt the Devil's Soup Bowl on your right (3.2 mi.) **[14]**. Grass Lake comes into view after you cross a road and walk through a small parking area (3.3 mi.) **[15]**. You skirt another logged area before crossing a footbridge (3.7 mi.) **[16]**. Note the beaver dam at the edge of the lake, regulating the flow of the water in the stream you are now crossing.

Stay right when the trail splits. Pass through red, then jack, pines. Cross a dirt two-track, then cross a clear-cut area now overgrown with ferns and aspen saplings (4.6 mi.) **[17]**. Descend and skirt a small, bowl-shaped wetland (4.7 mi.) **[18]** before passing by Ford Lake (4.8 mi.) **[19]**. Then climb to post #12 (4.9 mi.) **[20]**, turn left and make a steeper climb. Descend and climb again, before the trail levels out to cross Ford Lake Road (5.1 mi.) **[21]**.

A recently logged area, much of the next mile is reminiscent of a 1960s urban renewal project. Rather than rundown housing, large areas of trees have been leveled here, leaving gaping holes in the forest. At 6.1 mi. you reach the bluff overlooking the Pigeon River and the Pigeon River State Forest Campground **[22]**. The trail swings left, away from the bluff, and turns right into a red pine plantation. Descend along a cushion of pine needles to your vehicle below.

1. Trailhead
2. Crest
3. Equestrian trail
4. Dirt road
5. Mixed forest
6. Post #7
7. Section 4 Lake
8. Dirt road
9. Post #9, campground
10. Footbridge, beaver dam
11. Road crossing
12. Post #10, Grass Lake overlook
13. Post #11
14. Devil's Soup Bowl
15. Road crossing, parking area
16. Footbridge
17. Overgrown clear-cut
18. Wetland
19. Ford Lake
20. Post #12
21. Road crossing
22. Bluff

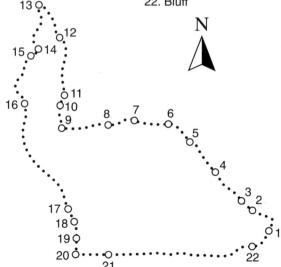

23. George Mason River Retreat Area

- Canoe the scenic South Branch Au Sable River.
- Try your luck at fly-fishing for trout.
- Visit the remains of Durant's Castle.

Park Information

The people of Michigan might thank the late George W. Mason as they fish, canoe, or hike along this stretch of the South Branch Au Sable River. Mason so loved this area that he bequeathed 1,500 acres to the state for preservation in 1954. Subsequent land acquisitions have nearly doubled the size of the area. Previously know as the South Branch Au Sable River Area, the site now is called the George Mason River Retreat Area, bearing the name of its benefactor.

Recognized for excellent trout fishing, the South Branch is also popular with canoers. Canoe landings are located at Chase Bridge on the south end and, 11 miles to the north, at Smith Bridge. A third landing is located at the Canoe Harbor Campground, the only campground in the area.

Directions: To reach the northern trailhead on M-72, head east from Grayling about 15 miles and turn south on Canoe Harbor Campground Road. Parking is on the left. To reach the southern trailhead from M-72, head east from Grayling about 12 miles and turn south on Chase Bridge Road. Go about 8 miles to the parking area. From Roscommon, take M-18 east 2.5 miles and turn left on Chase Bridge Road. Parking is 2 miles up the road on the right.

Hours Open: Open year-round.

Facilities: Hiking, cross-country skiing, fishing, hunting, canoeing, and camping (tent).

Permits and Rules: There is no visitor fee for the park. In state forest campgrounds, however, you must camp at a designated site, register, and pay the camping fee.

Further Information: Au Sable State Forest, 191 S. Mt. Tom Road, Mio, MI 48647; 517-826-3211.

Other Points of Interest

Canoe all or portions of the Au Sable River between Grayling and Oscoda. For canoe rental information, call the Grayling Area Visitor's Council at 1-800-YES-8837.

The **Wakeley Lake Foot Travel Area,** located on M-72 about 2 miles west of the Mason Tract Pathway, offers an extensive trail network for nonmotorized recreation. For information call the Mio Ranger District at 517-826-3252.

The **Midland–Mackinac Trail** passes just east of the Mason Tract Pathway. The trail was built by the Boy Scouts and approximates the old migratory route used by Native Americans. For more information call the Midland-Mackinac Trail Commission at 517-631-5230 or the Mio Ranger District at 517-826-3252.

The **Michigan Shore-to-Shore Riding and Hiking Trail** skirts the north end of the George Mason River Retreat Area. You may call the Mio Ranger District for more information.

George Mason River
Retreat Area

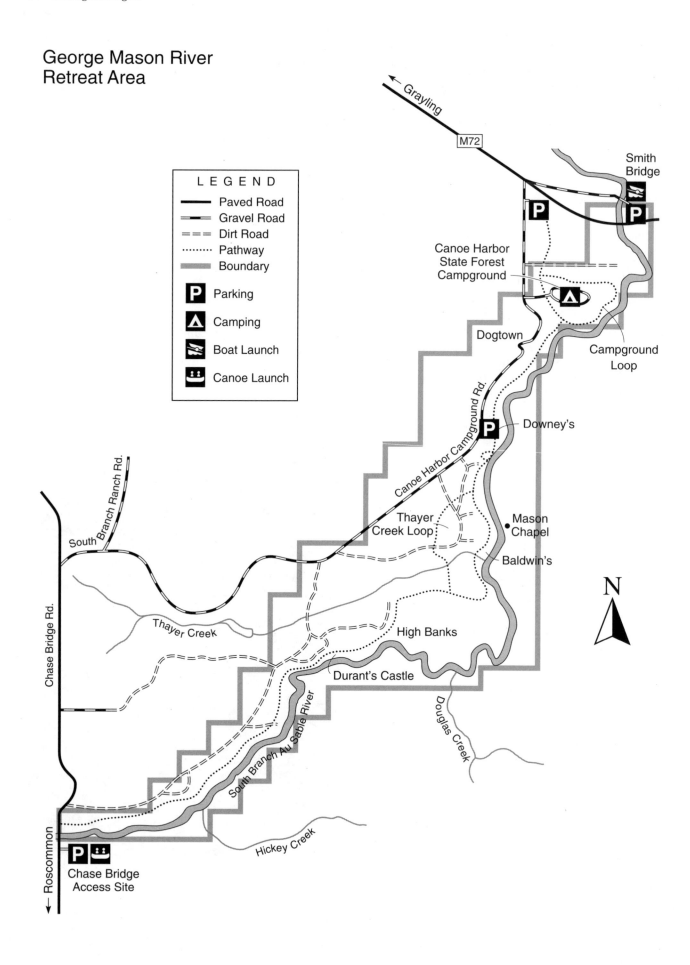

Mason Tract Pathway—North

Distance One-Way: 2.7 miles

Estimated Hiking Time: 1.5 to 2 hours

Cautions: Some sections of the trail have exposed roots and stumps. Watch your step and wear appropriate footgear. Take along insect repellent in the warm months.

Trail Directions: The hike starts at the north trailhead, which is on the east side of Canoe Harbor Campground Road, just south of M-72. This access covers the northern end of the trail as a point-to-point hike and provides an out-and-back day hike of reasonable length. You can also combine this trail with the southern route for an end-to-end hike of the 9.1-mi. pathway (or a very long out-and-back day hike).

Start at the east end of the parking area **[1]** and head south along the narrow path lined with blueberries and silvery-gray lichen. Jack pines sparsely cover the landscape, and the dry, gray trunks of long-dead trees lie scattered about. The area looks as though it was recently cleared, with some standing dead trees still spiking above the new growth. At .4 mi. you notice the fire scars **[2]**. Charred logs—still standing or scattered about—remain in a circular clearing. The carcasses of fallen trees lie gray and brittle, their branches turned upward like giant rib cages picked clean and left to dry.

At .5 mi. cross a sandy two-track **[3]** and pass jack pines before arriving at the Campground Loop (.7 mi.) **[4]**. If you are inclined to taking a side trip, this trail loops around the campground for almost a mile and skirts the river before rejoining the main trail. You'll see the river soon, however, if you continue straight. The trail passes the road into the campground at .8 mi. **[5]**, then gently rolls through ferns, jack pines, scrubby oaks and maples, and finally white pines. Just before you reach post #3 (1.1 mi.) **[6]**, a path cuts across yours. You can sit on a bench at the post, watching the river below from this ridge. From here, the trail swings right and begins to climb. Perched on a ridge, you view the river below (1.2 mi.) **[7]**.

As you continue, a feathering of white pines softens the scene. When you reach the aspen, listen to the quiet (1.3 m.) **[8]**. Strain to hear even the leaves shimmering in the breeze. Pass through red pines and a small parking area. Just before you reach post #4, which marks the parking area known as Dogtown (1.5 mi.) **[9]**, the river comes into view. Several paths lead from here down to the river. The trail undulates

along the river. At about 1.8 mi. you are on a ridge overlooking river debris **[10]**; trees and stumps pose minor obstacles to canoeists paddling down the river.

Your ridge walk ends, and the trail veers away from the river, continuing gentle undulations until it presents you with a fairly steep climb at 2 mi. **[11]**. At the crest is a seat, a small lot for parking, and a sign, "Quality Fishing Area." Pass through a couple of meadows, then climb up a red carpet of needles to walk the ridge above the river (2.4 mi.) **[12]**.

After another meadow, silvery lichen introduce you to a mixed forest before you pass an old fence post with rusty wire (2.5 mi.) **[13]**. The trail dips and then climbs up through the trees to another grassy area. Listen in the woods to the boughs moaning and creaking like a hinge on an old door. Below you, an old cement remnant clogs the river. Start watching for a post that marks a fork in the trail (2.7 mi.). A left turn here will continue you along the trail. A right leads you to the parking area, Downey's Access Site, the end of this trail **[14]**. If you haven't arranged for a driver to pick you up here, continue along the south end of the trail or turn and hike the 2.7 mi. back to the north parking lot.

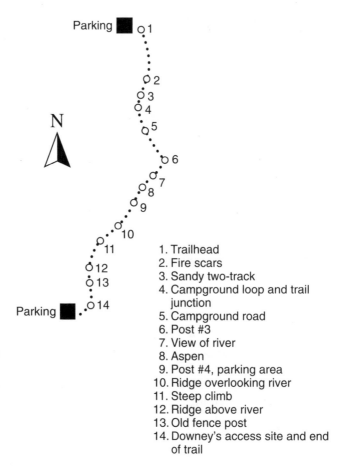

1. Trailhead
2. Fire scars
3. Sandy two-track
4. Campground loop and trail junction
5. Campground road
6. Post #3
7. View of river
8. Aspen
9. Post #4, parking area
10. Ridge overlooking river
11. Steep climb
12. Ridge above river
13. Old fence post
14. Downey's access site and end of trail

Mason Tract Pathway—South

Distance One-Way: 6.4 miles

Estimated Hiking Time: 3 to 4 hours

Cautions: Sections of the trail are overgrown. Wear appropriate footgear. Carry water and insect repellent.

Trail Directions: Start at Downey's parking area, 2.5 mi. south of the north trailhead [1]. The hike covers the southern end of the trail. Combine it with the north route for an end-to-end hike of the 9.1-mi. pathway or a very long out-and-back day hike.

Pass an overgrown foundation as you follow the trail that many anglers use to reach the river. You quickly find a less-worn trail that splits to the right. After investigating the river, take this less-worn path. The trail undulates through grass and past rows of red pine, crosses an old field, and skirts a dirt cul-de-sac to arrive at a stairway down to the river (.3 mi.) [2]. Go past the stairway to walk along an old field. After entering an aspen stand, you reach post #6 (.5 mi.) [3]. Go left.

View the river as you skirt a jack pine plantation. You pass some aspen with beaver scars, coming close to the river. At 1 mi. you reach post #7 [4]. Step to the left to stand alongside the river; then follow the trail away from the river, walking through a wet area. Cross a footbridge over Thayer Creek (1.1 mi.) [5] and climb to view the river from a bluff (1.2 mi.) [6]. The trail swings right and onto an overgrown forest road (1.3 mi.) [7] that snakes past a number of large red and white pines.

At 1.7 mi. you reach post #8, a junction for the Thayer Creek Loop [8]. Swing left past the bench and climb to cross a grassy field. Pass by more large red and white pines and eventually skirt a dirt cul-de-sac (2.3 mi.) [9].

When you reach a two-track, turn right and follow it briefly before veering left along the edge of a wooded ravine. You soon see the river below as you approach a stairway down to the river. This is the area known as High Banks (2.6 mi.) [10]. During the logging era, logs were rolled into the river here, then floated downstream to the sawmills.

Descend and walk through a wet stretch as you skirt a recently logged area (2.8 mi.) [11]. View the river through the brush before climbing to reach the remains of Durant's Castle (3.2 mi.) [12]. The dream of William C. Durant (of the Durant Motor Car family) became a nightmare when the 42-room mansion burned down shortly after its completion in 1931. The site now has a wooden canoe landing, an infor-

mation board, and vault toilets near an access parking area.

Continue along a two-track that runs through the woods across from the information board. Look for blue blazes, then walk through a burned area (3.3 mi.) [13]. At 3.6 mi., you reach a bench along a bluff [14], just before you swing left. Blackened trees contrast with the lush green ferns that dominate the landscape.

At 4.2 mi. walk the edge of a logged-out area where oak is growing back [15]. Swing right as you reenter the woods, then climb to the dirt cul-de-sac to post #11 [16]. The trail descends, and you eventually cross a boardwalk (4.8 mi.) [17]. Pass the bench while walking through maple, aspen, and red pine. The trail levels out, and you proceed through a number of wet areas with the river in view on the left. Swing right to cross several more boardwalks. Walk through mixed pine to arrive at #12, posted with its map on a tree at 5.5 mi. [18].

The trail here parallels a two-track. Skirt another parking area (5.7 mi.) [19] and follow the edge of a bluff. At 6.2 mi. cross a grassy opening [20] before swinging left past a number of fallen trees. The sound of passing cars signals that you are approaching Chase Bridge Road. At the road (6.4 mi.) [21], turn left and walk an additional .2 mi. to the southern trailhead parking area.

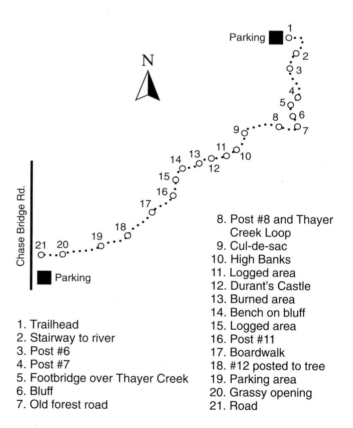

1. Trailhead
2. Stairway to river
3. Post #6
4. Post #7
5. Footbridge over Thayer Creek
6. Bluff
7. Old forest road
8. Post #8 and Thayer Creek Loop
9. Cul-de-sac
10. High Banks
11. Logged area
12. Durant's Castle
13. Burned area
14. Bench on bluff
15. Logged area
16. Post #11
17. Boardwalk
18. #12 posted to tree
19. Parking area
20. Grassy opening
21. Road

24. Hartwick Pines State Park

- Hike in the shadows of the largest stand of virgin white pine in the Lower Peninsula.
- Learn about the life of a lumberjack at the Logging Camp Museum.
- Pay your respect to the regal Monarch.

Park Information

This 9,672-acre park was donated to the state in 1927 by Mrs. Karen B. Hartwick in memory of her husband, Major Edward E. Hartwick. It is home to the largest stand of virgin white pines remaining in the Lower Peninsula. The park memorializes a 49-acre tract of white pines that survived the state's logging era of 1840 to 1910. So, too, are the "shanty boys," or the men who logged the trees, remembered. A reconstructed logging camp with bunkhouses, a mess hall, and other structures gives a sense of what these men's lives were like.

Four interpretive trails provide more than 6 miles for hiking. Some 10 miles of trails are groomed for cross-country skiing; these trails are open to mountain bikers in the warmer months. Limited trails are open for snowmobiles. An 8-mile scenic drive (located off M-93, about a mile northeast of the entrance to the Visitor Center) allows motorists to enjoy the environment.

The park's Michigan Forest Visitor Center offers audiovisual presentations, one of which depicts forest management now and in the logging era. Visit the towering trees on the Virgin Pines Trail. Most notable among them is the Monarch, which stretched upward to 155 feet before gusty winds trimmed 30 to 40 feet from it in 1992.

Directions: Hartwick Pines State Park is about 7 miles north of Grayling. Take I-75 to exit 259. Head north on M-93 about 3 miles to the park entrance.

Hours Open: The recreation area is open daily from 8:00 A.M. to 10:00 P.M. The Michigan Forest Visitor Center is open from 8:00 A.M. to 5:00 P.M., January through June and October to December. It is open from 8:00 A.M. to 7:00 P.M., June through September, and closed Mondays throughout the year. The Logging Camp Museum is open from 8:00 A.M. to 4:30 P.M. in April, May, September, and October, and from 8:00 A.M. to 7:00 P.M., June to Labor Day.

Facilities: Hiking, mountain bicycling, cross-country skiing, snowmobiling, fishing, hunting, camping (RV and tent), sanitation station, picnicking, cabin, interpretive trails, and interpretive center.

Permits and Rules: A park fee ($4 daily, $20 annually) is required for each motor vehicle. Motorized traffic is prohibited on trails; ride bicycles only on designated trails and roads.

Further Information: Hartwick Pines State Park, Route 3, P.O. Box 3840, Grayling, MI 49738; 517-348-7068 or call the Michigan Forest Visitor Center at 517-348-2537.

Other Points of Interest

Canoe all or portions of the **Au Sable** or **Manistee** rivers. For canoe rental information contact the Grayling Area Visitor's Council at 1-800-YES-8837. For information on state forest campgrounds accessible by canoe, call the Au Sable State Forest office at 517-826-3211.

Grayling is the midpoint of the **Michigan Shore-to-Shore Riding-Hiking Trail**. The trail stretches from Oscoda on Lake Huron to Empire on Lake Michigan. Contact the Au Sable State Forest office.

Park Trails

Mertz Grade Foot Trail 👢—2 miles—This interpretive trail starts in the picnic area, crosses the highway, and passes through the old campground (not used since 1993). It follows an abandoned railroad grade in an area where wildflowers and blueberries are prolific. It then loops through second-growth forest and returns to the picnic area.

Bright and Glory Nature Trail 👢—.5 mile—This interpretive trail starts near site #15 in the campground. It heads through aspen, twists through a blowdown area where a tornado cut a swath in 1994, lumbers by the gnawed remnants of a beaver's foraging, and cuts through dense swamp stands of Northern White Cedars near Bright and Glory Lakes.

Three additional trails are used for cross-country skiing and, in warmer months, for mountain bicycling. Trailheads are located at the north end of the Visitor Center parking area and the north end of the day-use parking area.

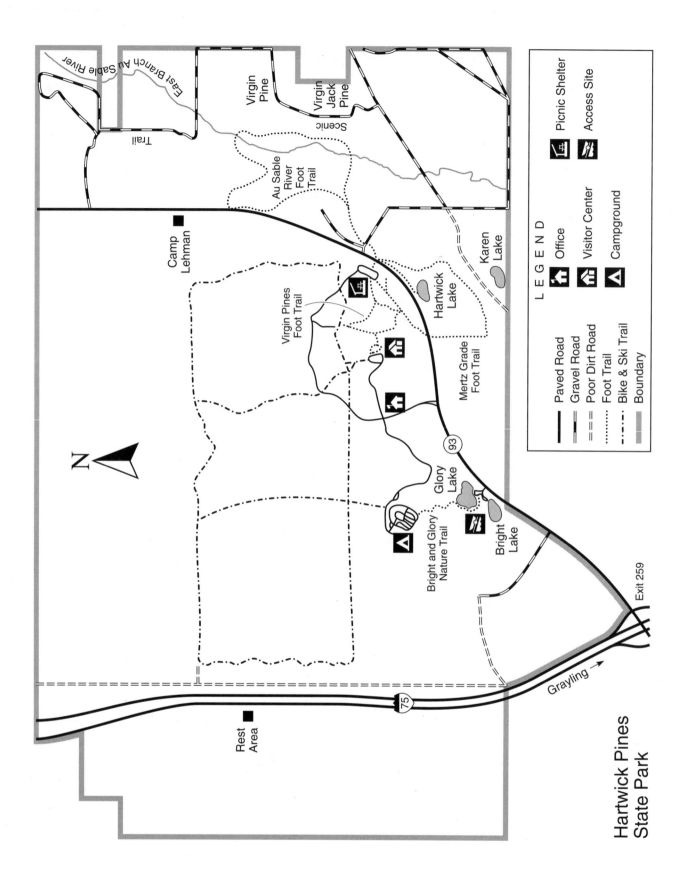

N

East Branch Au Sable River

Trail

Virgin Pine

Virgin Jack Pine

Scenic

Au Sable River Foot Trail

Camp Lehman

Virgin Pines Foot Trail

Hartwick Lake

Mertz Grade Foot Trail

Karen Lake

93

Glory Lake

Bright and Glory Nature Trail

Bright Lake

Exit 259

Grayling →

75

Rest Area

LEGEND

🛈 Office	Picnic Shelter			
Visitor Center				
Campground	Access Site			

Paved Road
Gravel Road
Poor Dirt Road
Foot Trail
Bike & Ski Trail
Boundary

Hartwick Pines
State Park

Virgin Pines Foot Trail 🥾

Distance Round-Trip: 1.2 miles

Estimated Hiking Time: 1 to 1.5 hours

Cautions: The paved trail often erodes at the edges, leaving a small ridge a couple of inches high. Be careful that you don't step or roll off the edges. To ensure a pleasant stroll, bring insect repellent during warm months: You don't want mosquitoes ruining an otherwise enjoyable hike through the old-growth forest.

Trail Directions: This interpretive trail starts out behind the Visitor Center, off the northeast deck **[1].** Pick up an interpretive map at the center so you may fully enjoy the 22 interpretive stops along this trail that takes you through a primeval pine forest and a logging camp museum.

Head down the trail, thick with beech, maple, and hemlock trees. These are trees of a climax forest, as you learn at post #1 (.1 mi.) **[2].** Continue descending as you pass under big, beautiful trees set in the rolling hillsides around you. Learn about the beech tree, then round the corner to the right and read about sugar maples before strolling through this forest. Savor the virgins that tower above you, admiring their stately stature. A bench at .2 mi. lets you do just that **[3].**

Not far from the bench is post #5, which describes two impressive hemlocks. Pass the explosion of growth on the forest floor among old logs strewn about like fallen soldiers. At .3 mi. a wood railing drapes around a majestic tree **[4],** like a courtier holding a robe and attending to his king, giving space for subjects to stand back and revere. This tree— known as the Monarch—has reigned supreme here, having reached a height of 155 feet. Its reign will end one day, with another tree replacing it. That day may come soon. Extremely high winds already toppled 30 to 40 feet from this white pine in 1992, and it lost the needles that reached for the sunlight. Weakened now, it is only a matter of time before this monarch will be replaced, but not without sadness—monarchs that serve well are not soon forgotten.

Wind through the old growth. Just after post #9, which points out the old growth that made fortunes for the early lumber barons, is a junction for the Mertz Grade Foot Trail (.4 mi.) **[5].** Turn left and make your way through the youthful growth of the 1950s and 1960s. Ferns carpet the floor, growing over the

rolling terrain and nature's plowing—fallen, rotting trunks of yesteryear. More of nature's work is evident at post #11, a stump that resulted from a 1941 storm, which produced hurricane winds that blew down almost half of the 86 acres of the old-growth forest (.5 mi.) **[6].** Forty-nine acres remain today.

You reach a junction at .6 mi. **[7].** A right leads to the day-use area. Turn left instead and climb up to the log church (.7 mi.) **[8].** Benches await you at the top if you want to rest before visiting the Chapel in the Pines. Head down, up, and down again to the Logging Camp (.9 mi.) **[9],** built in 1935 by the Civilian Conservation Corps as a memorial to those who labored in the Michigan forests. Turn right; wander through the mess hall and view the equipment (like the snow roller and sled) or investigate the mill. The buildings are open from June through October.

Turn around and head back up the trail past the big wheels that were once used to move the logs (1 mi.) **[10].** Stroll through the undulating woods, reaching the trail back to the Visitor Center at 1.1 mi. **[11].** Turn right and visit inside to enjoy the exhibits and hands-on displays of Michigan's forests.

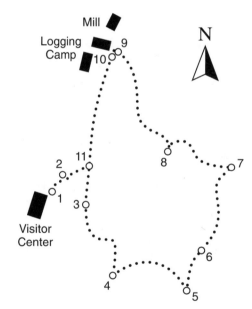

1. Trailhead
2. Post #1
3. Bench
4. Monarch
5. Mertz Grade Foot Trail junction
6. Evidence of winds
7. Junction
8. Chapel in the Pines
9. Logging Camp
10. Big wheels
11. Trail junction back to Visitor Center

Au Sable River Foot Trail 🥾🥾

Distance Round-Trip: 3.8 miles

Estimated Hiking Time: 1.5 to 2 hours

Cautions: This interpretive trail takes you over roots and through areas that are prone to flooding. Wear appropriate footgear and take insect repellent during warm weather.

Trail Directions: Start at the information board in front of the old Civilian Conservation Corps building at the south end of the day-use area parking lot **[1]**. Cross M-93, heading to the junction with the Mertz Grade Foot Trail and a pathway that leads down to Hartwick Lake. Continue straight into the original park campground. If you are lucky, you might spot a tombstone on your left that reads, "Hartwick Pines State Park Campground #1, 1929–1993" (.3 mi.) **[2]**. Pay your respects, then cross a dirt parking area, a sign announcing the trail, and a dirt road (.4 mi.) **[3]**.

Here you find a narrow, worn goat trail that widens when it enters a red pine plantation. At post #3, stay to the right as you follow the posts with blue boot prints and deer tracks (.6 mi.) **[4]**. Cross a two-track and go under a power line. Watch for exposed roots along the path otherwise cushioned by pine needles. You leave the pine plantation and enter a mix of trees just before arriving at a bench along the clear water of the East Branch Au Sable River (.9 mi.) **[5]**.

Cross two footbridges that sandwich a small island at the tip of a bend in the river. Once on the other side, you pass the location of the old swimming hole used by the Civilian Conservation Corps in the late 1930s and early 1940s. The trail swings north, and you hike in a mixture of pines and hardwoods. One type of tree stands out—not because of size but for its wonderful, fresh scent—the balsam fir that dominates the forest here (1.2 mi.) **[6]**.

At 1.6 mi., go under a large white pine (1.6 mi.) **[7]**, shortly before you pass a low bench. The trail swings left. You soon cross another footbridge over the East Branch Au Sable River (1.7 mi.) **[8]**. When this area was logged in the late 1800s, the logs were hauled out by sled across another bridge that existed at this location. Look north for evidence of this bridge; only the stringers remain

As you walk past the white cedar near the river, the trail is likely to be damp or muddy. At 2 mi. you enter a hemlock grove with a notable lack of growth on the forest floor **[9]**. Pass between large, white pines and the utility corridor and enter a red pine plantation (2.2 mi.) **[10]**.

At 2.5 mi. you will reach a sign and option: Continue straight to make a steep climb to an overlook or turn left to take the less difficult alternate route **[11]**. Go for the challenge. Climb steeply, switching back and forth up the side of a moraine (material deposited by the glaciers), through beech and maple trees, over roots and sand, and under a power line. When you reach the top, unfortunately, the overlook is seasonally obscured by the trees (2.6 mi.) **[12]**. Don't trip on the roots as you descend from the glacial hill into a red pine plantation. You cross the utility corridor again (which actually is the path of the less difficult route), and the alternate route merges back with the trail (2.7 mi.) **[13]**.

At 2.9 mi. cross an old corridor of a different type. Now hidden by the rows of red pine, the Mertz Branch of the Lewiston Railroad is slowly being reclaimed by the forest it had helped to clear during the lumber era **[14]**. You soon wind your way back to the first trail junction (3.2 mi.) **[4]**. Having completed the loop, retrace your steps to the parking area.

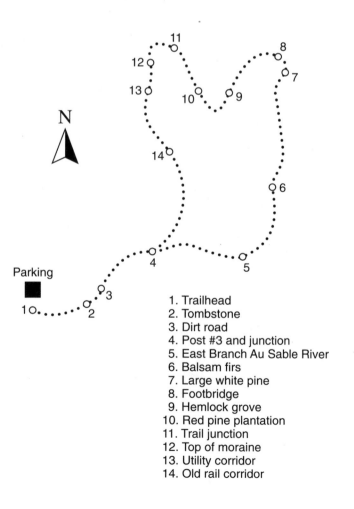

1. Trailhead
2. Tombstone
3. Dirt road
4. Post #3 and junction
5. East Branch Au Sable River
6. Balsam firs
7. Large white pine
8. Footbridge
9. Hemlock grove
10. Red pine plantation
11. Trail junction
12. Top of moraine
13. Utility corridor
14. Old rail corridor

25. Mill Creek State Historic Park

- Rediscover early log-cutting techniques at a reconstructed, 18th-century sawmill using water power.
- See the log-cutting and construction techniques of the beaver along the Mill Creek.
- Climb to an overlook of this beautiful park as well as Mackinac Island in the distance.

Park Information

This lovely park combines groomed nature trails, beaver dams, and scenic overlooks of the Straits of Mackinaw and Mackinac Island with an historic site depicting an industrial complex of the late 1700s.

Featured at this 625-acre park is a working replica of an 18th-century, water-powered sawmill. Archaeological excavation in 1972 revealed that this site had housed such a mill two centuries earlier. The park joined the Mackinac State Historic Parks in 1975. Development of the nature trails and reconstruction of the sawmill began in 1977; the park opened in 1984. Excavations are ongoing, as is the reconstruction of historic buildings.

Watch the water-powered saw biting through fresh logs, just as its predecessor did in the late-18th and early-19th centuries. You can also see two costumed interpreters depict the tedious method used to cut lumber before the water-powered saw was invented.

Five trails loop along 3.5 miles through aspen, along a bluff, around ponds, over footbridges and dams, and to overlooks for views of the Straits of Mackinac. Pack a lunch and picnic at a spot overlooking Mill Pond or visit the park pavilion.

Directions: Historic Mill Creek is located on US-23, about 3 miles southeast of Mackinaw City. From I-75 take exit 337 to US-23, and drive east to the park.

Hours Open: The park is open daily from mid-May through mid-October. Hours in May through June 14 and from Labor Day through mid-October are 10:00 A.M. to 4:00 P.M. From June 15 through Labor Day, the park is open from 9:00 A.M. to 6:00 P.M.

Facilities: Hiking, picnicking, interpretive trails, interpretive center, and historic demonstrations.

Permits and Rules: Admission is $5 for adults, $3 for children 6 through 12, and free for children 5 and younger. Combination packages, which allow seasonal access to Fort Mackinac, Colonial Michilimackinac, and Historic Mill Creek are available at $13 for adults and $7.50 for children.

Further Information: Mackinac State Historic Parks, P.O. Box 873, Mackinaw City, MI 49701-0873; 616-436-5563.

Other Points of Interest

Three other historic state parks are nearby: **Mackinac Island State Park** and **Fort Mackinac** (see park #1), and **Colonial Michilimackinac State Historic Park**. Colonial Michilimackinac offers a glimpse into the life of the British, French, and Native Americans in the 18th century. A 30-minute, guided walking tour allows you to explore the village within the fort. For more information contact Colonial Michilimackinac, c/o Mackinac State Historic Parks, P.O. Box 873, Mackinaw City, MI 49701; 616-436-5563.

From the glimmering beauty of the Straits of Mackinac to the history of Fort Michilimackinac, and, yes, even to the fudge, **Mackinaw City** has much to offer (see park #26). For information call the Greater Mackinaw Area Chamber of Commerce at 616-436-5574 or the Mackinaw Area Tourist Bureau at 800-666-0160.

About 11 miles west of Mackinaw City, **Wilderness State Park** (see park #27) offers 25 miles of Lake Michigan shoreline, modern campsites, sandy beaches, and some 12 miles of hiking trails. For more information contact Wilderness State Park, P.O. Box 380, Carp Lake, MI 49718; 616-436-5381.

Park Trails

Five trails that cover 3 miles loop through the park and flow along the Mill Creek. Three of the trails build on one another, whereas the other two are appendages off the far end of the longest loop.

Mill Pond Trail —.5 mile—The smallest, innermost circle, this loop takes you up to an overlook of the pond and historic buildings below, then down and across Mill Creek, over to another overlook, and circling through the main exhibit area.

Aspen-Wildlife Forest Trail —.5 mile—Accessed off the west end of the Beaver Pond Trail, this extension loops through aspen forest and exhibits aspen management techniques.

Mill Creek
State Historic Park

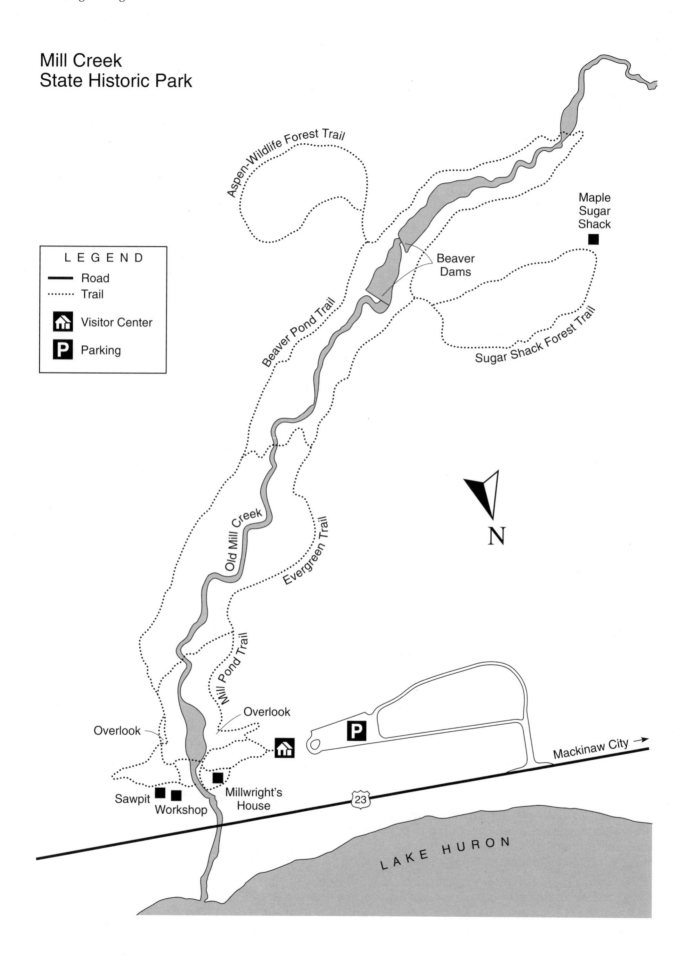

LEGEND
Road
Trail
Visitor Center
Parking

Aspen-Wildlife Forest Trail

Maple
Sugar
Shack

Beaver Pond Trail

Beaver
Dams

Sugar Shack Forest Trail

Old Mill Creek

Evergreen Trail

N

Mill Pond Trail

Overlook

Overlook

P

Overlook

Mackinaw City

Sawpit

Workshop

Millwright's
House

23

LAKE HURON

Evergreen Trail With Sugar Shack Forest Trail 👢👢

Distance Round-Trip: 1.9 miles

Estimated Hiking Time: 1 hour

Cautions: Roots, stumps, and rocks are embedded in the trail. Watch your footing. Some slopes are short but steep, and they are slippery when wet. Insect repellent is a must.

Trail Directions: Start this interpretive trail behind the Visitor Center at the kiosk **[1]**. Go right on the gravel path as it winds up to the observation deck (.1 mi.) **[2]**. From the deck you overlook the mill site, pond, and grassy picnic area below. You can see Mackinac Island in the distance.

Walk through mixed forest and over a small boardwalk. Signs along the way help you to identify trees as you stroll along, arriving at the junction for the Mill Pond Trail at .2 mi. **[3]**. A bench rests at the junction where steps lead down the short route. Continue straight under a thin canopy of trees. With more sunlight, ferns and foliage carpet the floor. Many roots and rocks web the trail through this stretch.

Pass by birches, then fallen trees. Foliage brightens the floor. Wind left and cross a boardwalk before passing velvety logs to arrive at the Evergreen Trail junction (.4 mi.) **[4]**. Go straight.

Soon you reach a fork that leads to a bench overlooking the creek. Listen to the trickle of the water as you view the creek with its debris of logs. Move along through the birch and maple trees. At .5 mi. an oak stands out from the crowd, having a trunk that branches out to form a crown of many trunks **[5]**. Veer left, past a pond that has the standing ghosts of trees in it. At .6 mi. an interpretive board by the pond discusses beavers and dams **[6]**. You can see the dam in the water. Climb the trail a couple hundred feet, pass a huge boulder, and arrive at the junction for the Sugar Shack Forest Trail.

Turn right. You soon see the large boulders beside the trail. These rocks aren't limestone like a majority of rocks in the area. They were transported from Canada by the glaciers, and they are called erratics. Near them, the trail forks. It's a loop. Follow to the right through sugar maples, beeches, oaks, basswoods, ashes, and hemlocks. Interpretive boards coach you on how the forest is managed.

Pass over moss-covered rocks. Look for rocks on your left the green color of an oxidized penny. Before you arrive at the sugar shack, read about maple syrup and how it is tapped (.9 mi.) **[7]**. Walk through the building, see the boiler, and get a taste for how maple syrup is made.

Rocks and boulders line the trail. Pass the huge Canadian imports again and arrive back at the trail at 1.2 mi. Head left, past the beaver dam and ghost trees, until you reach the Evergreen Trail junction (1.4 mi.) **[4]**. Turn right and step down the steep slope to cross the footbridge over Old Mill Creek. Wind your way to the main trail on the east side of the creek (1.5 mi.) **[8]**.

Turn left, brushing through lush ferns and thimbleberries. Cross a boardwalk and head over to a small sinkhole (1.6 mi.) **[9]**. Read the interpretive board to learn why the underlying bedrock eroded and then caved in. A series of boardwalks plank the next stretch of the trail. Just before you reach an overlook (1.8 mi.) **[10]**, you pass the Mill Pond Trail junction. From the overlook you can view the pond and the green bluffs along the west side of it.

Head down to the mill site. Stroll through the site and enjoy it now. If you prefer, you can return here after you cross the mill dam and bridge, wind through the picnic area, and stroll through the Visitor Center (1.7 mi.) **[11]**.

1. Trailhead
2. Overlook
3. Mill Pond Trail junction
4. Evergreen Trail junction
5. Oak crown
6. Beaver dam
7. Sugar shack
8. Main trail junction east of creek
9. Sinkhole
10. Overlook
11. Visitor Center

Beaver Pond Trail 👢👢

Distance Round-Trip: 1.7 miles

Estimated Hiking Time: 45 minutes to 1 hour

Cautions: This trail takes you over exposed roots and rocks. Some areas are apt to be wet and slippery: Wear appropriate footgear. Take along insect repellent in warm months.

Trail Directions: Start at the kiosk behind the Visitor Center **[1]**. You may want to start by watching the center's audiovisual presentation on the history and nature of Mill Creek. Follow the sign to the mill on the left. As you walk along the tranquil Mill Pond, you can decide if you want to visit the reconstructed mill now or when you return here.

As you cross the bridge at the end of the Mill Pond, water rushing over the mill dam below drowns out the sound of your footsteps. On the far bank, a left turn takes you past the sawmill and saw pit where log-cutting demonstrations take place. Check at the Visitor Center for the schedule of activities. A right turn has you climbing steeply to another kiosk (.1 mi.) **[2]**. Here, enjoy an overlook of Mill Pond and the bluffs on the west side of the creek.

Pass the junction with the Mill Pond trail, then cross a series of boardwalks designed to keep your feet dry on this lush, wet section of the trail. An interpretive board explains what caused the formation of that small sinkhole you're peering into (.3 mi.) **[3]**. Take a deep breath to savor the fresh pine scent of the forest before you pass the junction with the Evergreen Trail (.4 mi.) **[4]**.

Some large boulders at .5 mi. **[5]** signal (like the slap of a beaver's tail on water) that you are entering beaver country. Just past the rocks, a bench overlooks a beaver dam. At another dam a short distance farther, marvel at the size of the trees felled by beavers (.6 mi.) **[6]**. Continuing on, with beaver ponds on your right, cross a boardwalk. After the Aspen-Wildlife Forest Trail splits off to the left, you reach an overlook of a large beaver dam and then an interpretive sign about these industrious engineers (.7 mi.) **[7]**. Have a seat on the bench overlooking the beaver pond.

At .8 mi. you reach an overlook and interpretive sign that highlights the beaver lodge **[8]**. Cross a boardwalk where many large trees are being gnawed by the local beavers, swing right, and descend to the edge of the creek where there is, yes, a beaver dam. As you reach the far end of the loop, you cross a boardwalk and a footbridge over Mill Creek (.9 mi.) **[9]**. Yet another interpretive stop here describes the abandoned beaver dam. Abandon this site and climb the steps to reach the top of the embankment on the west side of the creek.

Now heading back toward the Visitor Center, you pass several large old stumps alongside and in the trail. At 1.1 mi. you reach the junction with the Sugar Shack Forest Trail **[10]**. Pass a large boulder and descend to the next interpretive sign for the beaver and dams (1.2 mi.) **[11]**.

Climb back onto the bluff and reach a fork in the trail (1.3 mi.) **[12]**. To the right is a side spur to a bench and an overlook of the creek. Listen to the trickle of water as you view the creek with its debris of logs and surrounding trees. Next follow the trail as it undulates. You pass the junction with the Evergreen Trail, cross a boardwalk, pass the junction with the Mill Pond Trail, and arrive at the overlook of Mill Pond (1.7 mi.) **[13]**. From the deck you can see not only the mill site but also the Grand Hotel on Mackinac Island across the straits.

Turn left and descend down to the Visitor Center. From here you can leave, hit the refreshment stand, or go visit the historic sites if you missed them earlier.

1. Trailhead
2. Kiosk and overlook
3. Sinkhole
4. Evergreen Trail junction
5. Large boulders
6. Beaver dam overlook
7. Beaver dam interpretive sign
8. Beaver lodge interpretive sign
9. Footbridge
10. Sugar Shack Forest Trail junction
11. Beaver dam interpretive sign
12. Fork, bench, and overlook
13. Mill Pond overlook

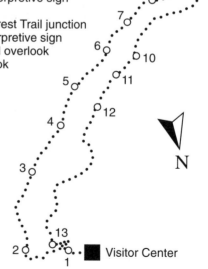

26. The Village of Mackinaw City

- Discover how 18th-century colonists lived at Colonial Michilimackinac.
- Watch freighters pass under the Mackinac Bridge.
- Ferry over to Mackinac Island.

Village Information

The old adage—location, location, location—holds true for Mackinaw City. Situated at the northernmost tip of the Lower Peninsula, at the southern end of the Mackinac Bridge, and by the Straits of Mackinac where Lake Michigan and Lake Huron meet, Mackinaw City is truly the crossroads of the Great Lakes.

A growing demand for fur led the French to build Fort Michilimackinac in 1715 at the site of present-day Mackinaw City. Trade flourished here because the site was conveniently located near three lakes, making it an easy rendezvous spot for the Indians. From fur to fudge, trade to tourism, Mackinaw City's location has been central to natural and manmade attractions, making as ideal a place for today's tourists as it was for earlier Native Americans. The village's population of about 800 swells on Labor Day as some 40,000 to 60,000 tourists rendezvous here.

Directions: Mackinaw City straddles I-75 at the northernmost tip of the Lower Peninsula.

Hours Open: The village is open all year. Check the diverse attractions for varying hours; many are seasonal.

Facilities: Hiking, bicycling, mountain bicycling, cross-country skiing, snowshoeing, snowmobiling, swimming, fishing, camping (tent and RV), picnicking, boat launch, minicabins, interpretive trails, interpretive center, and historic sites and museums.

Permits and Rules: Check with village.

Further Information: Greater Mackinaw Area Chamber of Commerce, 616-436-5574; Mackinaw Area Tourist Bureau, 800-666-0160.

Other Points of Interest

In addition to **Colonial Michilimackinac State Historic Park**, which is within the village limits, Mackinac State Historic Parks comprise three other sites in the Straits of Mackinac region: **Fort Mackinac** and **Mackinac Island State Park** (see park #1) on Mackinac Island, and **Historic Mill Creek** (see park #25), east of Mackinaw City. For more information contact Mackinac State Historic Parks, P.O. Box 873, Mackinaw City, MI 49701-0873; 616-436-5563.

For a unique way to experience the mighty **Mackinac Bridge**, join some 50,000 other participants in the Annual Labor Day Bridge Walk. For information on this event and other occasions that involve crossing the Mackinac Bridge, call the Greater Mackinaw Area Chamber of Commerce, 616-436-5574, or the Mackinaw Area Tourist Bureau, 800-666-0160.

Camping and other facilities are available in the Upper Peninsula's **Straits State Park,** which has an awesome view of the Mackinac Bridge (the bridge is lit up at night). Across I-75 from this unit is the **Father Marquette National Memorial and Museum**, administered by Straits State Park and dedicated to Jesuit priest Father Jacques Marquette. For more information call Straits State Park, St. Ignace, MI 49781; 906-643-8620.

About 11 miles west of Mackinaw City, **Wilderness State Park** (see park #27) offers 25 miles of Lake Michigan shoreline, modern campsites, and sandy beaches and about 12 miles of hiking trails. For more information contact Wilderness State Park, P.O. Box 380, Carp Lake, MI 49718; 616-436-5381.

Park Trails

The Mackinaw City Historical Pathway, highlighting landmarks and historical sites throughout the village, is being completed in three phases. The first phase or section covers about 2 miles. Additional phases will extend the pathway west along Fort Michilimackinac and east along the State Dock.

Mackinaw City Historical Pathway 🥾

Distance Round-Trip: 2.2 miles

Estimated Hiking Time: 1 to 2 hours

Cautions: Take care when crossing streets. Take plenty of cash, especially in warm months.

Trail Directions: This trail passes through the business district of Mackinaw City, along Lakes Huron and Michigan and near many tourist attractions as it leads you to information boards that depict the village's history. Start at the Visitor Center for Fort Michilimackinac, under the Mackinac Bridge **[1].**

Head east along the Lake Huron shoreline. As the waves roll onto the shore, take the time to read the history presented on the boards, or marvel at the impressive Mackinac Bridge as freighters pass by.

Visit the old Mackinaw Point Lighthouse that houses the Maritime Museum (.1 mi.) **[2].** Or, rest at the bench at .2 mi. **[3],** where you get a different perspective of the bridge. Learn about shipwrecks, among other things, from the nearby information board. Wind right to the kiosk, which adds information about voyageurs, glaciers, and the Straits Bottomland Preserve.

Turn left and stroll past residences; within .1 mi. reach the first of three boulevard parks (.4 mi.) **[4]** that line the shore. A larger park, Wawatam, awaits you at .6 mi. **[5],** where you'll find several picnic tables, interpretive boards, and a wood carving of Chief Wawatam.

Tour Mackinaw's first business district (.7 mi.) **[6].** Farther along business picks up—at Huron and Central Streets. Past the ferry dock, read the historical plaques about transportation. When you reach the road, follow the brick pathway past benches, a modern dock, and a board full of insights about railroad ferries (.9 mi.) **[7].** Learn about ice harvesting, then pass the Mackinaw City Pier. Future plans will extend the Historical Pathway around the pier. Before crossing Wendell Street (1 mi.) **[8],** another board tells a history of auto ferries.

Read about the history of the miniature golf site (1.2 mi.) **[9]** before continuing along to the old railroad depot at 1.3 mi. **[10].**

At the corner of Huron and Central, read a spelling lesson about Mackinaw, Mackinac, and Michilimackinac before crossing Central (1.4 mi.) **[11].** This boulevard is lined with interpretive boards. As you weave along this tourist mecca, learn its history. Pass the first board when you cross Central. Then head west. While weaving back and forth across what is now your main trail, Central, you might as well take in the tourist and fudge shops, restaurants, and ice-cream parlors.

Cross Nicolet to Indian Pathways Park for another history lesson. Head north, and where I-75 starts asceding into Makinac Bridge, cross Huron and walk under the bridge (2.1 mi.) **[13].** You can feel the thunder from the vehicles above. Stroll the few feet along Lake Michigan's shore before taking the few steps back to the Visitor Center (2.2 mi.) **[1].** Now is as good a time as any to visit the fort.

1. Trailhead
2. Mackinac Maritime Museum
3. Bench
4. Boulevard park
5. Wawatam Park
6. First business district
7. Railroad ferry plaque
8. Wendell Street
9. Miniature golf
10. Railroad depot
11. Cross Central
12. Indian Pathways Park
13. Bridge

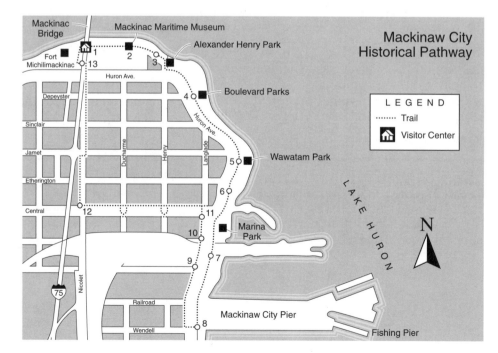

27. Wilderness State Park

- Hike through stands of virgin hemlock trees.
- Enjoy scenic views of Lake Michigan, the Straits of Mackinac, and the Mackinac Bridge.
- Swim or walk along a sandy Lake Michigan beach.

Park Information

Combine sandy beaches and rocky shores with rugged backcountry; add views of Lake Michigan and you get a general picture of Wilderness State Park. Throw in camping facilities, a boat launch, and a habitat suitable for bobcats, beavers, and bears, and you've got plenty of reasons to visit this 8,000-acre park.

Directions: Wilderness State Park is about 11 miles west of Mackinaw City. Follow County Road 81 and continue west along Wilderness Park Drive.

Hours Open: The park is open daily from 8:00 A.M. to 10:00 P.M.

Facilities: Hiking, mountain bicycling, cross-country skiing, snowmobiling, swimming, fishing, hunting, camping (tent and RV), picnicking, boat launch, and interpretive trails.

Permits and Rules: A park fee ($4 daily, $20 annually) is assessed per motor vehicle. No hunting is allowed within the marked safety zone. Snowmobiles and bikes are allowed only on certain trails (the contact station can tell you which trails these are).

Further Information: Wilderness State Park, P.O. Box 380, Carp Lake, MI 49718; 616-436-5381.

Other Points of Interest

East of the park are the four Mackinac State Historic Parks: **Fort Mackinac** and **Mackinac Island State Park** (see park #1), **Mill Creek State Historic Park** (see park #25), and **Colonial Michilimackinac State Historic Park**. For more information contact the Mackinac State Historic Parks, P.O. Box 873, Mackinaw City, MI 49701-0873; 616-436-5563.

From the glimmering beauty of the Straits of Mackinac to the history of Fort Michilimackinac and, yes, even to the fudge, **Mackinaw City** has much to offer (see park #26). The Greater Mackinaw Area Chamber of Commerce (616-436-5574) and the Mackinaw Area Tourist Bureau (800-666-0160) can supply more information.

The **Mackinaw/Alanson Trail** is a 24-mile rail-trail that starts in Mackinaw City. For information contact the Mackinaw State Forest, P.O. Box 667, Gaylord, MI 49735; 517-732-3541.

Park Trails

Big Stone Trail —.75 mile—Starting across from the picnic area, this trail leads almost to the southeast point of the Pines Campground. It links up with the Red Pine Trail and the Pondside Trail.

East Boundary Trail —1.8 miles—Start on the south side of Park Drive Road and head south to access the North Country Trail and the South Boundary Trail, which plunges through a wet area.

East Ridge Trail —1.4 miles—Beginning near the East Boundary Trail off Park Drive Road, the trail links with the east portion of the North Country Trail and with the Nebo Trail.

Hemlock Trail —.6 mile—You can reach this trail, which loops Mt. Nebo, either by continuing east along the Red Pine Trail or from the Nebo Trail.

Nebo Trail —2 miles—This trail heads south from the access road and descends through woods to the South Boundary Trail.

Pondside Trail —.5 mile—Starting across from the Pines Campground to the southeast, the Pondside Trail loops around Goose Pond.

Red Pine Trail —1.3 miles—Start from the Pondside Trail, south of the dam. It links with the Nebo and Hemlock Trails.

South Boundary Trail —1.5 miles—Start from the Sturgeon Bay, Swamp Line, Nebo, and East Boundary Trails.

Sturgeon Bay Trail —2.25 miles—Start south of Park Drive Road, east of the Station Point Cabin. It crosses the Big and Little Sucker Creeks and provides access to the west portion of the North Country Trail, Swamp Line, and South Boundary Trails.

Swamp Line Trail —2 miles—This trail follows south from the access road to the Pines Campground. It passes through cedar and aspen, and overlooks beaver ponds.

North Country National Scenic Trail —5.5 miles—This trail incorporates sections of the others on its planned 872-mile trek through Michigan.

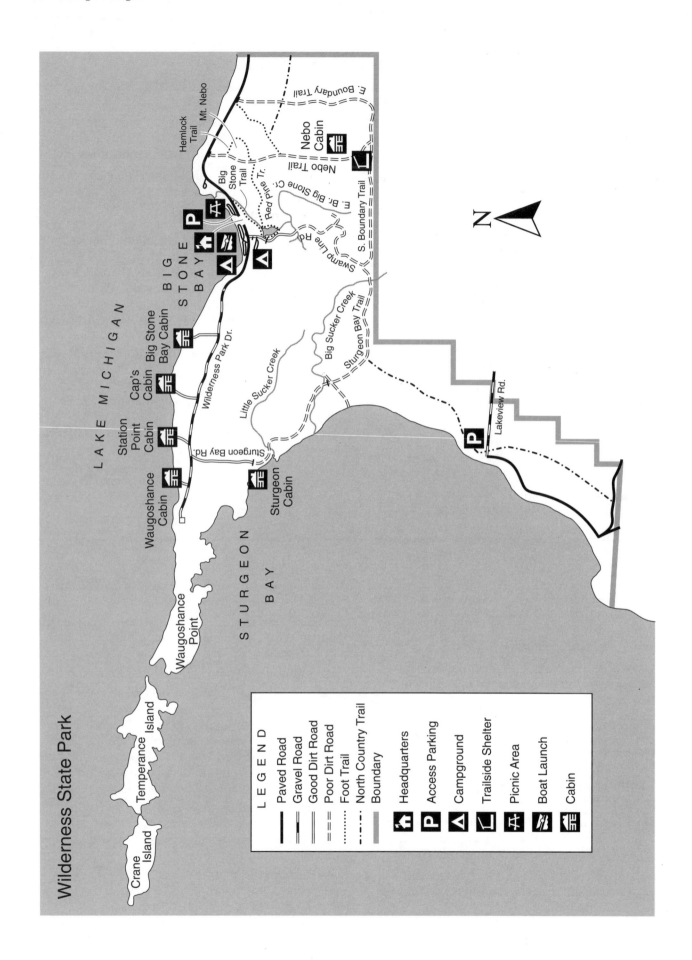

Wilderness State Park

N

LAKE MICHIGAN

BIG STONE BAY

STURGEON BAY

Temperance Island

Crane Island

Waugoshance Point

Waugoshance Cabin

Station Point Cabin

Cap's Cabin

Big Stone Bay Cabin

Sturgeon Cabin

Sturgeon Bay Rd.

Wilderness Park Dr.

Little Sucker Creek

Big Sucker Creek

Sturgeon Bay Trail

Big Sucker Creek

Swamp Line Rd.

S. Boundary Trail

E. Br. Big Stone Cr.

Red Pine Tr.

Big Stone Trail

Hemlock Trail

Mt. Nebo

Nebo Cabin

Nebo Trail

E. Boundary Trail

Lakeview Rd.

LEGEND
Paved Road
Gravel Road
Good Dirt Road
Poor Dirt Road
Foot Trail
North Country Trail
Boundary

Headquarters
Access Parking
Campground
Trailside Shelter
Picnic Area
Boat Launch
Cabin

East Ridge/Nebo/S. Boundary/ E. Boundary Trails Loop

Distance Round-Trip: 4.6 miles

Estimated Hiking Time: 2.5 to 3 hours

Cautions: This trail has exposed roots, and it cuts through wet areas. About .25 mi. on the East Boundary Trail will be wet or may even be flooded. Wading through water may not be for everyone. To avoid this stretch, consider hiking up to East Boundary Trail and then turning back. This round-trip makes a 5.6-mile hike, and it is only of average difficulty. Wear proper footgear and take along insect repellent during warm months.

Trail Directions: Park on the south side of Wilderness Park Drive to access the East Ridge and East Boundary Trails. The hike starts along the East Ridge Trail, heads southwest into the designated wilderness area **[1]**, and rolls through a forest carpeted with pine needles. The dark forest, hills, and low, lush areas along the East Ridge make this area feel like wilderness.

Leave pine perfume behind and blaze along a trail overgrown with vegetation (.2 mi.) **[2]**. A tree stump presages the logs that soon litter the trail. Eventually you reenter the cover of trees, and later you pass moss-covered logs while crossing a boardwalk (.3 mi.) **[3]**. The trail narrows and the forest darkens. Maples mingle with varied floor foliage. Velvety moss-covered logs (.4 mi.) **[4]** and lush foliage draping the trail give the area an eerie feeling.

A wetland (.5 mi.) **[5]** accompanies you on the left as you hike along a ridge, announcing the junction for the North Country Trail, which you reach at .6 mi. **[6]**. Your trail veers right and has you climbing.

Break out of the hills and to an open area to your right, and again climb. You encounter much the same terrain through ferns, mud, darkness, and wet areas. Wind your way up the trail, most likely not meeting a soul, and reach the Nebo Trail at 1.4 mi. **[7]**. Head left along this tree-lined two-track. Basically a level trail here, it cuts through wetlands and hills. At 2 mi. a silvery-green hill of lichen on your left precedes the Nebo Cabin **[8]**.

The trail winds before breaking into sunlight, only to reenter the shade of the forest. When you see a barrier to keep snowmobiles off the trail, you are near the trailside shelter (2.4 mi.) **[9]**. Soon the trail winds down to the South Boundary Trail junction (2.5 mi.) **[10]**.

Turn left and soon walk along a narrow meadow filled with wildflowers. This lovely little stretch of trail apparently gets little use. Darkness looms in the shadows of the forest that envelops the bright meadow corridor of wildflowers.

At 2.8 mi. the trail curves left and into the shadows of the East Boundary Trail **[11]**. This is a great place to turn back. You will get wet if you proceed. The grassy trail cuts through hardwoods that grow dense. Where the foliage is noticeably lush at 3.2 mi. **[12]**, you are nearing the wet area. It happens gradually as you pass through grassy areas until the water, depending on the season and weather, becomes almost unbearable at about 3.4 mi. **[13]**. For the next .2 mi., if you are lucky, you will trudge through mud. (If you are less lucky, roll up your pants because you are in for some wading.) Most of the flooding is passed by 3.6 mi. **[14]**. You still hike through reeds and grass, but they are manageable.

Pass four- to five-feet tall ostrich ferns just before you reach the North Country Trail junction (4 mi.) **[15]**. The trail widens. For a stretch, grasses and wildflowers grow in it. Pass through more pines before the trail takes you through the gate (4.6 mi.) **[16]** and back to your vehicle.

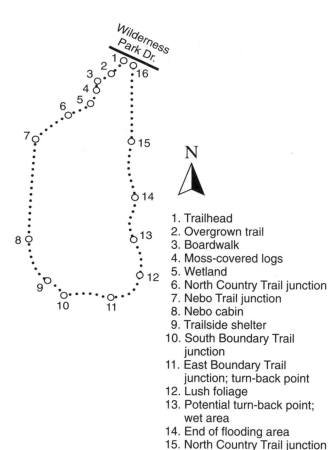

N

1. Trailhead
2. Overgrown trail
3. Boardwalk
4. Moss-covered logs
5. Wetland
6. North Country Trail junction
7. Nebo Trail junction
8. Nebo cabin
9. Trailside shelter
10. South Boundary Trail junction
11. East Boundary Trail junction; turn-back point
12. Lush foliage
13. Potential turn-back point; wet area
14. End of flooding area
15. North Country Trail junction
16. Gate

Big Stone/Pondside/Red Pine/ Hemlock Trails Loop

👢👢

Distance Round-Trip: 4.2 miles

Estimated Hiking Time: 2 to 2.5 hours

Cautions: This hike takes you through areas that are often wet or flooded, and it takes you over exposed roots. Wear appropriate footgear. Take along insect repellent in the warm months. Keep an eye on traffic for the mile you hike along Wilderness Park Drive.

Trail Directions: Parking for this hike is at the picnic area, northeast of the Lakeshore Campground and on the north side of Wilderness Park Drive. The trailhead is across the road, where a sign and map board are posted **[1]**.

Step past the trail sign into the woods and onto a cushion of pine needles. Turn right and walk parallel to the little stream called Big Stone Creek. Numerous trees have fallen into and around the creek, to the delight of the ferns now thriving in the sunlight. Shortly after a sign for the Big Stone Trail, you reach a point where the trail splits, providing a short alternate route for when the main trail is wet or flooded (.2 mi.) **[2]**. The main trail follows along the edge of the creek and has you stepping through mud, over roots and fallen trees, and past wildflowers.

After the alternate route rejoins the trail, note the white cedar on your left that fell years ago and whose individual branches have grown from the trunk to become trees (.3 mi.) **[3]**. Cross a clearing, go under a power line, pass a standing tree graveyard, and swing left back to the creek. You soon reach the dam at Goose Pond (.6 mi.) **[4]**. Turn right and circle the lily-covered pond on the .5-mi. Pondside Trail (or bypass the loop by turning left and heading east on the Red Pine Trail).

Turning right along the wood-chipped Pondside Trail, you pass interpretive posts that help identify some of the trees. Follow the trail as it turns south away from the Pines Campground; you pass between the pond and a parking area with a large map board of the park's trails (.7 mi.) **[5]**. The North Country National Scenic Trail merges into the trail where you swing left to cross a series of three footbridges at the south end of the pond. At the first two bridges beavers have built dams to complement the manmade dam on the north side of the pond (1 mi.) **[6]**.

When you arrive back at the manmade dam, turn right and start down the interpretive Red Pine Trail

(1.1 mi.) **[7]**. The trail crosses a low-lying wet area, and you soon walk through mud and over boardwalks and cut logs for nearly .5 mi. You then climb onto a ridge, passing the remains of several old, large trees (1.6 mi.) **[8]**.

The hike has been mostly level until now, when the trail undulates and you snake along the back of the ridge. You finally reach the red pine plantation, which gives the trail its name (2.1 mi.) **[9]**. Descend to skirt a small, bowl-shaped pond (2.2 mi.) **[10]**, and pass through a white cedar swamp to reach a trail junction (2.3 mi.) **[11]**. The North Country Trail splits off to the right, while your trail, the Red Pine, climbs to the left.

At 2.4 mi. you cross the Nebo Trail and continue your hike on the Hemlock Trail **[12]**. Climb gradually to reach the top of Mount Nebo (2.6 mi.) **[13]**, where the foundation of an old lookout tower remains. The trail then descends steeply, and you enter a forest with large hemlock trees (some of them 200 years old) that survived the lumber era (2.7 mi.) **[14]**.

When you reach the Nebo Trail again at 3 mi., turn right **[15]**, arriving at the Nebo Trail parking area on Wilderness Park Drive (3.3 mi.) **[16]**. Turn left here and follow the road, passing the big stone, a glacial erratic (3.4 mi.) **[17]**, on the hike back to the picnic area parking lot.

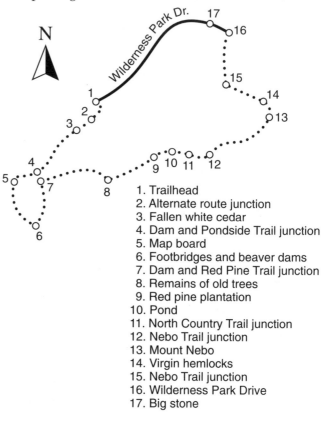

1. Trailhead
2. Alternate route junction
3. Fallen white cedar
4. Dam and Pondside Trail junction
5. Map board
6. Footbridges and beaver dams
7. Dam and Red Pine Trail junction
8. Remains of old trees
9. Red pine plantation
10. Pond
11. North Country Trail junction
12. Nebo Trail junction
13. Mount Nebo
14. Virgin hemlocks
15. Nebo Trail junction
16. Wilderness Park Drive
17. Big stone

28. Jordan River Pathway

- View the spectacular Jordan River Valley from the Deadman's Hill Overlook.
- Hike the pathway to appreciate why the Jordan River is a dedicated wild and scenic river.
- Camp at a hike-in only campground.

Park Information

Michigan's first waterway to be classified a wild and scenic river, the Jordan River unveils its natural beauty to viewers from the overlook at Deadman's Hill. To gain more than a glimpse of the scenic river valley, you can hike all or part of the 18-mile Jordan River Pathway, which winds through a portion of the Mackinaw State Forest, providing hikers an opportunity to become more intimate with the river and valley. The path traverses hills and spring-fed streams, low-lying wet areas, old logging railroad grades, and northern hardwoods and mixed pines. The North Country National Scenic Trail uses the northern portion of this trail for its route through the Jordan River Valley.

The pathway begins and ends at the parking area for Deadman's Hill. Backpacking the entire 18-mile trail takes two days, with an overnight at the Pinney Bridge Hike-In Campground. This rustic campground, which served as a logging camp in 1915, is located halfway along the hike and has a vault toilet and water pump. For shorter hikes, try the Deadman's Hill Loop or the half-mile round-trip hike to Deadman's Hill Overlook. You can customize your hike by using local county roads.

Directions: On US-131, go north 11.5 miles from Mancelona or south about 1.5 miles from M-32. Turn west on Deadman's Hill Road and drive about 2 miles to the parking area.

Hours Open: Open year-round.

Facilities: Hiking, snowshoeing, fishing, hunting, camping (backcountry), picnicking, and interpretive trail.

Permits and Rules: All hikers are asked to register. All campers are required to register and pay the fee. The maximum length of stay in any calendar week is two days. No campsite may be occupied by more than eight persons. Fires are prohibited except in designated fire circles in the campground. Do not bury garbage or refuse. No camping is allowed outside the designated campground.

Further Information: Mackinaw State Forest, 1732 West M-32, P.O. Box 667, Gaylord, MI 49735; 517-732-3541.

Other Points of Interest

Just north of the Jordan River Pathway sits the 3.8-mile **Warner Creek Pathway**. The North Country National Scenic Trail, which uses portions of both of these pathways, connects them with a 1-mile section of trail. For more information contact the Mackinaw State Forest.

Northwest of the Pinney Bridge Hike-In Campground is the **Graves Crossing State Forest Campground**. The campground is accessible from M-66 or from the Jordan River. Contact the Mackinaw State Forest for more information.

The **Grass River Natural Area** (see park #29) contains six interpretive trails bedecked with boardwalks, observation platforms, and footbridges with built-in benches, all designed to help visitors observe wetland flora and fauna. For more information contact Grass River Natural Area, Inc., P.O. Box 231, Bellaire, MI 49615; 616-533-8314.

Park Trails

Deadman's Hill Overlook 👢 —.5 mile round-trip— This trail takes you from the parking area to the Deadman's Hill Overlook for scenic views of the Jordan River Valley.

Deadman's Hill Loop 👢👢👢

Distance Round-Trip: 3.3 miles

Estimated Hiking Time: 1.5 to 2 hours

Cautions: This hike takes you over roots and rocks and through areas that are often wet or flooded. Wear proper footgear. Take insect repellent in the warm months. At one time this interpretive trail had 25 numbered posts that corresponded with an interpretive brochure. Many of the posts have fallen into disrepair; the staff of the Department of Natural Resources replaces these when they can.

Trail Directions: Start the hike by the foot trail arrow at the northwest end of the parking area at the end of Deadman's Hill Road **[1]**. Enter the cover of beech and maple trees and pass the vault toilets before you come to the junction of the Deadman's Hill Overlook and the Jordan River Pathway (.1 mi.) **[2]**. Turn left to walk the short distance to the edge of Deadman's Hill for panoramic vistas of the Jordan River Valley (.2 mi.) **[3]**. Here, an interpretive board gives the sad tale of the unfortunate lumberjack Big Sam and the event that cost him his life and gave this site its name.

Return to the junction (.3 mi.) **[2]** and start a long, steep descent, passing several tree identification markers before you reach the valley floor (.8 mi.) **[4]**. From a small clearing at the bottom, the North Country National Scenic Trail splits off to the right toward the Warner Creek Pathway. Turn left, however, and walk over sand and roots to reenter the woods. Climb along the edge of the hill before descending to an observation platform overlooking a small stream flowing down to the Jordan River (1.1 mi.) **[5]**.

1. Trailhead
2. Trail junction
3. Deadman's Hill overlook
4. Valley floor and trail junction
5. Observation platform
6. Trail junction
7. Trail junction, top of climb
8. Saw-eating maple

Step over a fallen tree; watch your step as you follow the sloppy trail, which undulates between the base of Deadman's Hill and the valley floor. Here, the trail takes you over gnarly roots, through mud, across trail logs, and teetering along the edge of eroded slopes. A swing right into ferns and aspen is your cue to look for the trail junction (where post #5 may or may not still be located) at 1.6 mi. **[6]**. At this junction you turn off the main trail. If you are feeling adventurous, hike up the main trail about .3 mi. to view an old beaver dam and pond where the trail follows the route of an old logging railroad grade.

Back at the junction, start your climb through ferns and an open area dominated by the silver and green patchwork of lichens. As you climb back up Deadman's Hill, notice that the trail is not as worn as the section of trail that you descended. Also, in addition to many small maple trees, you pass increasingly larger beech and maple trees the steeper the climb gets. When you pass a large boulder on the left, you have almost completed your climb. At the top, turn left at the trail junction, where a sign points you back to the starting point (2.2 mi.) **[7]**.

The remainder of the hike is fairly level; you snake through a forest of primarily beech and maple. Just before you return to your vehicle (and by post #24 if it is still in place), you should see a maple with a broken crosscut saw left in the crotch of the tree. As the tree grew, it slowly enveloped the saw (3.1 mi.) **[8]**.

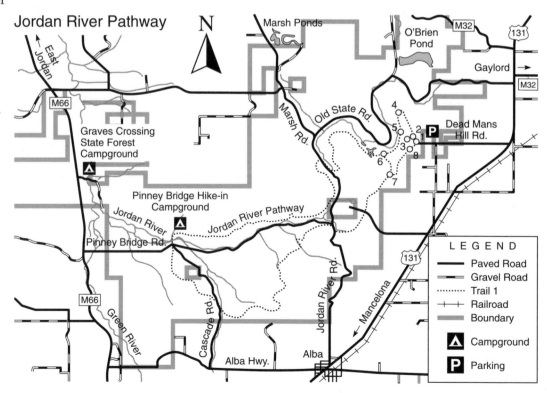

Jordan River Pathway

LEGEND
— Paved Road
—|—|— Gravel Road
.... Trail 1
+—+—+ Railroad
▬▬▬ Boundary
▲ Campground
🅿 Parking

29. Grass River Natural Area

- Hike an extensive system of boardwalks to observe wetland flora and fauna.
- View wildlife from wooden observation platforms.
- Sit atop Finch Creek on benches built into wooden decks that double as bridges.

Park Information

The more than 1,000 acres within this natural area produce diverse habitats: creeks, rivers, and wetlands; upland and marsh forests; and sedge meadows. These habitats are home to an even more diverse collection of plants, birds, reptiles, and mammals. Deer, beaver, loons, and eagles all are seen here frequently.

The Grass River Natural Area is a huge wetland drained by the Grass River and its tributaries. Two-and-one-half miles of the river connect Lake Bellaire and Clam Lake. Six interpretive trails, bedecked with boardwalks, observation platforms, and footbridges with built-in benches, flaunt the scenery and wildlife within the 225 acres that include the Education Site within the natural area. Visit the Grass River Natural Area Interpretive Center, which has displays, area information, and trail guides.

Directions: The Grass River Natural Area is about 8 miles west of Mancelona. At the intersection of US-131 and M-88 in Mancelona, go west on M-88 about 2.5 miles until the road bends north. Stay west on Alden Highway for another 5.5 miles to the access road, which is about .5 mile west of Comfort Road. Head north less than a mile to the parking lot.

Hours Open: The natural area is open daily from dawn until dusk. The Interpretive Center is open daily from 10:00 A.M. until 4:00 P.M., June through August. In May, September, and October, it is open on weekends from 10:00 A.M. until 4:00 P.M.

Facilities: Hiking, cross-country skiing, snowshoeing, fishing, hunting, canoeing, bridle path, interpretive trails, and interpretive center.

Permits and Rules: There is no fee, but donations are accepted. Hunting and horses are not allowed within the Educational Area. Please stay on trails and do not disturb plants. Do not litter, and leave pets at home. Open fires and alcoholic beverages are prohibited.

Further Information: Grass River Natural Area, Inc., P.O. Box 231, Bellaire, MI 49615; 616-533-8314. The phone number on-site is 616-533-8576.

Other Points of Interest

Antrim County has two chains of lakes—an upper and a lower chain. In addition to **Lake Bellaire** and **Clam Lake**, the Lower Chain of Lakes includes **Torch Lake**, **Lake Skegemog**, and **Elk Lake**. For information on canoe rentals or other interests in the area, call the Bellaire Chamber of Commerce at 616-533-6023.

South of Torch Lake and about 9 miles west of Kalkaska is the **Skegemog Lake Wildlife Area.** Here, the Skegemog Lake Pathway, via a rail-trail and an elaborate system of boardwalks, passes through a cedar swamp to an observation tower. For more information, contact the Kalkaska Forest Area, 2089 North Birch, Kalkaska, MI 49646; 616-258-2711.

Park Trails

Cabin Trail —.1 mile—This trail takes you from the parking lot to the cabin used as the Interpretive Center. It passes through an upland forest and an abandoned field and leads to the Sedge Meadow, Tamarack, and Fern Trails, which start at the cabin.

Sedge Meadow Trail —.7 mile—Start behind the cabin or pick it up off the Tamarack Trail. It loops through wetlands and has a spur that leads you to the dock on Grass River.

Tamarack Trail —.3 mile—This barrier-free trail starts at the cabin and loops through wetlands. You also may use this trail to reach the Sedge Meadow and Fern Trails.

Fern Trail —.5 mile—Begin off the Tamarack Trail and wind along Finch Creek, then cross it, and head back. You can also continue along the Woodland/Wildfire Trail.

Glacial Plain Trail —2 miles—Starting at the intersection of the Grass River Natural Area Road and the Grass River Natural Area Nature Trail, this trail follows the rail-trail less than a mile, turns south, crosses a boardwalk, and ends at an open field. Here you can explore the terraced hills, remains from the wave action of higher waters.

Grass River Natural Area Nature Trail —4 miles—This rail-trail curves along the south end of the natural area. It may be accessed from the south parking area, where the Glacial Plain Trail begins.

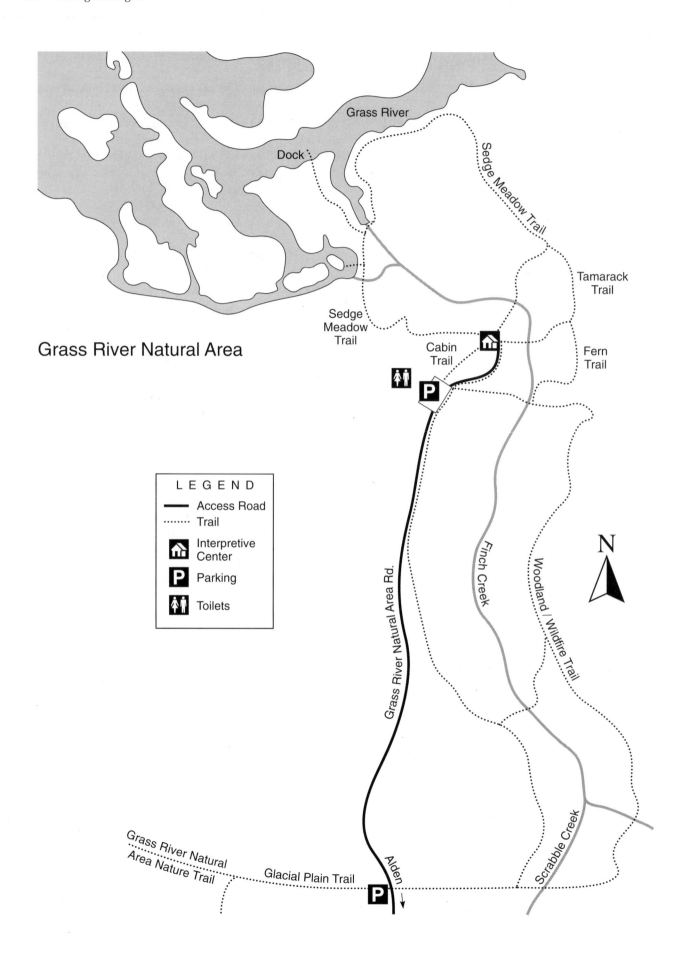

Grass River Natural Area

Grass River

Dock

Sedge Meadow Trail

Tamarack Trail

Sedge Meadow Trail

Fern Trail

Cabin Trail

LEGEND
—— Access Road
.... Trail
Interpretive Center
P Parking
Toilets

Finch Creek

Woodland / Wildfire Trail

N

Grass River Natural Area Rd.

Scrabble Creek

Grass River Natural Area Nature Trail

Glacial Plain Trail

Alden

Woodland/Wildfire Trail 🥾

Distance Round-Trip: 1.3 miles

Estimated Hiking Time: 30 minutes to 1 hour

Cautions: Some stumps and roots protrude from the trail and need a watchful eye. Watch also for low branches or fallen trees. Although wood chips carry some of your footsteps, not all the trail is cushioned this way. Some of the boards on the boardwalks give a bit, like a suspension bridge. Keep your balance. Take insect repellent in warm months.

Trail Directions: Park in the north lot, which serves most of the trails as well as the Interpretive Center. Start the hike across Grass River Natural Area Road, northeast of the parking lot **[1]**. Head east through the tall ferns (this portion of the path is shared with the Fern Trail). Your soft steps on wood chips soon turn to hard steps on wood boards, and you cross a boardwalk that evolves into an ornate footbridge over Finch Creek. Have a seat on one of the benches of this observation deck over the creek. Small islands of grass within the creek have trees growing from them.

Soon, you reach the junction where the two trails part (.1 mi.) **[2]**. Continue straight and pass moss mounds with trees sprouting from them. Walk through a stretch with scented trees tightly embracing the trail. At the end of the boardwalk veer left. Soon you see moss draping over roots and fallen logs. Cross first one short boardwalk, then another overlooking grass plumes that give a feathery softness against the darker draping moss and logs (.2 mi.) **[3]**.

The trail veers right, and you may notice more aspen, hemlock, and maple saplings. On another short boardwalk, view the vernal pond (.3 mi.) **[4]**. Pass by uprooted trees, dodging any stumps as the trail winds through the upland forest. At .4 mi. you reach what the interpretive guide calls a nursery stump **[5]**: From this white pine stump a new white pine grows.

You'll pass another nursery stump—a maple—and come to a small ridge. Forested hills envelop the trail. At .5 mi. you reach the shortcut junction **[6]**. Continue straight, winding your way through aspen, hemlock, and then white pine. At about .6 mi. reenter a wetland environment, taking the steps down to the boardwalk that keeps your feet dry as you walk by

lush grasses, moss, and ferns **[7]**. This boardwalk curves and leads to another elaborate footbridge with an observation deck. An old, wooden railroad trestle bridges over Finch Creek to your left. Plumes of grass islands sprouting trees also decorate this stretch of the creek.

The boardwalk soon ends, and the natural trail winds around, leading you to steps that take you up to the railroad grade. Once on the grade (.7 mi.) **[8]**, follow to the right along the raised ridge; around you maples give way to aspens and then white pines. Listen—you can hear the creek as you walk over it. At .8 mi. turn right at the sign and leave the abandoned rail corridor **[9]**.

Blaze down through a wall of ferns and back under maple cover. Cedars grow near the creek to your right. Pass the shortcut junction at .9 mi. **[10]** as the trail veers left and begins more undulations. It passes through low ferns and something a small sign identifies as "wood fungus."

The trail winds around a hemlock, then a maple, then passes through the spindly, leggy-like growth of youthful maples before it reaches the access road (1.2 mi.) **[11]**. Turn right and follow the road through its canopy of hardwoods until you reach the parking area. Visit the Interpretive Center or head out on one of the other trails for a view of the Grass River.

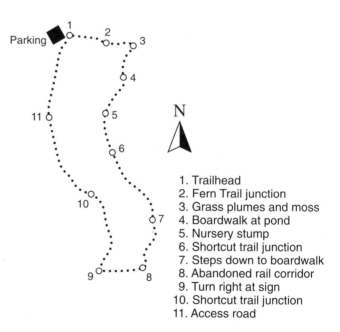

1. Trailhead
2. Fern Trail junction
3. Grass plumes and moss
4. Boardwalk at pond
5. Nursery stump
6. Shortcut trail junction
7. Steps down to boardwalk
8. Abandoned rail corridor
9. Turn right at sign
10. Shortcut trail junction
11. Access road

Cabin/Sedge Meadow/ Tamarack/Fern Trails Loop 🥾

Distance Round-Trip: 1.3 miles

Estimated Hiking Time: 30 minutes to 1 hour

Cautions: Some boards on this extensive system of boardwalks sag severely, and others give a bit when you walk on them. Watch your step. Also, watch your head under the low branches and trees leaning over the trail. Take insect repellent in warm months. Poison sumac and poison ivy are identified along the trail. Observe the signs and don't touch them.

Trail Directions: The Cabin Trail starts at the north end of the parking lot and heads toward the Interpretive Center **[1]**. Follow the wood-chip path past several interpretive markers as you traverse an abandoned field and pass fragrant pines to arrive at the center (.1 mi.) **[2]**, where you can view the displays and talk to the naturalist.

The Sedge Meadow Trail starts west of the center and heads into the woods. As you hike you see the habitat change from upland forest to swamp, and you soon step onto a boardwalk where white cedar dominates (.2 mi.) **[3]**. At Finch Creek, the boardwalk evolves into an ornate footbridge (.3 mi.) **[4]**. Sit on a bench placed on what has become an observation deck over the creek. If you're patient, you may see brook, brown, and rainbow trout.

Past the bridge, a spur boardwalk splits off to the left, taking you to an observation platform **[5]**. From it you overlook the open waters of Finch Creek, Grass River, and Clam Lake plus portions of the sedge meadow and the scrubby swamp forest. With such a diversity of habitats, this is a prime site from which to view wildlife or just sit back and enjoy the area's beauty.

Back on the main boardwalk, you reach another spur in less than .1 mi. that leads you across the sedge meadow to another observation platform **[6]** and a dock along the Grass River (.5 mi.) **[7]**. See how the Grass River got its name as you walk among the grass-like plants—reeds, rushes, and sedges—that aren't really grasses at all. Return to the main boardwalk, turn left, and cross a footbridge over a small branch of Finch Creek (.6 mi.) **[8]**. Look for marker post #10 where a white cedar blew over; each of its upraised branches is becoming a separate tree.

You pop out onto another section of sedge meadow before reentering the scrubby swamp forest to arrive at another observation platform (.7 mi.) **[9]**. This one is situated along the Grass River and provides an opportunity to view marsh hawk, osprey, and bald eagle as they feed. Poison sumac grows at this location, too, so be careful what you brush up against.

Continuing along the boardwalk through the swamp, you reach a covered bench (.9 mi.) **[10]**. This is also the junction with the Tamarack Trail. Turn left and follow the boardwalk for a short distance before you veer left to pick up the Fern Trail (1 mi.) **[11]**.

Passing moss mounds with trees sprouting from them, you turn right and then left when you reach the bench along Finch Creek (1.1 mi.) **[12]**. Turn right at the trail junction to cross Finch Creek. Once again the boardwalk evolves into an ornate footbridge with enticing benches (1.2 mi.) **[13]**. Leaving the bridge behind, you soon step off the boardwalk for the first time in just over 1 mi. Wood chips lead you to the road, which returns you to the parking lot.

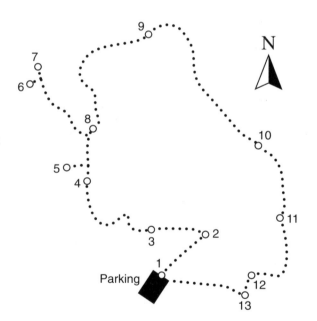

1. Trailhead
2. Interpretive Center
3. Start boardwalk
4. Ornate footbridge
5. Observation platform
6. Observation platform
7. Dock
8. Footbridge
9. Observation platform
10. Covered bench and Tamarack Trail junction
11. Fern Trail junction
12. Bench
13. Ornate footbridge

30. Leelanau State Park

- Climb to enjoy a scenic overlook of Lake Michigan.
- Tour the Grand Traverse Lighthouse and Museum.
- Stroll the Lake Michigan beach hunting Petoskey stones.

Park Information

If a quiet, sandy, Lake Michigan shoreline; secluded walks over wooded terrain; and inland lakes with views of migrating waterfowl pique your interest, this is the place to visit. Its two separate sections include the popular day-use, camping, and lighthouse-museum area and the undeveloped southern tract, woven with lightly used trails through woods and over dunes, marshes, and interdunal wetlands.

Leelanau State Park was established in 1932 when the U.S. Government gave 30 acres of this land to the State. Thereafter, more land was acquired until the park reached its current 1,300-plus acres. The northern section is located at the tip of the "little finger" of Michigan's Lower Peninsula, at the cusp where Lake Michigan meets Grand Traverse Bay. Here, Lake Michigan yields a rocky shoreline for hikers who can take advantage of one of the rustic campsites, enjoy the picnic areas, or enlighten themselves at the Grand Traverse Lighthouse, an interpretive maritime museum. Many people enjoy sifting through the rocks along the shoreline for Michigan's state stone, the Petoskey stone.

Four miles south of the developed section is the larger, southern section of the park, where about 1.5 miles of sandy Lake Michigan shoreline await you. More than 6 miles of trails loop through this tranquil part of the park. If you're up to it, climb the stairway to the top of a dune and an observation deck overlooking Lake Michigan. Or head inland to Mud Lake and view waterfowl during their spring and fall migrations.

Directions: The southern section of Leelanau State Park is located about 3 miles north of Northport. Take County Road 629 north from Northport 3 miles to Densmore Road (Airport Road), then head left to the parking lot. The northern section is another 5 miles north on County Road 629.

Hours Open: The park is open daily from 8:00 A.M. to 10:00 P.M. The Grand Traverse Lighthouse is open from 11:00 A.M. to 7:00 P.M. daily from Memorial Day weekend through Labor Day. After Labor Day it is open on the weekends from noon to 5:00 P.M.

Facilities: Hiking, cross-country skiing, swimming, fishing, hunting, camping (tent and RV), picnicking, and interpretive and historic centers.

Permits and Rules: A park fee ($4 daily, $20 annually) is required for each motor vehicle.

Further Information: Leelanau State Park, Route 1, P.O. Box 49, Northport, MI 49670; 616-386-5422 (summer) or 616-922-5270 (year-round). The park is administered by the Traverse City State Park, 616-922-5270.

Other Points of Interest

Bay Front Park in Northport sits on Grand Traverse Bay and has a small beach and playground. For information on Northport attractions call the Chamber of Commerce at 616-386-5806.

Hike along the Boardman River and stop for a picnic in the **Grand Traverse Natural Education Preserve**. This 370-acre preserve is 2 miles south of Traverse City, east of Cass Road. For more information contact the Grand Traverse Natural Education Preserve, 1125 W. Civic Center Dr., Traverse City, MI 49684.

Two area trails incorporate active or abandoned rail lines. The **Traverse Area Recreation Trail** (TART) is an asphalt-paved route within view of the Grand Traverse Bay. Contact Grand Traverse County Road Commission, 3949 Silver Lake Road, Traverse City, MI 49684; 616-922-4848. Under development, the 15-mile **Leelanau Trail** will stretch from just outside Traverse City to Suttons Bay. For more information contact the Leelanau Trails Association, P.O. Box 580, Suttons Bay, MI 49682; 616-271-4510.

Park Trails

The park's one loop has cutoff spurs that allow you to divide the large loop into four smaller loops. Two additional spurs lead to the beach on Lake Michigan and to an overlook. A small loop (.4 mile) wraps off the large loop on the east side. More than 5 miles of trails weave through the southern unit of the park. Two trails—Lake Michigan and Mud Lake Trail—are shown on the park's map boards, but the Maple Ridge Cutoff, Tamarack Cutoff, and the Pot-Hole Ridge Loop make for varying trail sizes from .8 mile to 3.2 miles.

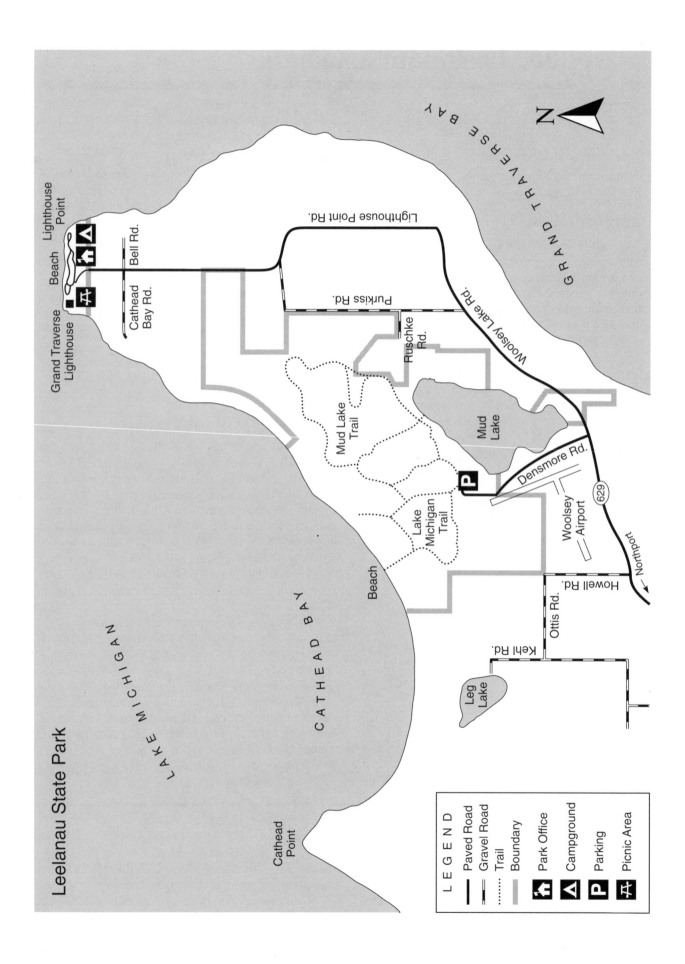

Leelanau State Park

LAKE MICHIGAN

Cathead Point

CATHEAD BAY

Beach

Grand Traverse Lighthouse

Lighthouse Point

Beach

Bell Rd.

Cathead Bay Rd.

Lighthouse Point Rd.

Purkiss Rd.

Ruschke Rd.

Woolsey Lake Rd.

GRAND TRAVERSE BAY

N

Mud Lake Trail

Mud Lake

Lake Michigan Trail

P

Densmore Rd.

Woolsey Airport

629

Northport

Howell Rd.

Ottis Rd.

Kehl Rd.

Leg Lake

L E G E N D

Paved Road
Gravel Road
Trail
Boundary
Park Office
Campground
Parking
Picnic Area

Lake Michigan Trail 👢👢

Distance Round-Trip: 2.4 miles

Estimated Hiking Time: 1 to 1.5 hours

Cautions: Watch for occasional exposed roots on the trail. You pass through dense woods, wooded dunes, and open, rolling sand; layer your clothing for the variations. Take sunscreen and insect repellent.

Trail Directions: All the trails start from the parking area off Densmore Road, about 4 mi. southwest of the campground. A map board shows the trails in various colors. The Lake Michigan trail, light blue, starts and ends at the northwest end of the parking lot **[1]**. The orange Mud Lake Trail has an access point there as well, so the entry post you see is tipped with orange. After a few steps, you notice a blue post off to the left. Follow it into the cool, dark shadows of the mixed forest. Under this thick canopy, the trail rolls through an undulating terrain.

The canopy breaks open at .4 mi. where a bench marks your entry to the flat, open area that the trail will encircle **[2]**. Reenter the cool cover of trees at .5 mi. **[3]** and continue along as the trail passes between wooded ridges.

After sliding through dunes resembling a bobsled bank, you reach the junction for the beach access. A map board shows your location, and a bench awaits your return from the beach (.7 mi.) **[4]**. Turn left at the gold-tipped post that marks the way to the beach, and roll along the trail as it descends through steep dunes. Your beacon to the beach is an arch of sunshine through a tunnel of trees. Step through the tunnel into the sunlight of the hot, sandy beach (.9 mi.) **[5]**.

Stroll down another .1 mi. over gently rolling sand, then stop and enjoy the solitude at Cathead Bay. Kick off your shoes and lie back a while before returning to the junction. Your trip back is uphill through open sand, so rest now and enjoy sunshine and the gentle rush of waves rolling onto the shore. Then head back through the tunnel and wooded dunes to the junction **[4]** where that bench is waiting. Next hike on straight, going through the forest. The trail bends left to cut over a footbridge that crosses over a small ravine (1.4 mi.) **[6]**. Shortly after walking over a small ridge braided with roots, you reach the overlook junction (1.6 mi.) **[7]**.

Turn left at the red-tipped post for a bird's-eye view of the bay. The trail along this spur rises (often over a series of stairs), culminating at the top of an observation deck (1.8 mi.) **[8]**. From this perch you overlook about .25 mile of rolling sand against a backdrop of the bay and sky—blue splashed with white. On a clear day, the Fox Islands add the final touches to the temporal canvas you view. Sit on a bench before you head back down the spur and continue straight past the junction (2 mi.) **[7]**.

Continue straight past the next junction, too, through the rolling woods. At 2.1 mi. birch logs are strewn about like fallen bowling pins cluttering the forest floor **[9]**. Soon after, the trail swings left and begins to climb. A steep hill flanks the trail in the distance, then you begin to wind down and reach the junction that brings your hike to a full circle (2.4 mi.) **[10]**. Turn left and walk the few steps back to the parking lot.

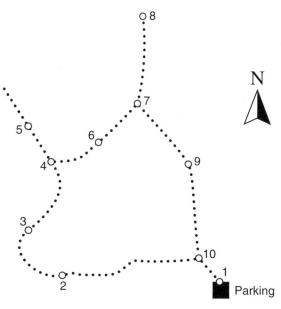

1. Trailhead
2. Bench
3. Cover of trees
4. Beach trail junction and bench
5. Beach
6. Footbridge
7. Overlook trail junction
8. Observation deck
9. Strewn logs
10. Trail junction to parking lot

Mud Lake Trail 👢👢

Distance Round-Trip: 3.2 miles

Estimated Hiking Time: 1.5 to 2 hours

Cautions: Low areas, especially along Mud Lake, are prone to flooding. Be careful walking among exposed roots and take plenty of insect repellent.

Trail Directions: Starting from the trail map board at the northeast end of the gravel parking area, you have the option of turning left to hike clockwise or right to hike counterclockwise. These trail directions go counterclockwise, so turn right **[1]**. All the trails, spurs, and cutoffs are color coded and marked by wooden posts with tips painted in the corresponding color. The Mud Lake Trail follows orange-tipped posts.

Your right turn takes you through a field of ferns; then the trail quickly breaks into the woods. Here the trail may be muddy or even under water. Forested dunes follow along on your left. To your right is Mud Lake, evidenced by many dead trees (most notably paper birch). You may have noticed these "ghost" trees as you drove to the trailhead along Densmore Road.

At .2 mi. you reach the Maple Ridge Cutoff **[2]**. Each trail junction has a map board showing your location, a bench, and color-coordinated trail posts that lead you in the right direction. You don't have to worry about getting lost on these well-marked trails. After you reach the Tamarack Cutoff (.5 mi.) **[3]**, the trail is sliced to a thin track running along the edge of the lake and the base of a forested dune. You soon leave this catwalk and feel you're venturing backstage at what appears to be a huge, natural amphitheater (.7 mi.) **[4]**. Enjoy the show before you swing right to stay near the lake and avoid a steep climb up a ridge.

After reaching the Pot-Hole Ridge junction (.8 mi.) **[5]**, the trail twists past fallen paper birch trees to climb a small ridge. When descending, swing left and inspect the neat rows of red pine standing at attention like wooden soldiers (.9 mi.) **[6]**.

Just beyond the second Pot-Hole Ridge junction, you reach a footbridge (1.2 mi.) **[7]** that carries you over a swamp and deposits you onto a pine-needle–covered bank. Turn left, and, with the needles cushioning your steps, follow along the swamp. Soon the trail swings right, away from the swamp, and climbs to a peak high above a natural bowl-shaped depression (1.4 mi.) **[8]**.

You reach the halfway point of your hike when you spot the trail marker that has a sign stating, "State Park Trail ends" (1.6 mi.) **[9]**. Turn left and continue your hike through the dense beech-maple forest as the trail snakes through the dune environment. A bench is set at 2 mi., and you can stop and enjoy the solitude of the forest **[10]**. Unless you've forgotten to bring insect repellent, sit back and enjoy the quiet.

Not long before you reach the northern end of the Tamarack Cutoff (2.4 mi.) **[11]**, the many fallen trees allow in the light—the trail seems to brighten. Bask in this rare window of sunshine. At 2.9 mi. you can turn right at the junction with the Lake Michigan Trail **[12]**. This route, with its light-blue-tipped posts, takes you to the scenic overlook of Cathead Bay and to a spur down to the beach. If you instead turn left, the Mud Lake Trail completes its loop and winds back to the parking area.

1. Trailhead
2. Maple Ridge Cutoff
3. Tamarack Cutoff
4. Natural amphitheater
5. Pot-Hole Ridge junction
6. Red pine stand
7. Footbridge
8. Natural bowl
9. Halfway point
10. Bench
11. Tamarack Cutoff
12. Lake Michigan trail junction

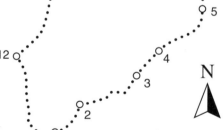

31. Sleeping Bear Dunes National Lakeshore

- Ascend the 130-foot Dune Climb of the Sleeping Bear Dunes.
- Ferry over to explore the Manitou Islands.
- Enjoy panoramic views of the dunes and lakes along the Pierce Stocking Scenic Drive.

Park Information

Comprised of more than 30 miles of mainland Lake Michigan shoreline, the North and South Manitou Islands, inland lakes, forests, rivers, cliffs, and towering dunes, Sleeping Bear Dunes is a national treasure. Several routes open up the park's treasures.

One of them, the 7.4-mile Pierce Stocking Scenic Drive, opens up views of the Lake Michigan shoreline. The Visitor Center houses a slide program and exhibits. In addition to 50 miles of mainland trails, South Manitou Island has 40 more miles and North Manitou Island has 20 miles plus many more miles that are not maintained.

Try canoeing the Platte or Crystal Rivers, swimming in Glen Lake, or visiting the Maritime Museum. And there's always the main attraction—the Dune Climb.

Directions: The park follows the Lake Michigan shoreline in Benzie and Leelanau counties, about 20 miles west of Traverse City. From US-31 you can access M-22, which is the main north-south road through the park. If you're coming from the east, M-115 and M-72 also lead to M-22. The Visitor Center is located on M-72, just east of M-22.

North and South Manitou Islands may be accessed by private water craft or from a ferry service out of Leland, off M-22. Ferry service is available from May to October for South Manitou and up to November for North Manitou Island. Check with the transit company for scheduling.

Hours Open: The park is open year-round. The Visitor Center is open daily from 9:30 A.M. to 4:30 P.M., with longer hours in the summer. It is closed on Christmas and New Year's Day. The Coast Guard Station Maritime Museum in Glen Haven has varied hours. Call ahead. The South Manitou Island Visitor Center is open daily from mid-June through Labor Day and on weekends during the rest of September. The Pierce Stocking Scenic Drive is open from mid-April through mid-November.

Facilities: Hiking, bicycling, cross-country skiing, snowshoeing, swimming, fishing, hunting, canoeing, canoe rental, picnicking, hang gliding, camping (tent, RV, and backcountry), bridle path, boat launch, sanitation station, interpretive trails, and interpretive center.

Permits and Rules: The fee for individuals is $5 per day, $7 for vehicles per day. The annual fee is $15. Dunes are unstable; don't venture onto them. Vehicles, including bicycles, are not allowed on the trails. Pets must be kept on a leash; they are prohibited on the Dune Climb and on the Manitou Islands. Do not collect plants or historical features.

Further Information: Sleeping Bear Dunes National Lakeshore, 9922 Front Street, Highway M-72, Empire, MI 49630-0277; 616-326-5134. The park concessionaire for ferry service to North and South Manitou Islands is at Manitou Island Transit, P.O. Box 591, Leland, MI 49654; 616-256-9061 (or 616-271-4217) during the off-season.

Park Trails

Old Indian Trail 👢 (Green Arrow) and 👢👢👢 (Black Arrow)—2.5 miles—Located north of Crystal Lake off M-22 at the south end of the park, this trail is two loops, one that builds slightly on the other.

Platte Plains Hiking and Ski Trail 👢👢—14.7 miles—This network of trails has many loops that are mostly level (except for some steep hills on the Lasso Loop). There are two trailheads: (1) Trail's End Road, west of M-22, and (2) Esch Road, west of M-22.

Empire Bluff Hiking and Ski Trail 👢👢—1.5 miles round-trip—This one-way interpretive trail cuts over hilly terrain through beech-maple forest and over fields and dunes to a boardwalk with an overview of Lake Michigan. It is located in Empire, south of the Visitor Center off M-22.

Dunes Hiking Trail 👢👢👢👢—3.5 miles round-trip—This one-way trail starts with the 130-foot high Dune Climb, then rolls over open dunes to Lake Michigan. Access is from the Dune Climb off M-109, north of Empire.

Duneside Accessible Trail 👢—.9 mile round-trip—Designed for visitors in wheelchairs and those with visual impairments, the trail goes through fields and woods. Start at the north end of Dune Climb.

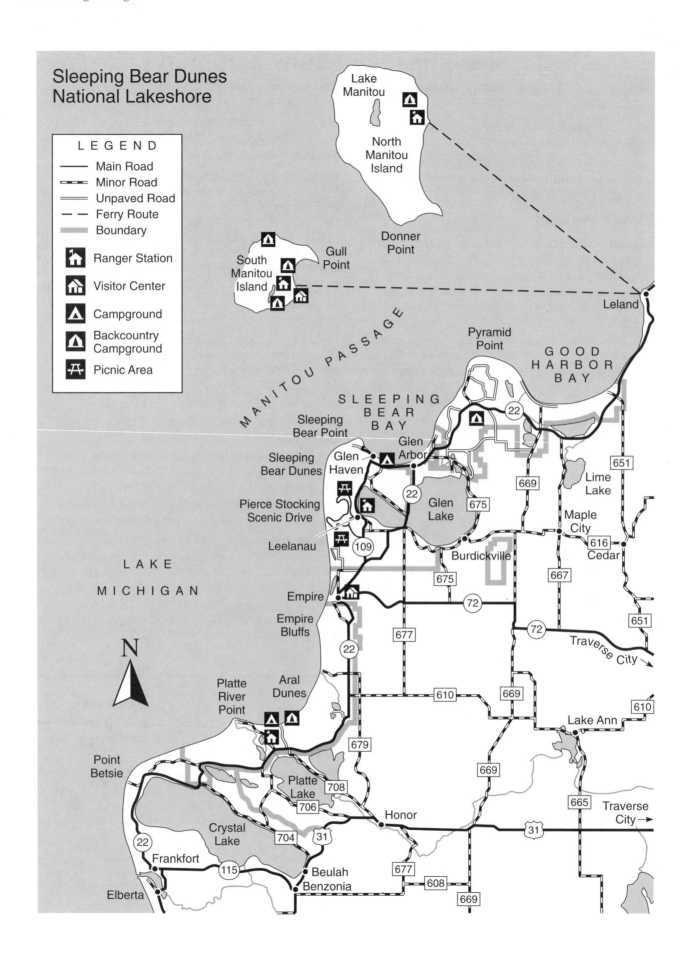

Sleeping Bear Dunes National Lakeshore

LEGEND

— Main Road
- ▪ - ▪ Minor Road
═ Unpaved Road
- - - Ferry Route
▬ Boundary

🏠 Ranger Station
🏠 Visitor Center
⛺ Campground
⛺ Backcountry Campground
🏕 Picnic Area

Lake Manitou

North Manitou Island

Donner Point

South Manitou Island

Gull Point

Leland

MANITOU PASSAGE

Pyramid Point

GOOD HARBOR BAY

SLEEPING BEAR BAY

Sleeping Bear Point

Glen Arbor

22

Sleeping Bear Dunes

Glen Haven

669

675

Lime Lake

651

Pierce Stocking Scenic Drive

Glen Lake

Maple City

Leelanau

109

Burdickville

616

Cedar

LAKE MICHIGAN

675

667

Empire

651

Empire Bluffs

22

677

72

72

Traverse City →

N

Aral Dunes

610

669

610

Platte River Point

679

Lake Ann

Point Betsie

708

706

669

Platte Lake

Honor

665

Traverse City →

Crystal Lake

704

31

31

22

Frankfort

115

Beulah

677

Benzonia

608

Elberta

669

Dunes—Sleeping Bear Point Hiking Trail 👢👢👢

Distance Round-Trip: 2.2 miles

Estimated Hiking Time: 1.5 to 2 hours

Cautions: This trail blazes across open sand. Stay on the marked path and beware of landslides on steep dunes. Some parts of the trail traipse through sand, which may be hot. You also go through forest, where roots and rocks may be exposed. Wear appropriate footgear. Insect repellent is a must in the warm months.

Trail Directions: The parking lot is off the gravel road, west of the Maritime Museum in Glen Haven. An information board at the northwest corner of the lot marks the trailhead **[1]**. You start this trail with firm footing, but the trail soon turns to sand and you get the first hint that this may be a trail of contrasts. It is. Open, desert-like stretches of dunes later give way to lush, cool, shady forests.

Plow up the slope through soft, deep sand to the first junction (.1 mi.) **[2]** and ask yourself, "Cool Lake Michigan waters or hot, open dunes?" Go for the cool. A spur to the right takes you to Lake Michigan by way of a climb up the sandy slope, past a blowout (the saucer-shaped depression in the sand, hollowed out by wind), and gently down past one of many walls of sand that characterize this dune environment (.3 mi.) **[3]**.

Kick off your shoes, pour out the sand, and dip your toes into the cool waters before heading back up to the junction. Near the junction, a look leftward shows the "fingers" of forested dunes in the distances. Back at the junction **[2]**, round the curve and blaze through grassy dunes. Occasional dips in the dunes along the shoreline offer profile views of the lake.

At .6 mi. a large blowout opens up a turquoise and deep lavender-blue Lake Michigan framed by a grassy dune **[4]**. Move on and the view is even better. Below you is a large, flat, sandy basin peppered with white. The ridges of sand surrounding it have battlement-like openings. Another contrast—but this castle in the sand is no fortification to wind and water.

The trail turns left, passing through grassy dunes. In the distance lies stark, barren sand. Start down a slope and arrive at this desert swath at .7 mi. **[5]**. A blue-tipped post guides you on your southwesterly trek. To your left are skeletons of trees. Pushed by the wind, these trees were buried by shifting sands, making ghost forests that offer the stark contrast of stability and change (.8 mi.) **[6]**.

Pass through another stand of ghosts standing upright like pencils in the sand, and step onto the sandy stripe that winds over the grassy dunes before you (1 mi.) **[7]**. Climb and wind to the left through rolling dunes blanketed by grasses and wildflowers. You pass an occasional blowout. At 1.3 mi. the grassy, rolling terrain is reminiscent of an Alpine meadow **[8]**.

The trail curves left again, wrapping itself around a small, crescent-shaped blowout. Then it comes to a T in the trail. Turn left and climb to a crest offering a panoramic view of the terrain (1.4 mi.) **[9]**. You not only get a different perspective of the barren sand and grassy dunes that you crossed, but you also can turn around for an interesting view of Glen Lake. Though it isn't a volcanic caldera that filled with water, like Crater Lake, this lake looks like one as it nestles beneath the wooded slopes that give it a bowl-shape.

Soon, the trail swings right and opens a view of sinuous rows of dunes (1.5 mi.) **[10]**. Concentric rows of forested dunes, one behind the other, get lighter in the hazy distance. At 1.8 mi., you reach another junction. Go down and left through juniper and ferns into the cool shadows of a forest **[11]**. The trail winds through the woods, so thick with ferns and juniper sometimes that there is only room enough for you to place one foot in front of the other. At 2.2 mi., place one foot in front of the other and break out of the woods back to the parking lot **[12]**.

1. Trailhead
2. Lake Michigan Trail junction
3. Lake Michigan
4. Dune-framed lake
5. Barren sand
6. Ghost forest
7. Grassy dunes
8. Alpine-like meadow
9. Panoramic view
10. View of wooded dunes
11. Forest
12. Parking lot

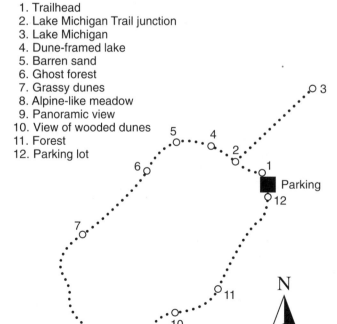

Pyramid Point Hiking Trail

Distance Round-Trip: 2.7 miles

Estimated Hiking Time: 1.5 to 2 hours

Cautions: At the scenic overlook, watch your step—it is a long drop to the lake. To protect the fragile bluff, and for your own protection, don't descend it. The hike finishes on Basch Road, where you should watch for traffic. Insect repellent is a must during the warm months.

Trail Directions: Heading northeast of Glen Arbor on M-22, turn left on Port Oneida Road. Continue north for 2 miles and turn right on Basch Road. In .3 mile you reach the parking area and trailhead on the left. There is a vault toilet at the parking area, but no water source. The trail begins at the northeast end of the parking area to the right of the trail board and map box **[1]**.

Your path angles northeast from the parking area and crosses a meadow. Before you climb into these woods loaded with paper birch, a less advanced trail splits off to the left. If you are not up to a steep climb, take the alternate route. You quickly reach the posted junction to the scenic Lake Michigan lookout near a boulder that stands out in stark contrast to its surroundings (.3 mi.) **[2]**. The alternate trail merges back with the steeper one here.

From the junction it is a .2-mi. climb through the woods to where the trail breaks out onto the sandy edge of a dune towering over Lake Michigan. Take your time to soak in the view. You should be able to see North Manitou and South Manitou Islands in the distance (.5 mi.) **[3]**. You may also see hang gliders preparing to launch themselves from the precipice.

Leaving the overlook, retrace your steps and descend to the marked trail junction, where you turn left. The trail continues to descend into the beech-maple forest; gradually it swings left along the backside of the dune. At 1.1 mi. the trail will turn sharply right away from the dune **[4]**. You'll see that many before you have been tempted to turn left and climb the steep sandy slope before moving on. Do the dune a favor; don't cave in to temptation.

At the next posted junction, one option is taking a shortcut back to the trailhead (1.2 mi.) **[5]**. The other is to continue on, the trail descending sharply and then leveling out to deposit you at the edge of a meadow (1.4 mi.) **[6]**. You turn right and follow along the tree line before bursting into the open meadow. After you cross the meadow and as you approach new tree growth at the edge of the forest, stop and look behind you. You should be able to see the top of the dune peeking over the vegetation (1.7 mi.) **[7]**.

Back in the woods, the trail swings right and climbs back onto the ridge you had previously descended to reach the meadow. At 2.1 mi. you meet the junction at the other end of the shortcut **[8]**. Turn left and make a steep climb along a ravine to Basch Road (2.3 mi.) **[9]**. Turn right on Basch Road and make a steep descent. This is a narrow dirt road, so be alert for traffic. You will reach the parking area in .4 mi.

1. Trailhead
2. Scenic overlook trail junction
3. Scenic overlook
4. Tempting dune climb
5. Shortcut trail junction
6. Meadow
7. Look back at dune
8. Shortcut trail junction
9. Basch Road

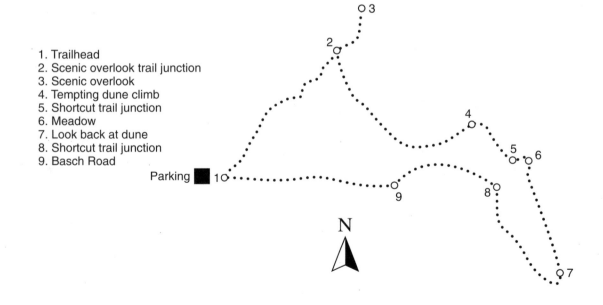

32. Nordhouse Dunes Wilderness

- Camp in backcountry on bluffs overlooking Lake Michigan.
- Swim or stroll along miles of sandy Lake Michigan beach.
- Enjoy more than 3,000 acres set aside as wilderness.

Park Information

Don't let the size of Nordhouse Dunes Wilderness—3,450 acres—belittle its unique characteristics. Distinguished as the only federally designated wilderness in Michigan's Lower Peninsula, the area has 3 miles of isolated Lake Michigan beach, dunes towering 140 feet high, extensive interdunal wetlands, and vegetation ranging from dune grass that tolerates desert-like conditions to a charming northern hardwood beech-maple forest.

Although no designated campgrounds exist in the wilderness, backcountry camping is allowed almost anywhere. Some limitations exist to help protect the environment and the wilderness experience. No water system is available, so plan on packing it in or purifying what you need. Better equipped, regular camping facilities are available, however, at the Lake Michigan Recreation Area that borders the northern end of the wilderness.

Roughly 15 miles of trails provide access to the varied habitats found at Nordhouse Dunes. Designation as a wilderness area is designed in part to provide a unique recreation experience for visitors. This designation means that the trail system is no longer maintained with signs or markers, though the trails still exist, and maps of the wilderness highlight their locations. What is missing is having the trail names specified on the new maps—monikers such as Dunes Edge, Algoma Ridge, and Nipissing. So, carry a map and compass, and pay attention to where you are hiking. You may also want to stop in at the Manistee Ranger Station for suggestions on routes and a schedule of guided hikes.

Directions: Nordhouse Dunes Wilderness lies between Manistee and Ludington. To reach the southern trailhead from US-31, turn west on Lake Michigan Recreation Road (FR 5629) for about 3 miles, then head south on Quarterline for a generous mile to Nurnburg Road. Head west about 6 miles to a small parking area. The Lake Michigan Recreation Area, at the northern boundary, is accessed from US-31 by following the Lake Michigan Recreation Road west about 8 miles to its end.

Hours Open: The park is open year-round.

Facilities: Hiking, cross-country skiing, snowshoeing, swimming, fishing, hunting, and camping (backcountry).

Permits and Rules: There is no fee. Motor vehicles and mechanized equipment, including mountain bikes and wheeled carts, are not permitted. Pack animals, including horses, are not allowed. Campfires and campsites must be more than 400 feet from Lake Michigan; no beach fires are allowed. Driftwood must neither be removed from the wilderness nor burned. Campsites along roads must be 400 feet from the wilderness boundary. Maximum group size is 10 people. Please pack out what you bring in.

Further Information: Huron-Manistee National Forest, Manistee Ranger Station, 412 Red Apple Road, Manistee, MI 49660; 616-723-2211.

Other Points of Interest

Bordering the Nordhouse Dunes Wilderness to the north is the **Lake Michigan Recreation Area**, which includes campsites, observation decks, an interpretive trail, mountain bike trails, and a swimming beach. The Nordhouse Dunes Wilderness is accessible from the recreation area. For more information contact the Manistee Ranger Station at the address and phone number mentioned earlier.

East of the Nordhouse Dunes Wilderness trailhead on Nurnburg Road sits the 100-acre **Hamlin Lake Marsh**. From Nurnburg Road, take Forest Road 5540 south to this little-used spot on the northern tip of Hamlin Lake. A small boat launch is located at this site. For more information contact the Manistee Ranger Station.

Ludington State Park (see park #33) borders the Nordhouse Dunes Wilderness on the south. This park has modern camping facilities, an interpretive center, beaches on two lakes, paved bicycling paths, and many miles of hiking paths. For more information contact Ludington State Park, P.O. Box 709, M-116, Ludington, MI 49431; 616-843-8671.

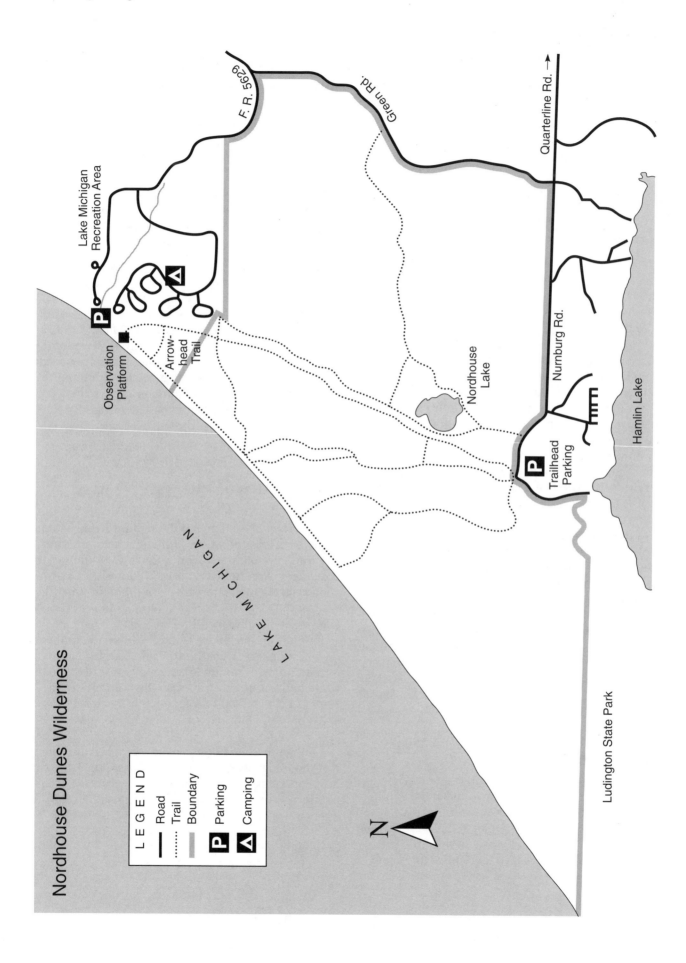

Nordhouse Dunes Wilderness

LEGEND

——— Road
········· Trail
——— Boundary
P Parking
▲ Camping

LAKE MICHIGAN

Observation Platform

Arrow-head Trail

Lake Michigan Recreation Area

F. R. 5629

Green Rd.

Quarterline Rd. →

Nurnburg Rd.

Nordhouse Lake

Trailhead Parking

Hamlin Lake

Ludington State Park

N

Four-Mile Loop 👢👢👢

Distance Round-Trip: 4.1 miles

Estimated Hiking Time: 2.5 to 3.5 hours

Cautions: The trails are worn and usually are easy to follow, but they aren't marked. Carry a map and a compass. You travel through sand and mud, over roots and rocks, and along ridges. Wear appropriate footgear. Take water and take insect repellent in the warm months.

Trail Directions: Park on Nurnburg Road, 6 mi. west of Quarterline Road. Start at the north end of the parking area, taking the left trail to the north **[1]**. Climb past the barricade and into the forest.

Wind around, gently ascending (.2 mi.) **[2]** the backside of a dune. Go through forested hills while ascending, passing grassy slopes that line troughs and the fern- and tree-lined slopes along the ravines. At .5 mi. a trail cuts in on the right **[3]**. It leads to Nordhouse Lake. Go straight.

The trail narrows, continuing its ascent. At .9 mi., a moss carpet **[4]** tips you off that dunes will soon appear. When the trail swings noticeably to the right, a gully begins to accompany you (1 mi.) **[5]**. Birch trees occasionally light up the woods.

Soon, you reach the left fork for the trail formerly known as Algoma Ridge (1.1 mi.) **[6]**. And a ridge it is. Climb. Climb past gnarly oaks with gaping holes and past grassy slopes. Keep climbing, after you think you've reached the crest with short, wind-cropped trees. Wind around wooded ravines, but keep climbing. Pass through an Alpine-like meadow, until you reach another crest at 1.3 mi. **[7]**. Trees are cleared here, and you get a panoramic view of Lake Michigan. Freighters are only hazy slits in the distance.

Cut back into the woods and break out at another clearing. Trees below you spill over the slope like carpeting, but four pines stand out (1.4 mi.) **[8]**, rising above the others, their branches extend out to the lake like arms readied in a welcoming embrace. Keep going, winding around a small blowout. Soon the trail narrows, goes through the woods, and starts down. Ferns line the way. Head back up, pass a sand bowl, and then climb down into shadows, only to rise again to a crest.

Lake Michigan comes into view at 1.8 mi., when you reach the final ridge that parallels it (1.8 mi.) **[9]**. A turn left here would take you for a ridge-walk parallel to Lake Michigan. Instead, turn right and head down to a set of steps. Take them down and turn left around an eroded area. Just past this area, blaze your way down the steep slope to the sandy shores of Lake Michigan.

Now—kick off your shoes and stroll to the west. Play tag with the water as it ebbs and flows. Listen to the waves and the seagulls. The next .5 mi. is yours to enjoy as you head west along the shore before reaching the point of reentry back inland (2.4 mi.) **[10]**.

Watch for an opening in the sandy dunes. Head inland. At the ridge you will pass a sign, "No horses," where steps lead up to the ridge (this is the trail that you could have taken). Go straight. The trail passes through a valley between dunes. You go by a graveyard of stumps; then hardwoods, cedars, and hemlocks perfume the way. A massive dune advances to your right, following along the trail's edge. Pass through a valley of ferns, roll along through hemlock, and reach a main trail junction at 3 mi. **[11]**.

Head left. You'll pass wetlands, ferns, maples, oaks, and hemlocks. The trail winds down around a wetland (3.7 mi.) **[12]**, and down even more to the parking area where you left your vehicle.

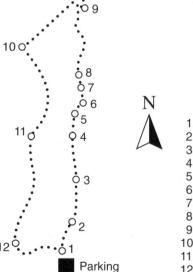

1. Trailhead
2. Gentle ascent
3. Trail junction
4. Moss on trail
5. Gully
6. Ridge fork
7. Crest
8. Pines with open arms
9. Trail junction, ridge
10. Reenter inland
11. Main trail junction
12. Wetland

Six-Mile Loop 👢👢👢

Distance Round-Trip: 5.9 miles

Estimated Hiking Time: 4 to 5 hours

Cautions: The trails are worn and usually easy to follow, but they aren't marked. Carry a map and a compass. Wear appropriate footgear. Take water and take insect repellent.

Trail Directions: Start near the information board at the southwest end of the parking area on Nurnburg Road, about 6 mi. west of Quarterline Road **[1]**. You start out on a wide, sandy path, climbing gently into the forest. Notice the large wetland on your right: Swing around to end up hiking north and climbing (.4 mi.) **[2]**.

Trudging along the sandy trail, shaded by mixed woods, you pass several small wetlands and an occasional side path. The trails aren't marked, so you're on your own for any side trips (which is, after all, in the spirit of a wilderness recreational experience—feel free to wander).

At 1.1 mi. turn right off the main trail and onto a less-used pathway **[3]**. Soon, you skirt a large dune in the forest on your left. As you continue north, you pass through cedar and hemlock trees that give way to maple. You also pass old stumps that stand like tombstones, a reminder of the forest that stood here prior to the logging era.

As you undulate along the trail, you eventually come to a little valley between a dune and a ridge. Follow the sometimes moss-carpeted trail to reach the edge of the Lake Michigan beach. On your right are steps leading up onto a ridge. (1.7 mi.) **[4]**. You have the option here of walking the Lake Michigan beach or the trail on the ridge that rises high above the lake.

Watch your step as you climb up the bluff and past any campers who might be set up on the ridge. Continue climbing, stopping now and then to enjoy a scenic view through the trees of Lake Michigan with its white, sandy beach. At 1.9 mi., after a steep climb and then a descent on steps, look to your left for an oak tree that blew down, whose upraised branches grew into trees **[5]**.

A trail will then merge from the right (2.1 mi.) **[6]**. Descend and skirt an eroded section of the bluff. A second trail then merges from the right (2.2 mi.) **[7]**. Continuing along the bluff, you eventually enter the Lake Michigan Recreation Area after you pass the Nordhouse Dunes Wilderness sign (2.8 mi.) **[8]**. You

reach the junction with the southern leg of the Arrowhead Trail at 2.9 mi.**[9]**. Continue along the bluff.

At 3.1 mi., the east leg merges from the right into the tip of the Arrowhead Trail **[10]**. Continue on to enjoy the observation platforms, boardwalks, trail to the beach, and interpretive markers at the Lake Michigan Recreation Area (3.2 mi.) **[11]**.

Back at the tip of the Arrowhead Trail (3.3 mi.) **[10]**, veer left and climb to an observation deck. Catch your breath, then catch the trail back by heading southeast. You pass two routes that descend to the campground. After the Arrowhead Trail splits, you pass a water-storage tank (3.5 mi.) **[12]**.

Soon reenter the Nordhouse Dunes Wilderness and pass a junction (3.6 mi.) **[13]**. The trail follows a bluff on the backside of the dunes, overlooking the interior of the wilderness. Another trail parallels your route using an old logging railroad grade, far below you on the left.

As the trail gradually descends, look for glimpses of Nordhouse Lake through the trees on the left. At about 5.2 mi. you have the option of turning left to descend to the lake or turning right to head back. Turn right **[14]** and hike the short distance to another trail. Turn left and descend to the parking lot.

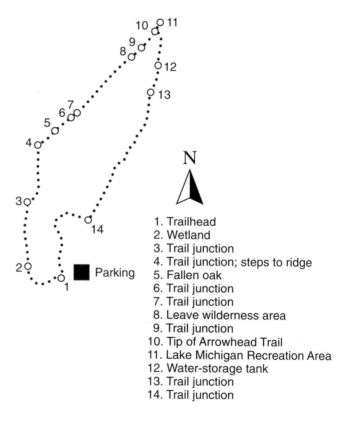

1. Trailhead
2. Wetland
3. Trail junction
4. Trail junction; steps to ridge
5. Fallen oak
6. Trail junction
7. Trail junction
8. Leave wilderness area
9. Trail junction
10. Tip of Arrowhead Trail
11. Lake Michigan Recreation Area
12. Water-storage tank
13. Trail junction
14. Trail junction

33. Ludington State Park

- Take in almost 6 miles of dune-lined Lake Michigan shoreline.
- Canoe or tube along the Big Sable River between Lake Michigan and Hamlin Lake.
- Follow the beacon—a number of trails guide you to the impressive Point Sable Lighthouse.

Park Information

This park's attendance ranks in the top ten of all Michigan state parks, with good reason. Almost 6 miles of Lake Michigan shoreline (connected by a river to an inland lake), rolling dune terrain, and an historic lighthouse provide the ingredients to satisfy any number of appetites for recreation. Two beaches —one on Lake Michigan and one on Hamlin Lake— encourage fishing, swimming, canoeing, and boating. Paved pathways along the river endow bicyclists with grounds for enjoyment. Some areas of the park are open to in-season hunting. Moreover, this 5,300-acre park is home to the Great Lakes Interpretive Center for exhibits, interpretive programs, and multimedia shows.

Although the camp and day beaches are usually crowded, plenty of acreage supplies opportunities to escape to more contemplative areas. Wilderness abounds to the north, extending from the park's own acreage to the neighboring Nordhouse Dunes Wilderness (see park #32). About 16 miles of cross-country ski trails glide over the park when the winter snows fall.

Directions: Ludington State Park is 8 miles north of Ludington. Take US-10 west into Ludington. Head north onto M-116 about 8 miles to the park entrance.

Hours Open: Open year-round from 8:00 A.M. to 10:00 P.M. The lighthouse is open from 10:00 A.M. to 4:00 P.M., except Wednesdays and Thursdays. On Sundays it is open from 1:00 to 5:00 P.M.

Facilities: Hiking, mountain bicycling, cross-country skiing, swimming, fishing, hunting, canoeing, picnicking, camping (RV and tent), boat launch, boat and canoe rentals, sanitation station, and interpretive center.

Permits and Rules: A park fee ($4 daily, $20 annually) is required per motor vehicle. Snowmobiles are not allowed in the park. Bicycles are allowed on paved roads and paths only.

Further Information: Ludington State Park, P.O. Box 709, M-116, Ludington, MI 49431; 616-843-8671.

Other Points of Interest

Hamlin Lake Marsh is east of Hamlin Lake on Forest Road 5540. Frequented by wildlife, its natural shoreline is favorable for wildlife viewing. For more information contact the Huron-Manistee National Forest, Manistee Ranger Station, 412 Red Apple Road, Manistee, MI 49660; 616-723-2211.

Park Trails

Although 11 hiking trails cover 18 miles, they are connector trails leading to one another. Park maps are available at the contact stations. Another possibility includes the 1.8-mile hike along the access road from the Pines Campground to the lighthouse.

Coast Guard Trail —1 mile—This trail, marked by black arrows, starts on the northwest end of the day-use area on Hamlin Lake. It takes you to a scenic viewpoint along Lake Michigan.

Ridge Trail —2.7 miles—This trail starts from behind the park store at the southwest end of the Cedar Campground. It traverses a ridge, following through woods.

Logging Trail —2.7 miles—Access this trail from the north end of the Pines Campground, near site #53. It is the remnant of an old logging road that climbs a ridge, descends into lowlands, and reaches hills and woods.

Beechwood Trail —1.5 miles—Start at the northeast end of the parking area for the Hamlin Lake day-use area. Veering northwest, it winds up at the Lighthouse Trail.

Skyline Trail —.5 mile—A scenic trail along a boardwalk, it loops around the Visitor Center and offers panoramic views of Lake Michigan and the Big Sable River.

Dune Trail —.7 mile—This trail starts behind the park store in the Cedar Campground.

Lighthouse Trail —1 mile—This trail is accessed via the Beechwood and Logging Trails or by the access road from the Pines Campground that leads to the lighthouse.

Eagle's Nest Trail —.6 mile—This trail is accessed by the Logging, Ridge, Beechwood, or Lost Lake trails.

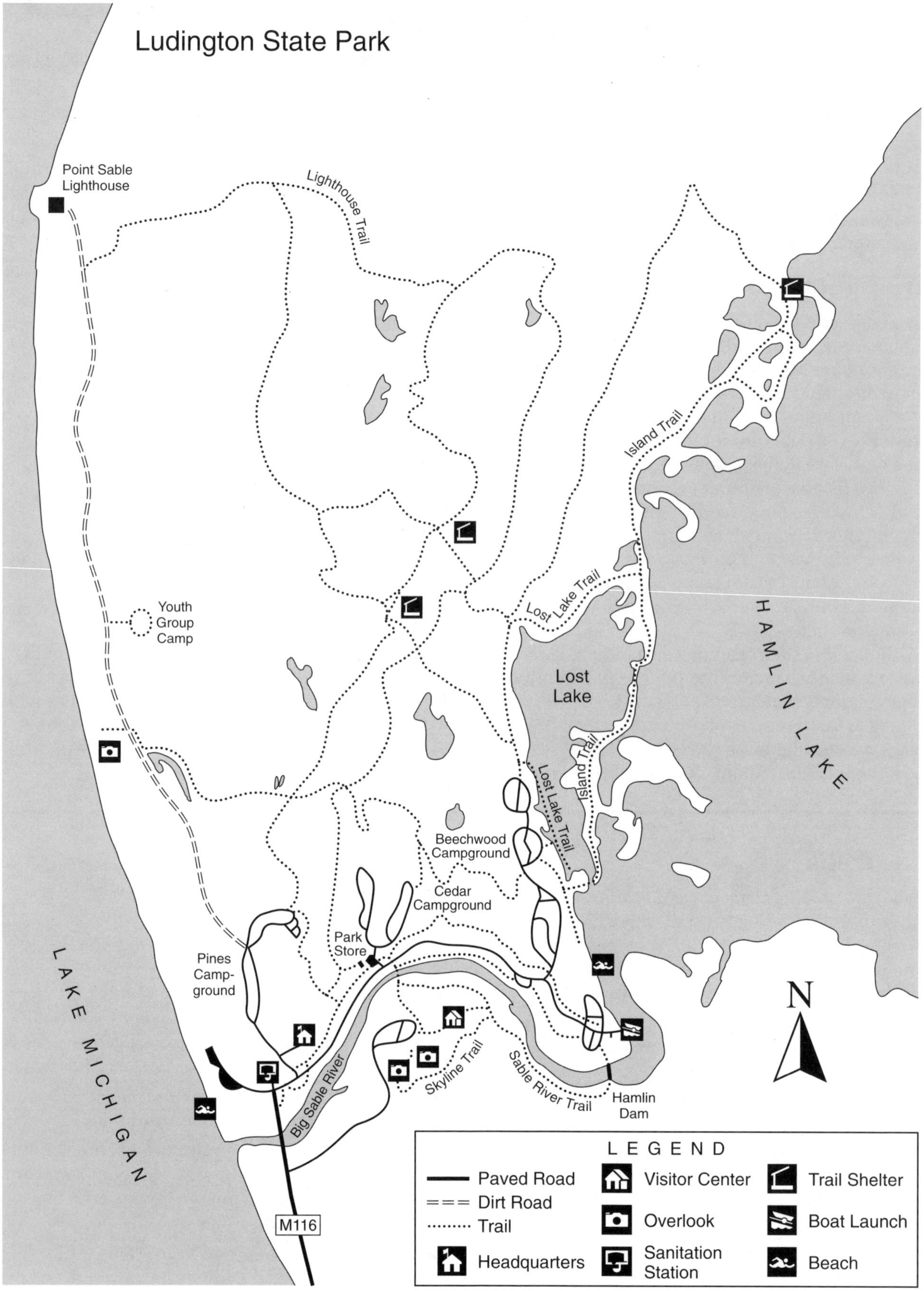

Ludington State Park

Point Sable
Lighthouse

Lighthouse Trail

Island Trail

Lost Lake Trail

HAMLIN LAKE

Youth
Group
Camp

Lost
Lake

Island Trail

Lost Lake Trail

Beechwood
Campground

Cedar
Campground

Park
Store

Pines
Camp-
ground

Big Sable River

Skyline Trail

Sable River Trail

Hamlin
Dam

LAKE MICHIGAN

M116

N

LEGEND

——	Paved Road	🏠	Visitor Center	◩	Trail Shelter
===	Dirt Road	⬛	Overlook	🚤	Boat Launch
⋯⋯	Trail			🏊	Beach
🏠	Headquarters	♲	Sanitation Station		

Skyline/Sable River/Island/ Lost Lake Trails

Distance Round-Trip: 3.7 miles

Estimated Hiking Time: 2 to 2.5 hours

Cautions: At times the trail narrows alongside the river. Roots are exposed and can be slippery. You will be in the woods, so insect repellent is a must during the warm months.

Trail Directions: The hike combines the Skyline, Sable River, Island Lake, and Lost Lake trails with a portion of a bicycle trail. You get overviews from boardwalks on bluffs, river walking, island hopping, and dock strolling. Start from the southwest end of the Visitor Center parking lot **[1]** to pick up the Skyline Trail, which takes you up a series of steps to a boardwalk on the bluffs.

At .1 mi. you see the Big Sable River **[2]**. Watch for the flotilla of Canada geese that take up residence in the park. At .3 mi. pass the staircase that leads down to the Visitor Center **[3]**. Views continue as you walk along the boardwalk to the Sable River Trail (.4 mi.) **[4]**. Turn right. The trail gradually takes you along the bank of the river, up root steps, and along the side of a wooded hill. Then it climbs and swings left over Hamlin Dam and Big Sable River (.7 mi.) **[5]**.

On the other side, cut through the Hamlin Lake Day-Use Area. Pass through the parking lot, by the concession stand, and after the swing set, swing near the beach and follow along the shore of Hamlin Lake (1 mi.) **[6]**. Soon you reach the junction for the Island Lake Trail (1.1 mi.) **[7]**.

Turn right onto the boardwalk through the cattails. At 1.2 mi. a footbridge crosses to one of the narrow islands separating Hamlin Lake and Lost Lake **[8]**. Notice the vast openness of Hamlin Lake and the narrow, river-like quality of Lost Lake. Follow the narrow strip of land and cross over to another narrow strip. Because of the island's irregular shape, lagoon-like pools are at your side. The irregularities continue to play, and you seem to pass open lakes, rivers, ponds, and lagoons. At times, the burnt-orange carpeting of pine needles underfoot offers a striking contrast with the dark-green canopies. Both lakes open wide. Continue along the strip of land between them, cross another bridge, then sit on the bench overlooking Hamlin Lake (1.7 mi.) **[9]**. More boardwalks await you before you arrive at the junction for the Lost Lake Trail (1.9 mi.) **[10]**.

Turn left, heading down between wetlands, then climb to a ridge from where you overlook Lost Lake (2 mi.) **[11]**. Roll along through the woods and arrive at a blowout-like slope that opens up another view of Lost Lake. Here, the trail veers right and soon brings you to the junction with the Ridge Trail (2.2 mi.) **[12]**. Although you should turn left here, the observation deck to your right (part of the Ridge Trail) is enticing, so catch a view from there before making your left turn along the Lost Lake Trail.

The Lost Lake Trail passes through mixed woods along a ridge above Lost Lake. At about 2.3 mi. a platform of steps assists you down to the lake level **[13]**. You can see the campgrounds up ahead as the Beechwood Trail merges in (2.5 mi.) **[14]**. Soon the trail arrives at a long boardwalk-dock that carries you along Lost Lake. At 2.7 mi. the boardwalk gives access to a small island where benches nestled under pines, hemlocks, and maples invite you **[15]**. At the end of the boardwalk, turn left and soon close the Island Lake–Lost Lake Loop. Retrace your steps to the Hamlin Lake Day-Use area, but instead of cutting across the park road back to the dam, turn right and follow the bike path along the north side of the river (3.1 mi.) **[16]**.

Just before you reach the Cedar Campground, you'll see the bridge that crosses over the river (3.6 mi.) **[17]**. Turn left and cross the park road and bridge. Pass through a short stretch of woods before arriving back at the parking lot.

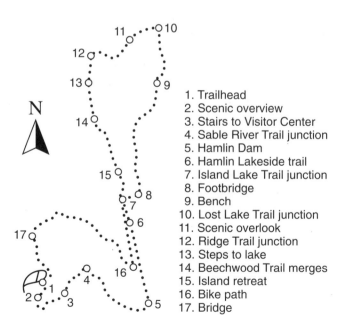

1. Trailhead
2. Scenic overview
3. Stairs to Visitor Center
4. Sable River Trail junction
5. Hamlin Dam
6. Hamlin Lakeside trail
7. Island Lake Trail junction
8. Footbridge
9. Bench
10. Lost Lake Trail junction
11. Scenic overlook
12. Ridge Trail junction
13. Steps to lake
14. Beechwood Trail merges
15. Island retreat
16. Bike path
17. Bridge

Big Sable Point
Lighthouse Loop 👢👢

Distance Round-Trip: 4.9 miles

Estimated Hiking Time: 2.5 to 3 hours

Cautions: The trail, a combination of the Lake Michigan shoreline and the Lighthouse and Logging Trails, takes you through a varied terrain. The trail may be hard to follow in the dunes. Look ahead and try to spot the next trail marker if you are unsure about where the trail is headed. Insect repellent is a plus for hiking the woods, as are sunscreen and a hat for the dunes and Lake Michigan shore.

Trail Directions: Parking is available north of the Big Sable River at the fish-cleaning station or at the bathhouse at the day-use area. The description here starts at the fish-cleaning station **[1]** and heads west along the drive to the bathhouse and beach.

North of the swimming area, the beach is wide and often covered with sun worshipers or people intent on using lake breezes to fly colorful kites. Hiking along the beach, you may even feel the pull of the lake and, depending on the weather, an uncontrollable urge to jump in. Plan ahead and wear your swimsuit. You can jump in now or wait until you've completed your hike.

At .9 mi. the silhouette of the black-tipped post marking the location of the Coast Guard Trail contrasts with the lightly colored sand of the dune **[2]**. You might use the Coast Guard Trail to access the service drive to the lighthouse if walking the sandy beach and listening to waves crashing onto the shore are not to your liking. At 1.2 mi. the Big Sable Point Lighthouse comes into view **[3]**. As you approach, its dark top rises above the light dune; it becomes your beacon, as it has been to others since it was first illuminated in 1867 (2 mi.) **[4]**. Owned by the Coast Guard, the lighthouse is being restored by the Big Sable Point Lighthouse Keepers, a nonprofit organization. The top of the lighthouse provides a spectacular view of the surrounding Lake Michigan shoreline and dunes environment.

When you leave the lighthouse, start out on the service drive and turn left at the post with the brown arrow (2.1 mi.) **[5]**. (Brown markers designate the Lighthouse Trail.) Head east into the dunes. It may be difficult to locate the trail in the open sand, so look ahead for trail markers across the open dunes. At 2.2 mi., after climbing a dune, take a parting look at the lighthouse nestled between the dunes and Lake Michigan **[6]**.

At the junction with the Beechwood Trail, stay to the left (2.5 mi.) **[7]** and prepare for a steep climb over the low point of a large dune. Before reaching the top, stop and look behind you for one last look at the dunes and Lake Michigan (2.6 mi.) **[8]**.

The trail swings right and descends sharply into a forest. You soon reach the end of the Lighthouse Trail and turn right onto the Logging Trail (2.9 mi.) **[9]**. Follow the green arrows as the trail rolls and snakes through the trees and past many old stumps left over from the logging era. At 3.6 mi. you reach the trail intersection with the Eagle's Nest Trail at the location of a hexagonal-shaped shelter built by the Civilian Conservation Corps in the 1930s **[10]**. Continue south and reach a second stone shelter at the intersection with the Beechwood Trail (3.9 mi.) **[11]**.

After passing two wetlands, you cross the junction for the Coast Guard Trail (4.3 mi.) **[12]**. Climb over a ridge and enter an area with fallen trees. Soon, you pass the Dune Trail and enter the Pines Campground next to site #54 (4.5 mi.) **[13]**. Turn right and hike through the campground to return to the parking area at the fish-cleaning station.

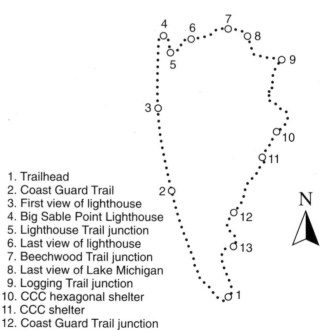

1. Trailhead
2. Coast Guard Trail
3. First view of lighthouse
4. Big Sable Point Lighthouse
5. Lighthouse Trail junction
6. Last view of lighthouse
7. Beechwood Trail junction
8. Last view of Lake Michigan
9. Logging Trail junction
10. CCC hexagonal shelter
11. CCC shelter
12. Coast Guard Trail junction
13. Campground

Southern Lower Peninsula

Michigan's south extends from the Indiana and Ohio borders to the imaginary line that corresponds to the knuckles of Michigan's mitten and includes the thumb.

Topography

The southern Lower Peninsula roughly includes that part of Michigan that used to be referred to as the industrial core of the United States and Canada. It contains the bulk of the state's population, all of its major urban areas, and its prime agricultural lands. Interestingly, it is also the only part of the state where the fossil remains of elephant-like mammals—the mastodons and mammoths—are found. As the glaciers receded, herds of these huge animals roamed southern Michigan. It is thought that these now extinct mammals were looking for life-sustaining salt seeps. An imaginary line called the Mason-Quimby Line marks the northernmost occurrence of mastodon and mammoth fossil finds and all of the recorded salt seeps, or shallow saline waters, in the state. It also corresponds to the area of transition between the north woods and the southern agricultural lands.

The present form of Michigan owes its shape to the last glacial retreat, which occurred between 10,000 and 35,000 years ago. The massive ice sheets transported large amounts of soil and rock, depositing them as moraines, serpentine eskers, elliptically shaped drumlins, kames, valleys, and hills of many shapes. An area of striking morainic development is found in Oakland and Washtenaw Counties, where two lobes of glacial ice collided and left a jumble of hills and lakes. Michigan's lowest elevation of 572 feet above sea level occurs along the shoreline of Lake Erie.

Famous for its sand dunes along the Great Lakes, Michigan also has dunes that lie far inland from the present shores. These inland dunes formed when the levels of the Great Lakes were higher. Many of these inland dunes are located well away from the shore of Lake Michigan. Another group of inland dunes

stretch west of Saginaw Bay almost as far as Clare. These inland dunes are less than 13,000 years old.

Major Rivers and Lakes

Lake Michigan borders the southern Lower Peninsula on the west; Lake Huron and Lake Erie are on the east. Canada shares the border with Michigan along Lake St. Clair and the St. Clair and Detroit Rivers. The Detroit River is the state's widest river, the Grand is the longest, and the Saginaw, with a length of 20 miles, is the shortest. The Saginaw, with its tributaries—the Tittabawassee, Shiawassee, Flint, and Cass Rivers—has the largest drainage basin in the state. Other significant rivers include the Muskegon, Kalamazoo, St. Joseph, and Huron.

Material carried by a river and deposited in a relatively quiet body of water forms a delta, which gradually grows outward from the shore. The St. Clair River delta, where the St. Clair River empties into Lake St. Clair, is the largest freshwater delta in the country.

As the glaciers receded, blocks of ice were left stranded. When these blocks finally melted, they left behind pits, or what are termed kettle holes. Many of these kettles holes filled with water and today are lakes. One of the greatest concentrations of kettle-hole lakes in Michigan occurs in a broad belt that stretches from just north of Pontiac and heads southwest to Jackson. This region contains many recreation sites important to the Detroit metropolitan area.

Common Plant Life

Michigan is a forest state. What early explorers noted first were the trees. Of the state's 37 million acres of land, 35 million were once forest. All of Europe has only 8 kinds of trees; Michigan has 83. The southern Lower Peninsula differs from the rest of the state in that it is not part of the transitional north woods. It is an area where hardwoods such as oak, hickory, maple, beech, ash, and elm dominate. Of the 83 tree types native to Michigan, 27 are found throughout the state. Thirty-three are abundant only in the southern half, and another dozen, like the paw paw, are considered unusual and are found only in the southernmost counties.

Beginning as early as April, wildflowers blanket the forest floor. The blue hepatica and bloodroot are among the early bloomers. Later, the trillium and yellow-flowered trout-lily bloom. In the summer, common meadow flowers like bergamot, brown-eyed Susan, teasel, chicory, and goldenrod are prominent.

Common Birds and Mammals

In southern Michigan, spring arrives when the state's bird, the robin, arrives. Other birds to look for include the red-winged blackbird, various warblers, eastern bluebird, chickadee, goldfinch, nuthatch, tufted titmouse, junco, tree sparrow, cardinal, blue jay, red-

tailed hawk, marsh hawk, kestrel, turkey vulture, sandhill crane, great blue heron, egret, woodcock, wood duck, mallard, Canada geese, great horned owl, swans, and various shorebirds.

Resident mammals include the white-tailed deer, raccoon, skunk, opossum, woodchuck, cottontail rabbit, red fox, coyote, muskrat, beaver, thirteen-lined ground squirrel, and chipmunk.

Climate

Michigan's south is in a climatic region identified as humid continental hot summer. Humid continental signifies that Michigan is a snow-forest region affected by a continental land mass and is constantly moist with enough precipitation to support trees. Hot summer refers to the warmest summer month, averaging above 71.6 degrees Fahrenheit.

Lake Michigan tempers the climate. A climatic subregion exists one to two counties inland from the lake. In this subregion, called the Fruit Belt, the temperatures are altered by the warm lake waters that cool more slowly than the adjacent land.

The average maximum January temperatures range between 28 and 32 degrees Fahrenheit, while the lows average between 13 and 18 degrees. In July, the average maximum temperatures range from 78 to 84 degrees Fahrenheit, with the lows averaging between 56 and 62 degrees. Annual precipitation ranges from 31 to 39 inches in the southwest to between 28 and 33 inches in the southeast. Annual snowfall totals vary from 93 inches at Muskegon to 29 inches at Ann Arbor. The longest growing season, 187 days, occurs in the southwest, near Benton Harbor.

Best Natural Features

- Three Great Lakes—Michigan, Huron, and Erie
- Sand dunes and sandy beaches along Lake Michigan
- Lake St. Clair
- St. Clair River delta—largest freshwater delta in the country
- Rolling landscape of Irish Hills
- Glacial features—kettles, kames, moraines, and glacial erratics
- Remnant pockets of prairie landscape

34. Sanilac Petroglyphs State Historic Park

- Study the petroglyphs—the only known rock carvings ascribed to prehistoric Native Americans in Michigan.
- Contemplate the history or just enjoy the quiet retreat the park offers.
- Stroll along an interpretive trail that crisscrosses a stream, meanders through forest, and weaves through open meadows.

Park Information

Sanilac Petroglyphs State Historic Park is an historic site that features petroglyphs, or aboriginal rock carvings. Archaeologists estimate that these carvings were chipped into exposed sandstone from 300 to 1,000 years ago. Fires that swept through the region in 1871 and in 1881 cleared the vegetation that had been protecting these impressions in sandstone over the years. Today, a pavilion protects the large slab of sandstone featuring dozens of carvings of animals, animal tracks, birds, and, most prominently, a bowman with arrow. A chain-link fence protects the pavilion.

The Michigan Archaeological Society raised private funds to purchase the 240-acre site; in 1970 it transferred the land to the State of Michigan. Although short on mileage, the 1.3-mile interpretive trail that weaves through the park is long on amenities. Not only does the nature trail educate you on the many historic facets within the park, including petroglyphs, Indian villages, and logging camps, but it also cuts across a branch of the Cass River, weaves through woods and open meadows, and meanders along a stream through rugged, scenic terrain. Beaver dams and animal prints abound along the stream's banks.

The site is rustic, the season and hours are limited, and there are no modern facilities. During the summer a tour guide is available, and the park features special events, such as presentations on Native American folklore and music. Call ahead to see what special events may be scheduled.

Directions: The Sanilac Petroglyphs Historic State Park is in Greenleaf Township about 13 miles south of Bad Axe. Take M-53 to the Bay City-Forestville Road. Head east about 4 miles to Germania Road. Turn south. The park entrance is about a half mile south of this intersection, on the west side of the road.

Hours Open: Hours vary; open from approximately Memorial Day to Labor Day, from 11:30 A.M. to 4:30 P.M., Wednesday through Sunday.

Facilities: Hiking, interpretive trail, and historic features.

Permits and Rules: There is no admission fee. This cultural resource is fragile. Keep off the rock carvings.

Further Information: Michigan Historical Museum, 717 West Allegan Street, Lansing, MI 48918; 517-373-1979.

Other Points of Interest

About 10 miles southwest of the park is the **Cass City Walking Trail**. This rail-trail, or trail created on an abandoned rail corridor, is 1.4 miles long. Open to hiking and cross-country skiing, it also gives access for fishing. For more information, contact the Village Manager at 6737 Church Street, P.O. Box 123, Cass City, MI 49726; 517-972-2911.

To the north, on the shores of Saginaw Bay, is the **Port Crescent State Park** (see park #35), which has camping, white beaches, dunes, and hiking trails. The Pinnebog River flows through the park and on to the bay. A private canoe livery, Tip-A-Thumb Canoe Rental (517-738-7656), rents canoes for leisurely paddling down the river. For more information contact Port Crescent State Park, 1775 Port Austin Road, Port Austin, MI 48467; 517-738-8663.

Located between Caseville and Port Austin, south of M-25 and east of Oak Beach Road on Loosemore Road, is the **Huron County Nature Center Wilderness Arboretum**. This 280-acre nature center has rolling dune ridges and shallow, wet depressions (swales), traversed by an interpretive trail system. Trees, plants, vines, and wildflowers are protected here for scientific and educational purposes. For more information call 1-800-35-THUMB.

The **Albert E. Sleeper State Park,** 5 miles east of Caseville, offers white, sandy beaches, camping and picnicking facilities, and about 4.5 miles of hiking trails. Within it, Ridges Nature Trail has interpretive markers, and a brochure is available for a self-guided tour. A good portion of this park is wild and undeveloped, for those interested in blazing their own trail. For more information contact the Albert E. Sleeper State Park, 6573 State Park Road, Caseville, MI 48725; 517-856-4411.

Petroglyph Park Nature Trail
👢👢

Distance Round-Trip: 1.4 miles

Estimated Hiking Time: 30 minutes to 1 hour

Cautions: Some portions of the trail have roots exposed, others are strewn with rocks and boulders: Watch your step. Parts of the trail may be muddy or flooded. Insect repellent is a must during the warm months. Pick up an interpretive brochure if you want to follow the numbered guide posts around the trail.

Trail Directions: Start at the map board on the west end of parking lot **[1]**. Wind through scrubby trees and into a field of wildflowers with reddish-orange petals and hairy stems. No, the flowers are not Indian paintbrush; they're hawkweed, or the devil's paintbrush. And they're the only devil's paintbrush that the legacy within this park needs: Respect the fragile artwork here and don't add any of your own.

Interpretive stop #1 shows off rocks that have bowl-shaped holes in them (.1 mi.) **[2]**. You'll see many more of these potholes along the trail. Glacial waters scoured the soft sandstones about 12,500 years ago to produce them. Up the trail, the pavilion shades the sandstones that bear the petroglyphs (.2 mi.) **[3]**. On the weathered stones, try to pick out the outlines of human figures, birds, and animal tracks.

Now follow to the right. You soon pass another outcrop of art before post #4 points out a path. A short walk through lush foliage takes you to the river and the remains of an old beaver dam.

Back on the trail, a path merges from the right that leads to more bowl-like impressions. Continue along the main trail, stepping over rocks and blazing through brush that tunnels around the trail. You soon reach marker #5 and more potholes in the rocks. Lichens on many of the rocks look like mint-green and white paint splatters from nature's palette.

The trail swings left through ferns, then you climb over large slabs of bedrock (.4 mi.) **[4]**. Pass marker #6, which exhibits rock carvings made by lumbermen in the 1870s. The trail now flows along a stream.

Fallen trees lie across the stream, and more huge outcrops of bedrock are exposed. Stroll along the stream banks. At .6 mi. cross the wooden footbridge over the stream, hanging on as it swings with your every step **[5]**.

Climb up to marker #7. The park brochure explains the remnants before you and their implications to the logging era. The trail, laden with rock, winds through ferns and young maples, which give way to mature maples and birches as you walk farther. Pass several low-lying depressions. Keep an eye out for animal tracks in the muddy trail.

Pass through a field of ferns, duck under the cover of mixed brush, and arrive at a broken tree that looks like a huge octopus (.7 mi.) **[6]**. Pass through mature maples, cross a boardwalk over a pool, and climb over boulders. Along this last stretch, you pass by what was once a Native American village. A path off to your left leads to a massive bedrock of sandstones; some look like sculptures in an open-air museum (1 mi.) **[7]**.

Cut through the ferns and across more rocks scattered along the trail until you reach marker #9, at a large pine that survived the 1881 fire (1.1 mi.) **[8]**. Another bridge awaits your footsteps to cross back over the stream (1.2 mi.) **[9]**. The rocky trail winds through ferns and maples, then breaks into the open at the pavilion (1.3 mi.) **[3]**. Retrace your steps on the short trail back to the parking lot.

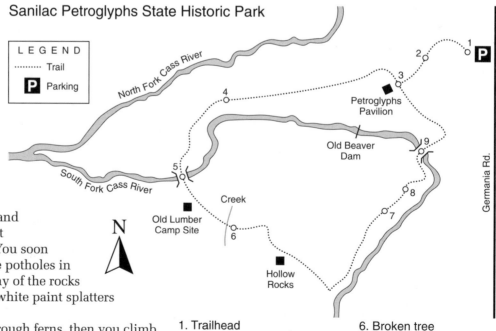

Sanilac Petroglyphs State Historic Park

LEGEND
········· Trail
P Parking

North Fork Cass River

South Fork Cass River

Petroglyphs Pavilion

Old Beaver Dam

Creek

Old Lumber Camp Site

Hollow Rocks

Germania Rd.

N

1. Trailhead
2. Marker #1 and potholes
3. Petroglyphs under pavilion
4. Bedrock
5. Footbridge
6. Broken tree
7. Sandstone sculptures
8. Marker #9 at large pine
9. Footbridge

35. Port Crescent State Park

- Picnic on one of the five decks overlooking Lake Huron.
- Traverse the crest of dunes from a 1,000-foot boardwalk.
- Canoe the winding Pinnebog River.

Park Information

This 565-acre state park gets a thumbs-up. Five picnic decks, interconnected by a 1,000-foot boardwalk, show off almost 3 miles of fine, white sand along the Lake Huron shoreline of Saginaw Bay. Dunes, impressive for the east side of Michigan, roll down to the shore. Additional water frontage is provided by the winding Pinnebog River as it carves the park into two major areas for camping and day use.

The east side of Port Crescent State Park is for camping, and it has individual sites and a campground for organized groups. Here, a 3-mile, figure-eight trail winds over wooded dunes, overlooks scenic viewpoints of Saginaw Bay, and crosses bluffs above the banks of the Pinnebog River. The day-use area on the west side of the park has 3.5 miles of trails over wind-blown dunes, and it features a .75-mile fitness trail with 10 exercise stations. Each of the two major trail systems, one in the camping area and one in the day-use area, has spurs for shorter routes. These spurs cut across from the southern and northern portions of each outer, or main, loop.

Directions: Port Crescent State Park is in the thumb area of Michigan, about 5 miles southwest of Port Austin on M-25.

Hours Open: Open daily from 8:00 A.M. to 10:00 P.M.

Facilities: Hiking, cross-country skiing, swimming, canoeing, fishing, hunting, camping (tent and RV), picnicking, sanitation station, and boat launch.

Permits and Rules: A park fee ($4 daily, $20 annually) is required for each motor vehicle.

Further Information: Port Crescent State Park, 1775 Port Austin Road, Port Austin, MI 48467; 517-738-8663.

Other Points of Interest

For leisurely paddling down the Pinnebog River, rent a canoe at **Tip-A-Thumb Canoe Rental;** 517-738-7656. The livery is located on M-25 at the Pinnebog River Bridge.

Five miles northeast of Caseville on M-25 is **Sleeper State Park,** a heavily forested state park with a half-mile beach on Saginaw Bay. The park features camping, swimming, bicycling, and cross-country skiing plus more than 4 miles of nature trails. The Ridges Nature Trail is an interpretive trail, and a self-guiding brochure helps hikers identify native trees, shrubs, and wildflowers (and describes how the Native Americans used them). For more information contact the Sleeper State Park, 6573 State Park Rd., Caseville, MI 48725; 517-856-4411.

The **Huron County Nature Center Wilderness Arboretum** is 9 miles east of Caseville. This tract with sand ridges and swales offers a network of trails. Enjoy one of the self-guided trails within the park. Take M-25 east from Caseville to Oak Beach Road and turn right to Loosemore Road. Turn left and continue to the park entrance. For more information call the Huron County Nature Center Wilderness Arboretum, 1-800-35-THUMB.

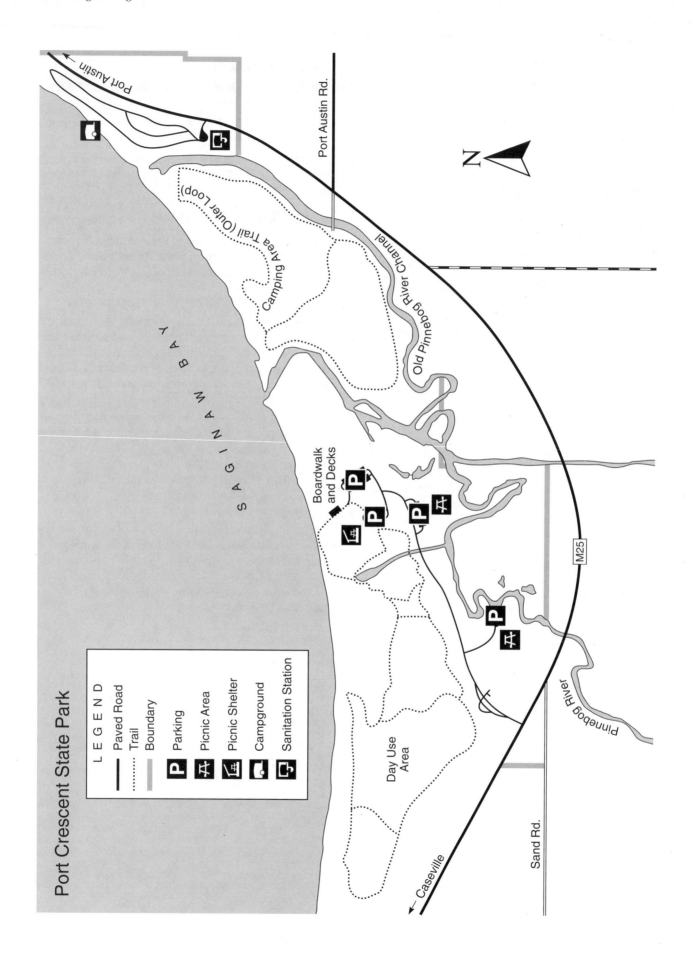

Port Crescent State Park

L E G E N D

Paved Road	—
Trail	··········
Boundary	
P	Parking
Picnic Area	
Picnic Shelter	
Campground	
Sanitation Station	

SAGINAW BAY

Port Austin

Port Austin

Port Austin Rd.

Camping Area Trail (Outer Loop)

Old Pinnebog River Channel

N

Boardwalk and Decks

Day Use Area

Pinnebog River

Caseville

Sand Rd.

M25

Camping Area Trail 👢👢

Distance Round-Trip: 2.1 miles

Estimated Hiking Time: 1 to 1.5 hours

Cautions: Several paths are not part of the official trail. This is especially true in the western portion of the trail. Keep an eye out for directional posts or paint marks on trees. The outer loop is made of two trails; the east side is marked by blue, and the west side is marked by red. Take along insect repellent.

Trail Directions: Start by the iron bridge on the northwest side of M-25, right across from Port Austin Road **[1].** A small lot, located about .3 mi. southwest of the campground entrance, provides a few parking spaces. Another trailhead may be reached from the beach area within the campground.

Head west over the bridge, crossing over the Old Pinnebog River Channel. Just past the bridge is the junction for the trail. Go right and follow along the outer loop, which mostly flows along with the three major water bodies that define this area of the park: Saginaw Bay, Pinnebog River, and Old Pinnebog River Channel. The Old Pinnebog River Channel is the first to accompany you through the canopy of trees along the narrow, gently rolling trail. Listen for splashes in the channel and look for what may be making them. Every so often, a break in the foliage allows you a view of the channel.

Just before you reach .5 mi. you come to a tender scene: A bent, crippled-looking oak tree wraps one of its branches around that of a smaller, younger tree; arm in arm, the youth appears to support the senior **[2].** Soon, the trail begins a gentle ascent, winding to the left. On your left is a post marking the trail's turnoff (.6 mi.) **[3].** You want to turn here, but wait. A few steps ahead, a bench overlooks the channel below. Have a seat—maybe someone will join you. East of this, a spur links the trail with the campground.

Return to the junction and follow the trail through the ravine-like trough in the hardwoods. Corrugated hills covered with trees envelop you as you wind your way. You pass between two large trunks poised tightly on either side of the trail like sentinels guarding their post (.7 mi.) **[4].** The post, with a blue diamond, reassures you that you are on the right trail. Watch for more such posts with blue diamonds as the trail winds again through undulating terrain before veering sharply to the north (right). Soon the trail winds left, and you get a view of Saginaw Bay (.9 mi.) **[5].**

A trail enters from the left. Stay straight, however, and the trail reaches another well-worn path. A right takes you to another overlook of the bay; a bench and another junction mark this spot, which separates the red and blue trails (1 mi.) **[6].** You could shorten your hike by taking a left here to go back to the bridge, but continue as you were walking, along the westerly route, where the trail will veer right. You reach a bluff where you see the bay and, in few more steps, the Pinnebog River spilling into the bay (1.2 mi.) **[7].**

Many paths cut through this area. Watch for red paint marks on the trees. Basically, the trail follows along the ridge over the Pinnebog River. Just before you reach 1.6 mi., a bench is set before the low-lying grasslands of the river valley **[8].** Not far away, a post marks a junction to your left, the trail's southerly turnoff. Turn left here, after you walk the few steps for yet another overview of the river. The trail soon swings east, and you're hiking through woods. When the path gets close to the organization camp, you'll know it—several trails cut through. Just watch ahead for the trees marked red. At 2 mi. the organization camp is visible **[9].** Go toward the camp; soon you'll come back to the iron bridge where you left your vehicle.

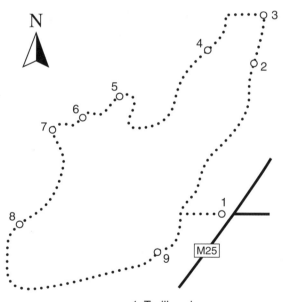

1. Trailhead
2. Supportive tree
3. Channel overlook; trail turnoff
4. Tree sentinels at post
5. Bay overlook
6. Short loop junction
7. Bay and Pinnebog River overlook
8. Bench
9. Organization camp

Day-Use Area Trail 👢👢

Distance Round-Trip: 2.8 miles

Estimated Hiking Time: 1.5 hours

Cautions: Low areas of the trail may flood seasonally or after periods of high rain. Wear appropriate footgear and take care when crossing planked, low areas. Stay on marked trails when you hike in the dunes. Take along insect repellent.

Trail Directions: The trail begins at the fitness trail sign board at the west side of the day-use area's west parking lot **[1]**. Heading right, along the crushed stone of the fitness trail, you reach the first exercise station on a rise overlooking the Pinnebog River Drain (.1 mi.) **[2]**. The trail then swings right, following the drain, providing scenic overlooks of Lake Huron. Descending the dune, you arrive at the 1,000-foot boardwalk that dominates the eastern end of the day-use area (.2 mi.) **[3]**. Continue on past the boardwalk.

At .3 mi. the trail cuts to the right, away from the fitness trail **[4]**. Denoting the hiking trail is a blue, Department of Natural Resources (DNR) triangle attached to a post. Now a hiking trail, the surface is made of natural material, and it guides you through jack pines.

After passing two sections (where the trail is sometimes under water), continue past an old two-track that swings sharply left. The trail now enters a sandy section and makes a hairpin turn to the right, along the backside of a dune (.8 mi.) **[5]**. Be sure to follow the trail markers, as the trail can be hard to spot in the sand. Plow a short distance through the sand, then follow the trail as it cuts left and climbs into a hardwood forest (.9 mi.) **[6]**. Stop to enjoy the view of Lake Huron to your right.

Shortly after you enter the woods, turn left to parallel the Lake Huron shoreline. As you walk through the woods along old beach ridges, the lake is often not visible. You will notice, however, a number of paths to gain access to the lake. At 1.3 mi. the trail swings left, almost reaching the westernmost end of the park **[7]**. As the trail loops back, it runs at an angle to the lake, parallel to M-25. It takes you up and over a series of old dune ridges and down into shallow wet areas, called swales. A boardwalk is located over one such swale (1.6 mi.) **[8]**. Others are bridged with logs. Be careful when crossing; some logs may be loose.

A notable bend in the trail occurs as it swings left, taking you along the backside of a ridge you've already climbed. Watch next for the trail markers at 2 mi. that lead you left (the ones to the right lead you to the gatehouse at the day-use entrance) **[9]**.

At 2.3 mi. the trail leaves the shelter of the woods and snakes its way across an open dune **[10]**. Soon you rejoin the fitness trail for the last leg of your journey (2.5 mi.) **[11]**. If you feel up to it, give stations #6 through #10 a workout. After station #7 you reach the boardwalk over the Pinnebog River Drain, a gentle reminder perhaps of the boardwalk at the beach (2.6 mi.) **[12]**. Grab your trunks and head for the water, after swinging left and returning to the day use parking area.

1. Trailhead
2. Pinnebog River Drain overlook
3. Boardwalk
4. Hiking trail leaves fitness trail
5. Hairpin turn
6. Enter woods; view of Lake Huron
7. Westernmost point of trail
8. Boardwalk
9. Gatehouse
10. Dune
11. Fitness trail
12. Boardwalk

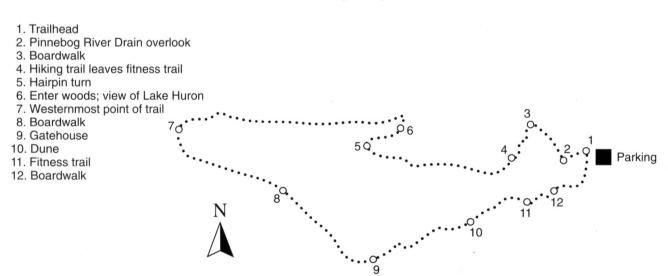

36. William P. Holliday Forest and Wildlife Preserve

- Visit a virgin forest of towering beech, maple, and oak trees.
- Look for signs of deer and other wildlife.
- Enjoy a quiet moment along Tonquish Creek.

Park Information

Established in the late 1950s, this site of 500-plus acres for decades served as southeast Michigan's only dedicated wildlife preserve. The park was a gift to the citizens of Wayne County from the late Arthur J. Richardson in honor of his uncle, William P. Holliday. Wayne County citizens recently came to the support of their parks by passing a millage request, and as a result the William P. Holliday Forest and Wildlife Preserve is to receive a long overdue facelift in 1997. Soon hikers along Tonquish Creek will have marked routes and will be able to cross Tonquish Creek on secure and safe bridges. New signs are planned to welcome them at the entrances, and the Nankin Mills Nature Center will reopen its doors.

The preserve is long and slender, like the creek it hugs. It contains six trails that wind through the varied habitats, including a virgin forest. Not all the trails are marked. Call ahead to check the status of the improvements to the trail network. Then plan to be surprised by the natural beauty preserved here.

Directions: To reach the east trailhead, south of Nankin Mills, exit on Farmington Road from I-96. Head south about 2 miles on Farmington Road to Joy Road. Turn right on Joy Road, and then left to access E.N. Hines Drive. Parking is available at Nankin Mills or in a small dirt lot across the street from the mill.

Hours Open: One-half hour before sunrise to one-half hour after sunset.

Facilities: Hiking and picnicking.

Permits and Rules: There is no admission fee. It is prohibited to possess alcoholic beverages; injure, deface, or disturb any structure; remove any trees, flowers, or natural objects; hunt, trap, or molest animals; have firearms, slingshots, or any other dangerous weapons; dispose of refuse; wander off established roads and trails; and disturb the peace. No pets are allowed. No swimming is allowed. Only pedestrian travel is allowed. Respect that any part of the park may be closed at any time.

Further Information: Wayne County Department of Parks and Recreation, 33175 Ann Arbor Trail, Westland, MI 48185; 313-261-1990.

Other Points of Interest

The east end of the preserve is connected to the **Middle Rouge Parkway**, also known as **Hines Park**. Hines Park has many varied recreational facilities. During the summer, a 6-mile section of Hines Drive is closed to traffic between Ann Arbor Trail and Outer Drive from 9:00 A.M. to 3:30 P.M. on the weekends: During that time the road is the domain of walkers, runners, cyclists, and skaters. For more information contact the Wayne County Department of Parks and Recreation at 313-261-1990.

Two driving tours highlight the mills that Henry Ford converted or established between 1919 and 1944. For information on the **Ford Heritage Trails**, contact the Wayne County Department of Parks and Recreation at 313-261-1990.

You can spend hours walking through the many buildings and artifacts collected at Greenfield Village and Henry Ford Museum. For more information call the Henry Ford Museum and Greenfield Village at 303-271-1620. For 24-hour taped information call 313-271-1976.

Park Trails

Mary Ellsworth Acorn Trail 🥾🥾—1.5 miles—Start this trail across the street from Nankin Mills. It follows the Middle Rouge River and loops through upland oaks.

Wildflower Trail 🥾🥾—1 mile—This unmarked trail starts from the Cowan Road entrance. Park across Cowan Road on the north side of the Service Merchandise parking lot. The trail comes alive with color in the spring.

Pheasant Run Trail 🥾🥾—2 miles—This unmarked trail also starts from the Cowan Road entrance. When bridge improvements are made, this trail will provide a loop along the Tonquish Creek.

William P. Holliday Forest And Wildlife Preserve

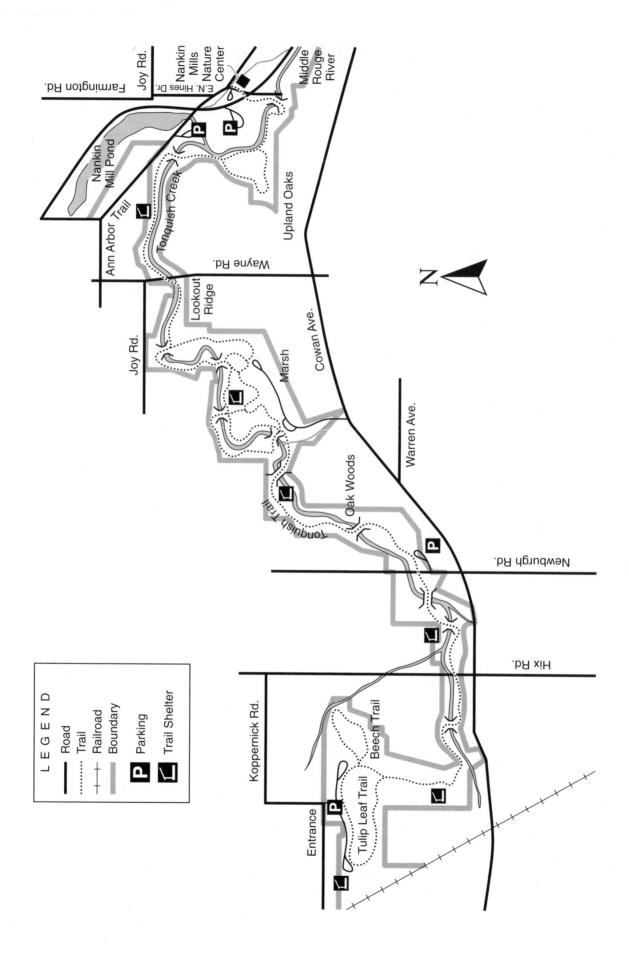

LEGEND

- Road
- Trail
- Railroad
- Boundary
- **P** Parking
- **L** Trail Shelter

Tulip Leaf/Beech Trails 🥾

Distance Round-Trip: 1.9 miles

Estimated Hiking Time: 1 hour

Cautions: The trail may be muddy or have exposed roots. You may have to walk on slippery logs or loose boardwalks. Poison ivy lines the trail. Take insect repellent in warm months.

Trail Directions: Park west of Hix Road on Koppernick Road in the gravel lot on the south side of the road. Start the hike from the southern barricade, heading southwest through something remarkable: a virgin forest with beautiful giants—namely, beeches, maples, and oaks **[1]**.

Follow the wide path that was once used as a drive to the picnic area. Crane your neck at the awesome beeches and maples. You may wonder if you're really in Wayne County. Violets and ferns soften the trail edges, and you marvel at the smooth, smoky-gray bark of the beeches. An occasional oak tree towers above you as well, such as the one to your right at .1 mi. **[2]**. Through the woods, you see residences. Okay, you are in Wayne County—but at least you are in rolling woods, where the massive elders of the woods seem to keep the outside world at bay.

The fork at .3 mi. **[3]** is an old cul-de-sac that led to the now overgrown and rusting picnic shelter. Whichever way you go, the trail winds up at the post for the old trailhead for the Tulip Leaf Trail. Embark on the narrow trail through the forest. Depressional pockets envelop the trail as you continue through the hardwoods, littered in places with fallen comrades (.4 mi.) **[4]**.

Veer left and pass another pocket of civilization. Notice a short stretch of mobile homes through the trees before veering away from them to reenter solitude. Pass more downed trees; large, sinuous vines drape from those that remain standing (.5 mi.)

[5]. Cross logs placed to steady your steps through low-lying wet areas.

The trail veers left, wrapping around a wetland where a tree has been uprooted. The woods are dense; boughs moan. Soon after you reach the junction for the Tonquish Trail (.9 mi.) **[6]**, you pass beech trees—the unfortunate, graffiti-boards of the lovelorn. Their size and smooth bark seem to invite the scarring of initials and hearts. Turn left.

At 1 mi. pass what may become the next fallen giant **[7]**. A gaping hole at the base of this tree makes you wonder how it remains standing. Veer left where ferns soften the turn. A post announces the Beech Trail (1.1 mi.) **[8]**. To your left, posts that once supported a picnic shelter now stand rusting and bare, like the lifeless ghosts of trees.

Turn right into the woods. Sassafras trees with mitten-shaped leaves grow beneath beeches, oaks, and maples. Loop around, pass another junction, and come upon a fence line of twigs. This is your cue that you are approaching a narrow plank to cross over a stream (1.3 mi.) **[9]**.

The trail veers sharply left (1.4 mi.) **[10]**; a stream to your right delineates the forest from commercial properties. Keep rounding the curve as your veiled view through the trees shows residences, then woods. Pass more beech graffiti-boards. Large vines snake over the trail before you cross some logs strewn over the wet-prone trail. Then walk the three-planked footbridge back over the stream (1.6 mi.) **[11]**.

A boardwalk assists you through the wetland. Reeds line the trail, and large vines drape from the canopies like sinuous netting. Brushy foliage closes in on the trail like a tunnel, and you break into the open at 1.7 mi. where restrooms once stood (only a ceramic tile floor remains) **[12]**. From here you can see the ghost of the picnic shelter. Cut over to the wide path and turn right back to the small parking lot (1.9 mi.) **[13]**.

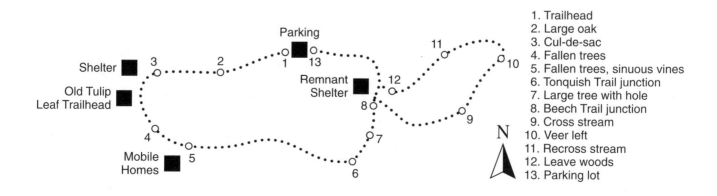

1. Trailhead
2. Large oak
3. Cul-de-sac
4. Fallen trees
5. Fallen trees, sinuous vines
6. Tonquish Trail junction
7. Large tree with hole
8. Beech Trail junction
9. Cross stream
10. Veer left
11. Recross stream
12. Leave woods
13. Parking lot

Tonquish Trail 👢👢👢

Distance One-Way: 5.8 miles

Estimated Hiking Time: 3 to 4 hours

Cautions: The trail is unmarked and rerouted due to nonexistent bridges. Poison ivy is present. Portions may be wet or flooded. Take insect repellent.

Trail Directions: Begin your adventure across the street from Nankin Mills. A brown post at the tree line identifies the starting point **[1]**.

Step into the woods and cross an intact bridge over the Middle Rouge River. Turn right as the trail splits, and teeter along the edge of the river. Walking up and down along the flood plain in the shade of a mix of trees, you pass what looks like an overflow channel at .1 mi. **[2]**. Swing left around a large cottonwood tree and onto a ridge. Continue through upland oaks to an unmarked junction (.2 mi.) **[3]**. Stay right and descend sharply to cross a small feeder stream, passing logs scattered about the flood plain. The trail is confusing here—follow the worn path as best you can.

After .5 mile, the Tonquish Creek merges from the west **[4]**. Veer left to follow the creek and arrive at the metal remains of a bridge at .7 mi. **[5]**. Hang on to the railing as you cross along the edge of the metal frame. Go left after crossing; scramble around a fallen oak tree. Then pass a rotting cottonwood. At 1 mi. you reach a dilapidated trail shelter **[6]**. Swing left at the creek bend, and edge along the eroding bank.

Ahead, vehicles intrude on your solitude as they rush by. Cross beneath the road, then cross the creek on an old bridge that stands in the shadow of its larger replacement (1.3 mi.) **[7]**. Turn right and follow the south side of the creek.

After edging along the creek, climb to walk along Lookout Ridge (1.5 mi.) **[8]**. When you reach the next skeleton bridge, don't cross. Instead, turn left and climb a bluff to hike a section of the Wildflower Trail (1.6 mi.) **[9]**. Stay to the right as the trail splits, high above the creek. As you skirt apartments, the trail splits right and descends through woods.

Go by the crumbling trail shelter, then past a skeleton bridge at 2.2 mi. **[10]** and another at

2.5 mi. **[11]**. Soon, the trail forks (2.6 mi.) **[12]**. Go right and descend to a drain that feeds into the creek. Turn left at the drain and look for a tree you'll use as a bridge to cross it. Then turn right to return to the creek.

Continue your urban trailblazing, crossing a reinforced bank. The trail soon deteriorates. Follow the orange ribbons in tree branches to reach another skeleton bridge (2.9 mi.) **[13]**. Cross carefully and turn left. Follow along the fence until you cross yet another bridge (3.4 mi.) **[14]**.

Proceed past a rundown trail shelter to arrive at a dirt parking lot (3.7 mi.) **[15]**. Follow the gravel drive to cross Newburgh Road. Look for the brown post at the tree line and reenter the woods. Soon, descend sharply and cross a bridge at 3.9 mi. **[16]** and another at 4.2 mi. **[17]**.

Pass a row of pines and teeter along a scenic stretch of the creek. Take a wide left and climb up steps to cross Hix Road (4.4 mi.) **[18]**. Descend into maples, snaking through the woods, to arrive at a bend in the creek. Ahead of you a bridge majestically spans the creek (4.6 mi.) **[19]**. Linger on the bridge before continuing on through aspen and climbing into maple. Swing left to parallel an old fence line, then skirt a field. Pine needles cushion your steps at 4.9 mi. as you turn right into red and white pines **[20]**.

Veer right and enter a mix of oak, hickory, and maple where you pass a moss-covered trail shelter (5.1 mi.) **[21]**. Wind through the majestic virgin beech, maple, and oak to arrive at the Tonquish Trail junction (5.4 mi.) **[22]**. Turn right, and continue through the trees, skirt a rundown shelter (5.6 mi.) **[23]**, and follow an old park drive to the parking area off Koppernick Road (5.8 mi.) **[24]**.

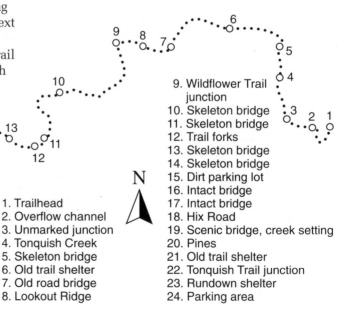

9. Wildflower Trail junction
10. Skeleton bridge
11. Skeleton bridge
12. Trail forks
13. Skeleton bridge
14. Skeleton bridge
15. Dirt parking lot
16. Intact bridge
17. Intact bridge
18. Hix Road
19. Scenic bridge, creek setting
20. Pines
21. Old trail shelter
22. Tonquish Trail junction
23. Rundown shelter
24. Parking area

1. Trailhead
2. Overflow channel
3. Unmarked junction
4. Tonquish Creek
5. Skeleton bridge
6. Old trail shelter
7. Old road bridge
8. Lookout Ridge

N

37. West Bloomfield Woods Nature Preserve

- View great blue herons nesting from a deck overlooking a rookery.
- Hike through the first site in Michigan recognized as an urban wildlife sanctuary.
- Stroll an interpretive trail where trains once rolled.

Park Information

Wandering over steep hills blanketed with oaks and hickories and past lush, wooded wetlands in this 162-acre site, it is hard to believe that you are only 20 miles from downtown Detroit. More amazing are the sights and sounds preserved at the great blue herons' rookery here, a major reason why West Bloomfield Woods Nature Preserve gained recognition as the state's first urban wildlife sanctuary.

A 2.2-mile interpretive trail meanders through the preserve, allowing visitors to seek nature on their own. Brochures, available at the trail kiosk near the preserve's parking lot, direct you to the 16 nature-interpretive sites located along the trail. A .5-mile section of the trail is designed for those with physical disabilities.

The preserve also serves as the western trailhead for the 4.3-mile West Bloomfield Trail Network, which follows the route of the Michigan Air Line Railroad, built in the 1870s. It cuts through several natural and man-made habitats. The trail has a surface of crushed limestone and is lined with 21 interpretive sites; brochures describing them are also available at the kiosk near the parking area.

Directions: From I-696, take Orchard Lake Road north about 6 miles to Pontiac Trail. Turn left and go 1.5 miles to Arrowhead Road. Turn left and go about .5 mile to the preserve entrance.

Hours Open: Open from 8:00 A.M. to sunset daily.

Facilities: Hiking, bicycling, and picknicking.

Permits and Rules: No fee is required. All pets must be on a six-foot leash. Please refrain from smoking. No bicycles or horses are allowed in the preserve, although bicycles are allowed on the rail-trail. No motor vehicles, hunting, weapons, fireworks, golf activity, or alcohol are allowed. Please don't remove plants.

Further Information: West Bloomfield Parks and Recreation, 4640 Walnut Lake Road, West Bloomfield, MI 48323; 810-738-2500.

Other Points of Interest

West of the preserve, along a stretch of the Huron River, is the **Proud Lake Recreation Area**. Eleven miles of hiking trails and 10 miles of bridle paths wander through the park's 3,700-plus acres, which include camping, canoeing, fishing, cross-country skiing, and picnicking facilities. For more information call the Proud Lake Recreation Area at 810-685-2433.

At the tip of a peninsula that extends into Cass Lake is the **Dodge No. 4 State Park,** a popular sandy beach and swimming area though it lacks camping facilities or trails. For more information call Dodge No. 4 State Park at 810-666-1020.

To the northwest lie some 6,000 acres of the **Highland Recreation Area.** Seventeen miles of hiking and bridle trails traverse the hilly terrain. Also available are a riding stable and facilities for camping, fishing, swimming, cross-country skiing, and picnicking. For more information contact the Highland Recreation Area, 5200 E. Highland Road, White Lake, MI 48383; 810-685-2433.

Courtesy of Oakland County Development and Planning Division.

West Bloomfield Woods Nature Preserve

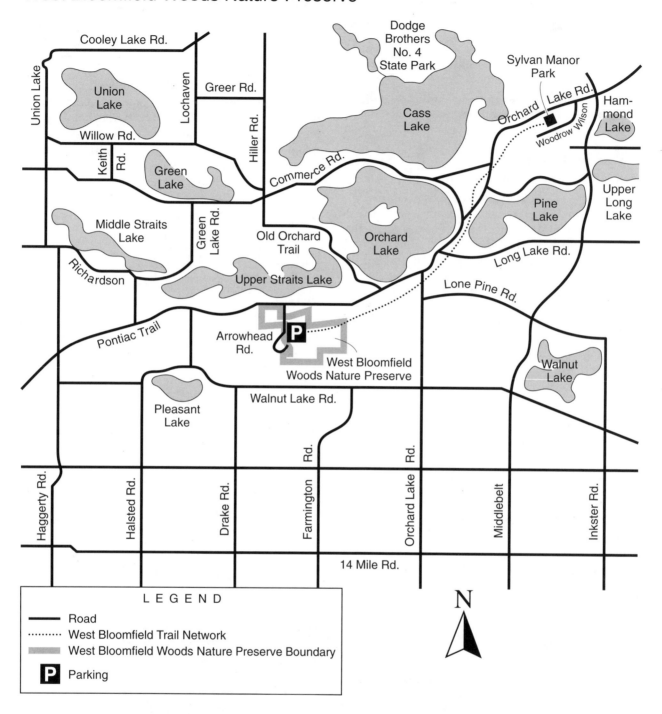

West Bloomfield Woods Nature Preserve Trail 🥾

Distance Round-Trip: 2.2 miles

Estimated Hiking Time: 1 to 1.5 hours

Cautions: Poison ivy lines the trail, so be careful. Take insect repellent in warmer months.

Trail Directions: Start at the information kiosk [1] and pick up an interpretive brochure before heading down the path to soon reach interpretive stop #1. Look carefully at the specimen—poison ivy.

A canopy of trees shades you, a pine-lined ridge accompanies you, and a green pool lies low to your right. Pass a large oak, one of many in this preserve, which has one of the oldest oak stands in southeast Michigan. Get a closer look at the green pool after you reach the junction at .2 mi. [2]. A boardwalk extends to an overlook for the pond; here you can watch and listen to wetland wonders from one of the benches built into the platform.

Continue east, onto wood chips that will soften your steps for almost 2 miles. The trail ascends. On your left, look for a blanket of wildflowers in the spring. Climbing through oaks, hickories, and maples, the trail veers right near post #6 (.3 mi.) [3]. Gently rolling woods envelop the trail.

You reach a junction at .4 mi. [4]. Stay straight, walking through old-growth, oak-hickory forest; past boulders and fallen trees; and down and left, bypassing post #8 and the pond it highlights. Planks keep your feet dry through a wetland. A bench gives you a quiet place to stop, or rest your elbows on the railing of the bridge that crosses a small stream (.7 mi.) [5].

The trail rolls through wooded hills. Round the curve to a green, lush pool (.8 mi.) [6]. Residences stand dignified on a distant hill, a reminder that the preserve is an urban one. Rest on the bench at an overlook and enjoy the vista of the river below, its narrow valley, and the dense cover of trees hugging the slopes (1 mi.) [7]. Pass through spruce trees lining the trail. The single ridge line becomes a terrace briefly; then you descend to a bowl-like depression before ascending to a junction (1.1 mi.) [8]. Straight ahead, you can see a building. A residential neighborhood, well-secluded by the dense cover of the forest, is beyond that. Turn left and wind down over a carpet of red-gold needles. Your descent culminates at the bridge (1.2 mi.) [9].

Pause as you cross over the river. Listen to the water and enjoy the irises and other foliage clumped together like green, feathery islands in the channel. The winding trail climbs before halting at another junction (1.3 mi.) [10]. Turn left and follow the ridge amidst the hardwoods.

Reach post #15 (1.4 mi.) [11], which refers your gaze over the ridge, beyond the trees, to the great blue heron rookery. These elegant birds have a haunting beauty, silhouetted in the trees with their scraggly nests. You won't see them from here, though, although you might hear their squawks in the springtime.

At 1.6 mi. a bench lets you contemplate the hill; the interpretive brochure informs you that this hill, a moraine, was shaped by mile-high ice [12]. This loop of the trail comes full circle just after 1.7 mi. [13]. Head right, retracing your steps to the pond overlook (1.9 mi.) [2]. Make the hairpin turn right and climb up and around to the West Bloomfield Trail Network (2 mi.) [14]. If you want, follow the line about .3 mi. to the right to reach the great blue heron rookery.

Otherwise, keep straight to walk through second-growth trees—quite a contrast to the old-growth forest you just exited. Wind around; the trees and brush gradually thin out, acclimating you to urban reality before you reach the parking lot at 2.2 mi.

1. Trailhead
2. Junction at overlook
3. Post #6
4. Junction
5. Bridge
6. Bench near pool
7. Overlook river
8. Junction
9. Bridge
10. Junction
11. Post #15
12. Bench, moraine
13. Trail junction
14. West Bloomfield Trail Network

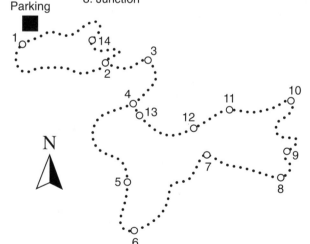

West Bloomfield Trail Network 🥾

Distance One-Way: 4.3 miles

Estimated Hiking Time: 1.5 to 2 hours

Cautions: The trail crosses busy Orchard Lake Road three times. A linear trail, you may turn around at any point to make this as short or long a distance (up to 8.6 miles) as you want. If you only want a one-way hike, secure your transportation at the end.

Trail Directions: Start at the trail kiosk on the south side of the parking area for the West Bloomfield Woods Nature Preserve **[1]**. An alternative starting point is the Sylvan Manor Park on Woodrow Wilson, south of Orchard Lake Road **[13]**. There are 21 interpretive sites along this former railroad corridor. Pick up a guide to the sites at the kiosk and head down the crushed-limestone path. Imagine a time when trains thundered along this corridor. Is that really a train whistle you hear in the distance?

Chug up the slight grade, noting the nature preserve on your right. Picking up speed, pass the first four interpretive sites and the junction with the nature trail at .1 mi. **[2]**. Stop at the decked overlook of the great blue heron rookery (.4 mi.) **[3]**. Spring is a time of great activity here.

Back on the line, pass the stand of spruces that helps buffer the rookery. Standing like a tombstone is a replica of a railroad mile-marker, set before you cross a local road (.6 mi.) **[4]**. This one is marked W.B. 42, representing the mileage to what used to be the terminal.

You soon reach a land bridge through a wet area (.9 mi.) **[5]**. Look for a blue heron standing along the edge of the wetland, waiting patiently to strike its prey. The trail crosses a dirt road and takes you under vegetation, reclaiming the air space over the old rail corridor. At about 1.2 mi. the trail skirts an aqua-green pond surrounded by palatial homes **[6]**. On your right, look for Canada geese on the lawn around a tennis court. Pass another tombstone (W.B. 41) before you reach the urban corridor along Orchard Lake Road (1.8 mi.) **[7]**. Jog left to cross at the light.

Beyond the urban corridor, the rail-trail becomes a land bridge and then seems to sink below grade as you approach a culvert tunnel (2.3 mi.) **[8]**. Listen to your footsteps echoing with metallic pings as you crunch through this safe passage under Long Lake Road. New human habitat is being developed on your

left. You see it at 2.5 mi., when you exit the tunnel and proceed to an area with an overlook deck on both sides **[9]**. To your left, in addition to the traffic whizzing by, you overlook a small wetland with Orchard Lake in the distance. On the right, a large cattail marsh sprawls out between you and Pine Lake.

Cross Orchard Lake Road for the second time and pass your third tombstone (W.B. 40) at 2.6 mi. **[10]**. Pass a ball field before crossing a dirt road and skirting the grounds of St. Mary's College. Arrive at Orchard Lake Road for your third, and last, crossing (3.4 mi.) **[11]**.

Grass now borders the trail; the green widens at the golf course. The corridor opens up on the left for a play lot and picnic area. Farther on is a bench. Press on and reach the last tombstone, W.B 39 (3.6 mi.) **[12]**. Pass another playground, then enter a tunnel of trees (4 mi.) **[13]**. The canopy opens, and the trail takes you behind a small commercial area. Swing right to avoid hiking down a section of the rail line that still operates. So, that really was a train whistle you heard in the distance.

This is the end of the line: Sylvan Manor Park (4.3 mi.) **[14]**. If you left a second car or made arrangements to get picked up here, your hike is over. If not, put your engine in reverse and head back to the nature preserve.

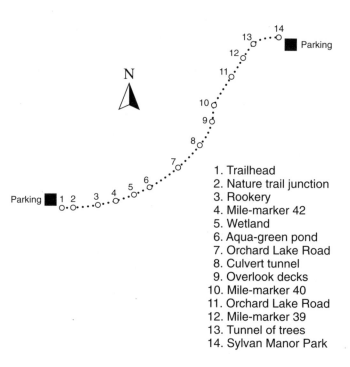

1. Trailhead
2. Nature trail junction
3. Rookery
4. Mile-marker 42
5. Wetland
6. Aqua-green pond
7. Orchard Lake Road
8. Culvert tunnel
9. Overlook decks
10. Mile-marker 40
11. Orchard Lake Road
12. Mile-marker 39
13. Tunnel of trees
14. Sylvan Manor Park

38. Indian Springs Metropark

- Visit the Huron Swamp—headwaters of the Huron River.
- Wind along a boardwalk through the swamp and past towering maple trees.
- Look for, and look out for, Michigan's only poisonous snake—the massasauga.

Park Information

One of 13 metroparks under the administration of the Huron-Clinton Metropolitan Authority, this 2,224-acre park stands out from the rest in that a large portion of it is dedicated to preserving and interpreting one of southeast Michigan's last great natural areas—the Huron Swamp. From the Huron Swamp flow the headwaters of the Huron River.

The solar-heated Nature Center at the park offers displays, exhibits, and programs that help to explain this unique wetland environment. Live and mounted pond creatures are featured. Park naturalists are on hand. Stop by and pick up maps or information about the services provided. The Center is the focal point for the three nature trails. Six miles of trails weave through swamps, meadows, fields, and woodlands, offering hikers an intimate experience with the area.

Additional features at Indian Springs Metropark include an 18-hole public golf course, picnic facilities with grills and shelters, and an 8-mile, barrier-free hike/bike trail for exploring the greater expanses of this exceptional environment. The Meadowlark picnic area within the park has a baseball diamond, a volleyball court, and a timber tot-lot.

In the winter, cross-country ski trails lace over the golf course or cut over select trails. On the weekends, ski rental equipment and food are available at the ski center located on the golf course. The Nature Center has a parking lot for sledding.

Directions: The park is about 9 miles northwest of Pontiac. From M-59, take Teggerdine Road north about 3 miles to White Lake Road. Head west for a little more than a mile to the entrance.

Hours Open: The park is open from 8:00 A.M. to 10:00 P.M. during the summer; at other times it is open from 8:00 A.M. to 8:00 P.M. The trails are open from daylight until dusk. Hours at the Nature Center are 10:00 A.M. to 5:00 P.M. daily during the summer. During the school year, it is open from 1:00 to 5:00 P.M. weekdays and from 10:00 A.M. to 5:00 P.M. on weekends.

Facilities: Hiking, bicycling, picnicking, golfing, cross-country skiing, sledding, and interpretive center.

Permits and Rules: A motor vehicle permit is required. A daily pass is $2 on weekdays and $3 on weekends and holidays. Wednesdays are free. Annual passes are $15. Please preserve property and natural resources. Adhere to posted regulations. If kept on a leash, pets are allowed in the park except at nature areas. Motor vehicles are allowed only on designated park roads and parking areas. Please remain on the nature trails when hiking them and picnic only at designated sites. Bicycles, horses, and motorized vehicles are not allowed on the nature trails. Leave natural things where they are.

Further Information: Contact Indian Springs Metropark, 5200 Indian Trail, White Lake, MI 48386; 810-625-7280. For information on all the metroparks, contact Huron-Clinton Metropolitan Authority, 13000 High Ridge Drive, P.O. Box 2001, Brighton, MI 48116-8001; 313-227-2757 or 800-477-2757.

Other Points of Interest

Just south of Indian Springs, and adjacent to it, **Pontiac Lake Recreation Area** opens up almost 4,000 recreation-packed acres for bicycling, hiking, horseback riding, fishing, hunting, swimming, and camping. For more information, contact Pontiac Lake Recreation Area, 7800 Gale Road, Waterford, MI 48327; 810-666-1020.

About 5 miles southwest lies the **Highland Recreation Area,** which has over 6,000 acres. Seventeen miles of hiking and bridle trails traverse the hilly terrain. Also available are camping, fishing, swimming, cross-country skiing, a riding stable, and picnicking facilities. For more information, contact Highland Recreation Area, 5200 East Highland Road, White Lake, MI 48383; 810-685-2433.

Park Trails

Pondside Trail 👢 —3 miles—This trail starts behind the Nature Center. The hard-surfaced trail loops around a pond. Benches allow visitors to sit and enjoy the setting.

Indian Springs Metropark

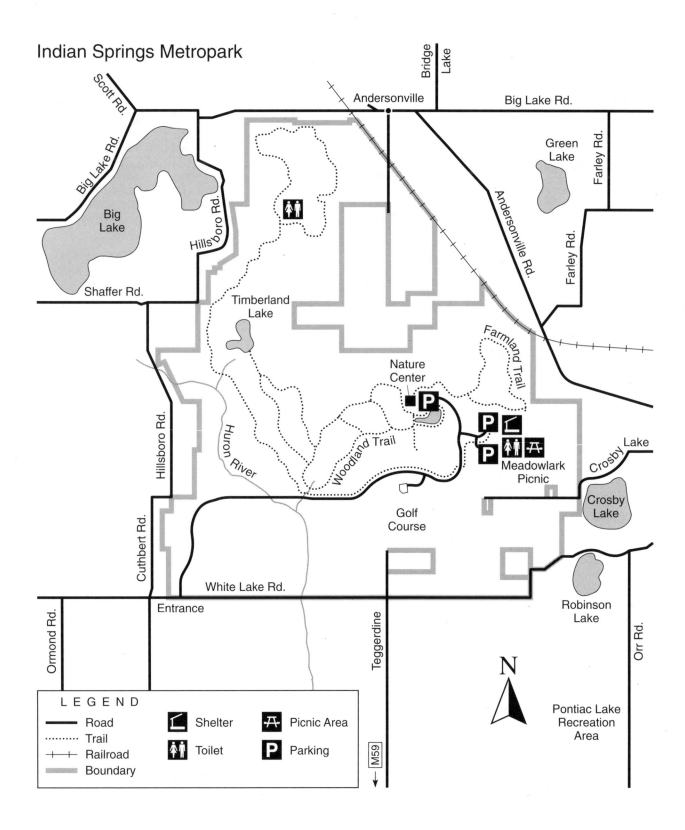

LEGEND

Road	
Trail	
Railroad	
Boundary	

Shelter
Toilet

Picnic Area
Parking

Woodland Trail 🥾

Distance Round-Trip: 3.7 miles

Estimated Hiking Time: 1.5 to 2 hours

Cautions: Bog mats will not support you; stay on the boardwalks. Wet environments are home to the only type of poisonous snake Michigan has—the massasauga. If you see one, leave this small, shy rattler alone. Take insect repellent.

Trail Directions: Start from behind the Nature Center **[1]**. Head west. The asphalt trail soon becomes a mowed swath through a meadow; then it goes under a canopy of trees.

An interpretive sign identifies the scraggly-looking conifer with eyelash starbursts of needles as a tamarack. This serves as a sentinel posted at the bridge. Cross over the Huron River, which is streamlike here at its headwaters (.1 mi.) **[2]**. The bridge evolves into a boardwalk.

A series of boardwalks takes you through luxuriant foliage and past green logs, softened with moss, that lie atop corrugated rollings of soil—the effects of the uprooting of trees, nature's way of plowing. More boardwalks carry you through the swamp. You reach the junction for the Crosscut Shortcut at .4 mi. **[3]**. Stay to the right. Sweet woodruff along the trail alerts you that you are in for a treat. High above you, the canopy is thick.

Pass Hunter's Ridge Shortcut (.6 mi.) **[4]** and cross between two pools littered with logs, grassy clumps, and green algae. The next stretch of trail alone is worth the hike. Tall stately trunks stretch high above you, silhouettes against the lighter greens of foliage in the background (.7 mi.) **[5]**. Maples. Huge. Impressive.

Wind through more pools and reach the Sawmill Shortcut at .8 mi. **[6]**. Stay to the right, curving around a boardwalk that makes a U-turn through the reeds and pools it crosses. Sinuous turns take you under impressive beech and maple trees and then over a boardwalk that wraps itself around a pool. Boardwalks lace through the wetland; one curves around to the junction for the Timberland Lake Walk (1.5 mi.) **[7]**.

Follow the curving boardwalk through lush foliage that hugs its sides. You see the small, intimate lake up ahead as you follow the boardwalk over a bog. The boardwalk becomes an overlook with benches at the lake's edge (1.6 mi.) **[8]**.

On the main trail, wind around onto a crescent-shaped boardwalk. Pass through woods, small clearings, and pools. At 2.1 mi., a bench announces the beginning of a long, S-shaped boardwalk that crosses a particularly large swampy area **[9]**. More boardwalks await you.

Large maples again grace you before you reach the Sawmill Shortcut junction (2.3 mi.) **[10]**. Turn right. Youthful growth follows; sumacs and grassy areas are prevalent. Near the bench at 2.4 mi., an interpretive sign points out a firebreak, a remnant from a fire that passed through in the late 1930s **[11]**.

Wind along and cross a footbridge over the Huron River; you soon walk under a canopy of mature trees (2.6 mi.) **[12]**. At 2.9 mi., a bench overlooks a small meadow **[13]**.

Cross the Hunter's Ridge Shortcut junction (3 mi.) **[14]**, passing through second-growth trees. More grasses and reeds envelop you, and then you pass the Crosscut Shortcut junction (3.2 mi.) **[15]**. The trail is now a mowed path; you see the hill you are about to climb. At the hill's junction (3.3 mi.) **[16]**, head up the mowed swath to reach the top (3.4 mi.) **[17]**, where you get a panoramic view of the park, its golf course, and the woods you just left. Enjoy the scene before heading down, passing the Pondside Trail, and arriving at the intersection of trails where you started.

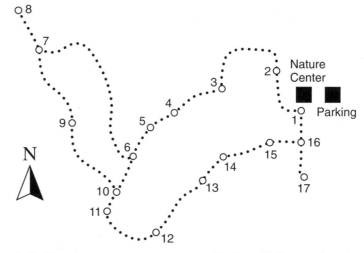

1. Trailhead
2. Bridge
3. Crosscut Shortcut junction
4. Hunter's Ridge Shortcut junction
5. Maples
6. Sawmill Shortcut junction
7. Timberland Lake Walk junction
8. Timberland Lake
9. Boardwalk
10. Sawmill Shortcut junction
11. Bench
12. Mature trees
13. Bench
14. Hunter's Ridge Shortcut junction
15. Crosscut Shortcut junction
16. Hill junction
17. Hill overlook

Farmland Trail 👢👢

Distance Round-Trip: 1.6 miles

Estimated Hiking Time: 30 minutes to 1 hour

Cautions: The park is home to the massasauga rattlesnake. Leave this small, shy snake alone. Poison ivy is along the trail. Be careful. Use insect repellent in warm months of the year.

Trail Directions: This interpretive trail starts at a map board near a shelter at the north end of the Nature Center parking lot [1]. Head east between the park driveway and a wetland.

After descending slightly, veer left, pass a large oak, and enter a fencerow of trees, where field stones are stacked to create a small wall. Ascending, you cut through an old fence line, the first of many you cross, before winding left to walk along an old drive. Along this trail you pass a number of temporary interpretive markers, like the one on the red squirrel. These markers change with the seasons and help you better understand the environment you are walking through.

The trail veers right to skirt the edge of a forest. Walking along the forest boundary, you make a wide left, pass an erratic (a boulder transported by a glacier) (.2 mi.) [2], and descend sharply around a wetland burrowed in among the trees.

Undulating along the transition area between forest and field, you cut through shrubs and skirt past blackberry, aspen, and gray dogwood. Then, cross a land bridge between two wetlands before climbing to a junction (.4 mi.) [3]. Stay left to hike the loop in a clockwise direction.

Following an old fence line, jog right and enter a field of goldenrod. A bench allows you to sit and enjoy the golden moment, and provides a base from which to identify the three types of goldenrod found here.

Cross the field; then cut through mixed hardwoods to reach a larger field. Just when you think you are about to cross the field, turn left to stay along the edge of forest and field. Don't sit down on that mound to your right. The ants won't appreciate it. Besides, after you make the right turn, pass more ant mounds, and stop to investigate a rusting piece of farm equipment, you arrive at a bench under a pine tree (.6 mi.) [4].

Pass more ant mounds, peer down a chipmunk burrow, and then turn right and cut through gray dogwood after passing even more ant mounds. The trail swings right, skirting a wetland, and takes you to a bench shaded by a green canopy (.8 mi.) [5].

Soon walk through youthful trees and brush. Near the sensitive fern interpretive stop, thoughtfully cross a small drain. At 1 mi., a bench is situated to overlook a field to the southwest [6]. Beyond this, discover an old plow. Then walk along a line of old oaks that witnessed the work of a relic farm implement when it was in its prime.

The trail makes a sharp right, crossing the fence line of large trees and field stones, to arrive at another collection of retired farm equipment (1.1 mi.) [7]. Roll with the landscape and veer left to cross a fallow field. Unlike the implements, keep plowing on. You don't want to rust like this fourth collection of farm equipment (1.2 mi.) [8]. Do have a seat on the bench, though, and watch for red-tailed hawks to circle overhead.

From here you have only to descend into some youthful trees and shrubs, cross another old fence line, and step past the bracken fern to arrive back at the junction that closes the loop. Turn left and retrace your steps along the transition area to the Nature Center.

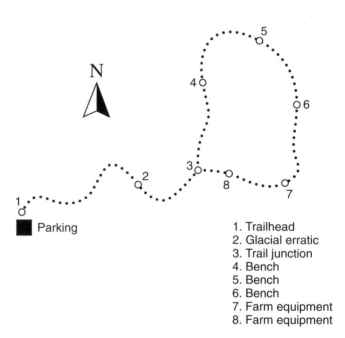

■ Parking

1. Trailhead
2. Glacial erratic
3. Trail junction
4. Bench
5. Bench
6. Bench
7. Farm equipment
8. Farm equipment

39. For-Mar Nature Preserve and Arboretum

- View live reptiles housed in the new Interpretive Center.
- Visit an Audubon bird exhibit with over 600 specimens.
- Hike the scenic and varied terrain along Kearsley Creek.

Park Information

About 380 acres, stitched together in a patchwork of woodlands, restored prairies, open fields, meadows, ponds, edges, and the Kearsley Creek, provide the main ingredients for the preserve. An arboretum, taking up about 100 of the acres, is planted with interesting trees, shrubs, and vines cultivated for the park. Seven miles of hiking trails weave through the diverse habitat. The preserve is named in recognition of the previous owners, Forbes and Martha Merkely.

In October of 1996, a new Interpretive Center had its official dedication. Interpretive programs, displays, live animals and reptiles, bird-viewing areas, and educational programs are offered. An Audubon bird exhibit, the Corydon E. Foote Bird Collection, contains more than 600 mounted birds that can be seen at limited viewing times. The exhibit building is located off Genesee Road north of the main entry.

Directions: The park is about 1 mile east of Flint. From I-75, head east on I-69 about 7 miles to Belsay Road. Take this north about 1 mile to Davison; then turn west for 1 mile to Genesee Road. Go north for about .2 miles. The main entry for most of the trails and for the new Interpretive Center is located here, on the east side of Genesee Road. The entrance for the bird exhibit is about .2 miles further north of this entrance.

Hours Open: The preserve is open from 8:00 A.M. until sunset. The Interpretive Center discretionally opens six days a week from 8:00 A.M. to 5:00 P.M. The staff are there then, but the hours are not guaranteed. Staff may be in the field with a group. To make sure someone will be there, please call ahead if you wish to visit. Hours for the bird exhibit are limited to Sundays from 1:30 to 4:30 P.M. from June through August. The rest of the year, the exhibit is open from 1:30 to 4:30 P.M.. on the first Sunday of every month.

Facilities: Hiking and interpretive center.

Permits and Rules: There is no fee at this Genesee County park. Please stay on the trails and leave pets, radios, and toys at home. Don't smoke, jog, or bicycle on the trails, and don't disturb plants or animals within the preserve.

Further Information: Contact For-Mar Nature Preserve and Arboretum, 2142 North Genesee Road, Burton, MI 48509-1209; 810-789-8567. You may also call Genesee County Parks at 810-736-7100.

Other Points of Interest

For a trip to the past, visit another Genesee County Park—**Crossroads Village** and **Huckleberry Railroad.** Crossroads Village offers a collection of 30 historic structures that, with the help of costumed interpreters, recreate the small-town days of early Michigan, circa 1860. Huckleberry Railroad leaves the Crossroads Depot for 35-minute excursions. The train, powered by an historic Baldwin steam locomotive, carries up to 500 passengers. Also featured in the park are rides on a 1910 ferris wheel and a 1912 carousel.

Hours and special programs for the Genesee County park vary. For fees, hours, and other information, call Genesee County Parks at 810-736-7100 or 800-648-PARK.

Park Trails

The 7 miles of trails form an intricate web of loops that are made up of wood-chipped paths, mowed swaths through grasses, service roads, and naturally beaten-down tracks. They are so interconnected that you may combine them any number of ways. All are relatively easy. Each individually is less than .5 mile in length.

A few of the trails are named. Their names generally reflect what they pass through: Ground Water Pond Trail, Young Woods Trail, Succession Trail, Hawthorn Trail, Edge of Woods Trail, Woodlot Trail (hazel trees), and Sugar Bush Trail. Several other trails have no names. Variations of the trails circle ponds, meander along Kearsley Creek, cross wooden suspension bridges, or cut through woods, wetlands, or prairies.

For-Mar Nature Preserve and Arboretum

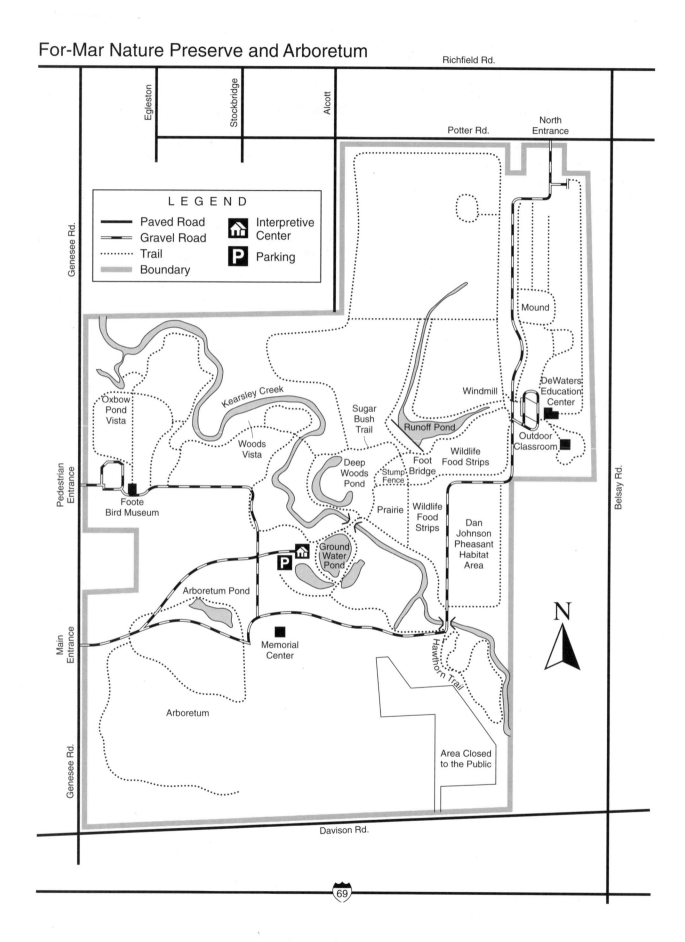

Ground Water Pond and Hawthorn Trail 🥾

Distance Round-Trip: 1.2 miles

Estimated Hiking Time: 30 minutes to 1 hour

Cautions: Poison ivy lines the trail and winds up into trees. Take insect repellent.

Trail Directions: Start from the east side of the Interpretive Center on the Ground Water Pond Trail **[1]**. The Interpretive Center is the focal point for many of the trails. Pass a black locust tree, the one with many small oval leaves drooping from one stalk. In the spring its fragrant flowers perfume the air.

Almost immediately, you reach a circle of benches. Behind them is the Ground Water Pond. The Hawthorn Trail goes right, past briers flowing down the bounds of the trail like prickly veils, and then through a blockade of trees. The grassy trail passes between two ponds. A bright green cover of algae shields the pond on the right. On your left, the pool is clear; plumes of grasslike reeds clump in islands. Watch for waterfowl making *V*s in the water.

The ponds end at a circle of grass (.1 mi.) **[2]**. Leave the Ground Water Pond Trail by cutting to the open field to the right. Turn left along the mowed swath that flanks the low-lying, grasslike wetland on your left. Grasses in the field stretch out on your right.

The trail wraps around the wetland, winding past goldenrod and shrubs, then approaches an edge of trees before reaching a service road (.2 mi.) **[3]**. Turn left. This serves as your trail.

Woods edge the trail on your left; a field of grasses and goldenrod stretches out on your right. Multiple trail choices await you at the end of the road (.3 mi.) **[4]**. The Hawthorn Trail is the grassy trail that cuts through shrubby growth at the end of the road. It takes you up for a sneak preview of Kearsley Creek, then winds down to the junction for the trail's loop (.4 mi.) **[5]**. Turn left here, cross a streambed, and then follow the loop to the right. A ridge rises tall and strong along the narrow channel, like a fortress wall that encloses this preserve; the trail follows along its bounds. A lone house sits high on the ridge (.5 mi.) **[6]**. Untamed roses, long and spindly, weave their own wall along the trail.

Soon the trail curves north, and you meet the creek that will follow along with you. A concrete culvert parallels the creek, ducking under a mound of earth to form another kind of ridge.

At .6 mi., the trail bends left **[7]**. The creek is in full view. Here, the corrugated spine of the culvert spills its contents into the creek. Now stroll with the creek flowing at your side before you wind back along the trail to close the loop. Head out onto the service road, where you turn right toward the bridge. Pass the intersection of trails **[4]**, and then step onto the wood planks to cross Kearsley Creek (.8 mi.).

Soon after you cross you reach an open prairie. Take the trail on your left that skirts through the trees edging along the creek. A prairie opens up to the north. You pass a mowed path that follows through it. Continue straight through a tunnel of trees and reach another junction (1 mi.) **[8]**.

Turn left and soon reach another junction. Follow left near the creek; the trail wraps around a large oak and then directs you to a wooden suspension bridge. Hold on to the railing; the arched bridge sways and wobbles as you cross over the water.

In a few steps you reach Ground Water Pond. Follow the north side of the pond and wind up to the circle of benches. From here, retrace your steps back to the Interpretive Center.

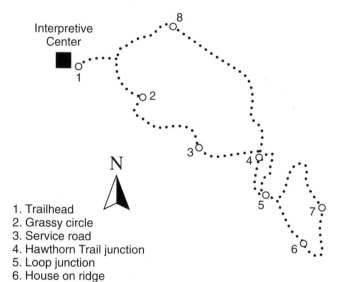

1. Trailhead
2. Grassy circle
3. Service road
4. Hawthorn Trail junction
5. Loop junction
6. House on ridge
7. Veer left
8. Trail junction

Ground Water Pond and Sugar Bush Trail 👢👢

Distance Round-Trip: .7 mile

Estimated Hiking Time: 30 minutes

Cautions: Sections of this trail are prone to be flooded or muddy. Wear appropriate footgear. Insects can be a problem in the warmer months. Take along insect repellent.

Trail Directions: Start from the east side of the Interpretive Center where a sign announces the Ground Water Pond Trail **[1].** Go past the sign and check out the bird feeders on your left. You can get an even better perspective from the viewing room in the Interpretive Center, but save that for later. The trail takes you to a circle of benches in a small grassy opening. Stay to the left under a canopy of trees and descend onto a ridge above Ground Water Pond.

You soon arrive at an observation dock that allows you to investigate the environment surrounding the murky brown waters of the pond. Keep an eye out for ducks, frogs, kingfishers, and other local residents that might be making a fuss over your presence.

Turn left at the dock and enter the woods to arrive at a pedestrian suspension bridge over Kearsley Creek (.1 mi.) **[2].** Hold on to the railing as the arched bridge bounces with your every step as you cross to the other side. Back on solid ground, turn left at the trail junction to parallel the creek. Pass an old stone barbecue that looks out of place among the ferns and horsetail; then walk up to the edge of the calm, algae-covered Deep Woods Pond. It offers a stark contrast to the flowing waters of the creek just a few feet away.

Snake between the creek and pond, ducking under vine-draped trees, and arrive at another junction (.2 mi.) **[3].** Turn right and cross an old bridge. Watch your step, both on and off the bridge and also as you wind around the small pools nestled here on the forest floor.

Pass an odd, casket-shaped, cement structure near a large oak. Don't worry. No one is missing. This structure was used back in the days when maple syrup was made from the sugar bush—the maple. Soon you arrive at a viewing platform on Deep Woods Pond. Have a seat on the bench and enjoy the unique setting.

Farther on, walk past a mature oak with a hollow trunk. You wouldn't want to stand under this hollow tree on a windy day. Reach the junction (.3 mi.) **[4]** just past a sign that announces the Sugar Bush Trail. Turn right, pass a bench, and start to climb up a ridge.

You reach another junction before you reach the top of your climb. Stay right and skirt an old field on your left. Descend through small trees and shrubs, where the trail becomes grassy. Pass another junction and descend to cross over a small creek on a footbridge (.4 mi.) **[5].**

Stay right as the trail splits, and hike through brush and small trees until you pass yet another junction. This one is near a stump fence. Follow along the old tree stumps and begin to descend along the edge of a bluff overlooking Deep Woods Pond (.5 mi.) **[6].** The ridge is lined with large oak and beech trees.

Railroad ties edge the bluff, and you descend past rustic log benches. Soon, reach another trail junction, turn right past an erratic—a boulder transported by a glacier—and then cut between a large oak and another erratic to arrive back at the pedestrian suspension bridge (.6 mi.) **[2].** Cross the bucking-bronco bridge and retrace your steps back to the Interpretive Center. Stop in at the Center and get a closer look from the viewing room at the birds that may be feeding outside. Or you can wander through the building studying the displays and exhibits on hand.

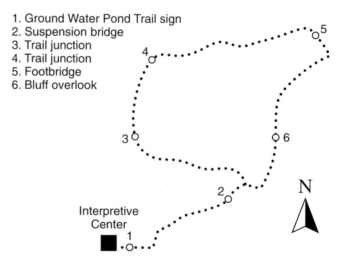

1. Ground Water Pond Trail sign
2. Suspension bridge
3. Trail junction
4. Trail junction
5. Footbridge
6. Bluff overlook

40. Parker Mill Park

- Tour a restored 19th-century gristmill.
- Walk the boardwalk along scenic Fleming Creek.
- Observe wildlife from a blind along the Huron River.

Park Information

Located along Fleming Creek just above the confluence with the Huron River, this Washtenaw County park preserves 44 acres of the original 1863 Parker family homestead. The county owns 26 acres, which include historic Parker Mill, the old millpond site, Fleming Creek forestlands, and a remnant tract of prairie-fen habitat. The remaining 18 acres, formerly known as Forest Park, are on permanent lease from the City of Ann Arbor. This parcel provides access to the Huron River.

The renovated gristmill, which began operation in 1873, is one of the oldest surviving sites in Washtenaw County. The mill is open for tours on weekends, but the hours are limited. Call ahead to confirm.

For day hikers, the park includes the recently completed Hoyt G. Post Trail, a barrier-free boardwalk trail complete with wheelchair curbs and state-of-the-art self-guided interpretive stations. There is a second, shorter trail called the Sugarbush. An asphalt trail that accommodates bikers, skaters, and joggers connects the park with Ann Arbor's Gallup Park along the Huron River.

Directions: From US-23, east of Ann Arbor, take Geddes Road east just past Dixboro Road. The park is located on the south side of Geddes Road.

Hours Open: The park hours are 7:00 A.M. to 8:00 P.M. from May through September, and 7:00 A.M. to 6:00 P.M. from October through April. The mill is open from 1:00 P.M. to 3:00 P.M. on Saturdays and Sundays. Call ahead to confirm.

Facilities: Hiking, bicycling, fishing, picnicking, interpretive trail, and historic site.

Permits and Rules: There is no admittance fee. Not permitted are fires, wading or swimming, picking or removing plants or animals, fishing except in designated areas, skateboards, alcohol, and hunting. Dogs, jogging, and bicycling are prohibited on Hoyt G. Post Trail. Elsewhere in the park, dogs must be on a leash. Pets, food, and smoking are prohibited in the buildings.

Further Information: Contact Washtenaw County Parks and Recreation Commission, 2960 Washtenaw Avenue, Ann Arbor, MI 48104; 313-971-6337.

Other Points of Interest

North of the park, on Dixboro Road, is **Matthaei Botanical Gardens.** In addition to a greenhouse with desert, temperate, and tropical rooms, the facility has four main trails. Ranging in length from .6 mile to 1.8 miles, the trails pass through marsh, prairie, and forest. For more information, call the Matthaei Botanical Gardens at 313-998-7061.

Just west of the park is Ann Arbor's **Gallup Park.** It has several loop and point-to-point trails including the Gallup Park Trail, which is a designated national recreation trail. Additional facilities include bike, paddleboat, and canoe rentals; picnic shelters; meeting building; boat launch; playgrounds; and interpretive displays. Adjacent to Gallup Park is a 48-acre natural area called **Furstenberg Park.** It features the most diverse flora of any park in the city. For more information, call the City of Ann Arbor, Department of Parks and Recreation, 313-994-2780.

West of Gallup Park is the 123-acre **Nichols Arboretum.** Maintained by the University of Michigan, the site features over 500 species of trees and plants and also offers scenic trails for walking and nature study. For a map, call the Ann Arbor Convention and Visitors Bureau at 313-995-7281.

North of Matthaei Botanical Gardens is the 87-acre **Marshall Park.** One of the wilder parks in the area, it includes a meadow, pine stands, and virgin oak/hickory forest. The trail that loops through the park is not clearly marked, so take a compass. For more information, call the Ann Arbor Department of Parks and Recreation at 313-994-2780.

Park Trails

Main Trail 👢—.7 mile—This asphalt trail starts at the park's parking lot and provides access to the Sugarbush Trail, the Hoyt G. Post Trail, and Ann Arbor's Gallup Park.

Sugarbush Trail 👢—.2 mile—This trail starts southeast of Parker Mill. It begins by crossing a bridge over Fleming Creek. It is intended for people with small children or for those on their lunch break who wish to enjoy a short walk.

Hoyt G. Post Trail 🥾

Distance Round-Trip: 1.6 miles

Estimated Hiking Time: 30 minutes to 1 hour

Cautions: There is poison ivy along the trail, so stay on the boardwalk and don't touch the vines in the trees. Take insect repellent during the warm months.

Trail Directions: Start by the information sign at the east end of the parking lot **[1]**. Follow the asphalt trail and swing right around the mill site, descending sharply to parallel Fleming Creek. Pass a junction with the Sugarbush Trail (.1 mi.) **[2]**. Soon you arrive at the trailhead for the Hoyt G. Post Trail (.2 mi.) **[3]**. Turn left onto the boardwalk; the trail leads you to an orientation deck.

At .3 mi. you reach interpretive station #1 **[4]**, which explains the link between the Fleming Creek Watershed and the postglacial landscape. From here you get a scenic view of the creek.

Following the boardwalk, swing away from the creek and walk through an old field. Invaded by non-native species of plants, this area will be managed to reestablish native flora.

The trail crosses an overflow channel and passes a large erratic (a boulder transported by a glacier). You reach the spur to the second interpretive station at .4 mi. **[5]**. It takes you to a creek-side platform with an interpretive board.

Continuing along the boardwalk, you pass large deadfalls, cross the overflow channel again, and arrive at a large, moss-covered deadfall next to the third interpretive station (.5 mi.) **[6]**, which explains the fallen trees in this floodplain environment. The reason isn't flooding; it is death by height. Winds topple whole trees over.

Arrive back at the creek for the fourth interpretive station. Soon, you reach a fascinating section of the trail. The boardwalk swings over Fleming Creek and runs under a limestone-arched railroad bridge that forms a shaded tunnel around the boardwalk (.6 mi.) **[7]**. When trains are overhead, the weight of the cars exerts enough pressure to cause air bubbles to fizz in the water. In the winter, icicles form, hanging like stalactites from the limestone blocks of the bridge.

Beyond the bridge, you enter the Huron River floodplain and walk through a sunny opening before entering a climax black maple forest. Stay to the right as the boardwalk splits; then you arrive at the spur to the fifth interpretive station (.7 mi.) **[8]**. This station is perched on a 100-foot-wide dome of peat that is being gently lifted by several artesian springs. Don't leave the deck; the mud is 5 to 12 feet deep in places.

Beyond the fifth stop you wander through a backup depression to a lagoon of the Huron River. This area floods anytime it rains. Those clumps of green are colonies of wild ginger. At .8 mi., you reach a spur to a wild-life blind on the Huron River **[9]**. In the spring, fall, and winter, it is possible to view large congrega-tions of water-fowl at this location.

From the blind, continue your hike along the boardwalk to complete your loop through this unique floodplain forest (1 mi.) **[10]**. Now, retrace your steps back to the parking area.

1. Trailhead
2. Sugarbush Trail junction
3. Beginning of boardwalk
4. Station #1
5. Station #2
6. Station #3
7. Tunnel
8. Station #5
9. Wildlife blind
10. End of loop

Parker Mill Park

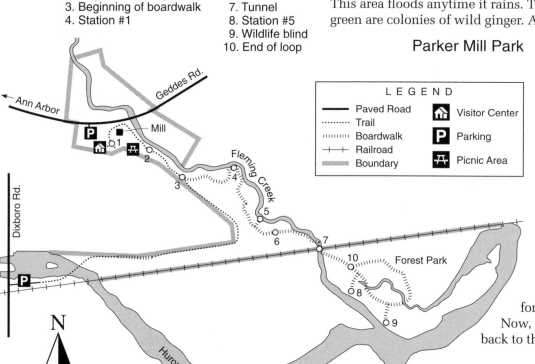

LEGEND

— Paved Road 🏠 Visitor Center
···· Trail 🅿 Parking
⊥⊥⊥ Boardwalk ⊞ Picnic Area
+—+ Railroad
▬▬ Boundary

41. Island Lake Recreation Area

- Catch glimpses of colorful hot-air balloons taking off from the Meadow Balloon Port within the park.
- Enjoy the river, two sandy beaches, and a springfed pond located in an open meadow.
- Stroll or canoe along the "Country Scenic" Huron River.

Park Information

Located in Livingston County, this park is bisected by the winding Huron River, which in 1977 was designated as "Country Scenic" under the Natural Rivers Act. The river flows through open meadows, fields, deep woods, and marshes. Portions of the 14 miles of hiking and biking trails traverse the river. For those who want a different perspective, canoes may be rented at Kent Lake at the northeastern end of the park for a leisurely paddle along the river through the park.

Three locations within this 4,000-acre recreation area provide opportunities for swimming: Island Lake, Kent Lake, and the springfed Spring Mill Pond. Picnic areas abound, and for an extra lift, the Meadow Balloon Port, which lies in about the center of the park, allows colorful views of hot-air balloons in the May-through-September flying season.

Two trails, covering about 14 miles, flow along and over the river, past lakes, through woods, and across meadows. Biking is restricted to a counterclockwise motion on the trails. A campground for canoeists is positioned along the Huron River.

Directions: The park is less than 2 miles southeast of Brighton. From I-96, go south on Kensington Road (exit 151) to the park entrance, which is on the east side of the road.

Hours Open: Open daily from 8:00 A.M. to 10:00 P.M.

Facilities: Hiking, bicycling, swimming, boating, fishing, hunting, canoeing, hot air ballooning, archery, camping (tent), picnicking, and snowmobiling.

Permits and Rules: A park fee is required per motor vehicle ($4 daily, $20 annually). Bikers must follow the one-way trail markings. Hunting is allowed from September 15 through April 1. The park is open to snowmobiling with four inches of snow on the ground; snowmobiles must have the State Park motor

vehicle permit. Spring Mill Pond has a special catch-and-release early trout season, beginning April 1. Only artificial bait is allowed at this time, and a trout stamp is required on fishing licenses.

Further Information: Contact Island Lake Recreation Area, 12950 East Grand River Avenue, Brighton, MI 48116; 810-229-7067.

Other Points of Interest

Heavner Canoe Rentals is the concessionaire for canoe rentals within Island Lake Recreation Area. The firm is open from Memorial Day to Labor Day, or at other times by advanced reservation. For more information, call 810-437-9406 or 810-685-2379.

Across I-96 and connected to Island Lake Recreation Area by Kent Lake is the 4,337-acre **Kensington Metropark.** This busy park offers a variety of hiking, biking, and bridle trails, a golf course, two swimming beaches, boat launches, rowboat rentals (for exploring the islands of Kent Lake), bike rentals, a farm center with animals, and numerous picnic areas. At the west end of this park is the less-congested Nature Study Area, which includes a nature center and several nature trails. Access fees to the park are $3 daily on weekends and holidays, $2 daily on weekdays, or $15 for an annual pass that may be used at all the local metroparks. The park headquarters is located at 2240 West Buno Road, Milford, MI 48380. For more information, call 800-477-2757.

About 3 miles southwest of Brighton is another state park, **Brighton Recreation Area.** This 4,947-acre park offers a rolling terrain composed of moraines, lakes, and woods that set the stage for varied recreation opportunities. The park has 7 miles of hiking/biking trails, several lakes for fishing, picnic facilities, campgrounds, about 18 miles of bridle paths, and a concession-operated riding stable. For more information, contact Brighton Recreation Area, 6360 Chilson Road, Howell, MI 48843; 810-229-6566.

Just south of Brighton is the **Huron Meadows Metropark.** This 1,539-acre park, located along the Huron River, offers picnic facilities, an 18-hole golf course, boat rentals, fishing opportunities, and about 9 miles of hiking or cross-country ski trails. For more information, contact Huron Meadows Metropark, 8765 Hammel Road, Brighton, MI 48116; 810-231-4084.

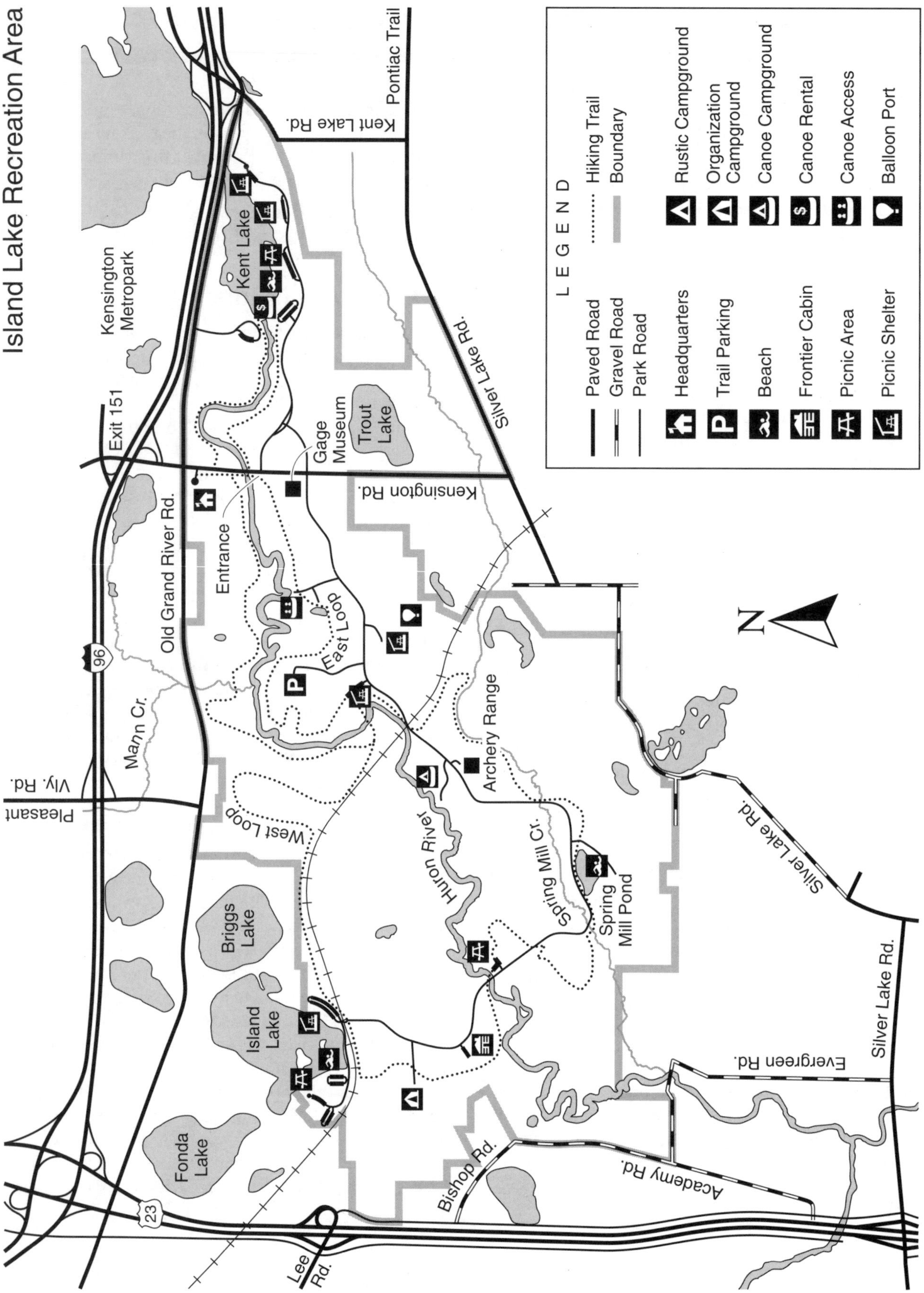

Island Lake Recreation Area

LEGEND

Paved Road		⋯⋯	Hiking Trail	
Gravel Road			Boundary	
Park Road				

Headquarters	Rustic Campground
Trail Parking	Organization Campground
Beach	Canoe Campground
Frontier Cabin	Canoe Rental
Picnic Area	Canoe Access
Picnic Shelter	Balloon Port

Kensington Metropark

Kent Lake

Trout Lake

Gage Museum

Entrance

Old Grand River Rd.

East Loop

West Loop

Mann Cr.

Pleasant Vly. Rd.

Exit 151

Kensington Rd.

Silver Lake Rd.

Kent Lake Rd.

Pontiac Trail

Archery Range

Huron River

Spring Mill Cr.

Spring Mill Pond

Briggs Lake

Island Lake

Fonda Lake

Bishop Rd.

Academy Rd.

Evergreen Rd.

Silver Lake Rd.

Lee Rd.

96

23

N

West Loop 👢👢

Distance Round-Trip: 9.5 miles

Estimated Hiking Time: 4 to 5 hours

Cautions: Hiking and biking are permitted. A couple of short sections have two-way traffic. Take along insect repellent.

Trail Directions: Both the West and East Trails start from the northwest end of the hiking/biking parking lot. Start out along the East Loop **[1]**, winding through woods and wetlands. Turn left at the junction (.1 mi.) **[2]**. The trail passes through the oak/hickory forest and grassy meadows; then it wraps around a stand of red pines. Descend gradually, and then make a steep drop into mixed woods (.3 mi.) **[3]**.

Swing left at .4 mi. **[4]**. Turn left at the fork and come to an intersection of trails. Stay straight and eventually wind around to cross the drive for the Riverbend Picnic Area (.6 mi.) **[5]**. For .1 mi., you stroll along a ridge overlooking the Huron River (.7 mi.) **[6]**. At the road, turn right, walk under the railroad trestle, and climb up the slope to the railroad grade to start your walk along the ridge above the railroad corridor. You leave the rail line at 1.1 mi. **[7]**, descending sharply to skirt the bottom of a steep, grassy hill and then following alongside Spring Mill Creek.

At 1.6 mi., cross a dirt road **[8]**. You veer away from the creek at 1.8 mi. and wind down a steep slope **[9]**. The trail rolls gently past wetlands, then parallels a road before crossing over the creek (2 mi.) **[10]**. The trail loops away from the road, cuts through a small wetland, and then, for the next .7 mi., takes you through hills that are reminiscent of grass-covered dunes. You skirt Spring Mill Pond at 2.7 mi. **[11]** and then veer left to parallel the road. The trail winds over another creek, and then cuts through rejuvenating fields and forests.

Wind and roll through meadows and forests. Make a sharp right at 3.7 mi. **[12]**. The trail cuts right

again, and you walk high on a ridge. At the junction at 3.8 mi. **[13]**, descend steeply toward the road (3.9 mi.) **[14]**. Follow the expansive loop around the Placeway Picnic Area. At the picnic area (4.7 mi.) **[15]**, head for the Huron River. Take the bridge over the river and pick up the trail on the west side of the road at 4.9 mi. **[16]**. Head up the steep slope to the ridge overlooking the river. Just beyond the massive common junipers you pass a rustic cabin (5.2 mi.) **[17]**.

The trail swings wide around the cabin. Cross the organization camp drive at 5.7 mi. **[18]**, and arrive at a junction (5.9 mi.) **[19]**. Turn right and follow much of the same winding terrain, reaching the park road at 6.2 mi. **[20]**.

Head north and pick up the trail across the road along the north side of the tracks. The next .3 mi. is a trail-with-rail walk. Veer away from the tracks, walk down the spiral root staircase, and climb back up to a junction in the woods (6.7 mi.) **[21]**, where you turn right and edge back near the rail corridor. Walk this line, passing a string of cottages and a rejuvenating field. Veer left around the field at 7.1 mi. **[22]**.

After .1 mi., you leave the field and roll through meadows and woods. Eventually, maples and oaks form a canopy and you hike another ridge. Wind down to cross a junction (7.6 mi.) **[23]** near the ravine; thereafter climb up to the left through the forest.

The trail passes a green pool, and then bends back so you roll along the railline (8.3 mi.) **[24]**. Head down, through a tunnel of brush, to merge with other trails (8.6 mi.) **[25]**. Veer right to cross the bridge over the river. Make a hairpin turn near the picnic shelter (8.8 mi.) **[26]**. Soon you reach the intersection that you passed early on in the hike (8.9 mi.) **[27]**. Go straight and zigzag up the narrow trail to the parking lot.

1. Trailhead	15. Placeway Picnic Area
2. Junction	16. Pick up trail
3. Steep descent	17. Rustic cabin
4. Veer left	18. Organization camp drive
5. Riverbend Picnic Area drive	19. Junction
6. Ridge overlook	20. Park road
7. Leave rail line	21. Junction
8. Dirt road	22. Veer left
9. Leave creek	23. Junction/veer left
10. Spring Mill Creek	24. Follow railline
11. Spring Mill Pond	25. Trails merge
12. Sharp right	26. Picnic shelter
13. Junction	27. Trail intersection
14. Cross road	

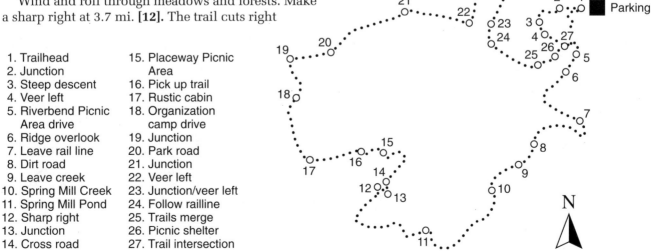

East Loop 👢👢

Distance Round-Trip: 5.6 miles

Estimated Hiking Time: 3 to 4 hours

Cautions: Hiking and biking are permitted. Bicyclists must travel counterclockwise, so travel clockwise.

Trail Directions: Start from the northwest end of the parking lot. Follow the sign for the East Loop and head into the woods **[1]**.

Turn left at the first junction (.1 mi.) **[2]**. Pass through an oak/hickory forest and grassy meadows before winding around a stand of red pine. You soon drop sharply into mixed woods (.3 mi.) **[3]**.

Swing left at .4 mi. **[4]**. You then reach a fork. Turn left and come to an intersection of trails. Turn right and skirt the Riverbend Picnic Area. Then make a hairpin right turn (.5 mi.) **[5]**, and cut through a low-lying wet area, to arrive at an old cement bridge spanning the Huron River (.6 mi.) **[6]**.

From the bridge, head right and climb along a ridge that parallels the river. Stay right at a trail junction (.7 mi.) **[7]**, and continue your climb along a gully-eroded section of the trail. You top out in trees along the edge of an old field. The trail winds and undulates as you pop in and out of mixed stands of hardwoods and pine and skirt old fields. At 1.4 mi., you reach a 5-mi. distance marker that is oriented for bicyclists traveling in the opposite direction **[8]**. Roll through pines and make a steep descent, leveling off where you can see traffic on Old Grand River Road.

Make a sharp right, then a sharp left, to eventually teeter over a creek on a small footbridge (1.7 mi.) **[9]**. A boardwalk then takes you across a low-lying area to the base of a bluff.

Zigzag up the steep slope. Then wind through an oak/hickory forest. You pop out of the trees briefly and pass the 4.5-mi. marker. Then it's back into the woods, where you descend to make a hairpin turn to skirt a wetland (.2 mi.) **[10]**.

Walking along a tree line, go left near the 4-mi. marker (2.4 mi.) **[11]** into an old field now sporting pine and maple. Cross the field, veer right, and climb steeply to a clearing (2.5 mi.) **[12]**. Back along a tree line, you are near the edge of a bluff. Then turn left to cross an old field. Descend and roll across the open hillsides before sharply descending to Kensington Road (3 mi.) **[13]**.

Turn right before crossing the road and follow the power-line corridor to the bank of the Huron River (3.1 mi.) **[14]**. Turn left and cross the river on the Kensington Road bridge, then veer right to pass a sign identifying the trail as multiuse. You now can see old farm buildings as you follow along the edge of old farm fields. At 3.4 mi., you pass the 3-mi. marker **[15]**, then skirt a stand of pine bordered by aspen. Eventually you climb away from the old field onto a ridge with a tree-lined view of the river (3.7 mi.) **[16]**.

At 3.8 mi., you reach a canoe access site along the river **[17]**. A little farther on you reach another scenic stop at a small pond just off the trail (3.9 mi.) **[18]**. A picnic table is located here.

You reach the 2-mi. post (4.2 mi.) **[19]** as you skirt around a large bowl that dominates the terrain on your right. You bottom out near cattails, only to climb a wide sandy path to break out of the trees into a clearing on top of a ridge (4.3 mi.) **[20]**. The trail undulates and descends into aspen. Turn left and skirt past an open hillside into young trees and shrubs that give way to large oak and hickory trees. Turn right and begin a long descent through the forest (4.5 mi.) **[21]**.

At 5.1 mi., you reach what might have been the foundation of a small cottage near a bend in the river **[22]**. Climb to walk along an old access drive where you pass a stone wall that is being reclaimed by the forest vegetation (5.2 mi.) **[23]**. Stay to the right as the trail splits, and walk along a ridge high above the river. The trail tops out at a picnic table and grill. This overlooks an overgrown bluff above the river (5.4 mi.) **[24]**. Now wind your way through the forest back to the first junction (5.5 mi.) **[2]**. Turn left to return to the parking area.

1. Trailhead
2. Trail junction
3. Steep descent
4. Veer left
5. Hairpin turn/picnic area
6. Huron River
7. Trail junction
8. 5-mile post
9. Footbridge
10. Wetland/hairpin turn
11. 4-mile post
12. Open field
13. Kensington Road
14. Huron River
15. 3-mile post
16. Ridge
17. Canoe access site
18. Pond
19. 2-mile post
20. Ridge
21. Oak/hickory forest
22. Old foundation
23. Stone wall
24. Picnic table/grill

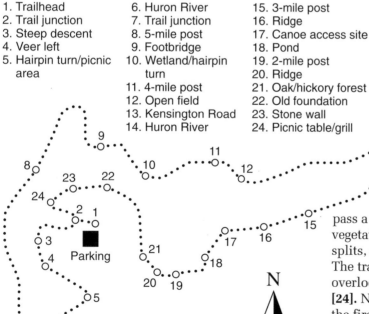

42. Bay City State Recreation Area

- Embrace nature with reverence from a board-walk and observation dock built over wetlands.
- View waterfowl from two 30-foot towers that overlook marshes and lagoons.
- Wade the shallow waters of Saginaw Bay.

Park Information

Initially connected by the Frank N. Andersen Nature Trail, the Bay City State Park and the Tobico Marsh State Game Area became one in July of 1995. The union resulted in the creation of the 2,800-acre Bay City State Recreation Area.

The former state park contributed its recreational amenities of camping, a soft, sandy beach along Saginaw Bay, and the former Jennison Nature Center. Newly named the Saginaw Bay Visitor Center and enlarged to three times its former size, the Center has displays that depict life in the wetlands and Michigan ecology. The facility is a combination of laboratory, museum, and classroom. Two trails are accessed from within the former state park: One, designed for people with visual and physical disabilities, forms a loop just outside of the Visitor Center, and the other, a 2-mile loop, encircles the Tobico Lagoon.

Tobico Marsh contributed its legacy as a wildlife refuge. This area, the largest Great Lakes coastal marsh, is a resting place for thousands of migratory waterfowl. It provides refuge for over 100 species of birds. More than 5 miles of trails, two 30-foot observation towers, and a 300-foot boardwalk and observation dock over wetlands await you here. Watch for, listen to, and take pleasure from the muskrat, deer, or beaver that may welcome you.

Still combining recreation and refuge, the Frank N. Andersen Nature Trail allows for a contemplative transition as you stroll from recreation to reverence in the refuge. This 1.6-mile trail, which largely follows along an abandoned rail grade, has occasional interpretive plaques, observation decks, and benches to enhance your enjoyment of the surroundings.

Directions: The Bay City State Recreation Area is located about 5 miles north of Bay City. Take I-75 to exit 168 and head east along Beaver Road for about 6 miles.

Hours Open: The recreation area is open daily from 8:00 A.M. to 10:00 P.M. Saginaw Bay Visitor Center is open Tuesday through Sunday from noon to 5:00 P.M. It is closed on Mondays.

Facilities: Hiking, bicycling, cross-country skiing, swimming, fishing, camping (tent and RV), sanitation station, picnicking, interpretive trails, and interpretive center.

Permits and Rules: A park fee is required per motor vehicle ($4 daily, $20 annually).

Further Information: Contact Bay City State Recreation Area, 3582 State Park Drive, Bay City, MI 48707; 517-684-3020. Or call the Saginaw Bay Visitor Center, 517-667-0717.

Other Points of Interest

Located in Bay City are the **Bay City Riverwalk** and the **Bay Hampton Rail Trail.** Two separate trails currently exist, one a 2.4-mile trail along the west side of the Saginaw River and the other a 2.3-mile rail-trail extending from Bay City into Hampton Township.

The existing Riverwalk takes you along the banks of the river to the 820-foot Riverwalk pier that extends out into the river. The Riverwalk crosses a pedestrian bridge (submitted to the *Guinness Book of Records* as the world's most crooked bridge) over to a small island in the middle of the river and passes through the Veterans' Memorial Park and the Liberty Harbor Marina. This trail, like the Bay Hampton Rail Trail, is constructed of seamless asphalt or concrete to accommodate walking, in-line skating, bicycles, strollers, and wheelchairs. For more information, call the Bay Area Community Foundation, 517-893-4438, or the Bay Area Convention and Visitors Bureau, 517-893-1222.

Park Trails

Chickadee Trail 👢—.5 mile—This trail loops behind the Visitor Center. It was designed so that those with visual and physical disabilities may enjoy the natural beauty here. Paved, it has a guide rope, and Braille signs along the way help to explain the natural history of the area.

Tobico Lagoon Trail 👢—2 miles—This trail has a hard surface with about .2 miles of boardwalk. Access is from the Visitor Center. From there the trail heads north to begin its loop around Tobico Lagoon.

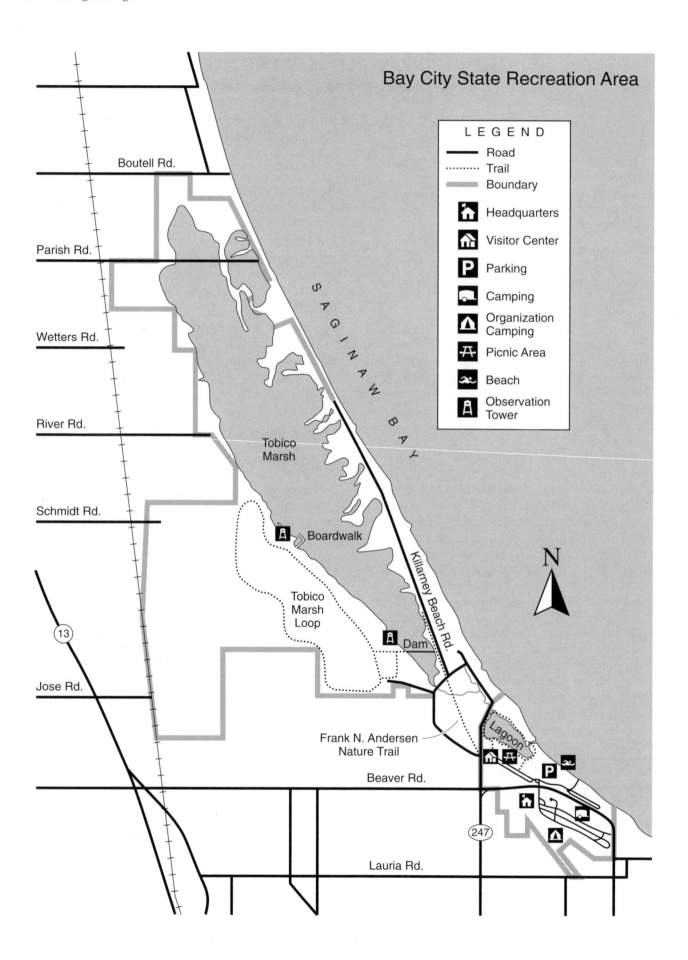

Bay City State Recreation Area

LEGEND
Road
Trail
Boundary
Headquarters
Visitor Center
Parking
Camping
Organization Camping
Picnic Area
Beach
Observation Tower

Boutell Rd.

Parish Rd.

Wetters Rd.

River Rd.

Schmidt Rd.

Jose Rd.

Beaver Rd.

Lauria Rd.

SAGINAW BAY

Tobico Marsh

Boardwalk

Tobico Marsh Loop

Dam

Killarney Beach Rd.

Frank N. Andersen Nature Trail

Lagoon

N

13

247

Frank N. Andersen Nature Trail 🥾

Distance Round-Trip: 3.2 miles

Estimated Hiking Time: 1 to 1.5 hours

Cautions: Take insect repellent during the warmer months of the year. On sunny days, you may want to take along a hat and sunscreen. Bring binoculars to enhance your wildlife-viewing experience while you are on the trailside nature observation decks.

Trail Directions: The trail begins behind the Saginaw Bay Visitor Center, which is located at the northwest end of the park's day-use area **[1]**. For a perspective on the history and wildlife of the Saginaw Bay Area, plan to visit the Center's Jennison Exhibit Hall, which features interactive hands-on displays.

Behind the Visitor Center, go past the large sign announcing the trail and immediately cross Euclid Road. The asphalt trail follows the route of an abandoned Detroit and Mackinac Railway corridor for 1.2 mi.

You enter into a wooded area where a nature observation deck awaits (.2 mi.) **[2]**. The deck is a covered wooden shelter with benches and interpretive plaques about the plants and animals in the surrounding habitat. This one features the trees and birds that might be found here in the woodland zone. Have a seat and wait to see what might fly in to feast at the feeders.

Leaving the woods, you enter a large marsh area. Stop and read the interpretive marker on the evil purple loosestrife before you arrive at a second covered observation deck (.3 mi.) **[3]**. Here, the plants and animals of the marsh environment are highlighted.

You soon cross a small wood-decked bridge built on the back of the old railroad trestle. Then stop to read about the important role reptiles and amphibians play in Michigan's wetlands. At .5 mi., cross Killarney Beach Road as it swings to parallel the trail **[4]**.

When the trail splits (.7 mi.) **[5]**, you have the option of continuing along the old rail corridor or turning left to cross the marsh on a weir, or, more familiarly, a dam. Since this is an out-and-back trail, if you choose to go left you could shorten your hike to 2 mi. by crossing the marsh to the observation

tower and then retracing your steps to the Visitor Center.

Continuing along the corridor, you get exceptional views of the Tobico Marsh. Take your time and look for waterfowl floating or feeding in the water. When the asphalt ends (1.3 mi.) **[6]**, double back, return to the junction **[5]**, turn right to cross on the weir (1.9 mi.).

You quickly reach a wooden bridge with interpretive plaques at both ends. Then, in the cattails to your right, look for the beaver lodge (2 mi.) **[7]**. If you're lucky, you may even spot a beaver swimming in the water. Learn more as you pass a couple more interpretive plaques. Get another great view of the marsh, and then arrive at an observation deck on your right (2.1 mi.) **[8]**.

Once across the marsh, you arrive at a large, two-story observation tower (2.2 mi.) **[9]**. Make the climb up the tower's steps, catch your breath, and enjoy the sweeping view of the area. This is when you will be glad you brought your binoculars. Without them those specks in the water will remain just that, specks in the water. So lift up your glasses. What is that out there? Don't forget your bird identification book.

When you've had enough, climb back down and retrace your steps back to the Visitor Center. If you still want to hike, turn the page to read about the Tobico Marsh Loop. You can pick up this loop by heading west past the vault toilet and into the woods.

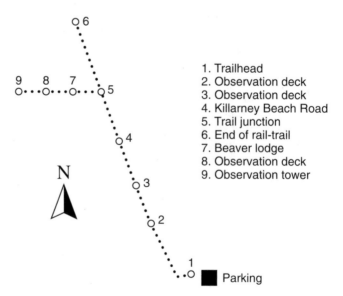

1. Trailhead
2. Observation deck
3. Observation deck
4. Killarney Beach Road
5. Trail junction
6. End of rail-trail
7. Beaver lodge
8. Observation deck
9. Observation tower

Tobico Marsh Loop 👢

Distance Round-Trip: 4.9 miles

Estimated Hiking Time: 1.5 to 2.5 hours

Cautions: Take insect repellent if you are here during the warmer months. Bring binoculars to enhance your wildlife viewing during stops at the trailside nature observation decks.

Trail Directions: Start behind the Saginaw Bay Visitor Center, which is located at the northwest end of the park's day-use area **[1]**. Take the asphalt-surfaced Frank N. Andersen Nature Trail, which you will follow for 1 mi.

Cross Euclid Road and you are on the route of an abandoned Detroit and Mackinac Railway corridor. This corridor transports you to a nature observation deck. Look around you and learn about the trees and birds found in this woodland zone (.2 mi.) **[2]**. Your next scheduled stop is at the second nature observation deck (.3 mi.) **[3]**. Here the plants and animals of the marsh are highlighted.

Cross Killarney Beach Road (.5 mi.) **[4]**. Turn left at the junction (.7 mi.) **[5]** to cross on a weir to the other side of the marsh. After crossing the wooden bridge surrounded by interpretive plaques, look to your right for the beaver lodge (.8 mi.) **[6]**. Then pass more interpretive plaques, view more marsh scenes, and arrive at another observation deck (.9 mi.) **[7]**.

Once across the marsh, you'll see a two-story observation tower overlooking the area (1 mi.) **[8]**. Climb up the steps, catch your breath, and enjoy the view. If you brought binoculars, this is a place to use them.

Your feet back on the ground, head past the vault toilet and into the woods where the asphalt ends; now your feet really are back on the ground (actually crushed stone). Soon the trail splits (1.1 mi.) **[9]** and you have the option of going either clockwise or counterclockwise. Turn right and head north through mixed hardwoods and the occasional pine.

At 1.8 mi., cross a clearing that exposes a vault toilet, and arrive at the second observation tower **[10]**. From atop this tower, your view of the marsh is much clearer than from the first tower. At the foot of the tower is a boardwalk that leads you out for more intimate interaction with the marsh. Have a seat on one of the benches built into the boardwalk and enjoy the setting.

The trail continues north from the tower. At 2.2 mi., the northernmost point of the hike, the trail swings left **[11]**. Now headed south, you pass between two wetlands where you view cattails silhouetted through trees (2.3 mi.) **[12]**. Hiking the lightly used west side of the trail, you pass through an open area (2.9 mi.) **[13]**. Continue strolling through woods and then cross a small wooden bridge (3.2 mi.) **[14]**.

Eventually a boardwalk takes you over the pool that has been paralleling the trail. Soon you arrive at the parking area that served as the original trailhead when this section of the park was on its own as the Tobico Marsh State Game Area (3.6 mi.) **[15]**. In addition to a shelter and vault toilets, there is a rock with a plaque that commemorates Tobico Marsh's designation as a registered natural landmark.

Continue north past the shelter. Turn right where the trail splits to cross the first of the three bridges that carry you over a series of old Lake Huron beach ridges. After crossing the last bridge (3.7 mi.) **[16]**, turn left and you will be quickly back at the weir (3.9 mi.) **[17]** that is east of the first observation tower. From here, retrace your steps for 1 mi. back to the Visitor Center parking area.

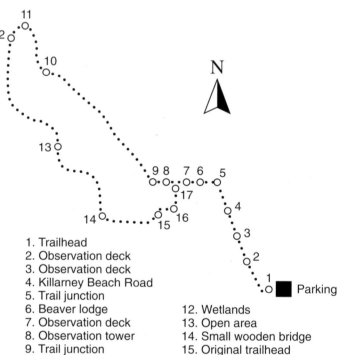

1. Trailhead
2. Observation deck
3. Observation deck
4. Killarney Beach Road
5. Trail junction
6. Beaver lodge
7. Observation deck
8. Observation tower
9. Trail junction
10. Observation tower
11. Northern end/swing left
12. Wetlands
13. Open area
14. Small wooden bridge
15. Original trailhead
16. Third bridge
17. Weir

43. Shiawassee National Wildlife Refuge/ Green Point Environmental Learning Center

- Enjoy one of the top 25 birding sites in America.
- Hike along dikes through forest, farm fields, and wetlands.
- View an abundance of diverse wildlife.

Park Information

Although the Shiawassee National Wildlife Refuge and the Green Point Environmental Learning Center are separate entities, they share a location near the confluence of four rivers: the Flint, the Tittabawassee, the Cass, and the Shiawassee, all of which combine to form the Saginaw River.

The refuge, with over 9,000 acres, was established in 1953 to restore an historically significant wetland area for the benefit of migrating waterfowl. In the first two weeks of November about 23,000 geese and from 25,000 to 30,000 ducks may be seen at the refuge. Songbirds, wading birds, owls, hawks, and even bald eagles either call the refuge home or pass through at some time.

An observation deck and a wheelchair-accessible observation blind are strategically placed for prime wildlife viewing. Dikes, pumps, and gravity-flow structures flood and drain various areas, promoting the growth of seeds and invertebrates that wildlife use for food. Also, sharecrop farming, whereby farmers leave a certain percentage of their crops in the field, provides wildlife with a winter food source.

Adjacent to the refuge is the Green Point Environmental Learning Center. Owned by the City of Saginaw, but operated under a cooperative agreement with the U.S. Fish and Wildlife Service, this natural area provides another 76 acres of diverse habitat and has an interpretive center for learning about nature.

Directions: The refuge headquarters are located about 4 miles south of Saginaw. From M-13, turn west onto Curtis Road for about .5 miles. Green Point Environmental Learning Center is located at the end of Maple Street in the City of Saginaw. Take M-46 to South Michigan Avenue. Turn south and go about 1.5 miles to Maple Street and turn left (south). It's about .5 mile to the Center at 3010 Maple Street.

Hours Open: The refuge is open from dawn until dusk, seven days a week year-round. During hunting periods the hours are limited. Refuge headquarters are open from 7:30 A.M. to 4:00 P.M., Mondays through Fridays throughout the year. Floods are a possibility any time. Call ahead to check conditions. At the Green Point Environmental Learning Center, the trails are open daily during the daylight hours. There are times of the year when they are flooded. Hours at the Interpretive Center vary seasonally as well. It's best to call ahead.

Facilities: The refuge has hiking, biking, cross-country skiing, hunting, and interpretive trails. The Green Point Learning Center has hiking, cross-country skiing, fishing, and an interpretive center.

Permits and Rules: No fee is required at either facility. Stay on the established trails. No pets or motorized vehicles are allowed. Leave all plants and animals as you found them, and pack out your litter. At the refuge, observe the "Closed Area" signs. At the Learning Center, no bicycling is allowed on the trails.

Further Information: Contact Shiawassee National Wildlife Refuge, 6975 Mower Road, Saginaw, MI 48601-9783; 517-777-5930. Or contact Green Point Environmental Learning Center, 3010 Maple Street, Saginaw, MI 48602; 517-759-1669.

Park Trails

Woodland Trail 🥾—3.5 miles—This trail is in the north portion of the refuge. Drive west on M-46 from Saginaw to Center Road and turn south. Go about 2 miles to Stroebel Road. Turn left to the parking lot. This 3.5-mile loop travels largely through bottomland hardwoods and at times gets close to the Tittabawassee River. Part of the trail passes over an abandoned rail grade, a remnant from the coal-mining period in the early 1900s.

Wildflower, Turtle, Hawk, and Deer Trails 🥾—.2 to 1 mile—These trails are smaller loops off the longer Songbird Trail at the Green Point Environmental Learning Center. They all start with the Songbird Trail behind the Center and wander through bottom-land hardwoods.

Duck and Beaver Trails 🥾—.4 and 1 mile—These trails are extension loops at the southern end of the Songbird Trail, where a boardwalk continues the trail across a wetland. They provide wildlife-viewing opportunities along the Tittabawassee River.

Shiawassee National Wildlife Refuge

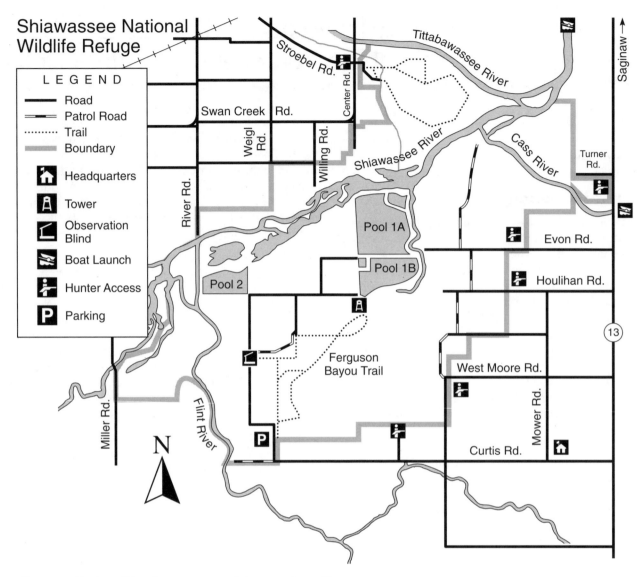

LEGEND
- Road
- Patrol Road
- Trail
- Boundary
- Headquarters
- Tower
- Observation Blind
- Boat Launch
- Hunter Access
- P Parking

Green Point Environmental Learning Center

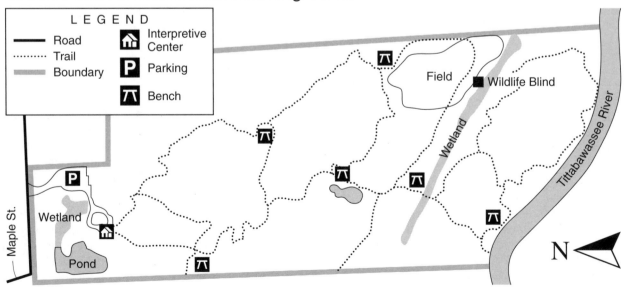

LEGEND
- Road
- Trail
- Boundary
- Interpretive Center
- P Parking
- Bench

Ferguson Bayou Trail 🥾

Distance Round-Trip: 4.8 miles (although a spur makes a shorter loop of about 1.5 miles)

Estimated Hiking Time: 2 to 3 hours

Cautions: The trail is prone to flooding. Take insect spray and call ahead to see what condition the trail is in. Keep an eye out for holes that have developed on the trail and for poison ivy.

Trail Directions: From M-13, take Curtis Road west about 4 mi. The trail starts at the northwest end of the parking lot, by the information board **[1]**. Take your first steps onto a dike system that supports the refuge, as well as your steps.

Grass cushions your steps as you head out through cultivated fields. Just before the service road, if the season is right, listen for bullfrogs in the pond to your right (.2 mi.) **[2]**. Follow the road to the right, then left, as it carries you above pools of water, until you arrive at a posted junction (.3 mi.) **[3]**. This marks the beginning and ending point for both the short and the long loop. Turn right along the gravel service road perched along the dike. Scan the field to your left for deer; the refuge is inundated with them.

Stop and take notice of your surroundings. It's not every day you get the opportunity to hike along a dike. From this elevated embankment, look to the pools below you to your right and the marsh to your left. Your adventure on this trail will occur atop these linear mounds. At the marsh, an interpretive sign discusses marsh ecology (.4 mi.) **[4]**.

A new environment awaits you at the upcoming junction—wooded wetlands (.5 mi.) **[5]**. Trees wade in dark pools occasionally lit by moss-green algae floating on the water's surface. Turn left; this wet, wooded wonderland flanks the trail as you walk to a bench at .8 mi. **[6]**, where a nest box is placed in the pool in front of it. Wood ducks or hooded mergansers are likely users of these nests.

The trail continues its wide, gravely way until you reach a posted junction at the water's edge (.9 mi.) **[7]**. Turn right and follow along this moatlike spur that is bordered by trees standing in pooled channels. Another bench and nest box (1.2 mi.) **[8]** await you just before the trail winds back to the main trail; there the spur for the short loop continues straight.

Turn right; the long loop continues on to a viewing tower. At 1.8 mi. is the junction for the tower loop **[9]**. Follow to the right under the dark canopy of trees along this swamplike corridor. Just before the trail takes a left, keep an eye out for cone-tipped stumps that look as though they've been through a huge pencil sharpener—evidence of beavers (1.9 mi.) **[10]**.

At 2 mi., a pile of rough-hewn twigs makes up a beaver lodge **[11]**. Wind around this loop. Just before stepping out of the shadows to climb the observation deck, there's another lodge (2.3 mi.) **[12]**.

The observation tower provides a panorama of the Shiawassee River Wetlands and its agricultural fields. A magnification scope helps to focus in on any wildlife that is near.

Head southwest past the field on your right that displays sharecropping. A sign interprets its benefits to wildlife. At 2.7 mi., a bench marks a junction with a service road, where the trail curves to the left **[13]**, and continues a short stretch until it returns to the tower loop junction (2.8 mi.) **[9]**. Turn right down the shaded corridor of the wooded wetland, emerging from the den of darkness at 3.1 mi. **[14]**. When you notice a bench up ahead, look closely to your left. Growths on either side of a maple tree give the impression that a bear and her cub are climbing it (3.3 mi.) **[15]**.

The trail turns left through grass, and then right, until you get to the spur to the observation blind (3.8 mi.) **[16]**. Turn left and pass a bench and the short-loop spur at 4 mi. **[17]**. It's a straight line back to the junction where you started the loop (4.5 mi.) **[3]**. You can retrace your steps back along the trail to the parking lot or follow the service road back.

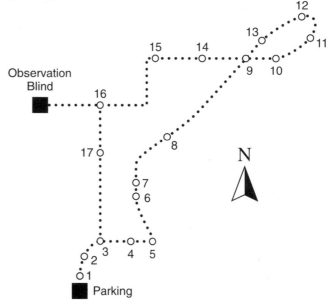

1. Trailhead
2. Pond
3. Junction
4. Interpretive sign
5. Junction
6. Bench
7. Junction
8. Bench/short-loop spur
9. Tower loop junction
10. Evidence of beavers
11. Beaver lodge
12. Beaver lodge
13. Bench/service road junction
14. Exit from woods
15. Bears climbing maple
16. Spur to observation blind
17. Bench/short-loop spur

Songbird/Duck Trails 👢

Distance Round-Trip: 1.5 miles

Estimated Hiking Time: 45 minutes

Cautions: Located in the floodplain of the Tittabawassee River, the trails at Green Point are prone to flooding, either seasonally or after periods of high rain. Wear appropriate footgear. Insect repellent is a must during spring and early summer. Poison ivy is widespread along the trail.

Trail Directions: All trails start from behind the Interpretive Center building. The trails can be accessed from either the east or the west end of the building. Where you start determines whether you walk in a clockwise or counterclockwise direction. The trail description here starts from the east end of the building at the signboard listing the rules and regulations **[1]**. Clockwise it is.

Just follow the blue songbird symbol located on the trail posts. Your first steps take you into the woods along the wood-chipped path. It shouldn't take long to realize why the Center's educational programs are based on the theme "Water, Wildlife, and You."

Soon after the beginning of the hike through this bottomland hardwood forest, the Wildflower Trail branches off to the right (250 feet) **[2]**. Shortly afterward, you come upon a large maple tree (.1 mi.) **[3]**.

Here a wealth of moneywort lines the trail; notice the coin-shaped leaves deposited along the forest floor.

At .2 mi. you reach a bench where the Turtle Trail heads off to the right **[4]**. The trail soon narrows. You then pass through a group of dead trees standing vigil over one of their fallen comrades. After rounding a bend, notice the tree with pockmarks—scars from woodpeckers. It bows to point your way.

Just past the junction with the Deer Trail, a second bench is near the opening to a field (.5 mi.) **[5]**. This is a good spot to stop and watch for wildlife. Continuing on, the trail parallels a drain before swinging right, along the other side of the field, to a wildlife observation blind overlooking a wetland (.6 mi.) **[6]**.

At about .7 mi. is the trail junction for the two River Trail loops **[7]**. The shorter of the two is the Duck Trail, which has a light blue symbol. Walking this loop will take you across a boardwalk and to a bench anchored securely on the bank of the Tittabawassee River (.9 mi.) **[8]**. A floating dock was also once located here, but it floated off to freedom in the flood of 1986. The Duck Trail loop is .4 mi. long.

When you return to the Songbird Trail at the junction with the River Trail, turn left, then right. You are now walking alongside a pond (1.2 mi.) **[9]**. Once past the pond, the trail enters the woods you started out in. You will encounter several large oak and maple trees and the junction to all the other woodland trail loops before you return to the Interpretive Center (1.5 mi.) **[10]**.

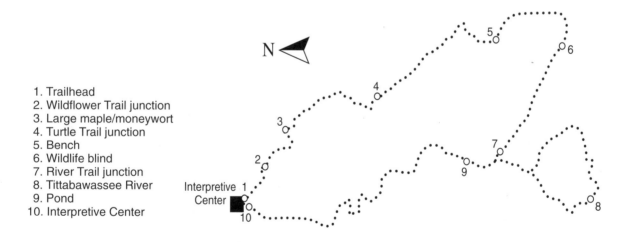

1. Trailhead
2. Wildflower Trail junction
3. Large maple/moneywort
4. Turtle Trail junction
5. Bench
6. Wildlife blind
7. River Trail junction
8. Tittabawassee River
9. Pond
10. Interpretive Center

Interpretive Center

44. Pinckney Recreation Area

- Traverse the rugged landscape shaped by glaciers.
- Climb to scenic overlooks.
- Experience a variety of wildlife as you hike past numerous inland lakes, ponds, and creeks.

Park Information

Created in 1944, the park encompasses over 10,000 acres. This acreage is scattered among numerous private landholdings. The park's rolling topography of numerous inland water bodies interspersed with hills and ridges is typical of formations shaped by glacial activity. Seven lakes, connected by streams and channels, form a chain that provides extended canoeing opportunities. The rolling, shaded landscape is popular with equestrians.

Six hiking trails weave through the park. All start from the Silver Lake day-use area. While the older trails are popular with mountain bikers, the three new Losee Lake Loops are closed to bicycles. The park also serves as the eastern terminus of the Waterloo-Pinckney Hiking Trail (see park #45).

Directions: The park headquarters, located at the Silver Lake day-use area, is 15 miles northwest of Ann Arbor. From US-23, head west on North Territorial Road about 10 miles to Dexter-Townhall Road, turn north for 1.2 miles, and then left at the Silver Hill Road where the park entrance is located. From I-94, head north on M-52 for 6 miles to North Territorial Road and turn right (east) for 6 miles to Dexter-Townhall Road; turn north for 1.2 miles and then left at the park entrance.

Hours Open: Open daily from 8:00 A.M. to 10:00 P.M.

Facilities: Hiking, bicycling, horseback riding, swimming, hunting, fishing, canoeing, boating, cross-country skiing, camping (tent and RV), and picnicking.

Permits and Rules: A park fee is required per motor vehicle ($4 daily, $20 annually). Motor vehicles permitted on established roads only. Camping permitted in established areas only.

Further Information: Contact Pinckney Recreation Area, 8555 Silver Hill Road, Route 1, Pinckney, MI 48169; 313-426-4913.

Other Points of Interest

The first 12.5 miles of the **LakeLands Trail State Park** opened in 1994 between the communities of Stockbridge and Pinckney. This rail-trail is operated by the Pinckney Recreation Area. It provides opportunities for hikers, mountain bikers, equestrians, and cross-country skiers. There is a separate fee for use of this trail. For more information, call 313-426-4913.

Washtenaw County's 205-acre **Park Lyndon,** while traversed by the Waterloo-Pinckney Hiking Trail, also has its own system of nature trails. Some of Michigan's rarest flora can be viewed from the park's trails. The park is located on North Territorial Road, 1 mile east of M-52.

Park Trails

Waterloo-Pinckney Hiking Trail 👢👢👢— The eastern end of the 36-mile Waterloo-Pinckney Hiking Trail is at the Silver Lake day-use area. This is typically the endpoint for people hiking the entire trail from its starting point at the Portage Lake day-use area in the Waterloo Recreation Area. See the featured trail write-ups for portions of the trail that go through the Waterloo Recreation Area (see park #45). Excellent day-hike opportunities exist on this point-to-point trail. Parking is available at Green Lake in the Waterloo Recreation Area, Washtenaw County's Park Lyndon, and at several of the dirt roads that the trail crosses.

Potawatomi Trail 👢👢👢—17.5 miles—This trail starts at the Silver Lake day-use area. The trail is so popular with mountain bikers that they are now required to travel clockwise. Hikers should travel counterclockwise. Through-hikers can camp at a walk-in campground on Blind Lake, roughly the halfway point of the trail.

Silver Lake Trail 👢👢—1.9 miles—This trail starts at the Silver Lake day-use area. You share this scenic trail with mountain bikers.

Losee Lake Hiking Trail—Blue Loop 👢👢— 1.5 miles—This trail starts at the Silver Lake day-use area and loops out to the boardwalk along Losee Lake. It is closed to bicycles.

Losee Lake Hiking Trail—Yellow Loop 👢👢— 2.5 miles—This trail starts at the Silver Lake day-use area and provides for an excursion past several wetlands and over the rolling landscape found in the park. The trail is closed to bicycles.

Pinckney Recreation Area

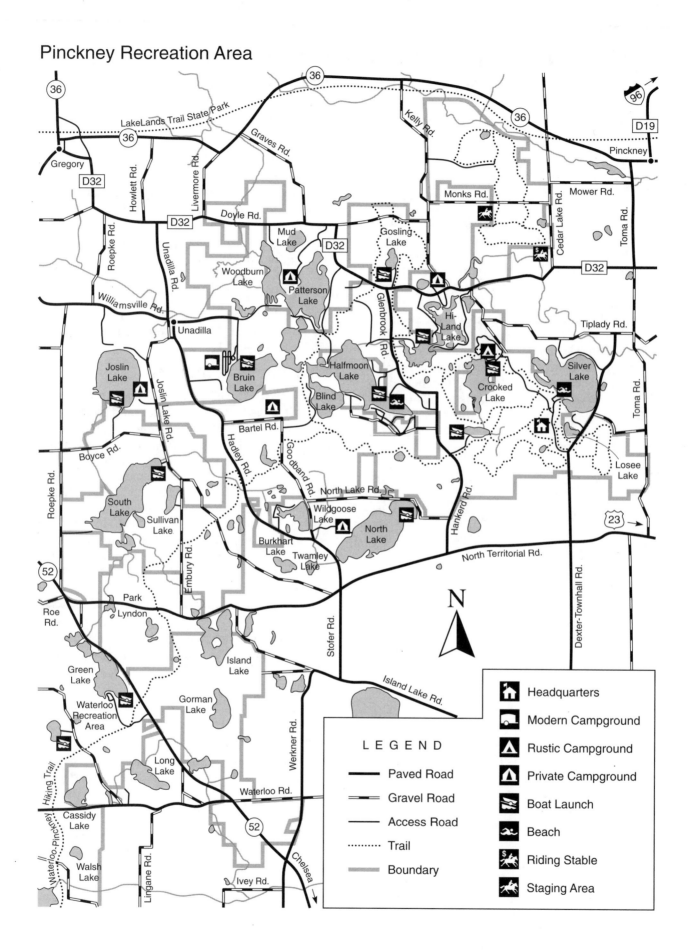

LEGEND

— Paved Road
= Gravel Road
— Access Road
······ Trail
━━ Boundary

🏠 Headquarters
🚐 Modern Campground
⛺ Rustic Campground
⛺ Private Campground
🛶 Boat Launch
🏊 Beach
🐎 Riding Stable
🐎 Staging Area

Crooked Lake Trail 🥾🥾🥾

Distance Round-Trip: 5.1 miles

Estimated Hiking Time: 2 to 3 hours

Cautions: Hiking and mountain biking are permitted on the trail. Mountain bikers must travel clockwise. Travel counterclockwise to avoid conflicts. Use insect repellent during the warmer months.

Trail Directions: The trail starts behind the wooden map board, "Pinckney Recreation Area Trails," located at the northeast end of the north parking lot of the Silver Lake day-use area **[1]**. The Potawatomi and Silver Lake Trails also start from this point.

Head northwest following the shore of Silver Lake. Your first steps are on a long boardwalk that takes you over a wet area. After you step from the boardwalk and make a short climb, you'll come to mile marker #36 (.1 mi) **[2]**. This marker is for hikers who have finished the Waterloo-Pinckney Hiking Trail (see park #45). Called the Ninawkee Trail by the Boy Scouts, it follows the Potawatomi Trail to the Bruin Lake Scout Camp, effectively extending the length of the Waterloo-Pinckney Hiking Trail to 46 miles.

Shortly thereafter, the Silver Lake Trail splits off to the left (.2 mi.) **[3]**. The posted trail directions may be confusing at this location; just stay on the trail to the right. The Crooked Lake Trail will eventually loop around and return to this spot from the direction in which the Silver Lake Trail is now heading.

At .5 mi., the trail swings west and climbs away from the lake **[4]**. Just before crossing Silver Hill Road, you will pass a sign directing cross-country skiers to the right. The trail then briefly parallels the road before heading west into the woods. After climbing gradually, at .8 mi. you climb steeply out of the woods to gain a peek at Crooked Lake **[5]**. You then cross the Crooked Lake access road and climb

steeply to a panoramic overlook of Crooked Lake and the surrounding countryside (1.1 mi.) **[6]**. Here a bench is positioned for your viewing pleasure.

Leaving the overlook, you begin a lengthy descent. At the bottom, you briefly skirt the bank of a creek before turning sharply to the left and crossing a small footbridge (1.5 mi.) **[7]**. After passing mile marker #38, you reach another trail junction (2.4 mi.) **[8]**. Here the Crooked Lake Trail turns left and heads south, away from the Potawatomi Trail. You then cross a wooden footbridge, climb a sandy slope, and cross Glenbrook Road.

On the other side of the road you will marvel at the awesome power that nature can unleash. A mature oak/hickory forest has been leveled by the destructive winds of a tornado that touched down during a storm in 1994 (2.8 mi.) **[9]**. As you walk through the downed trees, a trail splits to the right. It goes to the Halfmoon Lake beach, a 1 mi. round-trip.

Leaving the devastation behind, you again enter the woods and begin to veer to the left. Heading east you soon pass Pickerel Lake (3.3 mi.) **[10]**. A fishing pier is visible on the far side of the lake. At the east end of the lake, cross a footbridge over a channel that connects Crooked and Pickerel Lakes (3.6 mi.) **[11]**. Visible to the southeast is a footbridge on the Silver Lake Trail.

After climbing a couple of hills, you reach a junction with the Silver Lake Trail (3.9 mi.) **[12]**. Continue heading straight, or east, and soon you'll be on a ridge that rises above kettle ponds, first to your right and then to your left. There are a couple of steep climbs and descents before the trail drops sharply and then rises to cross Silver Hill Road (4.7 mi.) **[13]**. Turn right at the next junction and return to the parking lot on the section of the trail you started out on along Silver Lake.

1. Trailhead
2. Mile marker #36
3. Trail junction
4. Turn west
5. Peek at Crooked Lake
6. Scenic overlook
7. Footbridge
8. Trail junction
9. Tornado destruction
10. Pickerel Lake
11. Channel
12. Trail junction
13. Silver Hill Road

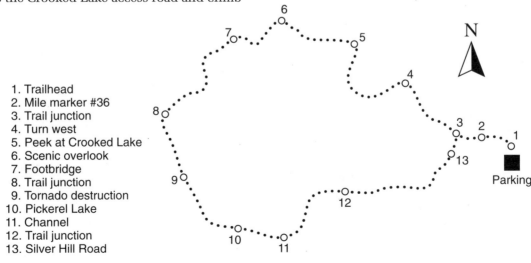

Losee Lake Hiking Trail— Red Loop 👢👢👢

Distance Round-Trip: 3.3 miles

Estimated Hiking Time: 1 to 1.5 hours

Cautions: This is a new trail. In addition to rocks and roots, watch out for small stumps. Some sections of the trail are wet. Wear appropriate footgear. Take insect repellent in warm months.

Trail Directions: Start at the east end of the lower parking lot near Silver Lake. A red trail marker is attached to the information board located between the parking lot and the lake **[1]**.

Head south past the information board, skirt the lake, and follow the edge of the mowed lawn up the side of a hill. Pass a bench before reaching a defined pathway cut through small shrubs and cedars. Still ascending, you soon make a sharp left (.1 mi.) **[2]** that takes you past small cedars and a bowl-shaped wetland (.2 mi.) **[3]**. Hike through a stand of red pines to arrive at a bench in a clearing (.3 mi.) **[4]**.

Now an old two-track, the trail splits left at a marker and you begin a descent. Turn left just before reaching the park's driveway, and descend sharply to a junction (.5 mi.) **[5]**. Stay to the right.

Skirting a wetland, you cross two small boardwalks before climbing a cedar-covered ridge. Descend to the junction with the Blue Loop. Stay right and cross Dexter-Townhall Road (.8 mi.) **[6]**. You soon walk a boardwalk between two wetlands. Then swing right and climb onto a ridge of red pine (.9 mi.) **[7]**. Turn left and approach a power-line corridor. Don't cross here; swing left back into the woods and approach it a second time. Cross near the large utility pole (1.1 mi.) **[8]**.

Descend sharply and veer right to climb steeply. A bench and a scenic vista of the rolling landscape to the south await you (1.2 mi.) **[9]**. The Yellow Loop junction is located here.

Descend into the shade of an oak/hickory forest. Swing left and find yourself alongside a wetland. Veer right and step down a small ridge to cross a boardwalk onto what is best described as a small island in a large wetland. Enjoy the setting at the bench (1.4 mi.) **[10]**.

Turn left and then left again to cross a boardwalk through cattails. Veer right past red pines, through cedars, and by a busy ant mound. After crossing a line of field stones, veer left to cross a boardwalk. Then climb a steep pine-covered hillside to a bench. (1.7 mi.) **[11]**.

Roll along open landscape through shrubs and small trees. Pass a bench, overlook a small pond (1.8 mi.) **[12]**, then begin a descent that leads you under the power lines (2 mi.) **[13]**. After bottoming out near several large cottonwood trees, the trail veers left into an oak/hickory forest.

Heading west, you can see Silver Lake through the trees to the north. Wind around a bowl-shaped wetland and pass through aromatic cedars to the junction with the Yellow Loop (2.3 mi.) **[14]**. Stay right and descend to a large wetland (2.4 mi.) **[15]**. Across the road is Losee Lake.

Climb a small ridge to get a great view of Losee Lake. The trail descends to cross Dexter-Townhall Road; then a boardwalk supports your steps through a wetland (2.5 mi.) **[16]**. Pass a bench overlooking the lake before the junction with the Blue Loop. Stay right and step onto a boardwalk that flows along the marsh perimeter of Losee Lake (2.6 mi.) **[17]**. From the boardwalk you climb to a bench, near a large oak tree, that faces the lake (2.7 mi.) **[18]**. Descend from the small ridge, winding around a wetland to the junction that leads you to the parking lot. Turn right and retrace your steps.

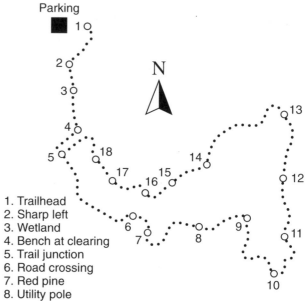

1. Trailhead
2. Sharp left
3. Wetland
4. Bench at clearing
5. Trail junction
6. Road crossing
7. Red pine
8. Utility pole
9. Bench/Yellow Loop trail junction
10. Bench in wetlands
11. Bench on hill
12. Bench overlooking pond
13. Utility corridor
14. Yellow Loop trail junction
15. Wetland
16. Boardwalk
17. Boardwalk
18. Bench at oak

45. Waterloo Recreation Area

- Experience geology hands-on at the Gerald E. Eddy Geology Center.
- Discover nature along interpretive trails.
- Escape to scenic overlooks, inland lakes, and deep woods.

Park Information

Covering almost 20,000 acres, this patchwork quilt of private and public landholdings is the largest state park in Michigan's Lower Peninsula. The park's terrain was shaped over 10,000 years ago in the last glacial period. Receding ice, often more than 1 mile thick, shaped the moraines (ridges), kames (hills), and kettles (lakes, ponds, and low-lying areas) that characterize the area, providing an abundance of recreational opportunities today. The terrain itself is a patchwork of remnant fields, upland oak/hickory forests, lowland beech/maple woods, and bogs.

The recreation area contains 17 lakes, numerous ponds and streams, four campgrounds, the Gerald E. Eddy Geology Center, several hiking trails, a 23-mile portion of the Waterloo-Pinckney Hiking Trail, a riding stable, bridle paths, and mountain bike trails.

Directions: West of Chelsea, head north from any of the six exits along I-94 that access the Waterloo Recreation Area. Take M-52 5 miles north to the Green Lake Campground. Follow Pierce Road north to the Cedar Lake Outdoor Center; north from there and west on Bush Road take you to the Geology Center.

To get to the park headquarters, go north on Kalmbach Road; then jog west on Cavanaugh Lake Road to north on Glazier Road, which curves west to Lowry. Head north to McClure Road; the head-quarters is west on McClure.

Access Sugarloaf Lake Campgrounds via Clear Lake Road north to Seymour Road. Turn east to Loveland Road, then south about .5 mile to the campground's entrance. Horseman's Camp is about .25 mile south from there.

Big Portage Lake Campground is located between Race and Mt. Hope Roads. Head north from either of these exits and turn onto Seymour.

Hours Open: Open daily from 8:00 A.M. to 10:00 P.M.

Facilities: Hiking, bicycling, horseback riding, cross-country skiing, snowmobiling, swimming, fishing, hunting, boat launch, camping (tent and RV), picnicking, interpretive trails, and an interpretive center.

Permits and Rules: A park fee is required per motor vehicle ($4 daily, $20 annually). Motor vehicles are permitted on established roads only. Camping and horseback riding are permitted in established areas only.

Further Information: Contact Waterloo Recreation Area, 16345 McClure Road, Route 1, Chelsea, MI 48118; 313-475-8307.

Other Points of Interest

The **Gerald E. Eddy Geology Center** features rocks, fossils, and glacial data. Slide shows, hiking trails, and interpretive programs help visitors understand the geologic history of the region. During the school year, hours are from 9:00 A.M. to 5:00 P.M. on Tuesdays through Sundays. From Memorial Day through Labor Day, hours are from 9:00 A.M. to 5:00 P.M. daily. For more information, call 313-475-3170.

The **Waterloo Area Farm Museum,** situated at 9998 Waterloo-Munith Road, serves as a memorial to the Michigan pioneer farmers. For more information, call 517-596-2254.

The **Riding Stable and Dude Ranch** offers guided trail rides. It is located at 12891 Trist Road, Grass Lake, MI 49240. For more information, call 517-522-8930.

View the fall migration of sandhill cranes at the **Haehnle Sanctuary,** which adjoins the recreation area. The sanctuary is located on the north side of Seymour Road, about 1.5 miles west of Race Road in Jackson County. For more information, call 517-886-9144.

Park Trails

Bog Trail 👢👢—1.5 miles—This linear trail starts at the Geology Center. It passes through forested wetlands and a mature beech/maple forest, and ends at a boardwalk that extends over a floating bog.

Hickory Hills Nature Trail 👢👢👢—1 miles—Start from the Park Headquarters on McClure Road. This hilly interpretive trail passes through an oak/hickory forest, skirts the shore of Crooked Lake, and putters through the remnants of a 1920s golf course.

Waterloo Recreation Area

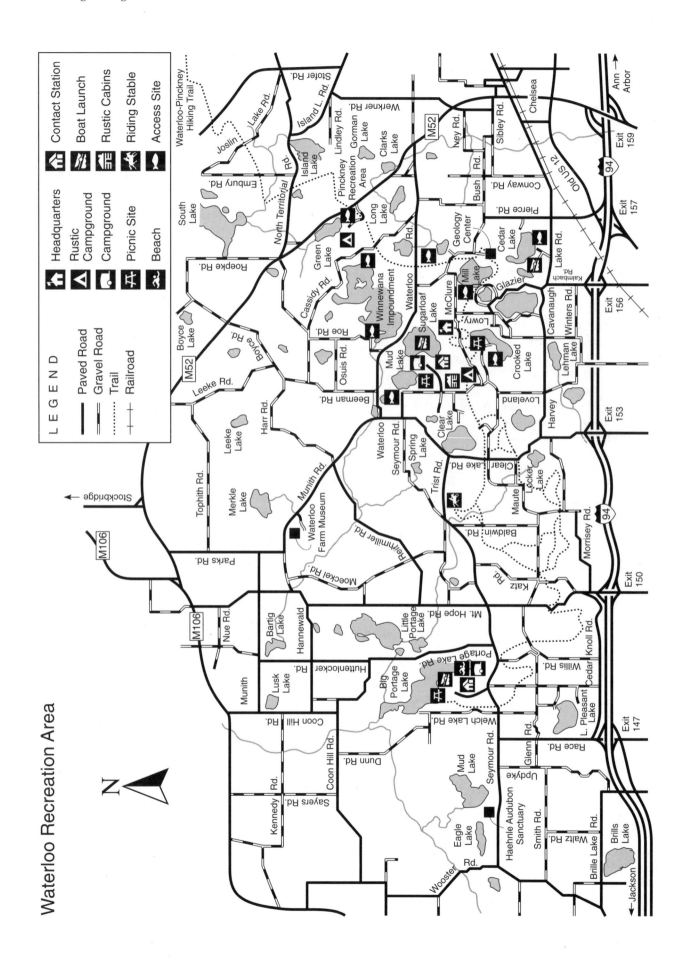

Waterloo-Pinckney Hiking Trail—Portage Lake to Sackrider Hill 👢👢👢

Distance: 5.9 miles one-way

Estimated Hiking Time: 3 to 4 hours

Note: Not many people will hike the Waterloo-Pinckney Hiking Trail from end to end. Because of all the day-hike opportunities it possesses, we've included two sections here. You may park at a number of crossroads. This is as close to a wilderness experience as you will find in southeast Michigan.

Cautions: Some swampy areas are inadequately planked, so wear proper footgear. The wet areas also attract seasonal insects. Be prepared. Various trails weave across this one, and not all are marked. Follow directions and the posted markings, and, usually, watch for the direct, well-worn path.

Trail Directions: Start in the northwest end of the Portage Lake boat launch parking area **[1]**. The trail takes you along a ridge overlooking the lake, dips to cross a stream on wood planks, then flows westward in gentle undulations until it bears south, away from the lake, and then climbs into the woods **[2]**.

At the fork (1.2 mi.) **[3]**, stay right. The trail descends, then climbs steeply, wrapping itself along a ridge that commands a view of the pond below. After crossing Seymour Road (1.5 mi.) **[4]**, continue through a grassy area, pass a power line, then weave through clearings before reentering the woods in an undulating pattern of hills and ridges, marshes, or ponds. Shortly after the 2-mi. marker, veer right. A field momentarily interrupts the undulating pattern (2.4 mi.) **[5]**.

After you cross List Road (2.7 mi.) **[6]**, the area is predominantly low lying and wet until you reach an old road, now a two-track (3 mi.) **[7]**. Turn left and enter a grassy clearing. Veer to the right when the trail splits (3.3 mi.) **[8]** and continue on to Willis Road, which has a parking lot (3.4 mi.) **[9]**.

Across the road, a concrete dam secures your steps over a stream that drains the cattail-covered wetland. Climb steeply back into the woods. The trail intermittently dips into marshy and wet areas. At 3.7 mi., wooden planks guide you through a soggy stretch of lowland **[10]**. Follow as the trail snakes around the rolling terrain and then descends onto Glenn Road (4.3 mi.) **[11]**. Steep hills, blanketed mostly with oaks, envelop the trail as you climb. Ascents are more difficult and steep; eroded downslopes require extra precaution. A trail merges in at 4.7 mi. **[12]**.

Take a dizzying look over the edge of the steep, wooded ravine when you reach the crest (5.1 mi.) **[13]**. About .1 mi. farther, veer left at the fork and continue along a land bridge that rises above the forest floor. Descend at a steep angle before you wind around to begin a serious climb up Sackrider Hill. A white cross marks the top (5.7 mi.) **[14]**, and a decked platform provides a welcome and well-deserved panorama of rolling farm fields, hedgerows, barns, and woodlands. If you have made arrangements to get picked up at the end of your hike, continue on and descend steeply to the parking area at Mt. Hope Road (5.9 mi.) **[15]**. Otherwise, you may want to turn back here and avoid the hill.

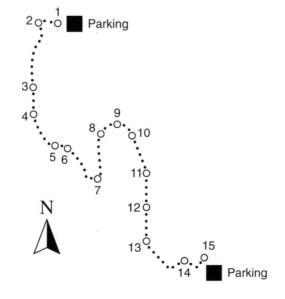

1. Trailhead
2. Entrance to woods
3. Fork in trail
4. Seymour Road
5. Field
6. List Road
7. Two-track
8. Split in trail
9. Willis Road/parking
10. Planked wetland
11. Glenn Road
12. Merging trail
13. Crest overlooking ravine
14. Sackrider Hill
15. Mt. Hope parking lot

Waterloo-Pinckney Hiking Trail—Horseman's Camp to Green Lake 👢👢👢

Distance: 8.3 miles one-way

Estimated Hiking Time: 3.5 to 4.5 hours

Cautions: The trail goes over roots and rocks, so wear appropriate footgear. Take insect repellent during the warm months. Various trails weave through that are not all marked. Pay attention to the posted markings; in most cases, watch for the direct, well-worn path.

Trail Directions: Start at the trail sign on Loveland Road about .25 mi. south of Horseman's Camp **[1]**. From here to the park headquarters, the trail winds its way through a heavily wooded and hilly landscape. There are some significant climbs up and over the hills. The trail snakes back and forth to cross McLure Road three times. Take care that you make a sharp left turn at a trail post located about .25 mi. past the first McLure Road crossing (.8 mi.) **[2]**.

A small stream is located at the second McLure Road crossing. Climb steeply away from the stream, and then descend sharply to merge with the Hickory Hills Nature Trail (1.9 mi.) **[3]**. Turn right. You soon reach steps made from railroad ties that guide you down to, and then up from, your third McLure Road crossing.

After a steep incline, Crooked Lake soon comes into view. After passing a bench, descend sharply to the lake. The stone foundation on your left (2.2 mi.) **[4]** once supported a pump house that supplied water to the Sylvan Estates Country Club, which went bankrupt during the Depression.

Rise steeply from the lake and enter what once was a golf course. Walk through the old fairway grass, then pass through trees to a parking area. Across the road is part of the old clubhouse for Sylvan Estates. It now serves as headquarters for the Waterloo Recreation Area (2.4 mi.) **[5]**.

From the headquarters to the Gerald E. Eddy Geology Center, the trail is an easy hike through woods and wetlands. Shortly after passing a metal barricade, you reach a junction (3.4 mi.) **[6]**. Turn left, and climb a small hill before descending into the woods. Soon you hike along a ridge above Mill Lake. Pass a bench to mile marker #18 (4 mi.) **[7]**.

At the next trail post, stay to the left and follow along the edge of a wetland. You may want to go right at the post, climb onto the back of the glacial feature

called an esker (a serpent-like hill created when glacial melt waters deposit sediments), and enjoy the panoramic view of a wetland.

Climb steeply to another overlook of Mill Lake. At the crest, the track joins a network of trails (4.2 mi.) **[8]**. Go left through a meadow, turn right at a parking lot, cross a road, and head into the woods. You soon reach a trail junction. Turn right. The next stretch takes you past the Mill Lake Outdoor Center and eventually to Bush Road, where a few cars can park (5.2 mi.) **[9]**. After a level stretch, turn left between two wetlands and rise sharply onto a ridge (5.8 mi.) **[10]**. Follow the ridge as it snakes its way to Waterloo Road (6.2 mi.) **[11]**.

The next section includes some steep climbs and descents through woods and wetlands. Eventually you snake your way down to cross Cassidy Road near a large wetland (7.7 mi.) **[12]**. Hike through several old farm fields, cross a footbridge, pass mile marker #22, and go under power lines into the woods that take you to the small parking area by Green Lake Campground (8.3 mi.) **[13]**. This is the eastern terminus of the Waterloo Recreation Area. The Waterloo-Pinckney Hiking Trail continues to the east for about 13 more mi. through Washtenaw County's Park Lyndon and the Pinckney Recreation Area (see park #44).

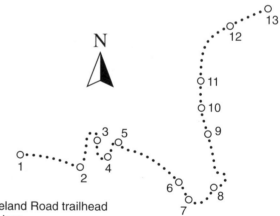

1. Loveland Road trailhead
2. Left turn
3. Hickory Hills Nature Trail
4. Stone foundation
5. Park headquarters
6. Trail junction
7. Mile marker #18
8. Trail junction
9. Bush Road
10. Left onto ridge
11. Waterloo Road
12. Cassidy Road
13. Green Lake Campground parking

46. Hidden Lake Gardens

- View the gardens from a series of winding, one-way drives set in the rolling Irish Hills.
- Visit the plant conservatory to enjoy tropical and arid plants as well as a variety of flowering houseplants.
- Test your plant identification skills on the thousands of trees, shrubs, and flowers that are labeled here.

Park Information

The 755-acre garden exhibits valuable plant collections and creates landscape pictures, fulfilling the objective of the Michigan State University-owned Hidden Lake Gardens. Open woodlands; native meadows; rolling hills; public gardens with natural and designed landscapes; and thousands of trees, shrubs, and flowers labeled for identification offer an incredible variety of landscapes for anyone interested in the outdoors.

Set in the glacially sculpted Irish Hills, this unique property has a plant conservatory that features tropical and arid plants. The Visitor Center has an auditorium, exhibits, meeting rooms, a gift shop, and a reference library. Some of the many plantings that color the landscape include a hosta collection, the Harper dwarf and rare conifer collection, a hill planted with various junipers, and a demonstration garden. Directing visitors to these, and numerous other features, are 6 miles of one-way drives. If that is not enough, five trails weave over 6 miles through woods and meadows, offering visitors a chance to get close to the natural environment.

Directions: Hidden Lake Gardens is 2 miles west of Tipton, or 7 miles west of Tecumseh. From M-52 head west on M-50 about 6 miles. The Gardens are located on the north side of M-50.

Hours Open: The Gardens and Conservatory are open from 8:00 A.M. to dusk in April through October and from 8:00 A.M. to 4:00 P.M. in November through March. The Visitor Center is open on weekdays during normal business hours and on weekends.

Facilities: Hiking and picnicking.

Permits and Rules: From April through October, the fee is $3 per person on weekends and holidays and $1 on weekdays. From November through March, the daily fee is $1 per person. Please preserve property and natural resources. Pets must be leashed and children must be kept under supervision. Please don't swim or boat; hunt or fish; park or drive vehicles or bicycles on grass, walks, or trails; picnic outside of the designated area; consume intoxicants; sunbathe; litter; ride bicycles on Sundays or holidays; have horses on the property; or use in-line skates.

Further Information: Contact Hidden Lake Gardens, Tipton, MI 49287; 517-431-2060.

Other Points of Interest

Bicentennial Woods contains the last stand of virgin beech/maple forest in Lenawee County. A short trail winds through the park. The park is on the west side of Tipton Highway, between Sheperd and Emery Roads, about 5 miles southwest of Tipton. For information, contact Building and Grounds Department, Lenawee County, 429 North Winter, Adrian, MI 49221; 517-264-4738.

Northwest of the Gardens, on US-12, is the **Walter J. Hayes State Park.** Rolling hills to trek through, two lakes to swim, boat, or fish, picnic areas, and camping facilities are what you will find here. For more information, contact Walter J. Hayes State Park, 1220 Wampler's Lake Road, Onsted, MI 49265; 517-467-7401.

At the junction of US-12 and M-50, visit the **Walker Tavern Historic Complex.** The tavern once served weary travelers as they journeyed along a stagecoach road that connected Detroit and Chicago. Exhibits, guided tours, and audiovisual programs help you revisit that time. For more information, contact Walker Tavern Historic Complex, 13220 M-50, Brooklyn, MI 49230; 517-467-7401. Or contact Michigan Historical Museum, 717 West Allegan Street, Lansing, MI 48918; 517-373-3559.

Park Trails

Kettlehole Plantings Walking Trail —.4 mile—Start from the parking stop along the 6-mile drive that is south of the Oak Upland Forest Tour. It loops through plantings.

Sassafras Trail —.7 mile—Start this trail along with the Pine-Tree and Hikers' Trails from the north end of the parking lot that is north of Hidden Lake. The trail loops through woods.

All Use Trail —.3 mile—Start from the northwest loop of the Sassafras Trail and wind through rejuvenating fields and woods.

Hidden Lake Gardens

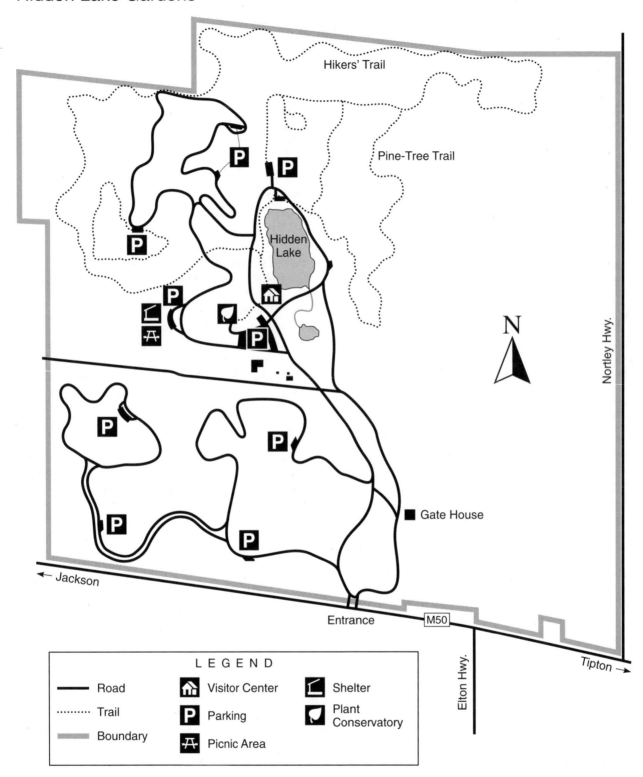

Hikers' Trail

Pine-Tree Trail

Hidden
Lake

N

Nortley Hwy.

Gate House

← Jackson

Entrance   M50

Elton Hwy.

Tipton →

L E G E N D

— Road

········· Trail

▬▬▬ Boundary

⌂ Visitor Center

P Parking

⊼ Picnic Area

◺ Shelter

❧ Plant
   Conservatory

Pine-Tree Trail 🥾🥾

Distance Round-Trip: 1.3 miles

Estimated Hiking Time: 30 minutes to 1 hour

Cautions: Poison ivy is present on the trail and hangs from trees. Portions of the trail are eroded; others have roots exposed or loose rocks. At times the trail narrows along ridges that angle down slopes. Watch your footing. Take insect repellent.

Trail Directions: Start the trail, along with the Sassafras, Hikers', and All Use Trails, from the north end of the parking lot that is north of the drive at Hidden Lake **[1]**. Head up the asphalt-paved trail, past the steep hill that is retained by rail ties. A strip of myrtle hugs the ground bordering the right side of the trail. This is only a teaser. On your drive through the grounds, you see this plant in full force as it spills down the slopes en masse in the "Ground Cover" area of the park.

The trail curves and you pass the All Use Trail junction (.1 mi.) **[2]**. The asphalt breaks up, and the trail becomes natural with roots, rocks, and erosional gullies. Climb the trail, accompanied by an old fencerow of trees. Glacial erratics, large boulders transported here by glaciers, show themselves erratically along the trail. A ridge rises alongside you. When your ascent tops out, notice the prevalence of oaks and hickories.

Pass a ravine in the woods. Post #7 is in its forefront. You'll pass many numbered posts; at one time there was a book that described the numbered sites. Soon you pass the junction for the Sassafras Trail, and then rock rubble—not unusual along fencerows or old property lines. Wind down and up to the junction for your turnoff (.3 mi.) **[3]**.

Turn right, wind down the narrow cobblestone trail, and pass a row of sassafras trees. Yes, the tree with mitten-shaped leaves is found along the Pine-Tree Trail. So are many old, gnarly crab apple trees. Watch for large vines wrapping themselves around the trees like stripes on a barber pole (.4 mi.) **[4]**.

Pass through a stand of red pines and then wind to the left. The trail descends, bottoming out near a large maple with several low branches like the arms of an octopus. Snake around with the trail and duck through a tunnel of shrubs and young maples; then walk along the narrow, tilted trail—perfect for a mountain goat—that skirts between a hill and a bowl-shaped depression. Soon, the trail makes a sharp right and heads down and past a large hickory. Watch for vines as large as tree branches that gnarl through the trees (.6 mi.) **[5]**.

Wind through thick shrubs, then down. Now you walk a narrow ridge with the hill on your right and a lowland to your left. The trail winds up and down and around the lowland, then makes a sharp right (.7 mi.) **[6]**, rounding the curve down to form the trek back to the north.

The trail undulates, descending rather steeply, and then winds around to more red pines to receive a carpeting of red-gold needles. Another steep descent, then gentle rolls, take you past a huge juniper (.9 mi.) **[7]**. At post #32, poison ivy takes over the bend—the trail veers sharply left. Walk the ridge along another goat trail between high and low lands.

Wind down and around through the wooded terrain, reaching a main trail junction at 1.2 mi. **[8]**. Head left and down the wide, eroded path. Your descent becomes steeper. Soon you reach the road, where you see swans delicately going about their business on Hidden Lake (1.3 mi.) **[9]**. From here you can see the road leading up to the parking lot where you left your vehicle. Take pleasure from the lake and the surrounding landscaping. Then head back up to your vehicle and slowly drive around the grounds to find unexpected beauty from the well-conceived landscapes.

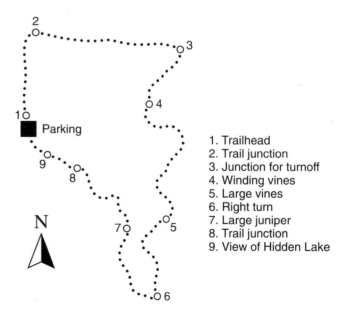

1. Trailhead
2. Trail junction
3. Junction for turnoff
4. Winding vines
5. Large vines
6. Right turn
7. Large juniper
8. Trail junction
9. View of Hidden Lake

Hikers' Trail 👢👢👢

Distance Round-Trip: 3 miles

Estimated Hiking Time: 2 to 3 hours

Cautions: The trail takes you over roots and rocks, and along narrow paths on ridges that angle down slopes. Watch your footing. There is poison ivy along the trail. Take insect repellent in the warmer months.

Trail Directions: Start the trail from the north end of the parking lot that lies north of the drive at Hidden Lake **[1]**. Head up the asphalt-paved trail.

The trail curves and you pass a junction (.1 mi.) **[2]**. Leave the asphalt and climb along an old fencerow as you step over roots, rocks, and erosional gullies. Glacial boulders show themselves erratically. A ridge, dominated by oak, hickory, and poison ivy, rises at your side.

You pass the Sassafras Trail junction, then rock rubble. The trail winds down and up to the junction for the Pine-Tree Trail (.3 mi.) **[3]**. Stay left, rise slightly into an open area, then descend to the lip of a deep wooded depression, the Butter Bowl (.4 mi.) **[4]**; this formation resulted from the melting of a huge hunk of buried glacial ice. Walk around the large bowl; then descend along a narrow path into it. Making a wide right, you pass moss-covered boulders as you skirt a rise on your left. Climb and follow along the lip of the bowl before making a sharp left through sumac and other brush (.6 mi.) **[5]**.

Heading east, wind and roll with the trail until it heads north and then west along the northern boundary. Trees frame the farm field on your right (.8 mi.) **[6]**. Look for the tree clutching a boulder (.9 mi.) **[7]**.

Winding your way through the woods, make a wide left to skirt a large, wooded depression (1.1 mi.) **[8]**. Have a seat on the boulder that split in such a way that it also provides you with a footstool (1.2 mi.) **[9]**. Then, start a gradual descent that becomes steeper and veers to the right. You bottom out at a gathering of field stones along an old fencerow (1.3 mi.) **[10]**.

Skirt the hill on your right and wind your way to peer over a fence at horses grazing on rolling pasturelands (1.5 mi.) **[11]**. Climb away from the pasture into lush foliage. At 1.6 mi., turn left where boulders **[12]** block your entrance into the woods and wind around another hill.

Having circled the hill, the trees become more impressive and the hills become more demanding. Descend sharply toward the drive, and then climb steeply to top out in the myrtle that spills down the slopes (1.8 mi.) **[13]**.

Roll through the oak upland forest and wind around a couple of depressions before breaking out into a field (2.1 mi.) **[14]**. Stay close to the tree line as you pass a large oak on the rise. Follow the worn path through the mowed field as you descend through the rolling landscape. Veer left behind several white pines; then wind down to parallel an old drainage ditch before climbing and cutting left across an old fencerow where the field stones are nearly buried (2.4 mi.) **[15]**.

Cross a field, and descend through sumac to reenter the woods (2.5 mi.) **[16]**. You soon teeter above a depression as you descend sharply to cross the drive to Juniper Hill (2.6 mi.) **[17]**. Keep descending until you find Hidden Lake (2.7 mi.) **[18]**.

Turn left and follow along the lake. Cut past myrtle to a small parking area on the north end of the lake (2.9 mi.) **[19]**. Stop and watch the swans before returning to your vehicle in the parking area north of the lake.

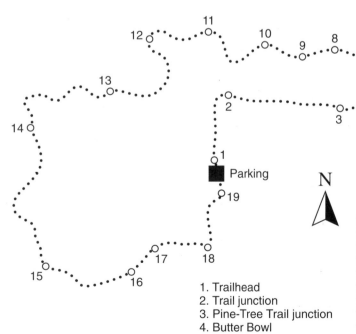

1. Trailhead
2. Trail junction
3. Pine-Tree Trail junction
4. Butter Bowl
5. Left turn away from bowl
6. Farm field
7. Tree gripping boulder
8. Wooded depression
9. Boulder
10. Field stones
11. Pasture
12. Boulders
13. Drive
14. Old field
15. Old fencerow
16. Reenter woods
17. Drive
18. Hidden Lake
19. Parking area

47. Chippewa Nature Center

- Explore almost 900 acres of woods, fields, rivers, ponds, and wetlands.
- Learn about the history and wildlife of the area at the Visitor Center.
- Visit the arboretum featuring native Michigan trees and shrubs.

Park Information

Start with a location at the confluence of the Pine and Chippewa Rivers; add a Visitor Center with museum, wildflower walkway, and wildlife-viewing area; and sprinkle in wetlands, and you've only skimmed the surface of programs or amenities available at the Chippewa Nature Center.

Over 14 miles of trails wind along the rivers, through forests and fields, and over wetlands (including remnant bog, oxbow, ponds, and marshes). Restored buildings—an 1870s homestead cabin, an 1880s log schoolhouse, and a sugarhouse—are all open seasonally. The Center offers more than a dozen school programs, a nature day camp, and nature walks.

Directions: From Midland, take M-20 to Homer. Go south to Prairie Road, then east to Badour to the Center. From US-10, take Business 10 west to Cronkright (Poseyville Road). Turn left on Cronkright, and go over Poseyville Bridge to St. Charles Street. Turn right and follow the signs 3 miles to the Center. From M-47, head northwest on Midland Road and turn left at Gordonville Road. Take this to Poseyville Road, turn right, and go to Ashby. Turn left on Ashby to Badour, where you turn right to reach the Center.

Hours Open: The Visitor Center is open Monday through Friday from 8:00 A.M. to 5:00 P.M.; Saturdays from 9:00 A.M. to 5:00 P.M.; and Sundays from 1:00 to 5:00 P.M. Call to find out holiday hours. The trails are open from dawn to dusk daily.

Facilities: Hiking, cross-country skiing, and interpretive center.

Permits and Rules: There is no admission fee for the Visitor Center or trails. No pets, smoking, alcohol, fishing, or hunting allowed. Bicycles and off-road vehicles are not permitted on the trails. Leave all plants, animals, and artifacts as you found them.

Further Information: Contact Chippewa Nature Center, 400 South Badour Road, Midland, MI 48640; 517-631-0830.

Other Points of Interest

Dow Gardens, located in Midland, features over 100 acres of various plants. The founder of Dow Chemical Company, Herbert Henry Dow, started the gardens in the late 1800s as part of the landscaping for his home. The facility is open daily from 10:00 A.M. until sunset, except on major holidays. For more information, contact The Dow Gardens, 1018 West Main Street, Midland, MI 48640; 517-631-2677.

The **Pere Marquette Rail-Trail of Mid-Michigan** is a 22-mile, asphalt-paved trail that has endpoints in Midland and Coleman. For information, contact Midland County Parks and Recreation Department, 220 West Ellsworth Street, Midland, MI 48640-5194; 517-832-6876.

Park Trails

Red Loop —2.5 miles—Start at the Visitor Center. It follows along the Chippewa River, then heads through sugar bush and beech/maple woods, and passes by the nature-study building and ponds.

Green Loop —2 miles—Start at the Visitor Center. It follows the river and through woods, passing the 1870s homestead farm and the log schoolhouse.

White Loop —1 mile—Starting at the Visitor Center, it follows the river, then cuts through an area near the arboretum before entering the woods and passing the Farmstead Foundation.

Yellow Loop —1.5 miles—This trail weaves through the wetlands area, which is located off the east side of Badour Road, south of Pine River Road.

Dorothy Dow Arbury Trail —.4 mile—This paved trail starts at the southwest portion of the Visitor Center parking area. It loops through pines, goes over a boardwalk near Arbury Pond, and has an observation deck overlooking the Pine River.

Meadow Trail —.6 mile—This trail is accessed from the parking area along Hubert Road, which is northwest of the Pine River. It passes primarily through a meadow.

Birch Trail —1 mile—Start from the parking area at Hubert Road. It cuts through mixed woods.

Meadow Mouse, Field, Wood Duck, and Fern Trails —.5 mile, .3 mile, .4 mile, and .1 mile, respectively—These trails are spurs off other loops.

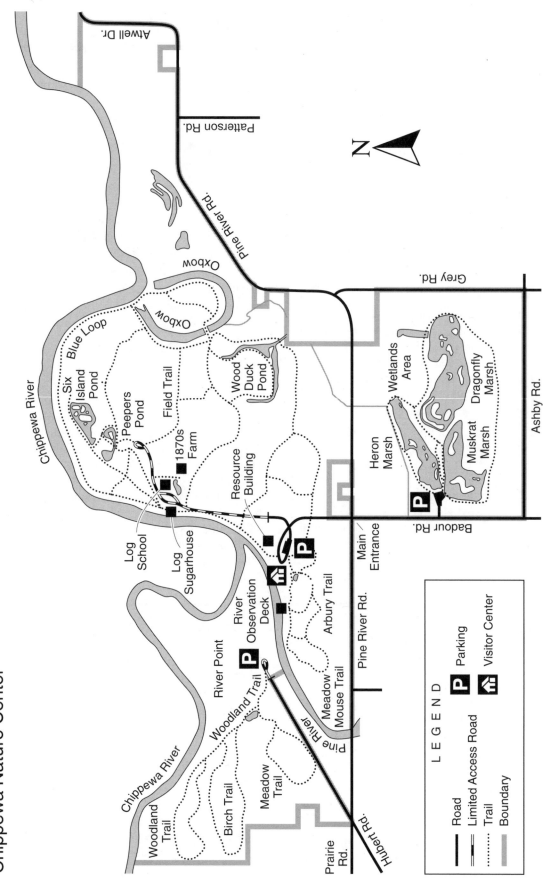

Chippewa Nature Center

Woodland Trail 👢

Distance Round-Trip: 2 miles (including the spur out to the loop)

Estimated Hiking Time: 1 hour

Cautions: Watch out for poison ivy, as well as for small stumps that may be protruding from the trail.

Trail Directions: The trail is located about .6 mi. northwest of the Visitor Center. Take Pine River Road west to Hubert and turn northeast. Hubert ends at a cul-de-sac. There are a few parking spaces here. The trail, along with the Meadow and Birch Trails, begins northwest of the parking area, just to the left of a garage. Watch for the "Trail Head" sign; then cut through the mowed path of grass **[1]**.

Don't let this grassy swath passing under transmission lines dissuade you. Soon the trail bends and you enter a canopy of trees, your gateway into a secluded environment (.1 mi.) **[2]**. The trail goes through a mix of mostly hardwoods and at .2 mi. arrives at a junction by a pond **[3]**. Follow to the right for the Woodland Trail, stepping on the planks over the stream that flows into the reflective pool to your left.

Shortly, you pass the first junction for the Birch Trail. Notice the stream that parallels the trail to your right, and thereafter the dark pool to your left. Just after the second Birch Trail junction, a small clearing is bright with the foliage of ferns (.4 mi.) **[4]**. After passing a wet area, the trail arrives at the junction for the Woodland Trail (.5 mi.) **[5]**. Go to the right and soon cross the planks over a low area that handles any overflow from the Chippewa River, which now flanks the trail to your right. The slightly undulating trail follows a ridge along the river, descends, and then veers left under the cover of trees before approaching intermittent clearings of ferns (.7 mi.) **[6]**.

Cutting through mature woods, the trail veers right; then, with its pine-needle carpeting, eventually bends left, dipping over a low, wet area to reemerge with a carpeting of moss (.8 mi.) **[7]**.

After passing through some hemlock, the trail turns left, rolling gently; then it passes through another wet area (1.1 mi.) **[8]** before taking another left to then undulate through wet, wooded lowlands. Look into the dark shadows of the trees. Is there wildlife there that you can't see, waiting for you to pass? Listen for the gentle sound of foliage being torn from a plant or the light snapping of a twig.

Light-tipped hemlocks line the way, and needles again soften the trail. At about 1.2 mi., a large conifer almost blocks your way **[9]**. Gentle undulations, like those at a miniature golf course, continue. The obstacles—white birch stumps, then a mix of other stumps—lie strewn beside the trail.

As you move along, the forest again becomes a mix of pine and hardwoods, and clearings of ferns give way to areas of sumac, which gives way to wetlands, which brings you to the close of the Woodland Loop (1.5 mi.) **[5]**. From here, retrace your steps for the .5 mi. hike back to the starting point of this trail.

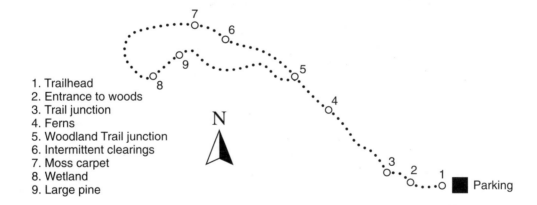

1. Trailhead
2. Entrance to woods
3. Trail junction
4. Ferns
5. Woodland Trail junction
6. Intermittent clearings
7. Moss carpet
8. Wetland
9. Large pine

N

Blue Loop 👢👢

Distance Round-Trip: 2.9 miles

Estimated Hiking Time: 1 to 1.5 hours

Cautions: Much of the trail is near water; bring your insect repellent. The trail is prone to flooding, so call ahead for trail conditions and wear appropriate footgear.

Trail Directions: The trail begins at the flagpole next to the Visitor Center **[1]**. Information boards are attached to the flagpole with updates on trail conditions and Nature Center activities.

Check the information board for trail conditions; then head north to the Pine River. You follow the river a short distance, to the point at which it converges with the Chippewa River. Benches are located along the bank so you can sit and watch the waters of the two rivers flow together (.1 mi.) **[2]**. When you continue your hike, the Chippewa River is at your side.

After passing a number of trail junctions that all go to the right, you reach an open area that serves as a pipeline corridor (.6 mi.) **[3]**. While this is not in keeping with the more natural setting of the Nature Center, keep your eyes open for wild turkeys. They have been spotted in the corridor.

The river soon swings to the right, and a number of houses come into view on the other bank. Along this stretch, near a culvert you cross over (.9 mi.) **[4]**, look for beaver in the little channel separated from the river by a sandbar. Geese, kingfishers, and muskrats also frequent this area.

At 1.3 mi., turn left at the trail marker and enter what once was the river channel **[5]**. A bench has been positioned nearby to allow you to sit and watch the Chippewa River flow by in its current channel. Beyond the bench, you reach the still waters of the old river channel, or oxbow lake (1.5 mi.) **[6]**. An oxbow lake is formed when the main channel is cut off, most likely during a flood event, as the river seeks a straighter or more direct path. The cutoff section of the channel forms the oxbow lake.

As you walk through the woods along the inside bend of the oxbow lake, look for snakes and turtles sunning themselves on exposed logs and branches. Swinging right, eventually you reach a land bridge that supports your steps across the oxbow and starts

you on your journey back to the Center (1.8 mi.) **[7]**. Immediately after crossing, turn left, then right. You may notice a number of tree stumps showing evidence of beaver activity here.

You soon find yourself walking along what looks like another old river channel. A wooden bridge provides a good platform from which to take in this scenic location called Wood Duck Pond (2.1 mi.) **[8]**. Large trees standing in algae-laden water dominate this area during periods of high water.

The trail then splits briefly. This provides you the option of taking the trail along a ridge or following the trail nearer the water. After the two trails reunite, turn left at the trail marker and enter an area where younger hardwood trees are mixed with pine. Not confined by water, the trail snakes its way through the trees and over a couple of boardwalks before reaching the trail sign that reads "Short Cut" (2.7 mi.) **[9]**. Resisting temptation, stay to the left and follow the trail over the Center's driveway, past the trailhead to the Dorothy Dow Arbury Trail, and back to the parking lot at the Visitor Center.

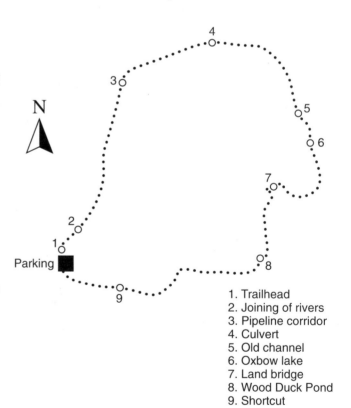

1. Trailhead
2. Joining of rivers
3. Pipeline corridor
4. Culvert
5. Old channel
6. Oxbow lake
7. Land bridge
8. Wood Duck Pond
9. Shortcut

48. Whitehouse Nature Center

- Hike four self-guided nature trails.
- Explore a tallgrass prairie restoration area.
- Visit an arboretum featuring Michigan trees and shrubs.

Park Information

Situated along the East Branch Kalamazoo River, only .25 miles from the main campus of Albion College, are the diverse lands of the Whitehouse Nature Center. Four self-guided interpretive trails lead you through a wide variety of natural and man-made habitats.

Dedicated in 1972, this 135-acre Nature Center, while owned and maintained by Albion College, is available for more than just college activities. Individuals of all ages are encouraged to make use of the Center's facilities and to participate in its educational programs and activities. Call the Center for information on adult education courses or on the public hikes that feature spring and summer wildflowers, birds, autumn trees and shrubs, and more.

Printed trail guides are available at the Interpretive Building. No, it is not a white house. The facility is named in honor of the 10th president of Albion College, Dr. William W. Whitehouse. While at the Interpretive Building, visit the observation room to see what might be feasting at the feeders. More than 175 species of birds have been sighted at the Center.

Directions: From I-94, take exit 124 to Albion. Go to the traffic light at Clark Street and turn left. Continue on Clark Street to a T-intersection at East Erie Street.

Turn right and proceed to Hannah Street. Turn left, cross the railroad tracks, and immediately turn left into a parking lot. Follow the signs through the parking lot to the Nature Center at the end of the athletic field.

Hours Open: The Nature Center's 135 acres are open seven days a week from dawn until dusk. The Interpretive Building is open weekdays from 9:00 A.M. to 4:30 P.M. and weekends from noon to 5:00 P.M.

Facilities: Hiking, interpretive trails, and interpretive center.

Permits and Rules: There is no admittance fee. The Nature Center does not permit bicycling, horseback riding, picnicking, camping, fire building, hunting, unattended dogs, consumption of alcoholic beverages, or motorized vehicles. Please do not take any natural materials from the Center or leave any unnatural materials.

Further Information: Call Whitehouse Nature Center at 517-629-2030.

Other Points of Interest

If it's history you seek, then a trip to **Marshall** is in order. Noted for its outstanding collection of Greek Revival and Gothic Revival homes from the 1840s and 1850s, the Marshall Historic Homes Tour is conducted annually during the weekend after Labor Day. For a do-it-yourself tour, a free walking-tour map is available. For the map, or for further information, call the Marshall Area Chamber of Commerce at 800-877-5163.

Park Trails

History Trail—Not a separate trail, the History Trail is a group of nine sites, scattered throughout the Nature Center, that are listed in a printed guide. As you walk the trails, you can refer to the guide for the history of a particular site.

Main Trail —.5 mile—The route of the old interurban trail bisects the Nature Center. All trails on the east side of the river loop off this historic corridor, referred to as the Main Trail.

McIntyre Marsh Trail —.5 mile—This trail is a boardwalk path through the marsh on the west side

of the river. The interpretive theme of the trail is marshland ecology.

Ecology Trail —2.4 miles, or 1.5 miles for the short loop—This trail is the longest at the Nature Center and features wildlife-viewing areas where various species occupy their open-field and fencerow habitats. Interpretive emphasis is on ecological principles and concepts.

Arboretum Trail —1 mile—This is the only trail within Whitehouse that is not self-guided. It passes through an area that features Michigan trees and shrubs.

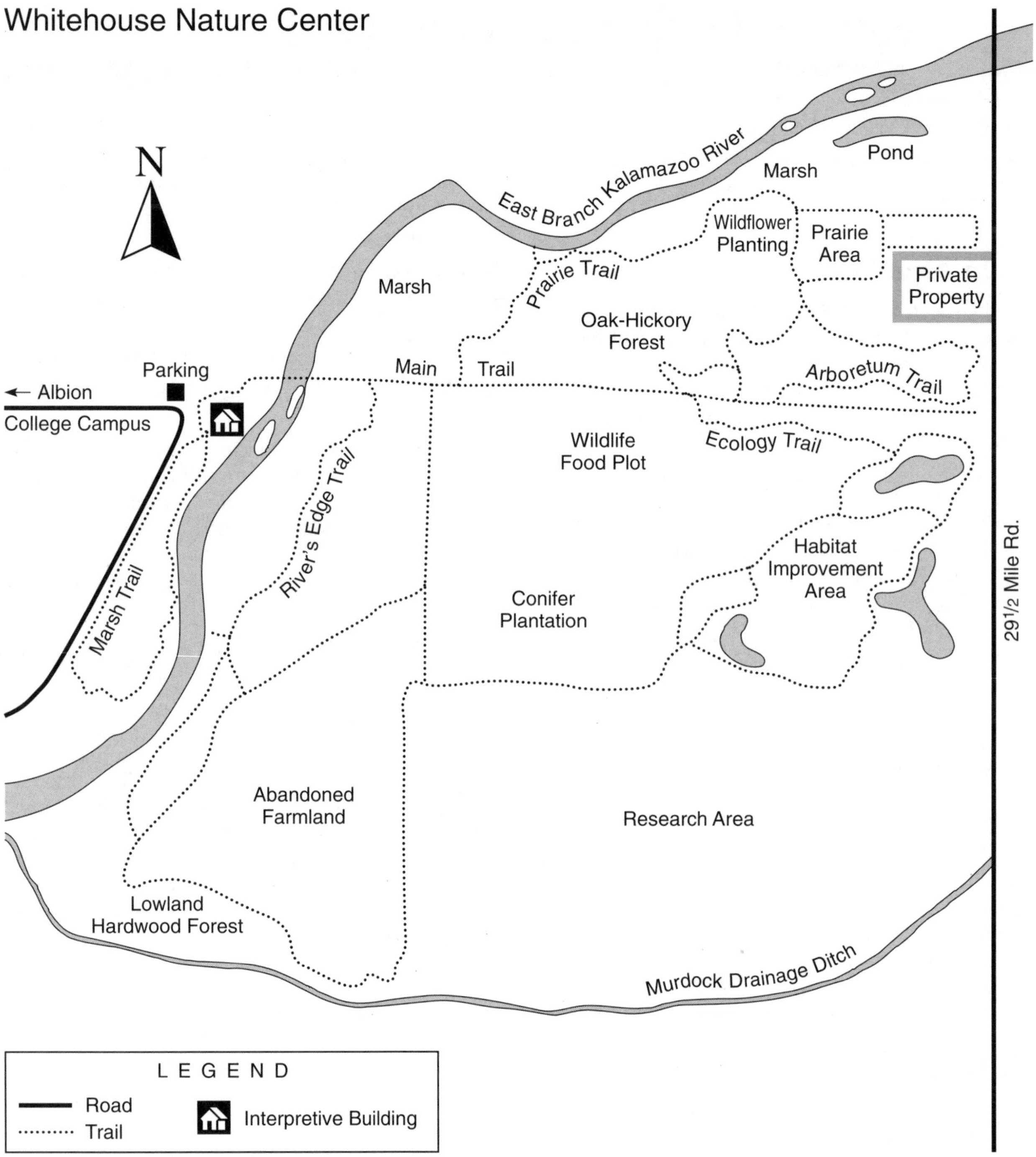

Whitehouse Nature Center

N

Parking

← Albion
College Campus

East Branch Kalamazoo River

Pond

Marsh

Wildflower
Planting

Prairie
Area

Private
Property

Marsh

Prairie Trail

Oak-Hickory
Forest

Main   Trail

Arboretum Trail

Ecology Trail

Wildlife
Food Plot

River's Edge Trail

Habitat
Improvement
Area

Marsh Trail

Conifer
Plantation

Abandoned
Farmland

Research Area

29½ Mile Rd.

Lowland
Hardwood Forest

Murdock Drainage Ditch

L E G E N D

——— Road

········· Trail

🏠 Interpretive Building

River's Edge Trail 🥾

Distance Round-Trip: .9 mile

Estimated Hiking Time: 30 minutes

Cautions: Take insect repellent during the warm months. Some sections of the trail may be wet or muddy. Wear appropriate footgear.

Trail Directions: The hike starts at the information board located at the east end of the parking lot near the Interpretive Building **[1]**. Stop in at the building for a trail guide.

Proceed to the left of the information board and follow the wood-chipped path past various wildflowers and the chatter of feeding birds. You then find yourself looking over the railing of a footbridge spanning the scenic East Branch Kalamazoo River.

The green corridor that stretches out before you once served as the rail bed for the interurban, Michigan Electric Railway, that operated between Detroit and Kalamazoo from 1904 to 1929. Now called the Main Trail, the corridor transports visitors, under their own power, to the Center's various nature trails.

The River's Edge Trail is the first stop (.1 mi.) **[2]**. Turn right and you will be on a narrow path that gives you a more intimate moment with nature than did the Main Trail. The canopy here is dense, an indicator of a floodplain forest where mucky soils promote this type of growth. Winding through the lush vegetation, you pass a number of interpretive stops on topics that vary from wood-rotting fungi to wild yams to wild plant communities. After you walk through a natural fernery, a spur trail splits off to take you to see what is happening at the river's edge (.3 mi.) **[3]**.

Back at the trail, you have the option of taking a shortcut through the woods or following the trail markers to the right. The shortcut saves you only about .3 mi. Either way, keep an eye out for blueberries. As you continue, a small ridge that has glacial erratics scattered among its vegetation rises on your left. At .4 mi., you can sit on one of the larger glacial boulders and watch the river flow by **[4]**.

Soon, turn left and climb away from the river to reach a trail junction (.5 mi.) **[5]**. Turn left and pull out your History Trail guide. You pass a place where Native Americans winter-camped about 500 to 1,000 years ago. You also pass the site of a sandstone quarry that was in operation in the 1840s.

After the shortcut trail merges back in from the left (.6 mi.) **[6]**, you will be skirting the Mouse Research Area. Here traps are set to monitor the fluctuations in the mouse population as part of a study into the ecology of populations. Please stay on the trail and don't tamper with the traps.

At the next trail junction, a stone bench waits (.7 mi.) **[7]**. Turn left and wind through the woods back to the old interurban, the Main Trail (.8 mi.) **[8]**. Turn left and retrace your steps back to the parking area.

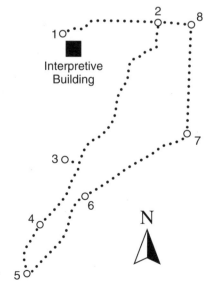

1. Trailhead
2. Trail junction
3. River
4. Glacial erratics
5. Trail junction
6. Trail junction
7. Stone bench
8. Interurban corridor

Prairie Trail 🥾

Distance Round-Trip: 1 mile

Estimated Hiking Time: 30 minutes

Cautions: Take insect repellent if you visit during the warm months. Some sections of the trail may be wet or muddy, so wear appropriate footgear.

Trail Directions: The hike starts at the information board located at the east end of the parking lot near the Interpretive Building **[1]**. Stop in at the building for a trail guide. Proceed to the left of the information board and follow the wood-chipped path past various wildflowers and the sounds of birds feeding. You will then be looking over the railing of a footbridge spanning the scenic East Branch Kalamazoo River.

While the bridge is a recent addition, the green corridor that bisects the Nature Center once served as the rail bed for the interurban, Michigan Electric Railway. This railway connected Detroit and Kalamazoo from 1904 to 1929. Now called the Main Trail, the corridor is a path that visitors take to the Nature Center's various nature trails.

The Prairie Trail is the first stop on the left. Turn and enter the oak/hickory forest. Duck under the fallen branch, caught in the crook of a tree, that is angled over the trail (.2 mi.) **[2]**. Then, swing right and wind through the forest to arrive at the river (.3 mi.) **[3]**. Within the Nature Center, marsh typically borders the river. Here the river has a sandy, rocky bank that enables you to get close for wildlife viewing.

Continue east to the native wildflower garden (.4 mi.) **[4]**. Most of the wildflowers you see here have been brought from other natural areas being faced with destruction. Since many of these wildflowers bloom before the trees leaf out and block the sunlight, the time to visit this area is in the spring. A small rock-bordered pathway loops through the garden to help you across the wildflowers. Just don't pick or remove any of them.

Just east of the wildflower garden is the Prairie Restoration Area. Dominated by grasses, this tallgrass prairie is best visited in the fall. Two loops from which you may view the prairie plants weave through the area. While they may look like weeds, prairie plants differ from weeds in that they are native plants; most weeds are plants that have been introduced into an area.

Having completed the inner loop, head south to the junction with the Ewell A. Stowell Arboretum Trail (.6 mi.) **[5]**. Turn right. Soon another junction gives you two options for getting back to the Main Trail. One is as good as the other. If you choose the one on the right, you weave through the woods. Once you are back to the Main Trail (.7 mi.) **[6]**, turn right and follow the old interurban corridor back to the parking area.

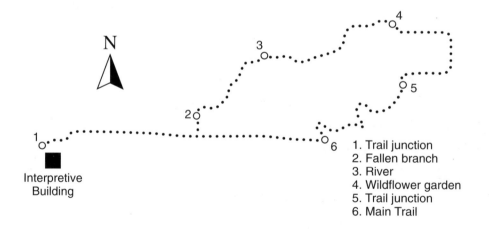

N

Interpretive
Building

1. Trail junction
2. Fallen branch
3. River
4. Wildflower garden
5. Trail junction
6. Main Trail

49. Yankee Springs Recreation Area

- Hike over rugged moraines to the Devil's Soup Bowl.
- Enjoy nine lakes, meandering streams, and numerous bogs.
- View wildlife in this recreation area and the adjoining Barry State Game Area.

Park Information

Over 5,000 acres of diverse terrain, once the hunting grounds of the Algonquian Indians, provide for varied recreation experiences. Nine lakes within the park boundaries offer opportunities for fishing, boating, swimming, and wildlife viewing. The largest, Gun Lake, is 2,500-plus acres. The site of Yankee Springs was established in 1835. Yankee Bill Lewis made the village famous by owning and operating an inn along the stagecoach run between Kalamazoo and Grand Rapids.

As with most of Michigan, the glacial period left its mark here. Features like the Devil's Soup Bowl, which is an old, dried-out kettle lake formation, and Graves Hill, a scenic overlook and one of the most popular of the rugged moraines that make for challenging hiking within the park, remind us of that period long ago.

Over 15 miles of hiking trails wind through the park to various points of interest. Additionally, there are 12 miles of biking trails and 12 miles of bridle trails.

Directions: The park is halfway between Kalamazoo and Grand Rapids, about 12 miles west of Hastings. From US-131, take exit 61 (County Road A42) east, following the signs for about 8 miles to the headquarters. From Hastings, take M-37 west to Gun Lake Road.

Hours Open: Open daily from 8:00 A.M. to 10:00 P.M.

Facilities: Hiking, mountain bicycling, cross-country skiing, snowmobiling, swimming, bridle trails, fishing, hunting, boat launch, camping (tent and RV), equestrian camping, picnicking, cabins, and interpretive trails.

Permits and Rules: A park fee is required per motor vehicle ($4 daily, $20 annually).

Further Information: Contact Yankee Springs Recreation Area, 2104 Gun Lake Road, Middleville, MI 49333; 616-795-9081.

Other Points of Interest

Adjoining the park is the **Barry State Game Area,** which offers more than 15,000 acres for wildlife viewing. For more information, contact the Barry State Game Area, 1805 South Yankee Springs Road, Middleville, MI 49333; 616-795-3280.

Park Trails

Chief Noonday Trail —4 miles—This trail begins off Chief Noonday Road. It takes you to the Devil's Soup Bowl and then returns. Along the way, you are afforded a panoramic view of the area from the McDonald Lake overlook.

Deep Lake Trail —4 miles—This trail begins and ends across from the campground office. It meanders around the bog area at the south end of Deep Lake, trudges across open fields and old farmsteads, and then winds around the smaller of the kettles at the Devil's Soup Bowl before returning north of Deep Lake. A portion of this trail is shared with mountain bikers, so take extra care and watch out for them.

Sassafras Nature Trail —.5 mile—This interpretive nature trail begins by the Gun Lake Campground office. Brochures are available for interpreting the signs that mark the way.

A portion of the North Country Trail, a National Park Service route, continues its trek through this park beginning south of Gun Lake Road. It follows along parts of the Chief Noonday and Hall Lake Trails.

Yankee Springs Recreation Area

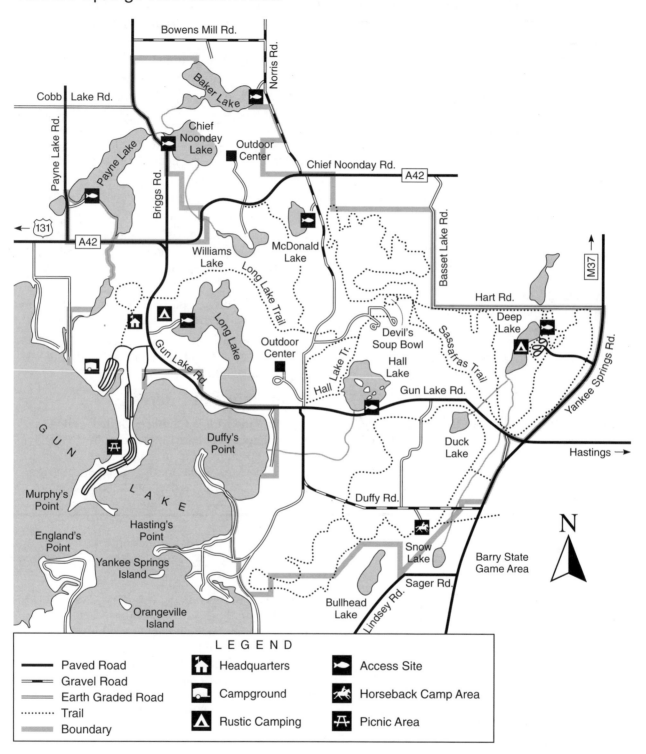

LEGEND

— Paved Road
 Gravel Road
 Earth Graded Road
······ Trail
 Boundary

Headquarters
Campground
Rustic Camping

Access Site
Horseback Camp Area
Picnic Area

Hall Lake Trail 👢👢

Distance Round-Trip: 3.7 miles (includes a hike around the Devil's Soup Bowl)

Estimated Hiking Time: 1.5 to 2 hours

Cautions: Watch for poison ivy along the trail. Around the soup bowls, a portion of the trail is shared with mountain bicyclists.

Trail Directions: The trail starts across from the entrance drive of the Long Lake Outdoor Center, which is north of Gun Lake Road **[1]**.

Just after embarking upon this trail, you come to a posted junction (.1 mi.) **[2]** that points the way to either Hall Lake or Graves Hill. Head to the right into the pines toward Hall Lake. Soon the trail veers to the left and you walk through small pines intermixed with mature hardwoods. The trail winds through rolling terrain until emerging into more mature pines (.2 mi.) **[3]**. After a short trek, look ahead of you to the left, where you catch your first glimpse of Hall Lake (.4 mi.) **[4]**. Thereafter, the trail swings left to begin traversing Hall Lake. A post to your left guides you over a short boardwalk that positions you between lake and wetland. In the springtime you'll be rewarded with an aquatic chorus as the frogs greet the season.

Soon you cross a footbridge over a small stream (.5 mi.) **[5]**. Look for the umbrella-like leaves on mayapples that clump near the stream. Shortly after that, a post reminds you that you are on a trail. Follow to the right and walk under the arch of a fallen tree.

Logs placed over a small stream remind you that you are still in a wetland environment (.7 mi.) **[6]**. Another reminder is the gentle sound of flowing water. Before starting up again, watch for turtles or other wildlife in the pond to your left or gaze out over Hall Lake to your right.

Now the trail begins its climb up. Stop along the way and take in a view of the lake from a high point (.9 mi.) **[7]**. Soon the trail begins a steep climb into mature pines. Near the top is a junction (1.1 mi.) **[8]**. Head straight to take in the view from Graves Hill, a moraine (a hill created from an accumulation of glacial deposits) (1.2 mi.) **[9]**. From here, view the interior of the park and a portion of Gun Lake before departing for the Devil's Soup Bowl.

To experience these kettles, or glacier-made depressions, continue straight on the Chief Noonday Trail. Follow as it winds around and then heads left to a parking area at a posted junction (1.3 mi.) **[10]**. The trail continues to the right of the parking area. Follow this up to the next parking loop (1.5 mi.) **[11]**, which overlooks the large soup bowl. From here you can look deep down the kettle created thousands of years ago from the weight of ice that broke off from glaciers. Don't be tempted to advance down the steep slope. Instead, follow the road to the left; this leads you to a continuation of the trail as it traverses the steep kettle and takes you to a junction along the ridge where you get the impact of the Devil's Soup Bowl (1.7 mi.) **[12]**. Large, deep depressions, more like kettles than bowls, lie before you.

Turn left, then right, following around the small bowl's edge until it eventually brings you to a ridge between the two kettles and circles back to the junction that directed you here (2.1 mi.) **[12]**. Turn left and retrace your steps back to Graves Hill (2.6 mi.) **[9]**. From here, backtrack the short distance to the post you passed earlier (2.7 mi.) **[8]**. Turn right and head down the slope along the Long Lake and Chief Noonday Trails. At the bottom, turn left at the posted junction. Soon you'll see a pond to your left (2.8 mi.) **[13]**, just before you climb up a short, steep hill, and then come to a posted fork (3 mi.) **[14]**. Stay to the right. The trail descends; then it veers left around a pond and brings you to another post (3.1 mi.) **[15]** before heading through small pines, then mature pines. Ski trails weave throughout this area, so be sure to stay on the main trail until you finally reach the junction that introduced you to the loop along the Hall Lake Trail (3.6 mi.) **[2]**. Turn right to head back to your vehicle.

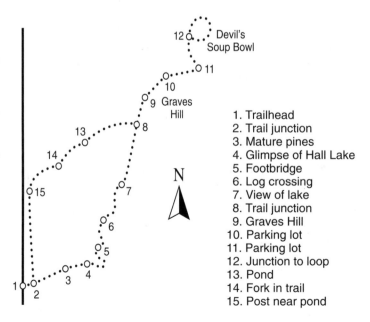

1. Trailhead
2. Trail junction
3. Mature pines
4. Glimpse of Hall Lake
5. Footbridge
6. Log crossing
7. View of lake
8. Trail junction
9. Graves Hill
10. Parking lot
11. Parking lot
12. Junction to loop
13. Pond
14. Fork in trail
15. Post near pond

Long Lake Trail 🥾🥾

Distance Round-Trip: 6.8 miles (which includes a hike around the Devil's Soup Bowl)

Estimated Hiking Time: 3 hours

Cautions: Watch for poison ivy along portions of the trail. Snowmobile and ski trails weave through the area. Their impressions are evident. Take care to stay on the main hiking trail.

Trail Directions: Start on the east side of Gun Lake Road, just north of park headquarters **[1]**. The trail is posted. You may park alongside of Gun Lake Road. (You may also start this trail from the north end of the Gun Lake campgrounds and follow along with the Sassafras Trail before cutting eastward across Gun Lake Road, which will add about .7 mi. round-trip.)

Head east from the road through a mixed forest until you come to a posted junction (.3 mi.) **[2]**. Turn left and follow along past stately pines until you reach the boardwalk that will support your steps over a beautiful bog (.6 mi.) **[3]**. In spring, this area lights up with the foliage and flowers from skunk cabbage, fiddleheads, and marsh marigolds—a stunning contrast to the dark, rich soil in this wet area and to the shaded woods at its periphery. The boardwalk winds around for almost .4 mi. before it ends (1 mi.) **[4]**. Continue along the ridge to the right as you traverse between a stream and rolling hills. Just after crossing a small plank over the stream (1.1 mi.) **[5]**, the trail ascends into a mixed forest.

Ultimately, the trail comes to a post (1.2 mi.) **[6]**, where you are directed to the right for Graves Hill, your destination. The path, now wide, is a remnant of an old wagon road that is believed to have been part of a stagecoach run from Kalamazoo to Grand Rapids.

At about 1.3 mi. a junction **[7]** directs you left to follow along a wetland. At about 1.8 mi., your path merges with a snowmobile trail **[8]**. Swing left

through a grassy area and begin a climb into pine-covered hills. Ski trails weave throughout the area. Stay straight on the main trail. At about 2.1 mi., you come to a posted junction **[9]**. Stay straight, following the Chief Noonday Trail, and soon you'll see another junction. Turn right, then cross the dirt road at about 2.2 mi. **[10]**.

The trail climbs into hardwoods and comes to another post at about 2.4 mi. **[11]**. Turn right and follow this south to cross another dirt road and soon reach a junction (2.5 mi.) **[12]**. Take the fork that climbs up the moraine and you soon reach another junction at the crest (2.7 mi.) **[13]**. Turn left, and within a few steps you arrive at Graves Hill, where you get a panoramic view of the park. Off to the southwest you can see a portion of Gun Lake.

From this overlook, continue straight along the Chief Noonday Trail and follow it as it winds around, then heads left to a parking area at a junction (2.8 mi.) **[14]**. The trail climbs to the right of the parking area to the next parking loop, which overlooks the large soup bowl (3.0 mi.) **[15]**. From here you can look deep down the glacier-created depression. You'll notice that others before you have trudged down the slope. Stay on the trail and take in the full impact of the glacial feature by following the road to the left, where it soon picks up the trail as it traverses the steep kettle. Follow along until you get to a junction along the ridge where you can get sweeping views of the Devil's Soup Bowl (3.2 mi.) **[16]**. These large, deep depressions, made from the weight of ice that broke off from glaciers, leave you in awe at the forces that shape the landscape.

Turn left, then right, following around the small bowl's edge until it eventually brings you to a ridge between the two kettles and circles back to the junction of the trail that directed you here. Turn left and retrace your steps back to Graves Hill and to the junction (4.1) **[13]** that takes you down the slope so you can head back along the Long Lake Trail. Your 2.7-mi. trek back may be enjoyed again, but from a different perspective.

1. Trailhead
2. Trail junction
3. Boardwalk
4. End of boardwalk
5. Plank over stream
6. Trail post
7. Trail junction
8. Snowmobile trail junction
9. Trail junction
10. Cross dirt road
11. Trail post
12. Trail junction
13. Junction at crest
14. Parking area at junction
15. Parking lot
16. Junction to loop/Devil's Soup Bowl

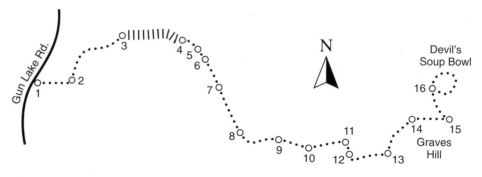

50. Kalamazoo Nature Center

- Explore 1,000 acres of thickets, meadows, farm fields, ponds, woodlands, and marshlands.
- Learn from old and new—view a restored 1850s homestead and farm, and learn about efficient solar energy.
- Visit the arboretum and botanical garden.

Park Information

With a mission to further the development of an environmental ethic in all persons within its reach, it is no wonder that the Kalamazoo Nature Center has so much to offer. An interpretive center features displays, a nature library, and a book shop. Field trips, training for teachers and naturalists, school curriculum programs, adult courses (nature photography, wildflowers, and gardening), and family activities (nature walks, summer camps, and excursions) are a few of the opportunities offered.

You can also wander the grounds and visit the DeLano Homestead, an 1858 homestead that has been restored and where activity demonstrations help visitors interpret the history of rural Michigan. You can learn how a pioneer farm functioned, or visit the farm and barnyard to understand modern organic farming techniques; you might explore a small, reconstructed prairie plot with some hundred species of native Michigan grassland plants. With so much to experience, you may need to come back to enjoy the arboretum and botanical reserve, the solar greenhouse, or the hummingbird-butterfly garden. Add to these resources 8 miles of nature trails through mature beech-maple forest; past ponds, marshes and streams; and over open fields, and you're sure to leave with a better appreciation of the environment.

Cooper's Glen, as the area used to be known, is named after James Fenimore Cooper, who visited the area in 1847 and 1848. While he pursued business interests in the vicinity, he collected information on natural features for a novel, *Oak Openings*.

Directions: The nature center is 5 miles north of Kalamazoo. From US-131, take D Avenue 3 miles east to Westnedge Avenue. Go south 1 mile to the entrance.

Hours Open: Monday through Saturday from 9:00 A.M. to 5:00 P.M. and Sundays from 1:00 P.M. to 5:00 P.M. The center is closed on Thanksgiving, Christmas Eve, Christmas, and New Year's Day. The west parking lot, near the DeLano Homestead, is open Saturday from 9:00 A.M. to 6:00 P.M. and Sunday from 1:00 P.M. to 6:00 P.M.

Facilities: Hiking, interpretive trails, and interpretive center.

Permits and Rules: No admission fee for members; $3.00 for nonmember adults and $1.50 for nonmember children or senior citizens. No pets are allowed.

Further Information: Kalamazoo Nature Center, 7000 N. Westnedge Avenue, Kalamazoo, MI 49004, or call 616-381-1574.

Other Points of Interest

Northwest of Battle Creek is the **Kellogg Bird Sanctuary,** at 12685 East C Avenue in Augusta, which is between Kalamazoo and Battle Creek. A unit of the Kellogg Biological Station of Michigan State University, the sanctuary is host to a variety of waterfowl. Stroll along the landscaped paths. Or head to the W.K. Kellogg Forest, where you may view the experimental stands of trees. For more information call Michigan State University at 616-671-2510 for the sanctuary or 616-731-4597 for the forest.

The **Kal-Haven Trail Sesquicentennial State Park** is a 33.5-mile rail-trail between Kalamazoo and South Haven. Contact the Van Buren State Park, 23960 Ruggles Road, South Haven, MI 49090; 616-637-4984.

Park Trails

Pioneer Woods Trail 👢👢—about 1 mile—This trail begins at the parking area south of West E Avenue and is open only on Saturdays from 9:00 A.M. to 5:00 P.M. and Sundays from 1:00 P.M. to 5:00 P.M. It traverses a beech-maple forest, circles the Pioneer Sugar Shack, and passes by the Pioneer Cabin and Barn and the DeLano Homestead.

Hawkridge Trail 👢—.3 mile, one-way—This trail begins southeast of the Family Farm Parking lot and may also be reached from the Fern Valley Trail. The trail's destination is an open, grassy area with a backdrop of tall trees.

Bluebird Trail 👢👢—.3 mile, one-way—Start from the south end of the Beechwood Trail and end at a gravel pit. From above the gravel pit the trail offers an overview of the Kalamazoo Valley.

Kalamazoo Nature Center

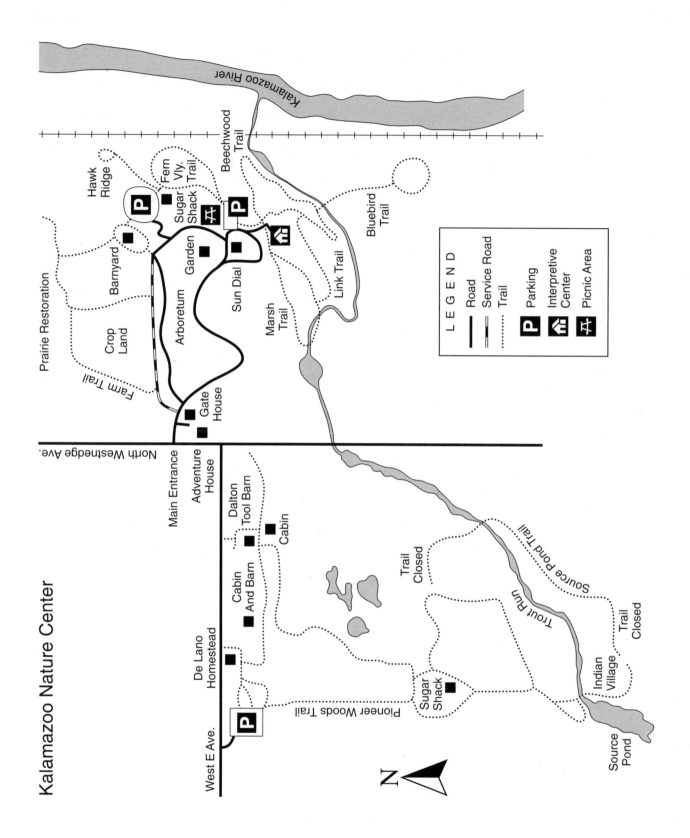

LEGEND

——	Road
═╪═	Service Road
····	Trail
P	Parking
🏛	Interpretive Center
🏕	Picnic Area

Kalamazoo River

Hawk Ridge

Fern Vly. Trail

Sugar Shack Trail

Beechwood Trail

Bluebird Trail

Link Trail

Barnyard

Garden

Sun Dial

Marsh Trail

Prairie Restoration

Crop Land

Arboretum

Farm Trail

Gate House

North Westnedge Ave.

Main Entrance

Adventure House

Dalton Tool Barn

Cabin

Cabin And Barn

De Lano Homestead

West E Ave.

Pioneer Woods Trail

Trail Closed

Source Pond Trail

Trout Run

Indian Village

Trail Closed

Sugar Shack

Source Pond

N

Beechwood Trail 🥾🥾🥾

Distance Round-Trip: .8 mile

Estimated Hiking Time: 30 to 45 minutes

Cautions: Watch out for poison ivy, as well as for small stumps that may protrude from the trail. Take along insect repellent.

Trail Directions: The trail starts at the information board located at the southwest corner of the interpretive center parking lot **[1]**. You can also start this trail from the interpretive center. A huge boulder welcomes you to the trail. Others line the trail as you enter the darkness of thick woods awaiting you after you turn left at the first fork (to avoid crossing the service road). Wind down and to the right, where the trail junction from the interpretive center joins in. Embedded in the ground here is a white and salmon–colored boulder. Turn left and head down to the start of the loop (.1 mi.) **[2]**. Take the southernmost trail down the stone-covered path that winds through rolling hills and mature sugar maples.

Step down stony stairs of railroad ties and pass the Link Trail that heads off to the right; wind down a second flight to a low area, and go on to a mossy graveyard of fallen trees (.2 mi.). You'll notice a large tree jutting into the trail **[3]**. Soon, you see the stream up ahead, Trout Run, and the trail makes a hairpin bend to the left. Trout Run stream runs along to the right of the trail. At .3 mi. a bridge fords the stream **[4]**, and another trail, the Bluebird, heads off there to the right, rolling through the wooded hills. The Bluebird Trail goes to the gravel pit, offering an overview of the Kalamazoo Valley.

Continue straight on the Beechwood, walking in the small valley that Trout Run stream cuts through. Impressive hills rise steeply from its banks. Just before you reach .4 mi., the trail winds left and up, soon rising above the stream. A wood-rail fence keeps you safely on the trail **[5]**. Stop here and enjoy the massive slopes before you.

Shortly, the stream widens to include wetland vegetation. When you come to a planked bridge, watch the small stream of water spilling down the hillside to your left. The stream and surrounding wetland vegetation widen subtly as you continue on. Watch for the horseshoe-shaped turn in the stream. Evidence of recent overflows suggest that a shorter, straighter path is being cut by the stream, perhaps to eventually cut off the horseshoe bend (or oxbow, as it is called).

So steep is the slope to the stream now that railroad ties brace the embankment from eroding into the stream. Just before the trail makes a sharp curve left up the hill, look down at the small valley. This area, once known as Cooper's Glen, used to be a favorite picnic and hiking stop of interurban and railroad passengers; a rail corridor remains (.5 mi.) **[6]**. You see it just before you make the sharp left and begin your steep climb up the moraine, or glacier-created hill. Every so often, stop and enjoy the overlook of the small valley below. Beyond the crest, the trail rolls through maple-covered moraines.

The forest thins, and you enter a thicket of small trees, wildflowers, and grasses where less than 40 years ago there was an open field and apple orchard (.6 mi.) **[7]**. Soon you come to the junction that closes the loop of this trail. Explore the interpretive center or turn right and retrace your steps to the parking lot.

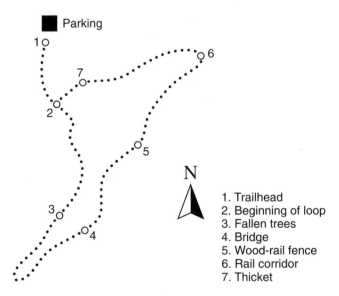

■ Parking

1. Trailhead
2. Beginning of loop
3. Fallen trees
4. Bridge
5. Wood-rail fence
6. Rail corridor
7. Thicket

N

Fern Valley Trail 👢👢👢

Distance Round-Trip: .6 mile

Estimated Hiking Time: 15 to 30 minutes

Cautions: Watch out for poison ivy, as well as for roots and rocks that may be exposed along the trail. Take along insect repellent in warm months.

Trail Directions: Pick up a brochure at the interpretive center before starting out on this trail. There are numbered stops along the path. The trail starts at the northeast corner of the eastern parking lot for the interpretive center **[1]**. A red oak serves as your trailhead post.

After only a few steps, you merge into the trail (which you may also start west of the picnic area). A sign instructs you to "follow the trail and learn about ground water." Turn right and sight a rock with a #3 on it. The brochure mentions recycling, rain, and hydrologic cycle.

Stroll down the grassy swath through mixed hardwoods. Soon you face a choice: right or left path. Jog to the right and cut into the woods. The natural trail descends, taking you past wild roses, Virginia creeper, and poison ivy. On your right, large rocks are strewn alongside the ridge. Can you pick out the pudding stone? Soon you reach rock #4. Lift up the wooden, cellar-like door and peer at the soil profile (.1 mi.) **[2]**.

The trail ascends and curves to the right, where a bench rests. You may rest, too, or wind down and around through the wooded hills. For the most part, a canopy shades out any intense sunlight, but small clearings occasionally let in streams of sunshine. The small opening at rock #6 is due to a spring, or, as the brochure says, "ground water flowing to the surface" (.2 mi.) **[3]**.

After bottoming out at the stream, the trail climbs, taking you through large beeches and maples. It veers left and parallels the rail track below to your right. Your loop continues to wind left. At .3 mi. steps made of railroad ties lead down the slope to a deck overlooking a small pond **[4]**. Marker #8 features the water pump here, not the pond. Why? Read up.

The trail wraps around the pond, which connects to a pool on your right. Listen. You can hear the water's passage as you step over its drainage stream. Wind up and around to get a perspective of the pond. Refer to #9 in the brochure and find out what makes a pond a pond.

Continue ascending past a junction, step up the rail-tie staircase, and arrive at #10. You don't need a brochure to know that these boulders are the matter of discourse: erratics—transported here by the glaciers. Keep climbing and get another view of the pond. Pass a moss-covered graveyard of logs, then reach the junction for the Hawk Ridge Trail. Go straight and ascend the hill to the sugar shack (.4 mi.) **[5]**. Sugar maples sweeten your climb with their cooling canopies.

The trail veers sharply to the left, ascends, and rolls through the forested terrain. At .5 mi., on your left, trees stand cloistered together making a cathedral **[6]**. One type of tree—small, with a spindly trunk, and huge leaves—is noticeable through this stretch of trail. So spindly is its trunk and so large are its leaves, the tree almost seems like a big-eared, long-legged, and awkward colt. The tree—the pawpaw—is native to the area.

Soon you walk around a large tree of many trunks, and the trail turns grassy. Shade from canopies gives way to sunshine. You are near your journey's end. Break out of the loop and onto the grassy, narrow lawn that you started from, soon returning to your starting point near rock #3. Turn left to the parking area. Stop by the Interpretive Center if you haven't already done so.

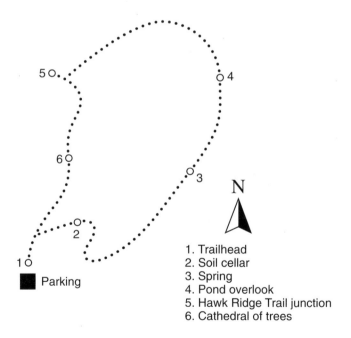

1. Trailhead
2. Soil cellar
3. Spring
4. Pond overlook
5. Hawk Ridge Trail junction
6. Cathedral of trees

51. Aman Park

- Hike through the rolling, wooded terrain shaped by Sand Creek.
- Enjoy a quiet corner of Grand Rapids far removed from the bustling urban center.
- View a spectacular springtime display of wildflowers.

Park Information

Although there is more history than meets the eye in how Jacob Aman's property ended up as part of Grand Rapids, it was his wish that the land belong to the city after his death. In a nutshell, that is why Grand Rapids has this city park located about 6 miles west of the city's limits.

Sand Creek has cut a narrow valley through the park's 331 acres. Trails wander ridges high above the valley. Other trails cut through marshes, bogs, forests, and fields. The six trails that weave over the rugged, yet peaceful, environment make a beautiful and stark contrast with the boisterous city nearby.

Wildflowers are spectacular in the spring, and the park's diverse terrain and varied plants produce continual showings throughout the year, from skunk cabbages and marsh marigolds to beeches and aspens, even to the gray of leafless branches pocketed with ice crystals. All seasons show off something in this retreat.

Directions: From I-196, take M-45 west about 6 miles. The park is on the north side of M-45, or Lake Michigan Drive.

Hours Open: The trails are open year-round from dawn until dusk.

Facilities: Hiking, fishing, cross-country skiing, and picnicking.

Permits and Rules: There is no fee. Enjoy the natural setting, but build no fires and pick no wildflowers or other plants.

Further Information: Grand Rapids Department of Parks, 201 Market St. SW, Grand Rapids, MI 49503; 616-456-3361.

Other Points of Interest

Pigeon Creek Park provides more than 10 miles of trails for hiking, mountain biking, cross-country skiing, and horseback riding. The park is about 12 miles west of Aman Park on Stanton Road. For more information call the Ottawa County Parks and Recreation at 616-846-8117.

Explore the **Frederik Meijer Gardens**, home of the state's largest tropical conservatory. Besides plants from around the world, the gardens feature waterfalls, streams, and winding, barrier-free pathways, to name but a few amenities. For more information call the Frederik Meijer Gardens at 616-957-1580.

Walk, skate, ski, or pedal along the 13 miles of the linear **Kent Trails**. Running partly along the abandoned Lakeshore and Michigan Southern Railway grade, the northern end of the trail can be reached from John Ball Zoo. For more information call the Kent Country Road and Park Commission at 616-242-6948.

Hidden within Grand Rapids is the 143-acre **Blandford Nature Center**. Nearly 4.5 miles of trails wind around the Center's woods, fields, ponds, and streams. Call the Blandford Nature Center at 616-453-6192 for more information.

Park Trails

The trails that loop through the park build on one another, weaving to Sand Creek or along the ridges high above the creek's valley. In 1997 a new interpretive trail is scheduled to open, which will add about .5 mile to the 5 miles already in place. Established trails will then feature identified wildflower areas.

Blue Trail 👢👢—1.2 miles—Access this trail from the Red Trail. It heads into the north end of the park along the west side of Sand Creek.

Green Trail 👢👢—.9 mile—Reach this trail also from the Red Trail. It loops over to the west side of the park, climbs out of the valley, and makes for an extended Red Trail walk.

Orange Trail 👢—.8 mile round-trip—This trail starts from the trail board north of the small parking area off the access road. It follows an edge separating field and forest, and culminates at Sweets Monument overlooking the Swan Creek and its valley before it heads back.

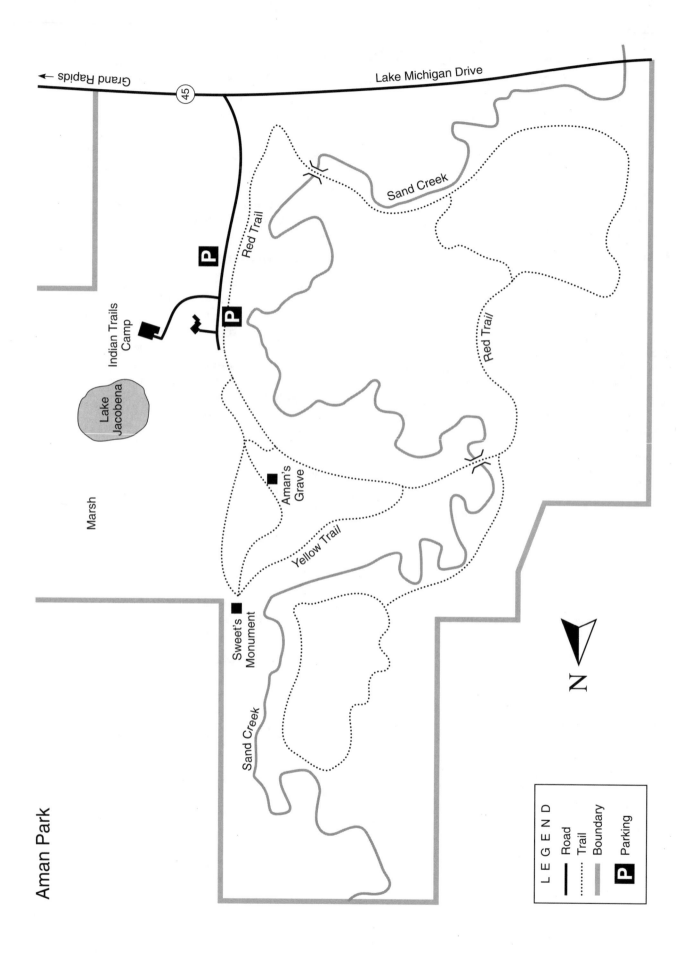

Aman Park

Grand Rapids ←
Lake Michigan Drive
45

Red Trail

P

P

Indian Trails Camp

Lake Jacobena

Marsh

Sand Creek

Red Trail

Aman's Grave

Yellow Trail

Sweet's Monument

Sand Creek

N

L E G E N D
Road
Trail
Boundary
P Parking

Yellow Trail 👢

Distance Round-Trip: 1.1 miles

Estimated Hiking Time: 30 minutes

Cautions: Parts of the trail are prone to erosion and parts have roots or rocks, so watch your step. Take insect repellent in warm months.

Trail Directions: Park in the small lot on the west side of the access drive, south of the trailhead. Start the trail along the west side of the map board that shows each trail by color **[1]**. Yours is the Yellow Trail. Your path is wide as you head through a canopy that includes oaks and hemlocks. A ravine is at your side as the trail winds around and passes a junction, which will be your return route (.2 mi.) **[2]**.

Still level, wide, and winding, the trail cuts through beeches and maples and gently descends. Just before you arrive at a junction (.3 mi.) **[3]**, pass the bench nature carved for you: a tree stump in the shape of a chair. Turn right at this junction, and follow along the trail as it takes you high on a ridge that overlooks a green pool in the valley below. On the ridge you walk through more hardwoods, oaks, and maples. The trail subtly ascends.

Pass some trees that have leaned too far over the slope and have fallen. (Now they lean on one another.) From your perch on the ridge, you can see green pools of water below (.5 mi.) **[4]**. The creek below teases as you walk along the ridge high above it—you hear the gentle ripples of its water before you catch the glisten of its surface water (.6 mi.) **[5]**. The slope down to it is steep.

Enjoy the sights and sounds. This point on the ridge is near a posted junction for you to follow. However, if you follow straight up the trail about a hundred feet, you get to Sweet's Monument, where a plaque on a boulder commemorates Edwin F. Sweet. Additional park plaques memorialize other honorable members of the Grand Rapids community. Head back to where you listened to the creek's music and follow the junction there to the southeast **[5]**.

Again the path is wide as you pass through large oaks, beeches, maples, and some pines. Although you are among giants here, there are no commemorative plaques. Your stroll through the woods takes you past a fork (.7 mi.) **[6]**, where you follow to the right. Soon after you pass a fallen tree, the trail veers left and brings you to Aman's Grave **[7]**. Here you see a large boulder with a plaque that describes Jacob Aman, another notable community member who happens to be buried beneath the rock. This spot was one of his favorite places and his choice for a final resting place.

The trail winds around through the woods and brings you to a junction with trails radiating from it (.9 mi.) **[8]**. Although a straight shot will take you back to the map board along the Orange Trail, the Yellow Trail makes a sharp right at this juncture and continues to wind you through the forest, reuniting you with the main trail **[2]**. Follow along to the left, retracing your steps out to the parking area.

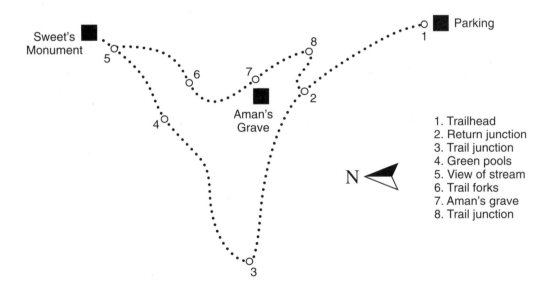

1. Trailhead
2. Return junction
3. Trail junction
4. Green pools
5. View of stream
6. Trail forks
7. Aman's grave
8. Trail junction

Red Trail 👢👢

Distance Round-Trip: 1.5 miles

Estimated Hiking Time: 30 minutes to 1 hour

Cautions: Some parts of the trail are eroding. Watch your step on the loose gravel or mud. Take insect repellent in warm months.

Trail Directions: Park in the small lot on the west side of the access drive, south of the trailhead. Start along the west side of the map board that shows each trail by color [1]. Yours is the Red Trail. The trail is wide as you head through a canopy that includes oaks and hemlocks. You swing to the west, following the ridge line, and pass a junction with the Yellow Trail (.2 mi.) [2]. Continue through beech and maple, and descend gently to where the Yellow Trail again splits off to the right (.3 mi.) [3].

Leaving the ridge line, note the large beech trees as you pick up speed in your descent. Spot a pond on your right, but watch your step along a section of the trail that is prone to erosion. The trail bottoms out at Sand Creek. Cross a cement bridge and quickly reach the junction with the Blue Trail (.5 mi.) [4].

As you walk across the forested flood plain, you swing south and pass several old channels of the creek. Just before climbing out of the valley, you'll pass a large oak tree on your right (.6 mi.) [5]. Now on the ridge, you leave the dense canopy of the forest and head east as the Green Trail splits off to your right (.7 mi.) [6].

If you packed a snack, several picnic tables are set along this section of the trail for your use. Beyond the picnic area, the trail swings right and briefly follows along the edge of a ravine before descending into the woods. At 1 mi. turn left at the junction with the Green Trail [7]. The trail again bottoms out. It takes you along the Sand Creek as it snakes toward the Grand River.

At 1.1 mi. take the footbridge across the creek near its elbow turn [8]. Get your knees ready for the climb up the bluff, which starts soon after you step off the footbridge—this is your steepest climb along the trail. At the top, turn left at the trail marker (1.2 mi.) [9], so M-45 is to your back. You now head north, with the ravine on your left and the driveway into the park on your right.

At 1.4 mi. a large oak tree marks a spot where you get a moving view of Sand Creek flowing below you in the valley [10]. Continue north to return to your vehicle or head back to the trailhead to try one of the other trails in this scenic park.

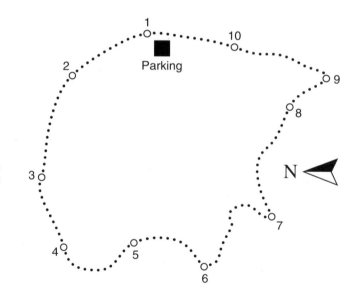

1. Trailhead
2. Yellow Trail junction
3. Yellow Trail junction
4. Blue Trail junction
5. Large oak
6. Green Trail junction
7. Green Trail junction
8. Footbridge
9. Trail marker
10. Scenic overlook

52. Saugatuck Dunes State Park

- Escape from the crowds and enjoy, in peace, the scenic Lake Michigan shoreline.
- Stroll over wooded dunes and sandy beaches.
- Walk softly and listen carefully; you may be rewarded with the sights and sounds of nature.

Park Information

About 1,120 acres of quiet, natural beauty await you at the Saugatuck Dunes State Park. Plan on hiking, if you want to enjoy and experience it. Acquired around 1977, this park is for day-use only. Adventure out over the 14 miles of trails that roll over wooded dunes and sandy Lake Michigan shores. And adventure out you must, if it's the shore you wish to enjoy. Lake Michigan awaits those who are not easily intimidated by the 1-mile trek over sandy dunes from the parking lot. The lake here is enticing if you like to escape beach crowds and yet enjoy the shore. The south end of this park is a designated natural area.

Three networks of trails lead toward the shore. The north trails are two loops, ranging from 2 to 2.5 miles in length, that weave through hardwoods and pines; cross over wooded, shrubby, and sandy dunes; then take you to a scenic view of Lake Michigan. The central, or beach, trails also range from 2 to 2.5 miles. They traverse wooded ridges and wind along a sandy dune overlooking Lake Michigan. The southern trails are two loops that offer 2.5- to 5.5-mile hiking opportunities. Yet another route over the dunes to Lake Michigan is the invigorating Livingston Trail.

Directions: The park is about 1 mile north of Saugatuck. From I-96, go west on Blue Star Highway (exit 141) to 64th. Head north about a mile to 138th Avenue, then turn west and follow the road to the park entrance.

Hours Open: Open daily from 8:00 A.M. to 10:00 P.M.

Facilities: Hiking, cross-country skiing, swimming; picnicking with grills, a shelter, and vault toilets.

Permits and Rules: A park fee ($4 daily, $20 annually) is required for each motor vehicle. This is a naturally managed, day-use park exhibiting classic dune succession; please make a special effort to respect all flora and fauna in this fragile place and stay on the marked trails.

Further Information: Holland State Park, 2215 Ottawa Beach Road, Holland, MI 49424; 616-399-9390.

Other Points of Interest

The City of Holland offers more than tulips and windmills. About 10 miles north of the park in Holland is the **De Graaf Nature Center Preserve**. This 16-acre nature preserve offers several short interpretive trails as well as an interpretive center. The small area hosts a wide variety of habitats. The center, operated by the City of Holland, is at 600 Graafschap Road, Holland, MI 49423. For more information call 616-396-2739.

South of the park in Saugatuck take a cruise down the Kalamazoo River and out into Lake Michigan on an old-fashioned sternwheeler, the **Star of Saugatuck**. Cruises are available from May through October. For more information call 616-857-4261 or write to 716 Water Street, Saugatuck, MI 49453.

Park Trails

Livingston Trail 🥾🥾🥾—2.5 miles round-trip—This point-to-point trail (marked by red) begins and ends at the southwest end of the parking area. Crossing over the wooded, sandy dunes is a challenge, but a reward awaits you—a scenic overview of secluded Lake Michigan. Huge grape vines twine along portions of the trail.

South Trails (Small Loop and Large Loop) 🥾🥾 and 🥾🥾🥾—2.5 miles and 5.5 miles—Both loops (marked by blue) begin and end at the south end of the parking lot. The large loop is a continuation of the small one, extending into the designated natural area of the park. Along its eastern leg, it passes mostly through climax forest. Closer to the lake, the trail undulates over varying dune ecology.

North Trail (Inner Loop) 🥾🥾🥾—2.1 miles—This trail (marked by white) begins and ends at the northeast end of the parking lot. It largely follows the same path as the outer loop: past a pond and wooded dunes, through mixed and pine forests, and up and down varying dune terrain. A shorter spur, however, bypasses a steep climb up a dune to one of the outer trail's scenic overlooks. If you want a spectacular view of Lake Michigan and you wish to experience a dramatic wall of wooded dunes, take the spur from the western point of this loop.

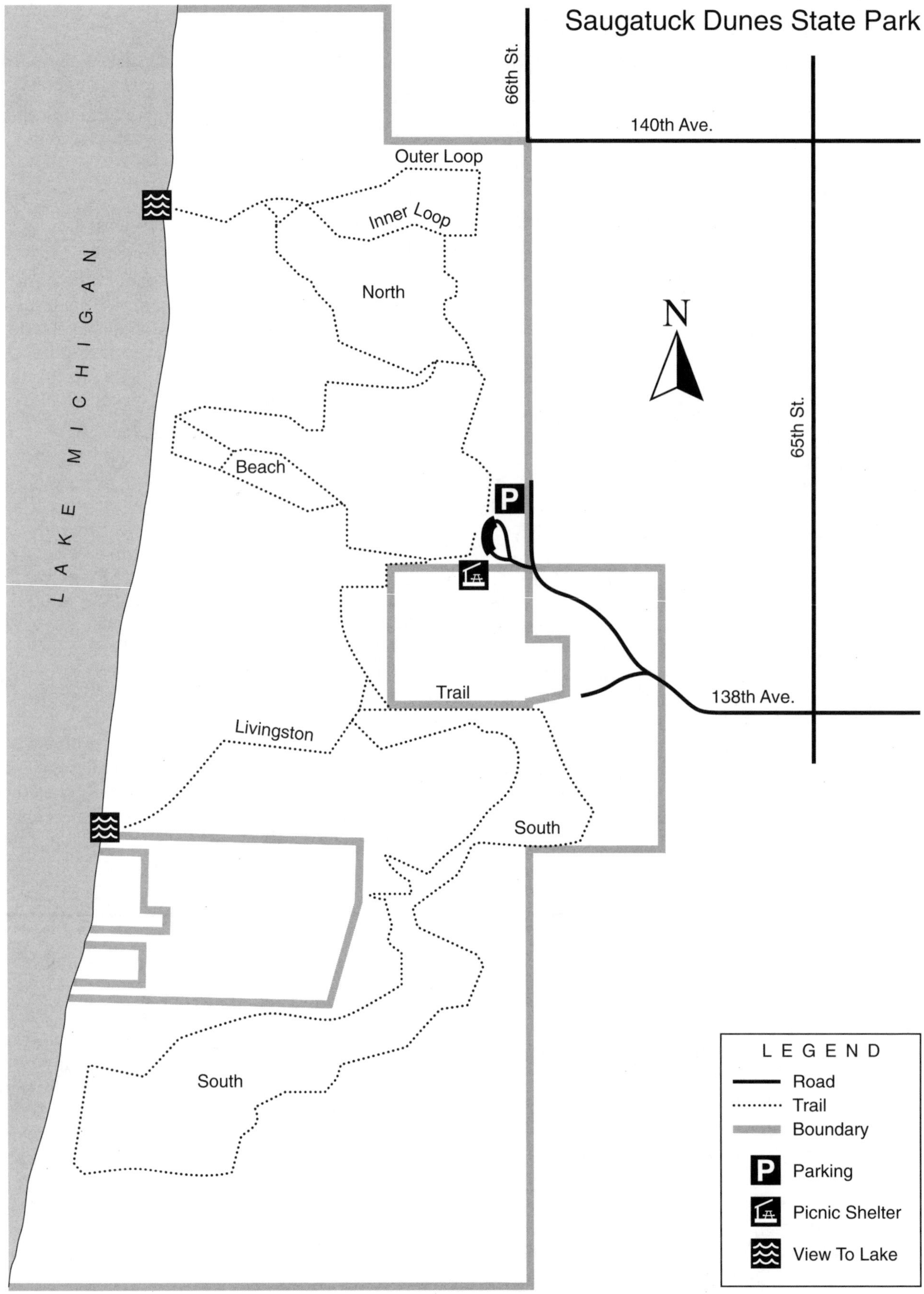

Saugatuck Dunes State Park

LAKE MICHIGAN

66th St.

140th Ave.

Outer Loop

Inner Loop

North

65th St.

Beach

N

P

Trail

138th Ave.

Livingston

South

South

L E G E N D

— Road

······· Trail

▬ Boundary

P Parking

Picnic Shelter

View To Lake

North Trail With Spur to Lake—Outer Loop

Distance Round-Trip: 2.9 miles

Estimated Hiking Time: 2 hours

Cautions: The trail (marked by white) is sandy and climbs up and down dunes (at times shaded by a canopy of trees, at times exposed to the sun). Wear sunscreen and proper clothing for climbing sandy hills. Take along some water. In the woods, watch your step; roots may be underfoot. Posts are colored: Follow your trail's color. Connectors of more than one trail show both colors. Green arrows point the way to the lake; red arrows point the way back to the parking lot. Watch out for poison ivy.

Trail Directions: This trail begins and ends at the northwest end of the parking lot and is well-marked **[1]**. It immediately enters the woods; from there a wide path takes you past wooded dunes. Stop and enjoy the pond to your right (.1 mi.) **[2]**. Walk softly, listen carefully, and enjoy the varied habitat at this edge between woods and pond. The spring bird migration can be particularly rewarding at this spot. As you continue on, let your gaze follow up the tall, wooded dune to your left.

Follow the trail as it climbs away from the pond and takes you to the next post, where the trail forks (.3 mi.) **[3]**. The post, tipped white, has a green arrow pointing left (west). Turn left and climb through a stand of red pines and mixed hardwoods of beech, maple, and oak until you reach a third post that marks a junction with the Beach Trails (.4 mi.) **[4]**. Take the North Trail (white) to the right, which soon takes you down a sandy slope and onto a carpet of needles that softens your steps. Walk slowly and enjoy the sights and smells as the trail undulates through dense pines until you reach post #4 (.8 mi.) **[5]**. Angle northwest for a short jog to the posted junction at 1 mi. **[6]**. Turn left. A massive wall of sand and woods rises steeply along- side you on this awesome spur to a bluff with a spectacular view of Lake Michigan (1.2 mi.) **[7]**.

Retrace your steps back to the post at the junction, but continue straight until you reach another posted junction (1.6 mi.) **[8]**, where you find several paths to follow. If you look to your right, you'll see another posted trail (which is the inner loop). To its right is another trail (which takes you back to the pine-carpeted trail you encountered earlier, hiking in). Take the path straight ahead through the open sand; climb through wind-swept dunes until you reach the junction at the bottom of a steep, sandy dune. Follow your gaze up the dune to the right where you'll see another post. The climb up the steep, sandy slope is worth the effort. The reward is a circular vista of varying dune terrain. You see sprawling forests, juniper, and grass-covered dunes (1.9 mi.) **[9]**. Look back the way you came. Lake Michigan is framed between sky, tree, and dune.

From this high point, follow the sandy trail as it drops sharply and takes you to another marker (2 mi.) **[10]**. This vantage offers rolling, grassy, wind-swept dunes. The trail turns sharply to the right, travels steeply down the slope, and makes another sharp right at the next post. From here, trudge back up a slope to a posted junction at the edge of the forest (2.3 mi.) **[11]**.

Turn left and enjoy the canopy of a mixed forest. The trail winds down until you reach the marsh that signals your approach to the junction where the North Trail began its loop (2.6 mi.) **[3]**. Continue straight and backtrack the first part of your journey down past the wooded dunes, the pond, and finally to the parking lot.

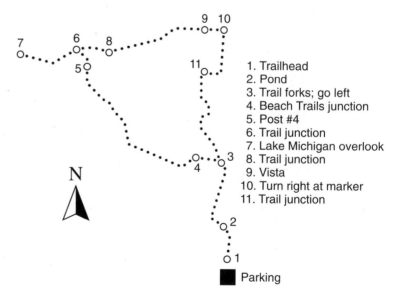

1. Trailhead
2. Pond
3. Trail forks; go left
4. Beach Trails junction
5. Post #4
6. Trail junction
7. Lake Michigan overlook
8. Trail junction
9. Vista
10. Turn right at marker
11. Trail junction

Beach Trail 🥾🥾🥾

Distance Round-Trip: 2.5 miles

Estimated Hiking Time: 2 hours

Cautions: The trail (marked by yellow) is sandy, and it climbs up and down dunes. Wear proper clothing for hiking sandy hills and bring along some water. Take extra care when hiking along the steep ridges. Follow your trail's posted color. Connectors of more than one trail show both colors. Green arrows point the way to the lake; red arrows point the way back to the parking lot. Watch out for poison ivy.

Trail Directions: Start northwest of the parking lot [1]. The first portion of the hike follows the North Trail. It immediately enters woods and then meanders past wooded dunes before arriving at a pond (.1 mi.) [2]. During the spring migrations, this wet area is a birder's delight. The trail climbs away from the pond and leads you to the first junction at .3 mi. [3]. Although the post is tipped white, turn left and continue along this joint venture with the North Trail.

The trail ascends through red pines and mixed hardwoods, and arrives at the parting junction for the North and Beach Trails. Take the Beach Trail to the left, which begins a climb up a ridge. At first, you'll notice the steep slope below you to the left. Soon, the trail rises above its surroundings, and you walk high along the ridge (.5 mi.) [4]. This natural land bridge supports your steps as you head west toward the lake. You catch a glimpse of Lake Michigan through the foliage (.7 mi.) [5] just before the trail takes a sharp turn to the left and descends the sandy slope to next enter the pine forest.

The descent continues; you wind through the woods before climbing steeply over a dune. This point is posted. Lake Michigan is before you. You can see the continuation of the trail through the trees to your left, and it's hard to resist heading west for the lake and scrambling up the next dune to perch higher for a Lake Michigan overview (1 mi.) [6]. A beaten down path leads you to this point, then heads south, following just inside a dune ridge that separates you from the lake.

The beaten path ultimately picks up the trail when it comes out of the woods (the woods you should have turned left into at the post to have stayed on the official trail). A post, tipped white on top and with yellow underneath, announces where you would have come from, had you chosen it. Don't veer back that way. Continue following the lake a few steps and you'll see the next post for your trek back through the woods (1.4 mi.) [7]. Turn left (an option would be to continue straight along the lake and pick up the next junction to the left, following along the outer Beach Trail) and start up the sandy incline to enter the hardwoods.

The terrain is rolling; it winds through woods until it reaches the posted junction at 1.7 mi. [8]. Veer left to stay on the inner, lower-lying loop. (A right would take you to the outer, higher loop.) Wooded slopes rise on either side until you begin the steep climb out of the bowl (1.9 mi.) [9]. The trails meet at a junction, where they now are joined as one (2.1 mi.) [10].

Wind around. Before long, notice that you are on a ridge overlooking the grounds of a refuge—first used as a seminary, later as a correctional facility (2.2 mi.) [11]. Tentative plans are in place to tear down the institutional facility and create baseball or soccer fields. Whatever the outcome, there still will be a refuge of sorts.

A few more steps bring you to a posted junction. The trail down to the right leads to the Livingston and the South Trails. Continue straight, with pines along your left. Soon the parking area will come into view, the trail veers sharply to the left, and eventually you reach the parking area just southwest of the picnic shelter.

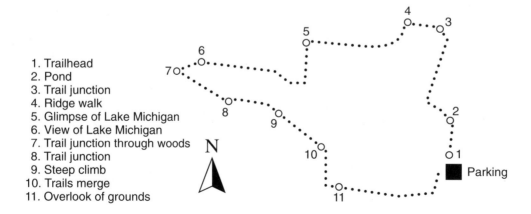

1. Trailhead
2. Pond
3. Trail junction
4. Ridge walk
5. Glimpse of Lake Michigan
6. View of Lake Michigan
7. Trail junction through woods
8. Trail junction
9. Steep climb
10. Trails merge
11. Overlook of grounds

N

53. P. J. Hoffmaster State Park

- Take the challenge of the Dune Climb Stairway to view Lake Michigan from an observation deck set high on a dune.
- Learn about sand dunes and their ecosystems at the E. Genevieve Gillette Visitor Center.
- Sink your toes in sand along the Lake Michigan shoreline.

Park Information

Encompassing almost 1,100 acres, the P. J. Hoffmaster State Park is a treasure trove packed with almost 3 miles of Lake Michigan shoreline, sandy beaches, and forested dunes. The trails that weave throughout the park give visitors a comprehensive experience of dune environments.

A vigorous hike along the Dune Climb Stairway to a platform on the top of a towering dune provides a panoramic overlook of the vast open waters of Lake Michigan. You also see the contrasting parallel line of dunes that run along the lakeshore: the foredune, sandy and somewhat barren-looking with dune grass and shrubs; and the backdune, lushly carpeted with beech and maple trees.

More than 8 miles of hiking trails are ample for you to sift through the park, lumber through a beech-maple forest, climb up and down dunes, and drift along the shore. Although the camp and day beaches are usually crowded, the south shore, which requires a dedicated effort to access, is often quieter. About 2 miles of bridle paths track through the southeastern portion of the park. In the winter, you can use about 3 miles of cross-country ski trails.

A different kind of crest is provided by the E. Genevieve Gillette Visitor Center, which is noted in the Midwest for its programs and exhibits that help visitors understand the unique dune environment. Named in honor of E. Genevieve Gillette, the Center is a tribute to her efforts in preserving unique natural areas in Michigan.

Directions: Hoffmaster State Park is 6 miles south of Muskegon. From US-31, take Pontaluna Road west about 2 miles. From I-96, take exit 4 and follow the signs to the park.

Hours Open: Open year-round from 8:00 A.M. to 10:00 P.M.

Facilities: Hiking, swimming, camping (tent and RV), bridle paths, cross-country skiing, picnicking, and an interpretive center.

Permits and Rules: A park fee ($4 daily, $20 annually) is required for each motor vehicle. Snowmobiles and off-road vehicles are not allowed in the park. Bicycles are allowed on paved roads only. It is unlawful to consume or possess alcoholic beverages within the campground area from April 15th to Labor Day and in the day-use area from April 15 to June 15.

Further Information: Hoffmaster State Park, 6585 Lake Harbor Road, Muskegon, MI 49441; 616-798-3711.

Other Points of Interest

The **E. Genevieve Gillette Visitor Center** provides a diverse range of programs for understanding the ecosystem of the sandy, linear mounds outside its door. These programs include exhibits, multimedia presentations in an 82-seat auditorium, and an art gallery. The center is open seven days a week from Memorial Day through Labor Day. It is open except on Mondays the rest of the year. For more information call 616-798-3573.

Located north of Muskegon, along the north shore of Muskegon Lake, is **Muskegon State Park**. This park caters to fishers and boaters with its piers and a channel connecting Muskegon Lake and Lake Michigan, and it also offers more than 10 miles of hiking trails and a scenic drive along the coastline. Plus it is home to the Muskegon Winter Sports Complex, which features a luge run and lighted cross-country ski trails for night skiing. A short, steep climb from Scenic Drive within the park takes you to the Blockhouse, a two-story log structure poised on top of a wooded dune. The park is at 3560 Memorial Drive, Muskegon, MI 49445. For more information call 616-744-3480.

Between Muskegon and Ferrysburg is the **Kitchel Dune Preserve**. Self-guiding brochures describe paths that weave through oaks, pines, interdunal ponds, and dune grasses that showcase the dune ecosystem. The landscape is fragile; please stay on the trails. For more information contact the City of Ferrysburg, 408 Fifth St., Ferrysburg, MI 49409; 616-842-5950.

Loop of Homestead, Quiet Area, and Dune Climb Stairway 👢👢👢

Distance Round-Trip: 2.6 miles

Estimated Hiking Time: 1.5 to 2 hours

Cautions: Roots are often exposed. Some portions of the trail go through poison ivy. Insect repellent is a must during warm months.

Trail Directions: Start the trail from the south end of the Visitor Center parking lot **[1]**. Climb a forested dune through beech, maple, and pine trees to the crest, where you find the spur to the Quiet Area.

Follow down the spur past velvety, green logs spilling along the slopes, and head through a valley of dunes. A wildlife botanical experiment soon emerges (.2 mi.) **[2]**. Two areas hang onto the slope; one is fenced, the other is not. The experiment is about deer-feeding habitats and wildflower population. The spur ends shortly thereafter as you reach a tree graveyard. Turn and go back up to the Homestead Trail (.5 mi.) **[3]**.

Head south down the main trail through the woods, passing many beech trees. Roll through low dunes and along a ridge with bowl-shaped depressions at your side; then descend and pass a steep ravine and arrive at a junction with the ski trails (.8 mi.) **[4]**. Turn right and hike down along the ridge through the oaks and maples. You pass through intermittent short, open, sandy stretches.

After a prominent right swing in the trail, you reach a large, forested dune (1.2 mi.) **[5]**. A sign here says "No horses." Climb up through mixed hardwoods for about .1 mi. and then start descending past oaks and beeches and along hills and ravines.

At 1.4 mi. a steep, sandy dune stands before you **[6]**. At the base, the trail swings back into the woods, and then onto a ridge. Quiet evolves into the lapping of waves. The trail leaves the woods, and through the shadowed tree trunks you see Lake Michigan. Step down onto the sandy beach (1.5 mi.) **[7]**.

Turn right and follow the shore. Look behind you at the Grand Haven Lighthouse. Ahead of you are sand, waves, and a ridge of dunes. A wooden fence (2.1 mi.) **[8]** is your beacon to turn inland. Head up the sandy slope. Steps assist you. Note the observation deck high above and the bowl-shaped sand blowout to your right.

Step into the shade along the boardwalk. An interpretive board describes the dune environment. Compare what's on the diagram with what surrounds you. Continue along a series of steps. At the end of the boardwalk, climb up the slope; a mountainous dune accompanies you. Cross boardwalks that pass interpretive signs identifying plants nearby. You reach the junction to the Dune Climb Stairway at 2.4 mi. **[9]**.

Wind your way up almost 170 steps for a sweeping view of the lake and dunes. A plaque at the overlook identifies as Mt. Baldy that mountainous dune you passed while climbing up. Ahead of you, a caldera-like dune (one with a blowout) frames Lake Michigan. Catch your breath before heading down to the trail; it is only a short distance to the Visitor Center (2.6 mi.) **[10]**.

P. J. Hoffmaster State Park

1. Trailhead
2. Wildlife experiment
3. Homestead Trail junction
4. Ski trails junction
5. Forested dune
6. Sandy dune
7. Lake Michigan
8. Wooden storm fencing
9. Dune Climb Stairway junction
10. Visitor Center

LEGEND
— Paved Road
······· Trail
— Boundary

🏛 Headquarters ⌂ Picnic Area 🏕 Modern Campground
🏠 Visitor Center 🎪 Picnic Shelter ♻ Sanitation Station
🅿 Parking 🏊 Beach 🚻 Toilet/Shower

54. Sarett Nature Center

- Explore more than 5 miles of trails with a park naturalist or on your own.

- View nature from elevated platforms, towers, boardwalks, and wood-chip nature trails.

- Take a specialty class on photography, canoeing, or nature awareness.

Park Information

Almost 600 acres, blanketed by upland meadows, swamp forests, marshes, and dry forest, are open to exploration via an elaborate trail system. You cross boardwalks, bridges with benches, and overlook towers, walking along wood-chip and natural trails. You meander on ridges high above the Paw Paw River and cut through wetlands in this variety of habitats. Bring a camera or just bring yourself. Come and learn more about the environment.

Sarett Nature Center offers more than trails to help you discover the natural world. Naturalists at the center are available to educate visitors on a variety of environmental topics—bird study, wilderness appreciation, and winter ecology, to name but a few. Many public programs are offered, including guided field trips and extended outings. Call for an extensive list of programs and classes. The center features exhibits, meeting rooms, a bookshop and library, and an observation room for viewing the birds attracted to the feeders outside.

Directions: The nature center is about 8 miles northeast of Benton Harbor. From east of Benton Harbor, at the junction of I-94 and I-196, head north on I-196/US-31 for about a mile to the Red Arrow Highway. Head southwest on Red Arrow Highway for about one-eighth of a mile to Benton Center Road. Turn north (right) and go about three-quarters of a mile to the entrance of the nature center, located on the west side of the road.

Hours Open: The trails are open year-round from dawn until dusk. Hours at the Nature Center vary. Tuesdays through Friday it is open from 9:00 A.M. to 5:00 P.M.; Saturdays it is open from 10:00 A.M. to 5:00 P.M.; and Sundays it is open from 1:00 P.M. to 5:00 P.M. It is closed on Mondays.

Facilities: Hiking and interpretive center.

Permits and Rules: No fee is required. Sarett is a private, nonprofit organization, supported by donations, contributions, and membership. Your support is vital to the continuation of the programs offered at the center. Visitors are encouraged to join. Enjoy the natural setting, but do so without pets, without picnicking, and without picking wildflowers or other plants.

Further Information: Sarett Nature Center, 2300 Benton Center Road, Benton Harbor, MI 49022; 616-927-4832.

Other Points of Interest

Two public beaches in St. Joseph are available for swimming, picnicking, boating, and pier strolling. **Tiscornia Park,** located north of the St. Joseph River Channel, provides easy access for a stroll along North Pier, which has two lighthouses. **Silver Beach County Park** is located on Lake Michigan and has a beach boardwalk, amphitheater, and access to the 1,000-foot South Pier. For more information on these and other parks, contact St. Joseph Today at 616-923-6739.

Lake Bluff Park has a scenic walking area through sculptures, overlook benches (overlooking Lake Michigan), and gardens. Information on walking tours or on St. Joseph may be obtained from St. Joseph Today at 616-923-6739.

Park Trails

West Marsh Trail 👢—.2 mile—Start from the west end of the Lowland Trail. It weaves through a marsh and goes out to the West Marsh Tower, which overlooks the west marsh and its cattails and sedges.

Ridge Loop 👢—.1 mile—Acccess this trail from the Upland Trail. It follows a boardwalk on the ridge connecting with overlook decks on the Upland Trail.

Cottontail Trail 👢—.2 mile—Accessed off the Upland Trail, it combines well with the Upland Trail to make a delightful .5-mile hike.

River Trail 👢👢—1 mile—This is the main path that stretches eastward through the park. It leads to the River Tower, where you view the surrounding wetlands and slow-moving waters of the Paw Paw River and on to the river itself. About .3 mi. along the River Trail, there is a spur to the North Marsh Tower. This area overlooks the marsh that gets flooded by the Paw Paw each spring. In addition to cattails and sedges, two other plants to watch for here are the arum and the arrowhead.

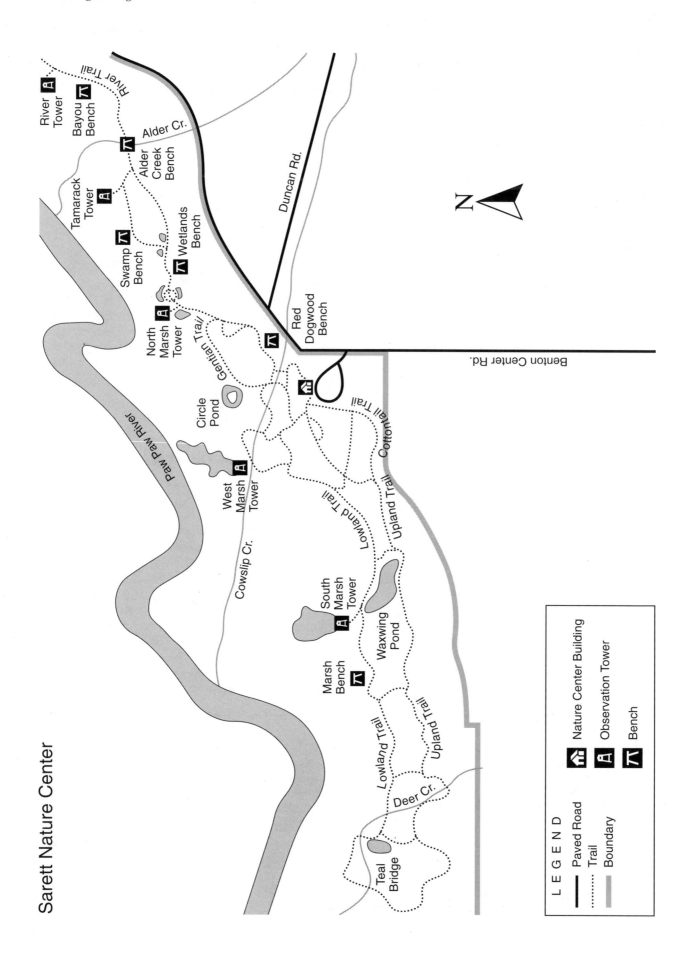

Sarett Nature Center

LEGEND

Paved Road
Trail
Boundary

Nature Center Building
Observation Tower
Bench

River/Gentian/Two-Board Trails Loop 👢👢

Distance Round-Trip: .6 mile

Estimated Hiking Time: 30 minutes

Cautions: Take insect repellent in warm months. You should also bring binoculars to enhance wildlife viewing. Watch your step so you don't end up off the edge of the boardwalk and in the fragile, wet environment along the trail.

Trail Directions: Begin at the west end of the Nature Center parking lot **[1]**. Be sure to stop at the Center for advice on what might be blooming and what trail will get you in viewing sight of it. You can also look out the Center's viewing windows to observe birds and small mammals at the feeders, taking in the panoramic view of the Paw Paw River valley in the background.

Head west from the parking area and quickly reach a junction. Turn right and descend from the bluff on steps. A bench waits under the large oak tree, if you want to sit a moment and catch your breath. Follow the River Trail as it splits right and passes a splash of wildflowers that precede a footbridge over the Cowslip Creek (.1 mi.) **[2]**. After crossing the creek,

continue straight on the Gentian Trail, as the River Trail splits right and the Treehouse Path goes left.

Pass through cedars to reach a lush, open area on the right. In August and September look for wildflowers such as fringed gentian (a protected Michigan wildflower), the pitcher plant (a threatened specie), turtleheads, and the showy, scarlet-red cardinal flowers. Stop at the observation deck to view wildlife at the algae-covered Circle Pond (.2 mi.) **[3]**. Then, briefly step off the boardwalk for a short walk through tall grasses. Step back on the boardwalk by the black willow tree and find yourself again under fragrant cedar trees. Take note as you pass other plants in the marsh, to spot iris, arrowhead, and skunk cabbage.

Turn right when you reach the River Trail, which is roughly the halfway point of the hike (.3 mi.) **[4]**. Then turn right to walk the unmarked trail known as Two-Board. It is called Two-Board because it is only two boards wide, rather than the usual three boards of other trail boardwalks. Cattails and lilies stand out here, and you get a view of the Nature Center up on the bluff to the south.

Turn right when you again reach the River Trail. The path may be spongy here as you walk through the thick shrubs and grasses. At .4 mi. you reach the Red Dogwood Bench **[5]**. This raised bench structure provides a good platform from which to sit quietly and watch wildlife atop the surrounding shrubs.

When you are back on the trail, you quickly cross a small footbridge and snake through small willows to arrive at a trail junction. Turn left onto an unnamed connector path and cross over the Cowslip Creek to arrive at the campfire area (.5 mi.) **[6]**. Then begin to climb back up the bluff and arrive at the east end of the Nature Center. Check what's growing in the Prairie Patch before heading left to the parking area.

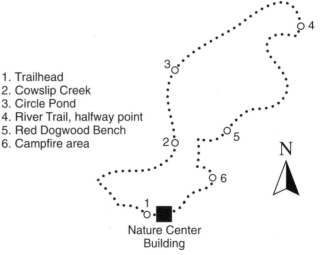

1. Trailhead
2. Cowslip Creek
3. Circle Pond
4. River Trail, halfway point
5. Red Dogwood Bench
6. Campfire area

N

Nature Center
Building

Lowland/Upland Trails Loop

🥾🥾🥾

Distance Round-Trip: 2 miles

Estimated Hiking Time: 1 hour

Cautions: The trail crosses boardwalks that sometimes give way like car shocks. The boardwalks are slippery when wet. At places roots are exposed. Poison ivy grows along the trail; don't brush up against it. Take insect repellent in warm months.

Trail Directions: Start at the west end of the Nature Center parking lot **[1]**. Cross a small boardwalk and immediately pass the junction for the Cottontail Trail to arrive at an information board. Many trails converge here. Turn right to follow along the Lowland Trail.

Head for the low land by stepping down the rail-tie steps past a bench resting among mayapples, past a huge oak, past a junction, and past a soil cellar (or a contraption that looks like a cellar). Stay to the left at the West Marsh Trail junction, then duck under a canopy of trees.

Pass the second spur for the West Marsh Loop (.1 mi.) **[2]**; climb up the hill and begin to walk along the ridge over the floodplain of Cowslip Creek. The trail continues to rise, and you pass a switchback spur (.2 mi.) **[3]**, and head down steps to the lowland. Soon, moss cushions your steps. Skunk cabbage announces the beginning of a planked boardwalk (.3 mi.) **[4]**.

Walk the planks through ferns and irises. Pass the Waxwing Path and the overlook for the Waxwing Pond (where wax-like lily pads cover the surface). At .4 mi. you arrive at the spur for the South Marsh Tower **[5]**. It's just a short stretch out to the overlook where the decking stands high above the swamp, home to silver maple, willow, elm, and alder trees.

Continue on the main boardwalk through the lush wetland. Benches overlook the cattails and willows of the marsh (.4 mi.) **[6]**. Soon you duck through a wall of shrubs, cross a small stream, and enter woods. At .6 mi. pass the Marsh Marigold spur and step off the boardwalk to continue along the Lowland Trail **[7]**.

A ridge rises to your left. The trail climbs and swings left just before you pass Hickory Path (.7 mi.) **[8]**. Head down and cross over the watercress-clogged Deer Creek. Pass Deer Creek Path (.8 mi.) **[9]**, an algae-laden pond, and cross planks back over Deer Creek.

The trail cuts through a meadow, and you reach a lowland with rich, dark soils. Cross Deer Creek again, over the Teal Bridge (.9 mi.) **[10]**. Step off the boards, climb a slope, and wind around and up steps (1 mi.) **[11]**. Next you walk high among youthful oaks and pass a metal truckbed with "Michigan Fruit Canners" whispering through its rust. At 1.1 mi. you reach the Deer Creek Path **[12]**.

Stay straight along a ridge until it cuts down to a boardwalk and back over Deer Creek. Climb back to a ridge, passing Hickory Path before winding down a steep switchback. At 1.4 mi. you pass the Marsh Marigold Path **[13]**. Step back onto a boardwalk. Ferns blanket the trail, and you again pass the green Waxwing Pond (1.6 mi.) **[14]**. Soon, the trail climbs high to a ridge.

Break out of the woods; at 1.7 mi. you reach the Cottontail Trail junction **[15]**. Go left, cutting through a field before reentering the woods. After the junction for Woodchuck Run you pass through a hallway of shrubs. You then reach the boardwalk and overlook (1.9 mi.) **[16]**.

Have a seat and soak in the view of the floodplain and the river valley below, or enjoy the view from another overlook platform a few steps farther. Look over the lowland where you hiked earlier; then head back to the Center.

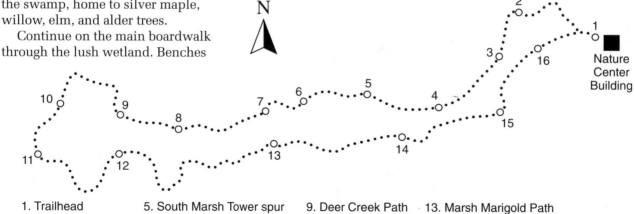

N

1. Trailhead
2. West Marsh Loop
3. Switchback spur
4. Boardwalk
5. South Marsh Tower spur
6. Benches
7. Marsh Marigold spur
8. Hickory Path
9. Deer Creek Path
10. Teal Bridge
11. Crest of hill
12. Deer Creek Path
13. Marsh Marigold Path
14. Waxwing Pond
15. Cottontail Trail junction
16. Boardwalk and overlook

55. Warren Dunes State Park/ Warren Woods Natural Area

- View the creation that wind, water, and sand have shaped—the Great Warren Dunes.
- Experience one of Michigan's most beautiful beaches.
- Stroll through majestic hardwoods.
- Revere one of the last-known stands of virgin beeches and maples in southern Michigan.

Park Information

Although Warren Dunes State Park and Warren Woods Natural Area are two distinct units separated by some 7 miles, they are united not only in name but also in origin. Both parks evolved through the foresight of Edward K. Warren, who, in the 1870s, purchased the land that is now called Warren Woods Natural Area. His effort preserved one of the few remaining virgin beech-maple forests in Michigan; the area was later designated a National Natural Landmark. He continued to purchase undeveloped land, including the land that eventually (about 1930) became Warren Dunes State Park. Both areas are administered by Warren Dunes State Park.

Warren Dunes State Park contains 1,507 acres that stretch along 3 miles of sandy Lake Michigan shore. Home to wind-blown dunes and hilly terrain blanketed with oaks and hickory, the Warren Dunes offer a superb study of plant succession. Dunes rising up to 240 feet provide spectacular viewing, climbing, and, for the experienced, hang gliding. Almost 7 miles of trails traverse the varied terrain.

Warren Woods Natural Area is for day-use only. About 1.5 miles of well-worn paths loop through the natural area, across and along the Galien River. Virgin hardwoods provide spectacular colors in the fall.

Directions: From I-94, Warren Dunes State Park is about 12 miles south of St. Joseph. Take exit 16 and follow the Red Arrow Highway south to the park entrance. Warren Woods Natural Area may be reached from exit 6 and by heading east on Elm Valley Road to the posted entrance. Call ahead if you wish to hike there, though. A bridge was washed out at the time of this writing, separating the parking area from the trail. An alternate parking area is on Warren Woods Road, which is 1 mile north of Elm Valley Road and can be reached via Three Oaks Road.

Hours Open: Open from 8:00 A.M. to 10:00 P.M. April 1st to September 30th, and from 8:00 A.M. until dusk from October 1st through March 31st.

Facilities: Warren Dunes State Park: hiking, swimming, fishing, hunting, cross-country skiing, hang gliding, camping (tent and RV), picnicking, and interpretive trails; Warren Woods Natural Area: hiking and picnicking.

Permits and Rules: A park fee ($4 daily, $20 annually) is required for each motor vehicle. Pets must be on a six-foot leash. Dogs are not allowed on the beach. Alcoholic beverages are prohibited from March 1 through September 30.

Further Information: Warren Dunes State Park, Red Arrow Highway, Sawyer, MI 49125; 616-426-4013.

Other Points of Interest

Grand Mere State Park, a day-use park, is located about 4 miles north of Warren Dunes. It, too, offers Lake Michigan beaches and access to three inland lakes, a picnic area, and hiking trails. Day passes may be obtained from Warren Dunes State Park.

Park Trails

Yellow Birch Loop 👢—1 mile—Start this trail west of the parking area on Floral Lane, which is off Red Arrow Highway, north of the park entrance. The trail passes through meadows, bottomland hardwoods, and wetlands. A new boardwalk welcomes you.

Golden Rod Loop 👢—.3 mile—This trail starts at the parking area on Floral Lane. It, too, passes through meadows and bottomland and is a favorite for bird-watchers.

White Tail Loop 👢👢—.8 mile—Start the loop off the Nature Trail, just northwest of the organization campground. It climbs up into the natural area.

Red Squirrel Trail 👢👢—.7 mile—This trail may be accessed from the Nature Trail near the organization camp. It climbs through hardwoods and passes through the park's natural area open dunes to exit along the Blue Jay Trail.

Oak Ridge Trail 👢👢—.2 mile—This trail links the Red Squirrel Trail and the Blue Jay Trail, passing through woods and onto open sand.

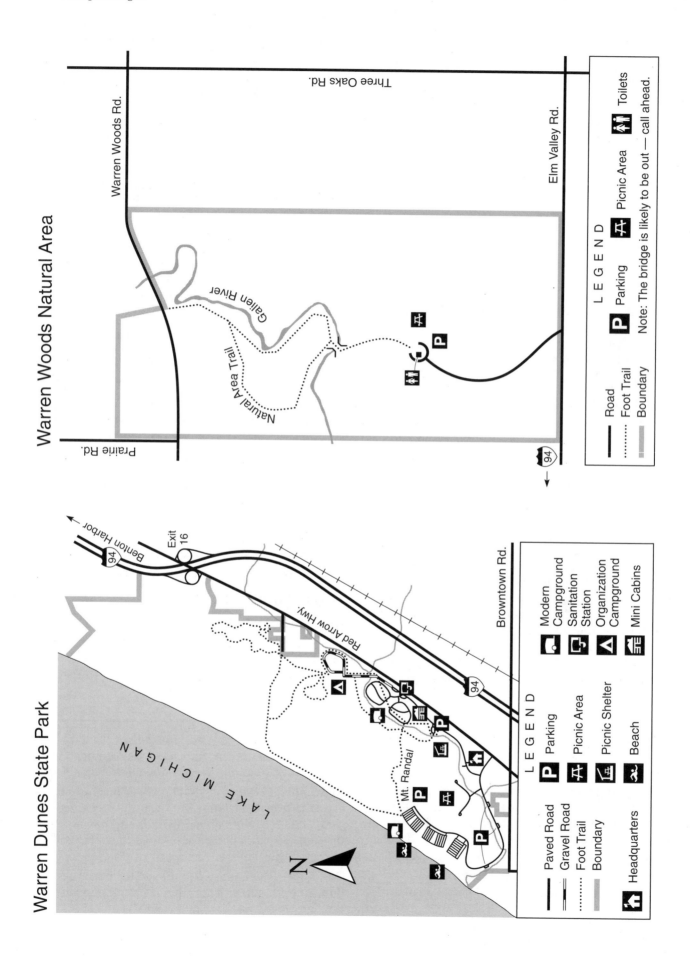

Nature/Blue Jay/Beach/ Mt. Randal Trails Loop 👢👢👢

Distance Round-Trip: 3.8 miles

Estimated Hiking Time: 2 to 2.5 hours

Cautions: Portions of the trail are apt to flood, so wear proper footgear. Layer your clothing to prepare for changing conditions. At times you will be hiking up or down sandy dunes, in and out of a canopy of trees. Have sunscreen and insect repellent handy and watch for poison ivy along the trail.

Trail Directions: The trail starts at the west end of the picnic-shelter parking lot (which is about halfway between the park's entrance and the campgrounds) **[1]**. It starts out on the Nature Trail, which has interpretive posts. Pick up a brochure at the contact station to follow along.

Head west over Painterville Creek to the fork. Turn right into the hardwoods along the backside of a dune. Flanking the creek, the trail is prone to flooding. Transient paths that swing up the backside of the dune (called Mt. Randal) help to divert you around any water. Don't climb what seems like a path up Mt. Randal's steep, sandy backside to view Lake Michigan (.2 mi.) **[2]**. You'll reach other overviews that won't require quite the strain to yourself or to the dune. Keep going past the Mt. Randal junction.

The trail passes another wet area, bypasses the campground, and merges with an old road (.8 mi.) **[3]**. The organization camp is nearby, as are the junctions for the White Tail, Red Squirrel, and Oak Ridge Trails. Continue along the backside of a dune. At 1.3 mi. you reach Floral Lane **[4]**.

Turn left along the Blue Jay Trail and begin a gentle climb around a wooded slope and into the Warren Dunes Natural Area. The trail climbs steeper and rises above the ravine to your right. Your first real climb, however, comes at 1.4 mi. when you trudge through sand **[5]**. Pass the Oak Ridge spur, then rise to a crest to take in the Lake Michigan view (1.5 mi.) **[6]** before descending the trough. Follow this wave of dunes toward the lake, stopping to notice the sandy blowout at 1.6 mi. **[7]**. Feel the breeze that helped to shape this bowl.

At 1.8 mi. you arrive at the last crest before the lake **[8]**. You could step down and follow along the shore, but you'd miss the blowouts you can see from the vantage point along the ridge of the Beach Trail. Turn left and reach the first beach blowout at 1.9 mi. **[9]**. As you scan the bowl of sand, look for vultures in the trees.

At about 2.2 mi. you get to dip your toes into the water if you choose; the trail slips off the ridge and onto the beach **[10]**, which it then follows for about .2 mi. Watch for the tree line to gradually taper down to the bare, sandy ridge. Take the unmarked path there back onto the ridge **[11]**. Soon, you pass the second blowout. Wind around on the ridge, passing the third bowl of sand, and then enter the woods. As the trail winds around, you can see the beach campsites. To your left is a sign, "Foot Trails." Climb up the sand, reenter the woods at this sign, and follow the Mt. Randal Trail (2.8 mi.) **[12]**.

The trail adventures back across the wave of dunes, mostly through oak-hickory forest, and at times it teeters along ridges above steep ravines. Stairways in the forest, made either by the roots of trees or by man, at times ease the stress of climbing up and down the crests and troughs. A final series of steps winds down to a bench where Mt. Randal sweeps up to your right (3.4 mi.) **[13]**. The trail continues winding down, passing a bench that offers relief for your knees as well as your eyes (it overlooks a pond). Sit and enjoy the respite before heading down again and reaching the Nature Trail junction at 3.6 mi. Turn right and head back to the parking lot.

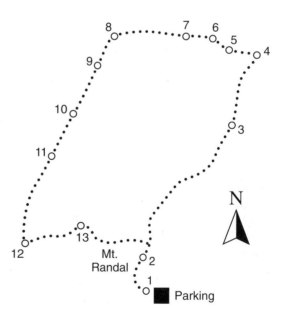

1. Trailhead
2. Steep slope of Mt. Randal
3. Old road
4. Floral Lane
5. Ascend dune
6. View of Lake Michigan
7. Blowout
8. Lake Michigan
9. Beach blowout
10. Beach walk
11. Back on ridge
12. Mt. Randal Trail
13. Bench

Warren Woods Natural Area Trail 👢👢

Distance Round-Trip: 1.2 miles

Estimated Hiking Time: 30 minutes to 1 hour

Cautions: Portions of the trail are apt to flood. Some sections along the Galien River have eroded into the river, making the path precariously narrow. Wear proper footgear and be careful. The bridge from the parking and picnic area has washed out (1996). It may take some time for the bridge to be repaired; call ahead to check on its status.

Trail Directions: Park on Warren Woods Road if the bridge is closed. The trail starts on the south side of the road, west of the Galien River **[1]**. Ignore the sign on the board telling you, "Please use developed facility on Elm Valley Road, one mile south"; until the bridge is repaired, this is where you start.

Pass through the entry post of trees with moss tucked onto their roots, like lint cotton balls between toes. Head straight; a rotting red log points the way down a staircase to the river. If you want, go down to the water (remembering that you do have to climb back up). You'll get another chance for that water visit farther along the hike. Follow the trail to the right and have a seat on the bench that overlooks the Galien River below.

Wind along the undulating trail of roots. The trail passes by huge beech trees that, thanks to Mr. Edward Warren, were spared the ax. Some of the trees are so big that two adults would have a hard time hugging one of them. These trees have been around a long time. It's okay to feel heartache when you see some of these trees that have ancient scars—hearts surrounding initials that were carved in decades ago. Ouch! They may have been spared the ax, but they were not spared the Swiss army knife. Beech trees aren't the only virgins in these woods; maple trees stand pure, but love-scarred, along with them.

Cross a streambed at .1 mi. (it may be dried out when you hike) **[2]**, and stretch your neck way back to look up at the huge beech on your left—good exercise to get your neck in shape for the many giants in this primeval forest. Pass a bench among the fallen giants, then come to an overview of the river (.2 mi.). **[3]**. You'll see youthful maples scattered about the

floor as you walk on and pass one of the giants that fell over toward the river. At .3 mi. you pass by a wall of roots, just before the trail splits **[4]**.

Follow to the right along the now narrow trail under a cover of smaller beeches and maples. Break out into the sun where a downed tree opens the canopy. Notice the ravine to your right (.4 mi.) **[5]**. Turn left at the deadfall, which takes you past another giant.

Go a short distance to the trail alongside the river. Follow left along the ridge, and take the root steps down past a large beech to arrive at the bank of the river. This area is prone to flooding, so you may have to roll up your pant legs. Tiptoe over logs through the wet stretch, pass a hollowed-out giant, follow along the river's edge, and pass the washed-out bridge (.6 mi.) **[6]**.

At times the trail is wet from the river spilling over. When you cross a small stream at .7 mi. **[7]**, look in the mud at the myriad tracks. The trail bends with the river. At .8 mi. the trail narrows where a tree fell over the bank, taking some of the trail with it **[8]**.

The trail becomes laden with roots. Pass through fallen trees that take their neighbors with them (.9 mi.) **[9]**. Soon the trail winds up to close the loop **[4]**. Follow the trail back to the road, where you left your vehicle.

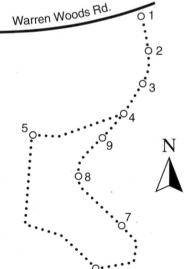

1. Trailhead
2. Streambed
3. Overview of river
4. Wall of roots
5. Ravine
6. Washed-out bridge
7. Cross stream
8. Trail narrows
9. Fallen trees